THE CAMBRIDGE COMPANION TO SHAKESPEARE'S LANGUAGE

The power of Shakespeare's complex language – his linguistic playfulness, poetic diction, and dramatic dialogue – inspires and challenges students, teachers, actors, and theatregoers across the globe. It has iconic status and enormous resonance, even as language change and the distance of time render it more opaque and difficult. *The Cambridge Companion to Shakespeare's Language* provides important contexts for understanding Shakespeare's experiments with language and offers accessible approaches to engaging with it directly and pleasurably. Incorporating both practical analysis and exemplary readings of Shakespearean passages, it covers elements of style, metre, speech action, and dialogue; examines the shaping contexts of rhetorical education and social language; test-drives newly available digital methodologies and technologies; and considers Shakespeare's language in relation to performance, translation, and popular culture. The *Companion* explains the present state of understanding while identifying opportunities for fresh discovery, leaving students equipped to ask productive questions and try out innovative methods.

LYNNE MAGNUSSON is Professor of English at the University of Toronto. Her ground-breaking articles and chapters treat topics such as the grammar of possibility in Shakespeare's language and the social rhetoric of Renaissance letters. She is the author of *Shakespeare and Social Dialogue: Dramatic Language and Elizabethan Letters* (Cambridge University Press, 1999).

DAVID SCHALKWYK is Professor of Shakespeare Studies at Queen Mary University of London. He is a leading Shakespeare scholar and author of *Shakespeare, Love and Service* (Cambridge University Press, 2008) and *Shakespeare, Love and Language* (Cambridge University Press, 2018).

A complete list of books in the series is at the back of this book.

T0349205

THE CAMBRIDGE
COMPANION TO
SHAKESPEARE'S
LANGUAGE

EDITED BY

LYNNE MAGNUSSON

University of Toronto

with DAVID SCHALKWYK

Queen Mary University of London

CAMBRIDGE
UNIVERSITY PRESS

CAMBRIDGE
UNIVERSITY PRESS

University Printing House, Cambridge CB2 8BS, United Kingdom

One Liberty Plaza, 20th Floor, New York, NY 10006, USA

477 Williamstown Road, Port Melbourne, VIC 3207, Australia

314–321, 3rd Floor, Plot 3, Splendor Forum, Jasola District Centre,
New Delhi – 110025, India

79 Anson Road, #06-04/06, Singapore 079906

Cambridge University Press is part of the University of Cambridge.

It furthers the University's mission by disseminating knowledge in the pursuit of
education, learning, and research at the highest international levels of excellence.

www.cambridge.org
Information on this title: www.cambridge.org/9781107131934
DOI: 10.1017/9781316443668

© Cambridge University Press 2019

First published 2019

Printed in the United Kingdom by TJ International Ltd, Padstow Cornwall

A catalogue record for this publication is available from the British Library.

Library of Congress Cataloging-in-Publication Data
Names: Magnusson, Lynne, editor. | Schalkwyk, David, editor.
Title: The Cambridge companion to Shakespeare's language /
edited by Lynne Magnusson with David Schalkwyk.
Description: Cambridge, United Kingdom; New York, NY:
Cambridge University Press, 2019. | Includes bibliographical references and index.
Identifiers: LCCN 2019000707 | ISBN 9781107131934 (hardback) |
ISBN 9781107583184 (paperback)
Subjects: LCSH: Shakespeare, William, 1564–1616 – Language. |
Shakespeare, William, 1564–1616 – Literary style.
Classification: LCC PR3072.C36 2019 | DDC 822.3/3–dc23
LC record available at https://lccn.loc.gov/2019000707

ISBN 978-1-107-13193-4 Hardback
ISBN 978-1-107-58318-4 Paperback

CONTENTS

CONTENTS

CONTRIBUTORS

AMY COOK, Stony Brook University

HUGH CRAIG, University of Newcastle, Australia

DIRK DELABASTITA, University of Namur

JEFF DOLVEN, Princeton University

SETH FREY, University of California at Davis

JONATHAN HOPE, Arizona State University

ALYSIA KOLENTSIS, St. Jerome's University, University of Waterloo

DOUGLAS M. LANIER, University of New Hampshire

PETER MACK, University of Warwick

LYNNE MAGNUSSON, University of Toronto

OLIVER MORGAN, University of Geneva

RUTH MORSE, Université-Paris-Sorbonne-Cité

CAROL CHILLINGTON RUTTER, University of Warwick

DAVID SCHALKWYK, Queen Mary University of London

JAMES SIEMON, Boston University

For much of the twentieth century, the close reading of Shakespeare's language played a central role in shaping literary education. With a complex array of established concepts and vocabulary to call on, close reading became the calling card of the discipline of English. And at the centre of that practice, Shakespeare's brilliant language routinely served as the testing ground for innovative approaches and the occasion for so many virtuoso interpretive performances. English studies has since opened its embrace to other disciplines and to what for many have seemed more burning issues than how the language works. The focus has often been much more on cultural and political contexts than the linguistic details of Shakespeare's dramatic texts, increasingly on how the plays speak to questions of gender and race, war and religion, or nationalism and colonialism. The traditional methods of formal text analysis appeared to have little to tell us about these issues. Today, however, more than a little paradoxically, we are being called back more and more to the explication of Shakespeare's language, sometimes by admiration, sometimes by incomprehension, sometimes by a recognition that language use or misuse has an active role in constructing cultural phenomena like race and gender, or war and religion. How can the plays speak to us at all if we forget their language?

The power of Shakespeare's complex language both inspires and challenges today's students and teachers, actors and directors. It has iconic status and enormous resonance, even as language change and the distance of time render it more and more difficult. *The Cambridge Companion to Shakespeare's Language* orients students to important contexts for understanding Shakespeare's experimentation with the English language and offers a range of approaches to enable readers and theatregoers to engage with it directly and pleasurably. Each of the fourteen chapters in the volume incorporates practical analysis and exemplary readings of passages from Shakespeare's plays, carefully modelling the approach under discussion. These up-to-date approaches aim to facilitate students – to be both accessible and stimulating. Accordingly, not only do our contributors explain the present state of play but they identify many places of opportunity for fresh discovery. The chapters equip students to ask productive questions, to try out innovative methodological frameworks, and to test-drive newly available digital technologies. The volume is organised into four parts – basic elements, shaping contexts, new technologies, and contemporary sites for language change.

Basic elements. The first six chapters treat the key elements of Shakespeare's language. They focus on style, words, speech acts, verse and metre, dialogue, and figures of speech. Jeff Dolven provides an overview of early to late Shakespeare as he explores what it means to think of literary language in terms of style, an important but not unproblematic category in use since Shakespeare's day. What many people think of when they think about linguistic creativity is vocabulary, the storehouse of words. Alysia Kolentsis asks what exactly it is that makes Shakespeare's words stand out? She qualifies some of the standard claims about how many words Shakespeare invented and helps students to appreciate his creativity with the existing resources of Early Modern English. Writing about speech acts in Shakespeare, David Schalkwyk invites us to consider dramatic utterance not in terms of words and stylistic ornamentation but instead as a serious – sometimes transformative – mode of action in the world. Treating verse and metre, Oliver Morgan pares down the complicated systems of scansion to some basic elements, showing readers how a minimalist prosody can yield a rich experience of Shakespeare's verse experimentation. Turning to language as interaction, Lynne Magnusson explores how to interpret Shakespeare's dramatic dialogue guided by the tacit knowledge of social conversation evident in our own highly skilled performances. Considering figures of speech 'at work' in Shakespeare, Ruth Morse takes a fresh look at metaphor and its relatives, encouraging us to see how we experience them not just as original surprises but through expectations set up by previous experience of inherited scenes.

Shaping contexts. The next two chapters consider early modern education and Elizabethan social organisation as shaping contexts for Shakespeare's language. Whereas many of the volume's chapters offer insight into the changing English language as a key resource for Shakespeare's verbal artistry, Peter Mack takes us back to the basics of the Latin-based humanist language arts that constituted the curriculum of Elizabethan grammar schools. His chapter on rhetoric as Shakespeare's boyhood guide to composition and as a useful approach to dramatic analysis emphasises what was actually taught in the schools rather than offering an idealised outline of classical oratory or concentrating solely on stylistic figures. (An appendix of useful figures and tropes based on a handlist by Mack appears at the end of this volume.) Clearly, Shakespeare's linguistic artistry was as deeply attuned to the social life of language in his time as it was to the classically inflected language arts of the schoolroom. Teasing out the many diverse social languages and dialects that Shakespeare's plays bring into conversation and collision, James Siemon's chapter gives us rich insights into the dramatist's heterogeneous and multi-languaged world of words.

New technologies. The next group of three chapters tests out new technologies and draws on concepts taking shape in emerging fields. Even as the passage of time and loss of historical grounding is making Shakespeare's language more challenging to the current generation of readers and theatregoers, the availability of digital tools, enabling lightning-swift counts and searches, is making it accessible and readable in wholly new ways. Jonathan Hope's two-part chapter on digital approaches provides, first, a how-to guide to methods one can learn quickly and use to make new discoveries now and, second, an account of more complex analytic tools and visualisation techniques that alter the object of study and that effect a conceptual shift in what it is to 'read'. Hugh Craig's chapter uses digital technology that was developed to answer questions about authorship attribution in order to 'read' large corpora of plays by Shakespeare and his contemporaries and to study their comparative styles. Amy Cook and Seth Frey offer an interdisciplinary experiment on experiential reading when they bring new work on the cognitive processing of language into conversation with ways that innovative literary scholars have engaged with Shakespeare's poetic artistry.

Contemporary sites for language change. The final three chapters turn to three sites – the theatre, translation, and popular culture – where Shakespeare's highly adaptable language is still living and speaking out today. Carol Chillington Rutter considers how Shakespeare, himself an actor, wrote lines and speech exchanges to serve the actors he knew so well, and she shows how that language also serves actors today, cueing performance. Dirk Delabastita reflects on what happens to 'Shakespeare's language' without the English words, translated to speak around the globe. Putting Shakespeare's writing in interlingual and intercultural dialogue can afford a 'stereoscopic reading', illuminating both the host language and Shakespeare's as its guest. In the concluding chapter, Douglas M. Lanier discovers method in how advertising and popular culture reread and adapt Shakespeare's phrases. While Shakespeare teachers and scholars (including many in this volume) often ask that we 'historicise' and read the words 'in context', Lanier takes an appreciative look at our love for Shakespeare's words let loose from history and contextual constraint and fitted to our own lives and often incongruous enterprises.

Thanks are owed and most gratefully offered to the Folger Shakespeare Library for hosting a symposium that was a seed for this volume; to the Social Sciences and Humanities Research Council of Canada for funding support; to Lindsay Mason for expert research assistance; to graduate students in repeated incarnations of 'Shakespeare's Language' at the University of Toronto; to Deirdre Baker and Carol Percy for encouragement and to Paul Stevens for generous advice; to the contributors for their patience and wisdom; and to our supportive Cambridge University Press editors, Sarah Stanton and Emily Hockley. For both editors of this volume, being in dialogue with one another about Shakespeare's language is an enduring pleasure.

Throughout this edition, act, scene, and line references (unless otherwise indicated) are to the volumes of the New Cambridge Shakespeare.

Lynne Magnusson

ABBREVIATIONS

Ado	*Much Ado about Nothing*
Ant.	*Antony and Cleopatra*
AYLI	*As You Like It*
Cor.	*Coriolanus*
Cym.	*Cymbeline*
Err.	*The Comedy of Errors*
Ham.	*Hamlet*
1H4	*The First Part of King Henry the Fourth*
2H4	*The Second Part of King Henry the Fourth*
H5	*King Henry the Fifth*
1H6	*The First Part of King Henry the Sixth*
2H6	*The Second Part of King Henry the Sixth*
3H6	*The Third Part of King Henry the Sixth*
H8	*King Henry the Eighth*
JC	*Julius Caesar*
John	*King John*
LLL	*Love's Labour's Lost*
Lear	*King Lear*
Mac.	*Macbeth*
MM	*Measure for Measure*
MND	*A Midsummer Night's Dream*
MV	*The Merchant of Venice*
Oth.	*Othello*
Per.	*Pericles*
R2	*King Richard the Second*
R3	*King Richard the Third*
Rom.	*Romeo and Juliet*
Shr.	*The Taming of the Shrew*
Temp.	*The Tempest*
Tim.	*Timon of Athens*

Tit.	*Titus Andronicus*
TN	*Twelfth Night*
TNK	*The Two Noble Kinsmen*
Tro.	*Troilus and Cressida*
Wiv.	*The Merry Wives of Windsor*
WT	*The Winter's Tale*

PART I

Basic Elements

I

JEFF DOLVEN

Shakespeare and the Problem of Style

How does Shakespeare speak of style? Among his twenty thousand or so words, 'style' is not especially prominent, occurring fewer than twenty times. The range of those few uses, however, is wide enough to show the complexity of the concept, and to suggest how vital it is for his work even when it goes unnamed. Take these two bantering aristocrats. They are talking about style as though it had an altitude:

> MARGARET   Will you then write me a sonnet in praise of my beauty?
> BENEDICK   In so high a style, Margaret, that no man living shall come
>   over it.   (*Ado* 5.2.3–6)

A high style, Benedick maintains, suits the elevated subject of love, and it vaults him above his competitors. He draws on the rhetoricians' traditional distinction of high, middle, and low. Another meaning of style must be in play when the word is used in the forest by a shivering courtier:

> AMIENS   I would not change it; happy is your grace
>   That can translate the stubbornness of Fortune
>   Into so quiet and so sweet a style.   (*AYLI* 2.1.18–20)

These lines address the exiled Duke Senior, who has been rehearsing the consolations of his new home in Arcadia. Amiens praises his eloquence, and also his forbearance, the ability to translate hardship into a melodious stoicism. Style is a quality as well as a measure, and a way of living as well as speaking. Such continence and self-control are the very opposite of what the courtier Boyet points out in the Spaniard Don Armado:

> PRINCESS   What plume of feathers is he that indited this letter?
>   What vane? What weathercock? Did you ever hear better?
> BOYET   I am much deceived but I remember the style. (*LLL* 4.1.87–89)

The blustering soldier has an epistolary style that gives him away, excessive, self-aggrandizing, and not altogether deliberate. Style can be particular to an individual, and it can be a vice. It can also tell time:

> But since he died, and poets better prove,
> Theirs for their style I'll read, his for his love.   (Sonnet 32, 13–14)

Poets are better now, at least in the present's judgement; it is the newcomers that the speaker will read for their style. Style can be a marker of historical time and seasons of fashion. It also seems to be a way of thinking about something that has been lost.

Style as skill, style as a way of living, style as identity, style as time. Style as choice and as compulsion. The meanings of style in Shakespeare's lifetime are various enough to wish that there were another word or two to keep them straight, so much more with the meanings of style today. The problem of style is just this, its tangle of internal contradictions. Style is teachable and demands a specialised vocabulary, but it is also social and occasional, and depends upon a feel for situations. Style is the way we recognise groups and movements, past and present, but it is also the way we pick particular voices from a crowd. Shakespeare exposes these contradictions with unique force. His voice is often said to dissolve into the voices of his creations, each character with a style of his or her own; and yet his own singularity must be a matter of sounding different from other writers of his age, and also of sounding like himself. Conviction in that singularity has gone hand in hand with three centuries of argument about what he wrote and what he did not. The work of this chapter will be to try to hold these meanings and questions together in a survey of Shakespeare's career; to provide an outline of the development of the style of the plays, but also to see them together as a long enquiry into the problem of style itself.

Early Plays: Style and Skill

Style is always to do with difference. Take the following two passages:

> I to the world am like a drop of water
> That in the ocean seeks another drop,
> Who, falling there to find his fellow forth,
> Unseen, inquisitive, confounds himself.   (*Err.* 1.2.35–38)

> The capon burns, the pig falls from the spit.
> The clock hath strucken twelve upon the bell,
> My mistress made it one upon my cheek.
> She is so hot because the meat is cold.   (*Err.* 1.2.44–47)

They are of palpably different styles; you can feel that difference, without immediately being able to say why. The study of style is always a negotiation between such impressions and the analysis that would explain them. The primary sense of the word in the period was technical, grounded in the ancient *artes* of grammar and rhetoric, arts – in the sense of a body of rules, descriptive and prescriptive – that remain the most basic resources for stylistic description. A modern reader might observe of the first passage that its single sentence is highly subordinated, with two nested, dependent clauses. (*Clausulae*, in sixteenth-century grammatical terminology.)[1] The final clause, beginning with 'who', is elegantly suspended, postponing the verb to the end in the manner of a classical period. To speak of a period is to cross from grammar, the rules of use, into rhetoric, the art of persuasion. A period is an orator's device, a show of skill, training, and perhaps fortunate birth. Rhetoric will also point to the formal analogy – *I am to the world as the drop is to the ocean* – and the parallelisms that define it. The choice of words, too, matters to the sense of a style. The diction is mostly plain, a run of good Anglo-Saxon, but the conspicuously Latinate 'inquisitive' has a prominent place near the close.

Grammar, rhetoric, diction. The second passage, by contrast, is paratactic: no suspension, just one clause after another. It is asyndetic: omitting conjunctions, to colloquial effect. Both terms come from classical rhetoric, though the lines they describe do not sound particularly Roman. The vocabulary is predominantly Anglo-Saxon and, with that already old-fashioned *-en* verb ending in 'strucken', even a little homely. That is not to say the lines are without patterns of language that the rhetoricians would recognise. Parallelism structures everything: the capon burning and the pig falling, the clock and the mistress striking, the cheek and the bell struck. The rhetoric handbooks of the time, in Latin and English, would call this balancing act *isocolon*. The parallels are tight, if crude, repetitive, and predictable. They are also urgent, energetic, and funny.

The differences are obvious, the more so when they are itemised. They are obvious in a different way when they are side-by-side in the second scene of *The Comedy of Errors* (1594).[2] The weary traveller Antipholus of Syracuse meets Dromio of Ephesus, the lost-twin servant of his lost-twin brother, for the first time. He mistakes the Ephesian for his own man, Dromio of Syracuse, whom he has just dispatched on an errand. 'What now? How chance thou art returned so soon?' says the disoriented Antipholus. 'Returned so soon? Rather approached too late' (1.2.42–43), replies the wrong Dromio. The reader with leisure to parse the sentences must remember that the grammatical and rhetorical contrast is embodied as a social encounter on the stage, where the differences are matters of character and station, coloured in with costume, gesture, posture, and accent. Still, a technical analysis is not beside the point, even for a theatregoer. Like the rest of the play, the scene hews close to the devices of Roman comedy, Plautus's *Menaechmi* in particular, and its most slapstick moments have a classical pedigree. The exchange is

stylised, as a modern would say; as Shakespeare's age would have it, artificial. Even for a contemporary audience member who could not hear the
Latin behind the English, it would have played both as a comic fiction of
authority and disobedience, and as an exhibition of joint skill in the arts of
language.

Such style-effects are among the reasons why the early Shakespeare is
sometimes called a literary dramatist. The humanist canon of Plautus and
Ovid and Virgil is prominent among his influences, and the names of the
rhetoricians' schemes and tropes sometimes hover over the action like
supertitles. That can be true even in moments of high tragedy, as when, in
Titus Andronicus, Titus's brother Marcus first sees his ravished, tongueless
niece Lavinia. Listen, again, for the parallelisms:

> Alas, a crimson river of warm blood,
> Like to a bubbling fountain stirred with wind,
> Doth rise and fall between thy rosèd lips,
> Coming and going with thy honey breath.   (2.4.22–25)

Rise and fall, coming and going; rosèd lips, honey breath. Such devices afford
a particular kind of pleasure, which Shakespeare stages for maximum contrast with the violent fiction. The actors are playing a game that members of
the audience can also play, the game of eloquence, and the theatre is at once
a field outside ancient Rome and a social space of shared skill. Tragic event
is also rhetorical occasion. One of the most important backgrounds for such
performances of style – almost superimposed as a second stage upon that
Roman field – is the Elizabethan schoolroom, where Shakespeare likely first
read his Plautus and his Ovid. He was one of a number of well-educated
playwrights emerging in the 1590s, which included men like Robert Greene,
Thomas Kyd, and George Peele, who had grammar school or even university training. The boys learned to imitate Roman orators and poets, and
to fill their commonplace books and their minds with the names of figures like *isocolon* and *anaphora* and *parataxis*. Frequent declamations and
disputations and even, in some schools, the staging of Latin plays made the
study of language into a performance, and behind Marcus's perverse fluency
are countless classroom impersonations of Dido or Hecuba.[3]

The coordinates of place, time, and station afforded by style can be
very precise, but the schoolroom imposed a gross measure that shaped the
period's consciousness of stylistic possibility. Style has three levels, or 'three
principal complexions', as George Puttenham put it in 1589: 'high, mean,
and base'.[4] The division had the authority of Cicero, who had given the
genera dicendi, or kinds of speech, their canonical formulations. The *genus
grande* has 'splendid power of thought and majesty of diction', sometimes

achieved by poised and rounded sentences, artefacts of masterful premeditation; sometimes by a rougher vocabulary and blunter, irregular sentence structures, made in the heat of an urgent occasion. The *genus humile* is good for 'explaining everything and making every point clear rather than impressive, using a refined, concise style stripped of ornament'. Between them lies a style '*medius et quasi temperatus*', moderate and tempered, the middle style, which uses 'neither the intellectual appeal of the latter class nor the fiery force of the former'. For some later theorists, this middle style could be 'flowery' or 'sweet', the idiom of lyric.⁵ The three would come to be identified with three motives: the high style, for moving its audience (*movere*); the middle, for pleasing (*conciliare* or *placere*); the low, for teaching (*docere*).

The levels of style are an ideology as much as an expressive repertoire. Together they project an ideal of decorum, the right level for every situation. Subject matter and speaker are both to be taken into account: 'It behooveth the maker or the poet to follow the nature of his subject', Puttenham advises, but it 'may it be said as well that men do choose their subjects according to the mettle of their minds' (234). When the style suits the occasion, when each interlocutor knows his or her place, society is integral and whole. The humanist ambition to unite eloquence and wise counsel is secure. When there is dissonance in the system it is a sign of dissent or injustice. *Love's Labour's Lost* (1594–5) is a particularly self-conscious laboratory for such stylistic adjustments, perhaps the play in Shakespeare's canon most *about* style. As the action begins, if 'action' is the right word, King Ferdinand and his attendant lords have pledged themselves to three years of scholarly austerity. Their idiom is wit, an agile middle style. The play derives much of its comedy from listening in as they trade their arch banter for the high-style Petrarchan flights of their sonnets, falling in love, one by one, with the Princess of France and her retinue, preparing the way for a quartet of dynastic unions. Unless, that is, Petrarchan poetry is better understood as a lyric middle style. In that case, a true high style goes missing in the play, a play in which the nobility have retired to the country, absent from their courts, and which ends by deferring those marriages for a year. The levels can be tricky to apply in practice. The system cannot clarify, let alone resolve, every situation.

That there are *genera dicendi*, however, and that the play negotiates among them, is clear enough. As though to contain the possible confusions, *Love's Labour's Lost* surrounds its aristocratic speakers with avatars of obvious stylistic excess. Don Armado's military high style is corrupt with bluster and the fashionable language of duelling manuals: 'the *passado* he respects not, the *duello* he regards not. His disgrace is to be called boy, but his glory is to subdue men. Adieu, valour; rust, rapier; be still, drum' (1.2.145–148). The punctiliousness of the schoolmaster Holofernes extends to pronouncing silent letters with special emphasis: 'I abhor such fanatical phantasimes, such insociable and point-device companions, such as rackers of orthography, as to speak "dout" sine "b", when he should say "doubt" … It insinuateth me of insanie. *Ne intelligis, domine?*' (5.1.15–21). The Don and the pedant are two versions of the high style gone wrong, and a well-schooled ear will pick out the vices, the comically exaggerated patterning, foreign words, over-weaning copia, and pretentious, undigested Latin. Minor characters are often defined by such stylistic rigidity. If the repertory of the levels promises the free choice of rhetorical virtuosity, such characters suggest something different, style as a compulsion.

The liberties and bondages of artifice are the problem of style for early Shakespeare. It is, again, a literary problem. When he was writing *Love's Labour's Lost*, he was still publishing narrative poems in his own name, *Venus and Adonis* in 1592–3 and *The Rape of Lucrece* in 1593–4. He was closely involved with the community of other playwrights. His debts to Marlowe are widely recognised; at times Shakespeare imitates him as he might have imitated Ovid in school. (Critics have heard the Tamburlaine and Barabas in his Aaron: 'Now climbeth Tamora Olympus' top, / Safe out of fortune's shot, and sits aloft, / Secure of thunder's crack or lightning flash' (*Tit.* 2.1.1–3).) The banter of the Antipholus twins or the French gentlemen would not be out of place in Peele or Greene. The early plays, that is, show a shared reliance on a style system to make character. Shakespeare inhabits that system with burgeoning virtuosity, but it is fair to say that through *Love's Labour's Lost* he distinguishes himself primarily by skill, rather than by the making of an outlying, tell-tale style. The received rhetorical accounts of high, middle, low, and their derivatives – 'the plain and obscure, the rough and smooth, the facile and hard, the plentiful and barren, the rude and eloquent, the strong and feeble, the vehement and cold' (234), as Puttenham puts it – those given styles, ingeniously managed, sometimes exaggerated and satirised, are nonetheless adequate, more or less, to the stories he wants to tell and the people with which he populates them.

Middle Plays: Style and Voice

It is a six-year leap from *Love's Labour's Lost* to *Hamlet*, and what has changed in the plays between – *The Merchant of Venice*, the Henriad, *As You Like It*, among others – can be heard when the prince first speaks. The scene is the Danish court, where Hamlet's uncle Claudius has gathered his council to act out what he hopes will be the final act of a comedy, in which a resourceful marriage, to his dead brother's widow, brings peace to the kingdom of Denmark.

> Therefore our sometime sister, now our queen,
> Th'imperial jointress of this warlike state,
> Have we, as 'twere with a defeated joy,
> With one auspicious and one dropping eye,
> With mirth in funeral and with dirge in marriage,
> In equal scale weighing delight and dole,
> Taken to wife.   (1.2.8–14)

Claudius writes his play in a high style: the masterful parallelism, the suspension of the periodic sentence, ending with an assertion as politically ruthless as it is syntactically elegant. The language of reconciled paradox prepares his audience to accept a union between 'uncle-father and aunt-mother' (2.2.344–345), as Hamlet later puts it. The new king meets no resistance until he looks to Hamlet himself. 'But now, my cousin Hamlet, and my son', he says, turning his arbitration of opposites into a claim of paternity. Hamlet interrupts: 'A little more than kin, and less than kind' (1.2.65). The line plays along with Claudius's parallelism, but barbs it with a pun, driven between kinship and kindness. The exchange is a patent collision of styles, like the high melancholy of Antipholus and the comic plainness of Dromio – but what is Hamlet's style? He manages to be both plain and opaque at once, a maximum refusal of his uncle's stylised manipulations. What level is that? He will not play in Claudius's play, and he will not articulate his speech to the speech around him.

To Hamlet we will return. In the meantime he can stand for a change in the way that the problem of style is posed in the middle plays. The traditional criteria of rhetorical skill become less important, or rather, they are submerged into a complex of plot and character that interacts with language in new ways, more dynamic and idiosyncratic. Five years before *Hamlet*, Shakespeare wrote a scene between King Richard II and the usurper Bullingbrook that reflects this evolving relation to the *genera dicendi*. Like Claudius, Richard is trying to conjure a sense of ceremony out of a broken custom – though he is not usurping the crown, but letting it go. He calls for a mirror, hoping it will show him who he has become.

RICHARD   Was this the face
> That like the sun did make beholders wink?
> Is this the face which faced so many follies,
> That was at last outfaced by Bullingbrook?

> A brittle glory shineth in this face.
> As brittle as the glory is the face,
> [*Smashes the glass.*]
> For there it is, cracked in a hundred shivers. (4.1.282–288)

There is something of the capable statesman's balancing act in the lines' parallelism and anaphora, but Richard is more poet than king, and his dignified cadences are shot through with more anarchic wordplay: 'face', 'face', 'outfaced'. Such punning is almost always in Shakespeare the resource of the disempowered. When Richard takes it up, he is laying down his claim to rule. Bullingbrook, who assumes the crown, began the play in overflowing outrage, but he has learned by Act 4 a new self-control. His answer here is terse: 'The shadow of your sorrow hath destroyed / The shadow of your face' (4.1.291–292). He echoes Richard's isocolon and anaphora and even his wordplay, but subjects them to the discipline of a new regime.

This basic plot of transition from a ceremonial order to the pragmatic language of a disenchanted *Realpolitik* is acted out again and again. In *Julius Caesar*, it can be heard in the words. The old-school Stoicism of Brutus is gradually suborned by the ambitions of Cassius as they conspire in the emperor's murder, and Cassius's new-fangled vocabulary insinuates itself in words like 'majestic' or 'indifferent'.[6] (When Brutus starts to waver, he muses, 'Fashion it thus' (2.1.30).) Style is doing its work of telling historical time. The same rough plot happens inside Prince Hal, Bullingbrook's son, in *Henry IV, Part 1*. The dialect Hal forsakes is the raucous prose of the Eastcheap Tavern, where he prides himself on his fluency: 'They call drinking deep "dyeing scarlet", and when you breathe in your watering they cry "Hem!" and bid you "Play it off!" To conclude, I am so good a proficient in one quarter of an hour that I can drink with any tinker in his own language during my life' (2.4.12–16). The dialect he takes up is the high ceremonial idiom of his ageing father. But he can sound like that pragmatic new man too. Consider his response to Falstaff's passionate self-defence in the second act's mock trial, a torrent of copious prose that concludes with three stirring lines of iambic pentameter: 'banish him not thy Harry's company, banish him not thy Harry's company. Banish plump Jack, and banish all the world' (2.4.396–398). Playing the part of his father, Hal's efficiency would make the Bullingbrook of *King Richard II* proud: 'I do, I will' (2.4.399).

Such characters shift stations and place themselves variously in time. It is not only the hierarchy of styles, however, that defines their differences. They also explore regions of a language-map that has become increasingly psychological as well as political and historical. Cicero, master of the *genera dicendi*, offers precedent for this notion of individual stylistic idiosyncrasy.

In his *De Oratore* he asks of the great orators, 'which resembles anyone but himself?'⁷ Shakespeare's characters sound different from themselves over time, too, whether because they are managing a complex stylistic repertory, like Hal or the aristocrats of *Love's Labour's Lost*, or because their voices alter under the pressure of events. In *Othello* the field of stylistic affinity and difference is as dynamic as the plot. The opening scenes make a statement of what G. Wilson Knight has called the 'Othello music',⁸ the confident, Marlovian high style that is the general at his most authoritative:

> Wherein I spake of most disastrous chances
> Of moving accidents by flood and field,
> Of hair-breadth scapes i'th'imminent deadly breach,
> Of being taken by the insolent foe
> And sold to slavery; of my redemption thence.   (1.3.133–137)

But there is another music in the play, the barbed wit of Iago, with its thrust-and-parry prose and the jangle of its rhyming. When Othello begins to succumb to Iago's hints about his wife's infidelity, his language crosses towards his tempter's, imagining the lovers 'as prime as goats, as hot as monkeys, / As salt as wolves in pride' (3.3.405–406). The fate of Antony in *Antony and Cleopatra* can likewise be told in his (Anthony's) stylistic volatility, the lavish high style of his self-abandonment ('Let Rome in Tiber melt' (1.1.35)); the terse, Stoic maxims with which he greets news of his wife's death ('She's good, being gone' (1.2.123)); the broken language of his shame after Actium ('Apace, Eros, apace! / No more a soldier. Bruisèd pieces, go' (4.15.41–42)). Cleopatra's magnificent oratory at his death is the synthesis of sensuosity and imperial grandeur that he himself could never quite sustain.

If individual voice is one of Shakespeare's great achievements – taking voice to be style, when it is attached to an individual – that achievement is a precarious one for his speakers. They move in and out of one another's fields of imitative influence, while vying for position on a grid of formal, rhetorical possibility. Features of style cross between scenes and acts, too, and it is possible to speak of the sound that pervades individual plays. In *Macbeth*, that sound is portentous, hypnotic antithesis: 'Fair is foul, and foul is fair' (1.1.12), 'To know my deed, 'twere best not know myself' (2.2.76), 'it makes him, and it mars him' (2.3.26). You could say that it is the sound of the play thinking, obsessively, about divided consciousness and divided time. Other plays have comparable devices, which sublimate a particular rhetorical figure into an encompassing atmosphere: hendiadys in *Hamlet*, as George T. Wright has shown ('the trappings and the suits of woe' (1.2.86)), or what John Porter Houston identifies as the fragmentary, dissociated copia, the 'inelegant abundance', of *Coriolanus*.[9] Style plays its role in world-making as it does in self-making. For just this reason, it recedes as a self-conscious category; or at least, it isn't as forward as the performative artificiality that pervades some earlier plays. The change is consistent with a phase of Shakespeare's career in which his great work is tragedy. The virtuosity of these plays it is not the kind that invites the wits in the audience to play along. The tragic predicament is always that we can only listen and watch.

Hamlet himself, that most charismatic of enigmas, is ever at the centre of all of such questions. His lines are a constant syntactic experiment. He is given to infolded brevity, but he can be garrulous and charming, as he is in welcoming the players. He sounds so modern, but has an apparent weakness for the fustian rhetoric of the old repertoire. He is a nimble mimic, whether he is ridiculing a slower wit like the foppish Osric or 'out-Herod[ing] Herod' (3.2.11). There are names for what his sentences do, like the anacoluthon of their self-interruption or the catachresis, the metaphorical abandon, of his more extreme conceits. Still there is something anti-rhetorical about the way it comes out, especially in the soliloquies: 'the syntax of shifting consciousness, not of logical development' (91), as Houston puts it. Puttenham reminds us that style is

> of words, speeches, and sentences together a certain contrived form and quality, many times natural to the writer, many times his peculiar by election and art, and such as either he keepeth by skill or holdeth on by ignorance, and will not or peradventure cannot easily alter into any other.   (233)

Is style at Hamlet's command, an artful choice; or is it something he cannot change, at the mercy of habit or mood or ancient injury? Is it artificial, or all too natural? A skill or a symptom? Does Hamlet sound like himself, or helplessly, variously like the world he so despairs of? In this sense the problem of Hamlet is also the problem of style.

Interlude: Counting Style

The *dramatis personae*, the juxtaposition of scenes, the sequence of plays: they are all fields for the perception of stylistic difference. The question so far has been how Shakespeare constructs these networks of affinity and distinction inside his fictions. What of the playwright himself, in the larger field of the language, where style can be a key to what he wrote, when he wrote it, and the place he made for himself among other playwrights? English as he had it over his lifetime was much less standardised than it would be even fifty years later. The first monolingual English dictionary was not printed until 1604. There was an English grammar in 1586, but it had no wide circulation, and there would not be another for thirty years. The language, meanwhile, was changing rapidly, carried into new tasks and territories by the rise of printing, widening trade networks, and the vernacular impulse of reformed religion. Many humanists, protectors of a culture of classical learning in the schools and universities, doubted that English could achieve the eloquence or poetic power of their Roman heroes. Others, like the poet George Gascoigne, defended its vulgar eloquence: 'You shall do very well to use your verse after thenglishe phrase, and not after the maner of other languages.'[10] The climate of debate and change meant that English was an instrument of great historical sensitivity. Expressive choices not only mapped the social landscape, but implied different visions of the national past and the national future.

Those choices begin with words, of which Shakespeare's dramatic vocabulary includes about twenty thousand. There has been a running argument among critics about how many he invented, as high as 2,200 if you count first recorded uses in the *OED*, though estimates have declined steadily as more period texts have been digitised and rendered searchable.[11] What can still be said with certainty is that he was an unusually vigorous participant in a culture of new coinage. Where to get the new words was a controversial question, with humanists tending to promote the archive of the ancient languages, Latin and Greek; others standing by the native, Anglo-Saxon roots of what Gascoigne called 'auncient English' (457). George Puttenham was a polemicist in the second camp. He offered new, English terms for the rhetorical figures, like *sage-sayer* for *sententia* and *trespasser* for *hyperbaton*. The humanists' Latinity was disparaged as 'inkhornism'. The diagnosis suits Holofernes: 'This is a gift that I have, simple, simple – a foolish extravagant spirit, full of forms, figures, shapes, objects, ideas, apprehensions, motions, revolutions' (*LLL* 4.2.59–61).

Shakespeare seems to have shared that scepticism about the inkhorn, and the plays often go in for mocking pedants. That is not to say he does not avail himself of a higher style. Holofernes's multiplication of near-synonyms is a parody of Erasmian *copia*, the humanist ideal of a various and plentiful eloquence. Claudius's parallelisms are a more controlled example; fat Falstaff incarnates an exuberant, vernacular translation. Doublings of the Anglo-Saxon and Latin arbitrate between these language-worlds, phrases like 'dull and long-continued' (*Tro.* 1.3.259) or 'wise saws and modern instances' (*AYLI* 2.7.156), often pairing a common and a hard word by way of definition on the fly. The nativist impulse is audible in inventive compounds, like Lear's 'thought-executing' or 'pent-up' (*Lear* 3.2.4, 55). Compounds tend to sound more German, less French or Italian or Latinate. (These modern romance languages are often treated, for comic effect, as pretentious.) Shakespeare also uses archaic forms, like Dromio's 'strucken', mostly to mark a speaker as un-cosmopolitan. He will occasionally put regional dialect in the mouth of a character like *King Lear*'s Poor Tom, who seems to come from the southern shires. There is little of what we would now call slang in the plays. Uneducated speakers, however, deform the language in haplessly ingenious ways.

Shakespeare is the master of a particular moment in the history of English vocabulary, one that was formative for the double nature of the language. He bounces Anglo-Saxon and Latin or romance lineages off one another in a constant play of high and low, abstract and concrete, fluent and terse. For all his free command, however, a couple of tendencies emerge. First, his vocabulary is somewhat less Latinate than that of his contemporaries, at least his contemporaries among the learned playwrights. If the Latin shows to effect, that is partly a consequence of vigorous and constant contrast. Second, in cases where older and newer forms are in free variation, Shakespeare has a discernible preference, throughout his career, for the past. The verb ending *–eth*, an older and outgoing form for the third person singular, is a good example. It is of service metrically, giving the poet an extra syllable when he needs it, but Shakespeare uses it more than other poets do. Something similar could be said about his syntax. Jonathan Hope and others have studied his use of auxiliary *do*, a grammatical construction that was unregulated in the period, meaning that it could be used, or not, in place of the simple past in phrases like 'mine eyes did see' or 'our ship did split' (*TN* 1.1.18, 1.2.8). In modern English, the form is used only for questions and specific emphasis (Did she go? – she *did* go!). The historical trend is strongly towards regulation even in 1600, and Shakespeare's contemporaries among the poets mostly went along. Shakespeare continued to use these auxiliaries all his life.[12]

There is a deep feeling for the old world in Shakespeare's work, the world whose loss he dramatised again and again at the hands of Bullingbrook and Octavius and Edgar and even perhaps Hamlet. His innovations feel to modern readers as though they point to the future. This may be perhaps less because of his pointing than our following. Whether or not he became newer, he did become increasingly different, increasingly experimental. The syntactic resources of the plays steadily expand, enriched and complicated with new techniques of dilation, fragmentation, and interruption. His metre changes, too. The handling of the iambic line in the early plays is indistinguishable from that of his contemporaries – quite regular, with lines syntactically end-stopped and frequently rhymed. Metre never does become a technique for differentiating character, but the total rhythm of the plays is more and more adventurous as time goes on, with more short lines, more lines shared between characters, more ambiguity in the scansion of syllables, and a general shift from the priority of the line to the priority of the phrase.[13] Such changes have all been of use to scholars dating the plays. Across all the registers of style there are gradual changes, the career of Shakespeare's style, within the larger, shared stories told by the history of the language.

Out of these countless choices or dispositions or tics, across so many registers, lexical, syntactic, rhetorical, metrical, it is possible to gather a sense of the style of the playwright, a style particular to Shakespeare himself – a voice. Confidence that his voice is recognisable among the differences of his characters has often underwritten claims about what he wrote and what he did not. The who-was-Shakespeare-really industry argues for his sounding like everyone from Marlowe to Bacon to the Earl of Oxford. (Not always wrongly; but that is not because they wrote his plays.) More convincing research has focused on identifying Shakespeare's voice in works he shared with others. Co-authorship was common during his theatrical career, and as many as half of the surviving plays were the work of more than one hand. His last two plays are now widely agreed to have been written with John Fletcher; others, such as *Titus Andronicus* and *Henry VI, Part 1*, and even *Macbeth*, contain passages by other writers. The history of *Henry VIII* is exemplary. As early as 1758, the poet and editor Richard Roderick observed the unusual incidence in the play of weak line endings, lines ending with an unstressed syllable, many more than usual even in late Shakespeare. In 1850, James Spedding made a speculative division of the play's scenes between Shakespeare and Fletcher, in an act of connoisseurship that relied on 'a general effect produced on the mind, the ear, and the feelings by a free and broad perusal'.[14] Style is an impression, after all. But he bolstered his hypothesis with a count of those weak endings, looking back to Roderick's observation, and his divisions have held up well.

Modern scholarship negotiates between intuition and quantification using an increasingly sophisticated set of computational tools for parsing the plays' language. The authorial signature can be tested by a variety of methods, including distinctive combinations of words, habits of grammar, counts of so-called 'function words', 'this's and 'with's. The computer can patiently weigh things that neither reader nor writer ever cared about, or knew they cared about, or at all events did not choose. Such tests have helped confirm, refine, and sometimes challenge traditional arguments about the dating of the plays. They have offered some evidence for the stylistic differences that obtain among characters. They also suggest that those differences begin to disappear in the later plays, that the traditional measures of style, bound up for a time with characterisation, begin to loosen those bonds.[15] Here, too, counting provides new evidence for some old impressions. It was in 1808 that Charles Lamb said that Fletcher 'lays line upon line ... adding image to image so deliberately that we see where they join. Shakespeare mingles everything, embarrasses sentences and metaphors; before one has burst its shell, another is hatched and clamours for this disclosure' (Vickers 362).

Late Plays: Style and Time

Consider a modern critic who takes a similar view of this mixing in late Shakespeare, Anne Barton. 'Over and over again', she writes, 'Shakespeare jettisons consistency of characterization because he is more interested in the impersonal quality of a moment of dramatic time'.[16] She points to Leontes's rant in *The Winter's Tale*, when he cries, 'I have drunk, and seen the spider' (2.1.45). It is an extreme performance, in its broken torrent of self-rebuke, but one that epitomises larger changes in the way the plays sound. He is only slightly less heated when he accuses his counsellor Camillo of disloyalty:

> To bide upon't; thou art not honest; or,
> If thou inclin'st that way, thou art a coward,
> Which hoxes honesty behind, restraining
> From course required; or else thou must be counted
> A servant grafted in my serious trust,
> And therein negligent; or else a fool. (1.2.239–244)

Modern editors are driven to desperate ingenuities of dash, semicolon, and comma to parse what is ultimately an unparsable onrush. Camillo begins his answer in a different style, making a list out of the king's rant – 'I may be negligent, foolish, and fearful' (247) – and then returning to each term in order, a careful *correlatio*: 'If ever I were wilful-negligent, / It was my folly; if industriously / I played the fool, it was my negligence ... if ever fearful ... 'twas a fear / Which oft infects the wisest' (252–259). But here he is in Act 4, trying to persuade the prince Florizel to go to Sicilia:

> A course more promising
> Than a wild dedication of yourselves
> To unpathed waters, undreamed shores – most certain
> To miseries enough; no hope to help you,
> But as you shake off one to take another;
> Nothing so certain as your anchors, who
> Do their best office if they can but stay you
> Where you'll be loath to be. (4.4.545–552)

Camillo claims to recommend the safer path, but his language has his old master's wildness. It seems to be something about the play that makes him sound this way.

What this wildness means is the great question of the romances. Some of Shakespeare's most radical experiments take place in the almost retrograde context of what Ben Jonson would call his 'moldy tales'. There is more of a consensus about how the late plays sound. The metre has become ever less regular, more freely enjambed, more phrasal in its rhythms. The syntax is more convoluted. As Russ McDonald puts it, 'the number of deformed phrases, directional shifts, and intricately constructed sentences is exceptional'.[17] McDonald also identifies such hallmarks as dropped connectives between clauses (as with 'miseries enough – no hope'); a heavy dependence on parenthesis; insistent, almost obsessive, repetition of letters, words, phrases, and rhythms; and a copia of dissociated metaphors, the hatching and clamouring of Lamb's account, like Leontes's whiplash transition above from hoxing (or hamstringing) an animal to grafting a plant. Modern critics turn again and again to that word 'experimental' to capture these changes, but if it fits, it is not exactly our idea of experiment, with its purposes and controls; more a kind of limit-seeking that remembers the etymological bond between 'experiment' and 'peril'.

It is tempting to take the mage Prospero as the avatar of this late transformation. He is the solitary maker writing the play of his own abdication, ventriloquising as best he can the other characters in pursuit of a resolution that embraces and transcends them all. His voice is the most prominent in *The Tempest*, and if the other characters sound alike, you could say it is because they sound like him. (Consider Miranda rebuking Caliban, incarnating all her father's anxious rage: 'When thou didst not, savage, / Know thine own meaning, but wouldst gabble like / A thing most brutish, I endowed thy purposes / With words that made them known' (1.2.355–358).) Prospero gives us the late style beloved of Theodor Adorno and Hermann Broch: Shakespeare as a kind of Beethoven, finally deaf to the world and listening only to himself; a man whose argument now is only with time, the still-unvanquished demon of the tragedies.[18] The compressed, elliptical, unpredictable lines are little models of the compressed, elliptical, unpredictable plots by which all the late plays find their way back to some chastened version of the consolations of comedy.

That said, *The Tempest* is not Shakespeare's last play. *Henry VIII* and *The Two Noble Kinsmen* were yet to come, the plays he wrote with John Fletcher. Brian Vickers, in his study of co-authorship, puts Fletcher and Shakespeare side-by-side to remind us of the difference in their voices (362–363):

> He counsels a divorce, a loss of her
> That like a jewel has hung twenty years
> About his neck, yet never lost her lustre.   (*H8* 2.2.29–33)

His highness, having lived so long with her, and she
So good a lady that no tongue could ever
Pronounce dishonour of her – by my life,
She never knew harm-doing.   (*H8* 2.3.2–5)

Two different characters, Norfolk and Anne Boleyn, are speaking of Queen
Katherine; but also two different playwrights. They are not easy to confuse: Fletcher's is perfectly good poetry, a thought evenly sustained through
a lucid image; in Shakespeare, the language breaks midway, tumbling from
the poised Latinity of 'pronounce dishonour' to the urgent, Anglo-Saxon
compound 'harm-doing'. It is all style, but by no means all surface. There are
ways, to be sure, in which these late plays might be said to show the influence of Fletcher on Shakespeare. Bart Van Es argues that the younger man
was associated with a growing fashion for an 'aestheticised, experimental'[19]
drama; the plays he wrote before his collaborations featured elements
of masque, magic, and meta-theatre that become especially important to
Shakespeare after *Pericles*. Such large-scale matters of plot and atmosphere
are part of style too, how we locate the plays in their social and professional
surroundings. The late Shakespeare is a playwright among playwrights, in
some ways a literary dramatist again. Still, he sounds different, and line by
line, he sounds like himself.

   Which is to say that however it may be explained, the problem of style
comes forward again at the end of Shakespeare's career. The skill of the early
plays is no longer an adequate measure. The late plays are transgressive, and
at their most characteristic they unfold without criterion. They may still
exploit the differences in style that partition the England of his audience
into its ways and stations, and they may still activate the principles by which
the rhetorical order of that society was understood. But their sound, in its
strange, pervasive music, is the sound of another world. The achievement
of the late plays is to overcome the antagonism between style and fiction,
the law by which awareness of style's surface suspends our imaginative
immersion. Style in a play like *The Winter's Tale* is a second nature, in something like Philip Sidney's sense, how the poet by the force of breath brings
forth things far surpassing nature's doings. 'Lie there my art' (*Temp.* 1.2.25),
says Prospero; he means his magical *techne*, his skill. But he never lays down
his style.

NOTES

1   Ian Michael observes, however, that the subordinate clause was rarely singled
    out in the grammatical theory of the period; *clausula* could refer to any part
    of a sentence. See *English Grammatical Categories and the Tradition to 1800*
    (Cambridge: Cambridge University Press, 1970), pp. 43–44.

2 All dates for Shakespeare's works are taken from Stanley Wells, Gary Taylor, John Jowett, and William Montgomery (eds.), *The Oxford Shakespeare: A Textual Companion* (Oxford: Oxford University Press, 1997), pp. 69–144.

3 These performances are the subject of Lynn Enterline's *Shakespeare's Schoolroom: Rhetoric, Discipline, Emotion* (Philadelphia: University of Pennsylviania Press, 2011).

4 George Puttenham, *The Art of English Poesy*, ed. Frank Whigham and Wayne A. Rebhorn (Ithaca: Cornell University Press, 2007), p. 234.

5 David Wilson-Okamura, *Spenser's International Style* (Cambridge: Cambridge University Press, 2013), pp. 79–85.

6 David Daniell makes this observation in his edition of *Julius Caesar*, Arden Third Series (Walton-on-Thames: Thomas Nelson, 1998), pp. 60–62.

7 Cicero, *On the Orator: Book 3. On Fate. Stoic Paradoxes. Divisions of Oratory*, tr. H. Rackham (Cambridge, MA: Harvard University Press, 1942), pp. 22–23.

8 G. Wilson Knight, 'The *Othello* Music', *The Wheel of Fire: Interpretations of Shakespearian Tragedy* (Oxford: Oxford University Press, 1930), pp. 97–119.

9 George T. Wright, 'Hendiadys and *Hamlet*', *PMLA* 96 (1981): 168–193; John Porter Houston, *Shakespearian Sentences: A Study in Style and Syntax* (Baton Rouge: Louisiana State University Press, 1988), p. 162.

10 George Gascoigne, 'Certayne Notes of Instruction', *A Hundreth Sundrie Flowres*, ed. G. W. Pigman (Oxford: Oxford University Press, 2000), pp. 454–462; p. 459.

11 David Crystal, *Think on My Words: Exploring Shakespeare's Language* (Cambridge: Cambridge University Press, 2008), pp. 8–11.

12 Jonathan Hope, *The Authorship of Shakespeare's Plays: A Socio-Linguistic Study* (Cambridge: Cambridge University Press, 1994), pp. 11–26.

13 George T. Wright, *Shakespeare's Metrical Art* (Berkeley: University of California Press, 1988), pp. 249, 116, 157, 213.

14 Brian Vickers, *Shakespeare, Co-Author: A Historical Study of Five Collaborative Plays* (Oxford: Oxford University Press, 2002), p. 336.

15 Michael Witmore and Jonathan Hope discuss the late plays holistically in 'Shakespeare by the Numbers: On the Linguistic Texture of the Late Plays', *Early Modern Tragicomedy*, ed. Subha Mukherji and Raphael Lyne (Cambridge: D.S. Brewer, 2007), pp. 133–153.

16 Anne Barton, 'Leontes and the Spider: Language and Speaker in Shakespeare's Last Plays', *Essays, Mainly Shakespearian* (Cambridge: Cambridge University Press, 1994), pp. 161–181; p. 167.

17 Russ McDonald, *Shakespeare's Late Style* (Cambridge: Cambridge University Press, 2006), p. 33.

18 Gordon McMullan discusses the category of late style, with some scepticism, in *Shakespeare and the Idea of Late Writing* (Cambridge: Cambridge University Press, 2007).

19 Bart Van Es, *Shakespeare in Company* (Oxford: Oxford University Press, 2013), p. 266.

2

ALYSIA KOLENTSIS

Shakespeare's Creativity with Words

What is more Shakespearean, in the popular imagination, than creativity with words?[1] Shakespeare's mythic gift for lexical invention underlies his enduring reputation as godfather of English literature and language, a writer whose work has apparently given us 'roughly one-tenth of all the most quotable utterances written or spoken in English since its inception'.[2] The reality of Shakespeare's lexical creativity is rather more earthbound. In recent decades, the standard narrative of Shakespeare's unsurpassed inventiveness has been challenged, thanks in part to the digitisation of early modern texts, renewed attention to the social and historical contexts of Shakespeare's life and work, and a recognition of the fertile linguistic milieu in which he came of age. This chapter considers the ways that Shakespeare's linguistic ingenuity is indebted to his attunement to the potential inherent in the existing resources of his language, and it offers an overview of various examples of his creativity with words, including his coinages, repetitions, puns, and etymological wordplay. It also considers the rich and dynamic English language that was Shakespeare's most valuable tool, as well as his immersion in a culture that took seriously the matters of teaching, critiquing, and listening to language.

Shakespeare's popular reputation is aligned with an exuberance and celebration of the power of words, yet the characters he created tend to express a more tempered view. Speakers frequently disparage words on Shakespeare's stage. Both Hamlet and Troilus speak dismissively of the potential emptiness and equivocation of 'Words, words, [mere] words' (*Ham.* 2.2.189; *Tro.* 5.5.107); Falstaff punctures the lofty aspirations of 'honour' by designating it a 'word ... a mere scutcheon' (*1H4* 5.1.132–137); and Cleopatra, with characteristic incisiveness, calls out Caesar's flattery by transforming the noun into a damning and original verb: 'He words me, girls, he words me' (*Ant.* 5.2.190). In these instances, words are figured as agents of misdirection, and language users must be alert to their inherently hollow or fraudulent nature. Even when the power of words is lauded, the praise is muted. In Sonnet 76, the poet-speaker professes anxiety about his ostensibly staid verse, his inability or reluctance to adopt the 'new-found methods' and 'compounds strange' of his contemporaries (4). Yet he locates the beauty and novelty of verse in his capacity to remake what is already there: 'So all my best is dressing old words new / Spending again what is already spent' (11–12). In a paean of sorts to an understated type of creativity, the speaker suggests that even those words that are 'old' and familiar have the capacity to signify in surprising and expressive ways. Shakespeare's particular linguistic skills are evident in the unadorned words that capture an astonishing array of emotion and encapsulate entire narratives – think of Prince Hal's 'I do, I will' (*1H4* 2.4.399) or Lear's 'O, you are men of stones' (*Lear* 5.3.231) – as well as in the unexpected dimensions he uncovers in even the simplest of utterances. An understanding of Shakespeare's lexical resources, and the linguistic climate in which he lived and worked, helps to illuminate the ways in which he was truly creative: not in an unparalleled knack for invention, but rather in a sharp attunement to the linguistic resources at hand.

In Shakespeare's lifetime, the status of English as a lowly vernacular was shifting. It was gradually moving towards written standardisation, and debates about the language's expressive and rhetorical capacity flourished. Late sixteenth-century England was saturated with foundational questions of language; the enduring Elizabethan interest in topics such as grammar, rhetoric, and linguistic change reveals a culture that was 'extremely self-conscious about its language'.[3] Such attention to language is not surprising, given that the English of this period was characterised by exceptional expansion. During Shakespeare's lifetime, loan words and new words formed from the building blocks of existing ones enriched the English lexicon at an unprecedented rate.[4] The remarkably generative nature of English allowed for ample choice and expressive potential among early modern speakers and writers. While Shakespeare was auspiciously positioned to take advantage of a language that had much to offer, he was not the singular neologiser enshrined in the popular imagination. The peak of vocabulary growth in Early Modern English coincided with the years that Shakespeare lived and wrote, but he was responsible for relatively few new English words.[5] Through analysis of newly available digital databases, scholars have made convincing claims that Shakespeare's language was not particularly exceptional. In an essay on the 'myths' and 'reality' of Shakespeare's vocabulary, Hugh Craig concludes that Shakespeare coined new words at a rate comparable to his fellow playwrights, just as his vocabulary was in keeping with those of others.[6] In fact, what is perhaps more interesting than the 'fact' of Shakespeare's word creation is what the capacity for invention tells us about the state of the English language. As Helen Cooper observes, Shakespeare's 'much commented upon neologisms (many of them in fact attested earlier) rely on the ease with which English can create new compounds or new usages from words already there, a process helped by the loss of many grammatical endings over the course of the Middle Ages'.[7] It is tempting to hold Shakespeare up as the vanguard of Elizabethan word coinage, but his reputation as such is unearned, and it tells us more about his larger-than-life cultural legacy – championed by Romantic poets, lexicographers, and Bardolators alike – than his actual creative output.

English is elastic by nature; purists today may complain about apparently repellent verbal constructions such as 'growing a business' and 'dialoguing with colleagues', but the process of functional shift, or conversion, that permits such usage is a paradigmatic feature of the modern language. One of the most prominent changes associated with the transition from Middle English to Early Modern English was the gradual loss of inflections. In linguistic terms, English began as what is called a 'synthetic' language, which uses inflections (prefixes or suffixes) to signal the relationship between words, before gradually transforming into an 'analytic' language, which depends on factors such as word order and particles such as prepositions to indicate parts of speech. In Old English, then, 'a noun is a noun because it has a noun-like ending'.[8] These specific and distinctive inflections meant that words remained rigidly categorised – the noun 'dialogue' could not be used as a verb because the language did not permit such boundary-crossing. Even in Middle English, as inflections declined, functional shift was rare; long-standing notions of strict grammatical categories seemed to linger despite the changes that were afoot. By Shakespeare's time, however, when parts of speech were no longer distinguished by inflections, functional shift was widespread – it was a favoured way to expand the expressive possibilities of English through its existing components and its unique state of flexibility. Thus, Shakespeare could use 'dialogue' in a way that could make present-day prescriptivists cringe, as when Apemantus asks Timon, 'Dost dialogue with thy shadow?' (*Tim.* 2.2.55). Indeed, principal parts of speech were more readily interchangeable in Shakespeare's England than they are today; 'such interchanges were particularly common between adjectives and nouns, adjectives and adverbs, verbs and adverbs, but even nouns and verbs exchanged functions'.[9] The new plasticity of Early Modern English meant writers such as Shakespeare understood lexical categories in a different way than those who came before or after, and in their hands parts of speech became malleable and productive resources.[10]

While functional shift was a key feature of Shakespeare's linguistic inheritance, familiar and available to speakers and writers of his time, he transformed it into a wellspring of creative expression. Shakespeare was certainly not the only poet and playwright of his time to exploit conversion for expressive ends, but he demonstrated an astonishing deftness and ease with arranging lexical building blocks to unusual and arresting effect. One of his hallmark manoeuvres is the conversion of a mundane noun into an unexpected verb. In *Coriolanus*, Menenius uses the arresting phrase 'cupboarding the viand' (1.1.83) to describe accusations of selfish hoarding, while in *The Tempest*, Alonso's lament for his presumably drowned son is framed in a viscerally suggestive verb: 'I wish / Myself were mudded in that oozy bed / Where my son lies' (5.1.150–152). 'Cupboarding' and 'mudded' derive their verve from specific affective and descriptive characteristics of their source nouns, unexpectedly transformed into forms of action. Such noun-to-verb conversion is particularly effective for the narrative demands of drama, which depends upon momentum-saturated dialogue. Consider, as well, how Shakespeare employs this strategy not only to invent a new word, but also to reimagine an existing word's function. Instances such as Gremio's sardonic assertion that 'Petruchio is Kated' (*Shr.* 3.2.234); Perdita's vow 'I'll queen it no inch farther' (*WT* 4.4.429); and Cleopatra's 'I shall see / Some squeaking Cleopatra boy my greatness' (*Ant.* 5.2.218–219) rely on the audience's surprise at a repurposed noun. Deployed as novel verbs, these words imbue Shakespeare's dramatic dialogue with captivating semantic force; a simple phrase such as 'boy my greatness' is extraordinarily apt, thanks in large part to a fresh verb redolent with associations of presumptive overreach and callow inefficacy.

Just as he recognises the expressive potential of a strategically altered noun, Shakespeare has a particular talent for converting a commonplace noun into a striking adjective. Again, functional shift enables Shakespeare to take advantage of his language's existing lexical stock and fluid grammar to create clever and evocative descriptors. In King Henry IV's maudlin description of his troubled kingdom, 'and, other times, to see / The beachy girdle of the ocean / Too wide for Neptune's hips' (*2H4* 3.1.48–50), the whimsy of the personified image is crystallised in the invented adjective 'beachy'. Functional shift from noun to adjective can also be playful – such as in Falstaff's encomium to the 'most comparative rascalliest sweet young prince' Hal (*1H4* 1.2.64) – and revealingly self-reflective, as when Berowne apparently renounces his attachment to 'Figures *pedantical* – these summer flies / Have blown me full of *maggot* ostentation' (*LLL* 5.2.407–408, emphasis added). Berowne's phrase highlights two different examples of effective nominal adjectives – 'pedantical' and 'maggot' – while at the same time it draws attention to a characteristic Shakespearean linguistic strategy: the transformation of an evocative noun to a startling adjective.

Here, the metaphor of flies infecting Berowne with his propensity for verbal pretension is emphasised by the lexical play. The noun 'maggot', with its visceral associations of decay and corruption, gains unsettling force through its unexpected pairing with the noun 'ostentation' (a discomfiting effect reinforced by the harsh staccato of hard 'g' and 't' consonants). The image is particularly fitting; to be 'full of maggot[s]' is to be irrevocably diseased, and, as this speech shows, Berowne is too far gone to notice that his earnest renunciation of verbal flourish is delivered in ostentatious sonnet form.

Another signature Shakespearean lexical skill, also reliant on the plasticity of his raw material, is the union of two words (often derived from different parts of speech) in an evocative compound. Several of Shakespeare's compounds have entered our collective lexicon – 'star-cross'd' (*Rom.* Prologue line 6); 'widow-maker' (*John* 5.2.17); and 'helter-skelter' (*2H4* 5.3.76) among them – and often these are the types of words that come to mind when we think of Shakespeare's creativity with words. Yet the sheen and novelty of these creative combinations make it easy to overlook their powerful expressive properties. The combination of noun and verb into a single descriptive word is particularly invigorating to dramatic dialogue, since it ensures that narrative momentum is present even in what appears to be a simple description. When Prospero, in *The Tempest*, describes the Milanese noblemen as 'sea-swallowed' (2.1.247), the effect cuts in various directions. The original, alliterative beauty of the word succeeds in making even grim death by drowning seem oddly beautiful. At the same time, the audience is subtly reminded of the pivotal plot point of the shipwreck contrived by Prospero; it is his magic that has compelled the sea to act. In *The Winter's Tale*, Camillo finds himself in the impossible position of being unable to either obey or disobey the king without the threat of punishment, he summarises his dilemma with the succinct 'to do't or no is certain / To me a break-neck' (1.2.358–359). Here, the invented noun 'break-neck' encapsulates the story behind Camillo's quandary by evoking an image of the gallows, while it also underscores the imprisoning nature of the situation, in which he has no real choice. In these and other examples, compounds effectively condense a wealth of aesthetic, dramatic, and narrative effects into a single, memorable word.

I have been focusing on how Shakespeare exploits the unique features of his language to add to its existing stock, in a way that both reflects the linguistic resources of his age and showcases his particular aptitude for mining its expressive possibilities. However, it must be emphasised that the politics of language use did not allow for an unfettered linguistic free-for-all. As Paula Blank notes, 'The so-called "linguistic exuberance" or "linguistic enthusiasm" of authors such as Shakespeare ... needs to be re-examined as an expression of an age engaged in a struggle for possession of the vernacular, a struggle in which linguistic authority was just as much at issue as linguistic freedom.'[11] The matter of linguistic authority is an important one, and evidence of its influence is embedded in Shakespeare's work. While certain speakers – and the poet and playwright himself – appear free to revel in the linguistic exuberance allowed by the rich, transitional state of Early Modern English, for many others the boundaries of acceptable language play are firmly policed. Characters who misuse language – in other words, those who stretch its flexible boundaries a shade too far – are scorned. The plays consistently highlight and lampoon characters who struggle to master the nuances of English, and who attempt to compensate for their deficiencies by overreaching.[12] Linguistic misfires, such as Dogberry's attempt at 'suspicious' – 'aspitious' (*Ado* 3.5.35) – are played for laughs. Indeed, a distinctive feature of Shakespeare's creativity with words is the way that he consistently holds up for attention the nuances of individual words and the conventions governing their use. Characters regularly linger over lexical associations, mock or deride perceived linguistic over-compensators, and throw into relief the peculiarities of usage. Hamlet famously resists Gertrude's exhortation that he temper his grief by correcting her terminology: 'Seems, madam? nay, it is, I know not seems' (*Ham.* 1.2.76). Coriolanus calls out the tribune Sicinius for his brazen and indecorous use of the formidable directive 'shall': '"Shall remain"? / Hear you this Triton of the minnows? Mark you / His absolute "shall"?' (*Cor.* 3.1.89–191). Even the verbose Polonius acts as an amusing linguistic arbiter; of an excerpt from Hamlet's letter to 'the most beautified Ophelia', Polonius declares that it is 'an ill phrase, a vile phrase' (*Ham.* 2.2.109–110). This type of commentary offers an interpretative model for Shakespeare's audience. Beyond the expressive properties and aesthetic pleasures of words, we are encouraged to pay close attention to the contextual factors that determine rules of usage. In watching speakers consider, critique, and spar over words, we witness the negotiation of status, power, and identity, and we are reminded that linguistic play is necessarily circumscribed.

Context of interaction is vital to understanding the ways that Shakespeare's speakers use and understand words; similarly, the social and historical context of Shakespeare's language must be brought to bear on his lexical creativity. For example, we must account for the gap between contemporary conceptions of words and those of Shakespeare's England. Words on Shakespeare's stage necessarily incorporated *vox*, or voice, which grounds words in the body: 'Speech is a material fact in Shakespeare – and a physical event.'[13] Elizabethans were attuned to the aural effects of words; in contrast with present-day speakers, they often 'read aloud or experienced words as they sound'.[14] The raucous punning and wordplay for which Shakespeare is famous is rooted not only in his exceptional skill, but also in his immersion in a linguistic climate that celebrated sound. Such an environment could not help but encourage lexical experimentation in an aspiring playwright, whose craft depends on attentiveness to the minutiae of dialogue. Shakespeare's virtuoso displays of punning demonstrate his keen ear for the aural properties of words. Puns in Shakespeare are often associated with comic characters whose speech is punctuated with wordplay rooted in lexical ambiguity: 'I from my mistress come to you in post. / If I return I shall be post indeed' (*Err.* 1.2.63–64). Yet puns are found across the spectrum of dialogue in Shakespeare, in linguistic exchanges that are variously heated, melancholy, and joyful. Hamlet's famous first words, 'A little more than kin, and less than kind' (1.2.65), feature a glum *paranomasia*, a form of punning which plays on similar sounds between words. Similarly, in a tense confrontation with Iago, Desdemona exclaims, 'I cannot say "whore": / It does abhor me now I speak the word' (*Oth.* 4.2.160–161). *Antanaclasis*, when a word is repeated with a second meaning, infuses Sonnet 136 with coarse humour: 'Will will fulfil the treasure of thy love, / Ay, fill it full with wills, and my will one' (5–6). In a starkly different context, this form of punning conveys an angry reaction in *King Lear*: 'Nothing will come of nothing' (1.1.85). Here, the expressive force of the puns derives both from their aural qualities and their semantic associations; the repetition of the word renders it familiar, but the shift in meaning pushes against such recognition. *Syllepsis*, a play on multiple meanings of a single word, is a favourite trick of Shakespeare's manipulative villains because it allows them to profit from the pun's implicit ambiguity. In *Richard III*, Richard's false assurances to Clarence are subtly revealed in a slippery word: 'Well, your imprisonment shall not be long. / I will deliver you or else *lie* for you' (1.1.114–115, emphasis added). While Clarence believes that Richard's promise to 'lie' on the executioner's block in his place is a pledge of his fidelity, Richard, of course, depends on the alternative association of deception. Indeed, Richard is uncannily alert to the ambiguity of even seemingly insignificant function words:

RIVERS   She may, my lord, for –
RICHARD   She may, Lord Rivers, why, who knows not so?
               She may do more, sir, than denying that.
               She may help you to many fair preferments,
               And then deny her aiding hand therein.   (1.3.92–95)

Here, Richard challenges Rivers's use of 'may' to indicate something that *can* be done by reminding Rivers that such a capacity involves not only the ability to carry out an action but also the socially sanctioned power to do so.[15] As with *antanaclasis*, Shakespeare's instances of *syllepsis* – often delivered onstage in a subtly emphatic or knowing tone – encourage the audience to linger over a word and to mine its rich associations.

In some important respects, Shakespeare's innovation with words is the product of his being born in Warwickshire, just past the midpoint of the six-teenth century. This serendipitous timing meant that Shakespeare effectively won the lottery of linguistic options. As Jonathan Hope notes, Shakespeare 'was born early enough, and far enough away from the more standardized London dialect, to learn the older forms while they were still vital, but late enough also to have access to the features that entered the standard'.[16] His gender and his class permitted him to take advantage of one of the most radical cultural advancements in early modern England: accessible educa-tion. Free grammar schools, the product of a humanist vision that promoted an ideal of universal education (in principle, if not in practice), proliferated in the years prior to Shakespeare's birth. As a result, Shakespeare had the opportunity to attend the King's Free Grammar School in Stratford-upon-Avon, a privilege that would have been unthinkable only a few decades earlier. The impact of grammar school on writers of Shakespeare's gener-ation is profound. Sixteenth-century English schoolboys were immersed in a world that celebrated and took seriously matters of style and rhetoric, and they learned early the power and potential of close reading and artful expres-sion. From an early age, training in humanist rhetoric and reading prac-tice encouraged students to become close readers, thanks to their exposure to foundational thinkers like the Dutch humanist Erasmus. Erasmus encouraged two different types of reading: a practical mode that allowed students to grasp the primary content, and an attentive mode akin to close reading, in which the student pays attention to the nuances of language and rhetoric. The latter mode, in Erasmus's view, helped to 'develop judgment, by observation and analysis, word by word'.[17] Students like Shakespeare were thus inculcated into a literary world where the ideal reader was active and collaborative, so that the practice of interrogating individual words and the artistry of language use became second nature.

The core tenet of humanist grammar schools, training in Latin, fostered several practices that provided a fruitful apprenticeship for novice poets and playwrights. In England's schoolrooms, which acted as 'a kind of daily theatre for Latin', the emphasis on imitation, performance, and self-monitoring in the learning of Latin instilled a strong foundation of theat-ricality in generations of early modern English schoolboys.[18] Young pupils, inculcated early into the culture of performance, apprehended a fundamental link between rhetoric and drama: to persuade is to perform, dazzlingly, and to enact the Horatian dictum to instruct and delight. Additionally, grammar school students of Shakespeare's generation were first-hand spectators to the gradual incursions of the vernacular into the formerly inviolable realm of classical language. Reformers of the late sixteenth century, many of whom were schoolmasters, sought for English to realise its potential as a sophisticated and authoritative language that was capable of holding its own among the ascendant vernacular tongues of other nations such as Italy and Spain. In his 1582 work *The First Part of the Elementarie*, Richard Mulcaster, headmaster at the distinguished Merchant Taylors' and St Paul's schools, famously argued for the attenuation of Latin instruction so that English schoolboys could become better acquainted with the beauty of their native tongue. Mulcaster derided the 'bondage' that saw English speakers become servants to Latin, while neglecting the 'treasur in our own tung'.[19] Central to these shifting notions about the status of English were debates about the relative merits of Latin and English. Vestiges of older beliefs – that systematised grammar rules were exclusive to Latin, and that English was a vulgar and disordered tongue – co-existed with burgeoning ideas about the capacity of English to have its own set of rules, different from but equal to those of Latin.[20] Language purists also discouraged the practice of importing new words from Latin and other Latinate languages, and instead advocated for speakers to coin new words from existing Saxon forms to augment the English lexicon. Sir John Cheke, a vocal proponent of native vocabulary-building, famously attempted to translate the New Testament using only English terms.[21] Other reformers focused on the English grammar school curriculum's dependence on Latin, and pedagogical treatises lamenting the lack of English in the classroom began to flourish.

Even in grammar school classrooms committed to the learning of Latin, pupils unwittingly gained an appreciation for the power of English. Latin and English were set alongside one another in textbooks and in exercises, a practice that invited comparison. This arrangement ostensibly confirmed the superior nature of Latin: it appeared elegant and organised while English, in contrast, seemed haphazard. Because spelling, pronunciation, morphology, and syntax were largely unstandardised, English was widely considered 'to be largely irregular and, many would have claimed, incapable of being reduced to a proper system and orderliness'.[22] Yet even Lily's *Grammar*, the ubiquitous textbook of the Elizabethan schoolroom, grants the familiar mother tongue the authoritative final word: 'English is given a peculiar form of subservient ascendency over its erstwhile master. Latin meaning is verified through the vernacular, and tested in the mind of the schoolboy by reference to vernacular forms.'[23] Another problem exposed by translation exercises is that correct Latin usage does not parallel that of English, a reality that undermined the sacred notion that Latin grammar provided an *ur*-model for the grammars of other languages. Indeed, the acknowledgement that English possessed a grammar of its own set the stage for its recognition as an estimable language; when English gained its own grammar, it secured 'a newfound and a potentially divisive power'.[24] And just as the schoolbooks exalting Latin inadvertently hinted at the power of English, the pedagogical drills used to instil Latin rules paradoxically served to expose the creative potential of the vernacular. One of the most striking of these exercises, used with even the youngest of schoolboys, was the practice of double translation, which required students to translate a passage of Latin into English, and then convert the English back into Latin without the benefit of the original. Such a practice, while surely vexing, encouraged an intimate awareness of the nuances of grammar, and at the same time introduced a sense of creativity and play into an ostensibly rigid framework: 'students keep inventing as they travel across the language barrier until they achieve a text that is at once their own voice and the re-creation of a pre-existing model'.[25] For schoolboys, the experience of learning Latin improbably served to accent the creative possibilities of English;[26] and for a generation of sixteenth-century English writers, the experience of grammar school bequeathed a lifelong appreciation of the origins of words.

The intensive Latin training that formed the cornerstone of early education, along with the public profile of language reformers who fought for the status of native 'Saxon' English, meant that former grammar school pupils such as Shakespeare were accustomed to the distinct features of and tensions between classical and native language. As Sylvia Adamson observes, there was 'a general awareness of the etymological origin of words and an appreciation that the Saxon and Latinate elements in the word-stock had different and complementary expressive properties'.[27] Shakespeare's work offers rich evidence of his attention to the origins of words, and it calls attention to distinctions between Latin and English overtly as well as subtly. Characters make reference to the experience of grammar school, and in particular to the Latin lessons that formed the cornerstone of the curriculum. In *Much Ado About Nothing*, Benedick quotes a passage from Lily's *Grammar* – the standard text embedded in the memories of generations of early modern English schoolboys – just as *Titus Andronicus*'s Chiron recognises 'a verse in Horace; I know it well, / I read it in the grammar long ago' (4.2.22–24). *The Merry Wives of Windsor* features a garbled grammar lesson delivered by the pedantic Sir Hugh Evans in which the declension of Latin verbs devolves into nonsense and double entendre (4.1.15–69). Indeed, Shakespeare regularly uses a tendency or fondness for amusing or arcane Latinate terms to signal a character's foolish pedantry. In *Love's Labour's Lost*, the plodding schoolmaster Holofernes's excessive Latinisms reveal him as a braggart and a blowhard: 'Yet a kind of insinuation, as it were, *in via*, in way, of explication, *facere*, as it were, replication, or rather *ostentare*, to show, as it were, his inclination' (4.2.12–14). Here, actual Latin terms are interspersed with Latin-derived words to amusing effect; rather than clarify and elucidate, Holofernes's accrued words muddy interpretation. He thus exposes himself as a pitiable figure, the inarticulate schoolmaster.

Shakespeare also mines the rich stock of native Saxon terms for novel and expressive ends. Reeling from Cressida's betrayal, Troilus decries her false love in stark Saxon tones: 'The fractions of her faith, orts of her love, / The fragments, scraps, the bits and greasy relics / Of her o'er-eaten faith' (*Tro.* 5.2.157–159). The potent, relatively uncommon monosyllables 'orts', 'scraps', and 'bits' are particularly fitting in this context. The Germanic staccato of 'orts', or table scraps, is at odds with the overwrought Latinate speech favoured by the play's pompous war heroes, and it captures in a single lexical item the play's consistent deflation of grandeur and idealism. Similarly evocative Saxon words – such as 'kibe' (*Temp.* 2.1.273); 'geck' (*Cym.* 5.3.144); 'plash' (*Shr.* 1.1.23) – serve both to offer variation in the lexical registers of dramatic dialogue and highlight the unique expressive properties of English. Adamson notes that we must be mindful of the different properties of Latin and Saxon words; while Latinate words tend to be learned through formal education, Saxon words 'are typically learned early … through speech and in the context of physical experience'.[28] As a result, heavily Latinate speech tends to be associated with a 'formal, public style', while Saxon words are linked to 'private and intimate discourse', encoding 'perceptions, emotions, evaluations'.[29] In addition, many standard elements of the English language – articles, conjunctions, and pronouns – are Saxon, and it is to be expected that Shakespeare's dramas, comprised of interactive dialogue, feature a high proportion of personal pronouns and other function words. Yet in the open class of words – nouns, verbs, and adjectives – 'significant choice can be made'.[30] Shakespeare had the creative advantage of a linguistic context in which multiple options were available, and the choices that he makes are telling.

The English language emerges as a formidable force in Shakespeare's sonnets, which consistently play on contrasting word origins.[31] In the bitter penultimate line of Sonnet 92, 'But what's so blessèd fair that fears no blot?' (13), the arresting 'blessèd' and 'blot', with their hard, voiced consonants, are both distinctively English words with no corresponding form in other Germanic languages. In a poem that reflects on the precariousness of 'love' that should endure 'For term of life' (2–3), these words act as anchors.

'Blessèd', rooted in the Old English *bloedsian* and cognate with 'blood', suggests a natural and inviolable bond, but it is uncomfortably close to its antithesis, the homophonic 'blot', which undoes the sanctity of this union. 'Blessèd', 'blot', and their shared root of 'blood' all encapsulate the conflict at the heart of this sonnet: the potential for betrayal is inherent in all bonds, no matter how consecrated or apparently secure. Similarly, Sonnet 5 highlights the eloquence of simple English words: 'A liquid prisoner pent in walls of glass, / Beauty's effect with beauty were bereft, / Nor it nor no remembrance what it was. / But flowers distilled, though they with winter meet, / Leese but their show; their substance still lives sweet' (10–14). The sonnet illustrates Shakespeare's characteristic ear for the idiosyncrasies of English; its effective use of rare regional variants such as 'pent' (10) and 'leese' (14) hints at the rich lexical stock of the English language.[32] The repeated Latinate 'beauty' of line 11 is eclipsed by the concluding Germanic 'bereft', just as the Latin-derived 'substance' of the closing line is trumped by the resonant English words 'lives sweet'. Also in the closing lines, the Latinate 'distill' is transformed into the English 'still', an echoing pair that draws out the word 'still', deepening its association with endurance, and using an expressive Latinate term as a vehicle to enhance the meaning of an English one. The sonnet thus closes with the concise, resonant impact of native words, a significant feature in a poem that draws attention to unusual English words in its lexical choices while, in its theme, celebrates unadorned and enduring beauty.

Just as Shakespeare's expressive play with Latin- and Saxon-derived words speaks to his grammar school experience, his remarkable achievements with the device of *synonymia* – the use of several synonyms at once, to amplify or explain – may be rooted in the formative books of his schooling. The inestimable influence of Erasmus's *De Copia* permeated English attitudes towards language both as a written and spoken practice and as an ideology. The ideal of *copia* was reflected, broadly, in the belief that linguistic proficiency was tied to a *modus vivendi* of liberality and expansiveness: 'The *De Copia* taught a generation of English schoolboys to define eloquence as the ability to speak as expansively as possible on any subject – and to identify that ability with a more literal freedom of movement, a protocosmopolitan approach to being at home in the world.'[33] At the level of composition, *copia* was celebrated in the ideal of variety, exemplified in the practice of *synonymia*. In some cases, Shakespeare's synonyms create a lexical reflection of the message being communicated by the speaker. When Macbeth confesses 'But now I am cabined, cribbed, confined, bound in / To saucy doubts and fears' (*Mac.* 3.4.24–25), the accumulated, alliterative descriptors of captivity produce an effect of confinement in the structure of the phrase: the sentence becomes an echo chamber – an apt site of inexorable 'doubts and fears' – where each successive word simply mirrors the one that came before. Similarly, Hamlet's famous lament 'How weary, stale, flat and unprofitable / Seem to me all the uses of this world' (1.2.133–134) demands that its audience pay close attention to the nuances of lexical usage and connotation. On one hand, these four adjectives convey the profound, ineffable extent of Hamlet's despair in something approaching *aposiopesis*, an abruptly broken-off sentence. No collection of adjectives, this string of words implies, can adequately capture the experience of living in a world upended by grief. Yet on the other hand, these descriptors comprise a curious set. While Shakespeare occasionally uses 'weary' to modify nouns such as 'night', and 'time', most often it is used to describe a person. In this case, the pairing of 'weary' with the nebulous 'uses of this world' is striking. 'Stale' and 'flat' are more flexible adjectives, but they share a common dependence on opinion; in this context, they declare a stance in a way that is not operative in describing something as, say, 'red' or 'wooden'. Finally, 'unprofitable' is the most overtly egocentric adjective of the lot: 'the uses of the world' do not profit Hamlet. What this set of adjectives shares is a strong tie to the stance of the speaker; taken together, they offer a perfect echo of the solipsistic and myopic state of grief.

Shakespeare's masterful lexical innovations extend far beyond his novel coinages. His creativity with words stems largely from his uncanny ability to elevate the ordinary, and to use the resources of his inherited language to produce fresh expressive effects. The plasticity of the English language – and the unusually flexible conditions of Early Modern English – meant that Shakespeare could revive existing words in unexpected contexts. Additionally, the experience of the Elizabethan grammar school ensured that young pupils such as Shakespeare were well trained in the etymological and grammatical properties of words as well as in the precepts of classical rhetoric. One of Shakespeare's best creative gifts was his capacity to attend to his varied and transitional linguistic contexts, and to find in the common language of his environment seemingly endless possibilities for wonder and renewal.

NOTES

1 Some of the ideas, examples, and discussion in this chapter have appeared elsewhere. Please see Alysia Kolentsis, 'Shakespeare's Lexical Style', *Shakespeare In Our Time: A Shakespeare Association of America Companion*, ed. Dympna Callaghan and Suzanne Gossett (London: Arden Bloomsbury, 2016), pp. 306–311; 'Shakespeare's Linguistic Creativity: A Reappraisal', *Literature Compass*

11.4 (2014): 258–266; and '"Grammar Rules" in the Sonnets: Sidney and Shakespeare', *The Oxford Handbook of Shakespeare's Poetry*, ed. Jonathan Post (Oxford: Oxford University Press, 2013), pp. 168–184.

2 Bill Bryson, *Shakespeare: The World as Stage* (New York: HarperCollins, 2007), p. 115.

3 Jane Donawerth, *Shakespeare and the Sixteenth-Century Study of Language* (Urbana: University of Illinois Press, 1984), p. 4; Russ McDonald, *Shakespeare and the Arts of Language* (Oxford: Oxford University Press, 2001), p. 23.

4 Terttu Nevalainen, 'Lexis and Semantics', *The Cambridge History of the English Language*, ed. Roger Lass (Cambridge: Cambridge University Press, 1999), vol. 3, pp. 332–458; p. 336. See also Ward E. Y. Elliott and Robert Valenza, 'Shakespeare's Vocabulary: Did it Dwarf All Others?' *Stylistics and Shakespeare's Language: Transdisciplinary Approaches*, ed. Mireille Ravassat and Jonathan Culpeper (London: Continuum, 2011), pp. 34–57; p. 35.

5 Nevalainen, 'Lexis', p. 337.

6 Hugh Craig, 'Shakespeare's Vocabulary: Myth and Reality', *Shakespeare Quarterly* 62.1 (2011): 53–74.

7 Helen Cooper, 'Introduction', *Medieval Shakespeare: Pasts and Presents*, ed. Ruth Morse, Helen Cooper, and Peter Holland (Cambridge: Cambridge University Press, 2013), pp. 1–16; p. 3.

8 S. S. Hussey, *The Literary Language of Shakespeare* (London: Longman, 1982), p. 123.

9 Anne Ferry, *The Art of Naming* (Chicago: University of Chicago Press, 1988), p. 2.

10 Ferry, *Art of Naming*, p. 3.

11 Paula Blank, *Broken English: Dialects and the Politics of Language in Renaissance Writings* (London: Routledge, 1996), p. 6.

12 Blank, *Broken English*, p. 42.

13 Donawerth, *Shakespeare and the Sixteenth-Century Study of Language*, p. 17.

14 Ferry, *Art of Naming*, p. 2.

15 For a detailed discussion of this example, see Lynne Magnusson, 'A Play of Modals: Grammar and Potential Action in Early Shakespeare', *Shakespeare Survey* 62 (2009): 69–80.

16 Jonathan Hope, 'Shakespeare's "Natiue English"', *A Companion to Shakespeare*, ed. David Scott Kastan (Oxford: Blackwell, 1999), pp. 239–255; p. 255.

17 Andrew Zurcher, *Spenser's Legal Language: Law and Poetry in Early Modern England* (Rochester: Boydell and Brewer Inc., 2007), p. 26.

18 Lynn Enterline, *Shakespeare's Schoolroom* (Philadelphia: University of Pennsylvania Press, 2011), p. 44.

19 Richard Mulcaster, *The First Part of the Elementary, 1582* (Menston: Scolar Press, 1970), p. 254.

20 Manfred Görlach, 'Regional and Social Variation', *The Cambridge History of the English Language*, ed. Lass, vol. 3, pp. 459–538; p. 482.

21 Celia Millward, *A Biography of the English Language*, 2nd edn (Orlando: Harcourt Brace, 1996), p. 230.

22 Görlach, 'Regional and Social Variation', p. 482.

23 Brian Cummings, *The Literary Culture of the Reformation: Grammar and Grace* (Oxford: Oxford University Press, 2002), p. 25.

24 Cummings, *Literary Culture*, p. 25.

25 Leonard Barkan, 'What Did Shakespeare Read?' *The Cambridge Companion to Shakespeare*, ed. Margreta de Grazia and Stanley Wells (Cambridge: Cambridge University Press, 2001), pp. 31–47; p. 35.

26 Catherine Nicholson, *Uncommon Tongues: Eloquence and Eccentricity in the English Renaissance* (Philadelphia: University of Pennsylvania Press, 2013), p. 12.

27 Sylvia Adamson, 'Literary Language', *The Cambridge History of the English Language*, ed. Lass, vol. 3, pp. 539–653; p. 573.

28 Adamson notes that native English speakers need not 'be told the meaning of *light* or *strong*; they consult their memories of all the experience with which the word is connected. Words like *illumine* or *energial*, by contrast, are learned late, learned through education' ('Literary Language', 573).

29 Adamson, 'Literary Language', p. 573.

30 Adamson, 'Literary Language', p. 574.

31 Bradin Cormack discusses Shakespeare's 'experimental philology' in his incisive essay on the tension between Latin and English in Shakespeare's sonnets. See 'Tender Distance: Latinity and Desire in Shakespeare's Sonnets', *A Companion to Shakespeare's Sonnets*, ed. Michael Schoenfeldt (Oxford: Wiley-Blackwell, 2010), p. 244.

32 Most modern editors emend 'leese' to 'lose', but the Quarto has 'leese', a variant that Shakespeare uses only here.

33 Nicholson, *Uncommon Tongues*, p. 16.

3

DAVID SCHALKWYK

The Performative Power of Shakespeare's Language

Sonnet 18 is one of Shakespeare's best-known lyrics. What is Shakespeare doing in it? How is he using language, and to what effect?

> Shall I compare thee to a summer's day?
> Thou art more lovely and more temperate:
> Rough winds do shake the darling buds of May,
> And summer's lease hath all too short a date;
> Sometime too hot the eye of heaven shines,
> And often is his gold complexion dimmed;
> And every fair from fair sometime declines,
> By chance or nature's changing course untrimmed:
> But thy eternal summer shall not fade,
> Nor lose possession of that fair thou ow'st,
> Nor shall Death brag thou wand'rest in his shade,
> When in eternal lines to time thou grow'st
> So long as men can breathe or eyes can see,
> So long lives this, and this gives life to thee.

The poem describes an especially beautiful person, and it does so through simile: the subject of the poem is compared to the loveliness of a summer's day. But the poem is not simply a description, even a fairly complicated and intricate one. First, it is addressed *to* someone: the person described is expected to respond to it. That response is not recorded in the sonnet – it happens offstage, as it were, but it is nevertheless implied by the direct address, offered in the form of a question: 'Shall I compare thee?' The sonnet therefore initiates an interaction between two people, in which one, the writer, is trying to get the other, the addressee, to do or to be affected in some way: to be delighted, flattered, feel admired and loved, and perhaps to love and admire in return. So, despite the fact that the poem appears to do no more than describe someone, it is a form of action. It is composed of *speech acts*: it performs things through the language it uses. Its speech acts navigate a set of feelings, attitudes, and relationships with another person

35

with whom they engage. Such language in action is called *performative*. This is a different sense of performative from the way in which actors perform on stage or in film, although performative speech acts in the sense I am using it invariably lie at the heart of histrionic performance. It's the *language* that acts, that changes attitudes, transforms relationships, as it is put to use in a particular context by a speaker.

Let us look briefly at some of the actions that the poem's speech acts perform. First, there is the opening question, 'Shall I compare thee?' Exactly what kind of question is it? Is it asking permission to draw the comparison 'May I compare thee'? Or is it saying 'Let me compare thee', which echoes the first line of another famous sonnet, 'Let me not to the marriage of true minds admit impediment' (Sonnet 116). 'Let me' is somewhat more assertive than the permission-seeking 'May I'. If it is asking for permission or agreement, it suggests an unequal power relationship between poet and addressee. But this suggestion is undercut by its use of 'thee', which indicates a greater degree of familiarity or intimacy than the more formal 'you', and therefore a less pronounced personal difference between speaker and addressee.[1] On the other hand, it may be saying 'If I compare you to a summer's day then the comparison does not really hold: you are more beautiful, less given to extremes; you give much more pleasure, you command much more admiration and wonder.' And that is indeed what each comparison concludes up to line eight, the end of the octave. Line nine introduces another use of the word 'shall', with which the poem begins: 'But thy eternal summer shall not fade.' Notice the ambiguity of the modal verb 'shall': is the poet *predicting* that the addressee's beauty will live forever, or is he *commanding* that beauty to endure? Furthermore, is he in a position either to predict or command? How does he know? What power lies in him to do any of these things? The couplet provides the answer: the very poem that the poet is writing will make the addressee's beauty live beyond the lease of a summer's day, or a single summer, or a succession of summers. He or she will live on in the lines of language, through the force of these words, reread and reinterpreted in the eyes of future generations.

Anyone reading the poem will be struck by the force of Shakespeare's claim, boast, or prediction. If you're reading the poem, then the beauty of the addressee does indeed live on, through the fact that language is essentially repeatable across time and is renewed through reiterated reading. However, Shakespeare may be able to out-boast death, but he cannot predict *how* his poem will be read, or what kinds of interpretation it will generate across time. That remains beyond his power. By asking whether the poet is begging or commanding, predicting or merely wishing, we are attending to the possible performative force of these uses of language as speech acts to affect, change, or transform relationships and personal status: to change the way the reader thinks or feels. And we are also forced to enquire about the speaker's standing or authority in the world: does he have the power to do the things he is trying to do with his speech acts? We will come back to this.

There is another term for what I am calling performative speech acts, and Shakespeare would have been steeped in its practice: *rhetoric*, the use of language to persuade or move a reader or audience. A number of chapters in this collection deal at length with the role of rhetoric in Shakespeare's education and the construction of his plays. This chapter offers a different perspective on the rhetorical use of language from a modern, philosophical perspective that, unlike traditional rhetoric, offers a distinction between different kinds of performative speech acts and their effects that classical rhetoricians ignore. The philosopher of speech acts, J. L. Austin, calls rhetorical uses of language '*per*locutionary' performatives. Stanley Cavell terms these 'passionate utterances' and the historian of emotions, William Reddy, calls them 'emotives': speech acts that are involved in the 'navigation of feeling'.² Perlocutionary or rhetorical speech acts transform relationships between people by moving an audience or reader emotionally and by persuading them to feel or act in certain ways or *not* to feel or act in others. An enormous amount of skill and practice is involved in such speech acts, and their effects may be considerable (compare Hitler and Churchill's speeches during the Second World War, those of President Lincoln or Martin Luther King in the United States). But they are also unpredictable. Their success or failure cannot be assured.

Such perlocutionary acts should be distinguished from those that are not merely rhetorical, which carry an internal force or power whatever the skill of their speaker. Austin calls these illocutionary performatives. Making a promise, saying 'I do' in a marriage ceremony, declaring someone 'guilty' in a court of law or 'out' in a cricket match – pronounced by properly constituted jury members or umpires – automatically produce the desired change or transformation. Once these words are pronounced, I am bound; I am married; I am guilty; I cannot carry on batting – *at once*, without delay or hesitation. The force of the performative comes into effect *in* the saying of the words, by linguistic and social convention: hence they are *il*locutionary. Also, such taking effect marks the end of the speech act. The speaker does not need to say anything more beyond making the promise, or saying 'out' to the batsman, or 'guilty' in a court of law, or 'I do' at their wedding for the speech acts to have their performative effect. These acts also require certain 'felicity conditions' to be valid or 'happy'. I have to be a properly appointed and authorised cricket umpire, judge, or jury for my illocutionary acts to have any effect.

Outstanding examples of the relationship between perlocutionary and illo-cutionary performatives in Shakespeare are Brutus and Antony's respective speeches to the citizens of Rome at Caesar's death in *Julius Caesar*, each displaying a different rhetorical strategy and a different mix of illocutionary and perlocutionary acts. Brutus, confident in the moral and political virtue of his motives in assassinating Caesar, cannot imagine the citizens opposing his deed, and is therefore happy to allow Caesar's friend, Mark Antony, to speak after him – 'as Caesar's friend' (3.1.104). Brutus's co-conspirator, Cassius, knows that this is extremely risky, because he understands the unpredictability of the outcome of perlocutionary acts. But Brutus overrides him, with catastrophic results. Brutus offers a speech that is not exactly rhet-orically incompetent, but it is much too complacent:

3 PLEBIAN	The noble Brutus is ascended, silence!
BRUTUS	Be patient till the last.
	Romans, countrymen, and lovers, hear me for my cause, and be silent that you may hear. Believe me for mine honour, and have respect to mine honour that you may believe. Censure me in your wisdom, and awake your senses that you may the better judge. If there be any in this assembly, any dear friend of Caesar's, to him I say that Brutus' love to Caesar was no less than his. If then that friend demand why Brutus rose against Caesar, this is my answer: not that I loved Caesar less, but that I loved Rome more. Had you rather Caesar were living, and die all slaves, than that Caesar were dead, to live all freemen? As Caesar loved me, I weep for him; as he was fortunate, I rejoice at it; as he was valiant, I honour him; but, as he was ambitious, I slew him. There is tears for his love, joy for his for-tune, honour for his valour, and death for his ambition. Who is here so base that would be a bondman? If any, speak, for him have I offended. Who is here so rude that would not be a Roman? If any, speak, for him have I offended. Who is here so vile that will not love his country? If any, speak, for him have I offended. I pause for a reply.
ALL	None, Brutus, none.
BRUTUS	Then none have I offended. I have done no more to Caesar than you shall do to Brutus. The question of his death is enrolled in the Capitol, his glory not extenuated wherein he was worthy, nor his offenses enforced for which he suffered death. (*JC* 3.2.11–34)

Brutus begins, questionably, by assuming that people he seeks to win over are inferior to him. He opens by presenting them with a series of *commands*:

'be patient ... hear me ... be silent ... believe me ... have respect to mine honour'. He doesn't realise that in this situation, having murdered their leader, he needs to convince them of his honour, persuade them to respect him, and re-establish his credentials with them. He cannot merely assume his standing of authority with them. We could say that all these commands are merely the prelude to his perlocutionary rhetoric in the rest of the speech, but such rhetoric needs to come *after* he has re-established his authority in their eyes, his right to have his orders obeyed.

Brutus enters a perlocutionary or rhetorical mode, a register of 'passionate utterance', when he builds up the force of his rhetorical questions through the patterns of parallel repetition: 'As Caesar loved me, I weep for him. As he was fortunate, I rejoice at it. As he was valiant, I honour him. But, as he was ambitious, I slew him. There is tears for his love, joy for his fortune, honour for his valour, and death for his ambition. Who is here so base that would be a bondman?' There is no assumption of the authority to command here, but rather the skilful patterning of language to change the thoughts and feelings of his audience. His repeated 'as he' affirms in its initial three iterations his love for Caesar – before suggesting, in 'As he was ambitious, I slew him', that the slaying was itself an act of love. Following that, his rhetorical question (one which not only expects no answer, but is devastated if one is offered), 'Who is here so base that would be a bondman?', manipulates his audience into a position where they could not possibly contradict him without damning their own servility. From that point Brutus seems to have the citizens in his hands. They appear to be his to manipulate and command.

But he underestimates Antony's much more adroit use of rhetoric (perlocutionary speech acts) to change the mood and attitudes and behaviour of the citizens. Antony begins with a single, resounding illocutionary act – the command: 'Friends, Romans, countrymen, lend me your ears' (one of the most well-known openings to any speech). Antony appears to follow Brutus by opening with a vocative address (the powerful 'Friends, Romans, countrymen' in contrast to Brutus's rhymically weaker 'Romans, countrymen, and lovers') and a command to listen to him, 'lend me your ears' (3.2.65). (Antony's greater rhythmical power stems in part from the fact that he speaks in blank verse, whereas Brutus remains in prose.) After this initiating illocutionary command, Antony does not presume upon his authority. Instead he uses a pattern of repeated affirmation, 'Brutus is an honourable man', to devastating effect, turning it through accumulated irony into the very opposite of what it appears to be say:

> Here, under leave of Brutus and the rest –
> For Brutus is an honourable man;
> So are they all, all honourable men –

> Come I to speak in Caesar's funeral.
> He was my friend, faithful and just to me,
> But Brutus says he was ambitious,
> And Brutus is an honourable man.
> He hath brought many captives home to Rome,
> Whose ransoms did the general coffers fill;
> Did this in Caesar seem ambitious?
> When that the poor have cried, Caesar hath wept:
> Ambition should be made of sterner stuff;
> Yet Brutus says he was ambitious,
> And Brutus is an honourable man.   (3.2.73–86)

By the time the speech ends, the citizens have been unleashed on the conspirators and Antony, whose position was precarious before the speech, has commanded a position of authority and power by putting words into action.

Such performative action changes the social world through a combination of linguistic and social convention embedded in a set of communal and historical relations between people. But we should keep in mind the different kinds of action perlocutionary and illocutionary speech acts perform. Cavell remarks that 'perlocutionary acts make room for, and reward, imagination and virtuosity' (as we see so clearly in the virtuosity of Antony's speech), whereas 'illocutionary acts do not in general make such room – I do not … wonder how I might make a promise or … render a verdict. But to persuade you may well take considerable thought, to insinuate as much as to control may require tact, to seduce or to confuse you may take talent … passionate expression makes demands upon the singular body in a way illocutionary force (if it goes well) foregoes' (Cavell 173).[3]

'Passionate utterances' in Cavell's sense are interactively dialogical; they always happen between two or more people. Such speech acts are an invitation to another to respond. A 'you' is singled out that 'comes into play in relation to the declaration of the "I" who thereby takes upon itself a definition of itself, in, as it may prove, a causal or a fateful form. A performative utterance is an invitation to participation in the order of law. And perhaps we can say: A passionate utterance is an invitation to improvisation in the disorders of desire' (Cavell 185). Cavell means by this distinction that the illocutionary force of a performative speech act is, in the right circumstances, the result of a rule or law in the language itself, apart from the skills of the speaker. If I promise you to be there at 2pm, then I am bound by the promise the moment I speak the words.

Perlocutionary speech (or Reddy's emotives), which change relationships *by* (Latin *per*) saying something rather that *in* saying something, are more intriguing. There is an external or unpredictable connection between words and effect in this performance *by* saying certain things (as opposed to the more predictable outcome *in* saying them), as we saw in the very different outcomes of Brutus and Antony's speeches. Perlocutionary performatives are the forms of language we use to change others' attitudes, behaviour, feelings (like the attitudes, feelings, or actions of the Roman citizens) – but without any certain result or outcome. The most obvious, overused, thread-bare of such uses are the words 'I love you'. The utterance seems to be a description of an inner state, but it is a declaration that demands a response. 'I love you' is never said without the expectation of the response 'I love you too'. Nor is that sufficient. Such a response is expected to put into effect a series of subsequent actions, commitments, engagements, and emotions. But how often does that declaration have its desired effect?

We are engrossed by the consequences of the speech act 'I love you' because it encapsulates our own desires, aspirations, and failures: to get someone else to bend to our desire, to return our love. Shakespeare's sonnet with which this chapter opens offers one way of saying 'I love you'. But we are never certain of the outcome of that speech act. And we hang on that uncertainty; we are intrigued and bewitched by it. 'I love you' brings into existence a relationship between two people – the 'I' who loves, and the 'you' who is loved. Perlocutionary performatives are therefore usually directed towards a 'you'. Austin suggests that illocutionary speech acts, on the other hand, are grounded in an 'I' which is empowered to be the centre of the performative force of the utterance: *I* promise; *I* declare you out; *I* judge you guilty; *I* agree to be your lawful wedded spouse. A *you* may be involved in each of these speech acts, but not all such performatives involve a human *you*: *I* call this ship the *Titanic*; *I* declare the meeting over; *I* call a curse upon myself. The perlocutionary nature of passionate utterances opens the speaker up to the *you* of the other, which, because it is always prone to mislocation or misdirection, makes demands upon the identity of the speaking *I*. That *I* always needs to 'single out' the *you* that is addressed, and it has to do so appropriately and in a way that stakes itself upon an always uncertain response for the other: '[F]ailure to have singled you out appropriately ... puts the future of our relationship, *as part of my sense of my identity, or of my existence* ... radically at stake ... The "you" singled out comes into play in relation to the declaration of the "I" who thereby takes upon itself a definition of itself, in, as it may prove, a causal or fateful form' (Cavell 184–185).

We now have two shiny tools to understand the complexity, range, and nuance of Shakespeare's uses of language in the mouths of his characters. They are useful because they sharpen our awareness of the ways in which we ordinarily use language to perform different actions (and Shakespeare's characters are imitations of such ordinary uses), and they allow us to follow the dialogical interaction between characters more succinctly and understand the demands of authority, power, and social expectation within those interactions and relationships.

Perlocutionary Speech Acts and the 'Disorders of Desire': *Much Ado About Nothing*

A scene in *Much Ado About Nothing* exemplifies the way in which the perlocutionary force of passionate utterances effect the 'navigation of feeling' between an *I* and a *you* where the *I* risks itself by singling out and engaging with another – a *you* who is invited and challenged to assume a fateful redefinition of itself. In the back-and-forth of performative speech acts each speaker navigates a course of feeling that is continuously responding and adapting itself to the other's speech.

Here is the scene. The apparent mortal enemies, Beatrice and Benedick, are left alone together after Benedick's closest friend, Claudio, and his commanding officer, Don Pedro, have publicly shamed Beatrice's cousin, Hero, instead of engaging in the illocutionary performatives of the marriage ceremony, the force of which would have bound Claudio and Hero together as husband and wife. Beatrice and Benedick's subsequent discovery and declaration of love for each other is thus framed by the *failure* of the play's central illocutionary event: the marriage of Hero and Claudio. The marriage is infelicitous (it is 'unhappy' or doesn't come off) because Claudio refuses to take Hero as his wife, accuses her of adultery, and abandons her by storming out of the church with his companions. Benedick, his closest friend, does not join them as we'd expect him to, but stays behind with Hero, her father, the priest, and Beatrice. Beatrice and Benedict then find themselves alone together. After this shocking turn of events, what do they say to each other? What *can* they say to each other? In the light of their earlier antagonism (even in play), the navigation of feeling here is peculiarly difficult. Benedick's companions have done the worst possible thing that anyone could do to a marriageable woman in Shakespeare's time, not only reject her at the altar, but also publicly brand her as a whore, thereby putting her beyond marriage altogether. What Claudio enacts is an anti-marriage, an illocutionary act that makes Hero unmarriageable.

In what way could Benedick possibly approach Beatrice under such circumstances? How could he navigate *towards* her? She is alone, weeping, traumatised by what has happened to her cousin:

BENEDICK	Lady Beatrice, have you wept all this while?
BEATRICE	Yea, and I will weep a while longer.
BENEDICK	I will not desire that.
BEATRICE	You have no reason, I do it freely.
BENEDICK	Surely I do believe your fair cousin is wronged.
BEATRICE	Ah, how much might the man deserve of me that would right her!
BENEDICK	Is there any way to show such friendship?
BEATRICE	A very even way, but no such friend.
BENEDICK	May a man do it?
BEATRICE	It is a man's office, but not yours. (*Ado* 4.1.248–259)

This is the first time Benedick addresses Beatrice by the honorific, formal title, 'Lady'. He thus imposes a respectful distance. His question about her crying is somewhat lame, but it also demonstrates concern and latches onto her apparent emotional state. Her response might be played defiantly or poignantly, but his next move, which inserts his own desires into the exchange, is sharply rebuffed by her insistence on her own agency and freedom – and her irritation at his presumption. Here Benedick might have stopped, drawn a line under their exchange, and rejoined his friends. But he doesn't. He now puts himself on the line – declaring his change of sides, his sympathy with her 'fair cousin'. Beatrice's immediate rejoinder betrays her frustration and sense of powerlessness as a woman in this society. She has no way of redressing the wrong herself; she, a woman who has throughout the play had little good to say about men in general and Benedick in particular, needs a 'man' to do it.

This is the opening Benedick is looking for. It gives him the opportunity to offer himself, crucially, as a 'friend'. But Beatrice doesn't take the bait. Even though he is careful to speak abstractly, she makes sure that he is again excluded from the possibility of acting as Beatrice and Hero's 'friend'. 'May a man do it?' is a further probe that registers the gender politics of the situation – it acknowledges that under these circumstances all men might be regarded as the enemy. Notice, in contrast with his earlier railing against love, women, and Beatrice in particular, how sensitively and tentatively he puts these questions. He knows that he cannot force himself into a position of trust and friendship. So delicate is the situation that he has to approach her obliquely. We see Benedick trying, with great care and sensitivity, to navigate a way into some kind of emotional reciprocity with a woman who ostensibly loathes him and his band of friends through perlocutionary acts: performative acts that attempt to create emotional space and express empathy and understanding. Finally, Beatrice seems to catch the direction of his questioning, and sharply and directly rebuffs him: 'It is a man's office, but not yours.'

At Beatrice's outright rejection ('not yours'), it would appear that Beatrice has ended any further interaction. Where could one go from here? What he does next is startling in its bold directness. He declares his love for her!

BENEDICK   I do love nothing in the world so well as you, is not that strange?

BEATRICE   As strange as the thing I know not: it were as possible for me to say I loved nothing so well as you, but believe me not, and yet I lie not, I confess nothing, nor I deny nothing: I am sorry for my cousin.   (260–264)

Beatrice is taken aback by this utterly unexpected, and in the context apparently inappropriate, directness. Her initial response seems to make no sense, but now she is the one who follows an indirect path as she tries to navigate a way of taking in his declaration, and then reciprocating it. Notice how she adopts the conditional: 'It *were* as possible.' She collapses into paradox and contradiction, before, finally, resetting her emotional focus on her cousin's suffering. The language performs the state of emotion and attitude, which betray what each person finds of value at any point, not only in the way it affects the hearer, but crucially in the way it creates and transforms feelings and attitudes. This is not a situation in which characters experience emotion and then find words to express it – the words they grasp at themselves form and reform the feelings.

In the conversation that follows, Benedick moves from his earlier reticence into increasingly assertive cliché, moving now from perlocutionary to illocutionary speech acts – oaths – that, he believes, will force Beatrice to accept his sincerity:

BENEDICK   *By my sword*, Beatrice, thou lovest me.

BEATRICE   Do not swear and eat it.

BENEDICK   *I will swear by it* that you love me, and I will make him eat it that says I love not you.

BEATRICE   Will you not eat your word?

BENEDICK   With no sauce that can be devised to it: I protest I love thee.
     (265–270, emphasis added)

Beatrice has always been suspicious of such oaths, and she reprises her earlier disparaging comments about Benedick's 'faith' in the opening scene by repeating her taunt, which turns the vapid emptiness of the oath into the material unlikelihood of his eating the sword by which he swears. But his affirmation has the effect he desires: Beatrice finally comes around to confessing her love for him, playing poignantly on the notion of protesting to admit her capitulation, but not before Shakespeare creates some suspense for both Benedick and the audience by having her ask for 'forgiveness':

BEATRICE	Why then God forgive me.
BENEDICK	What offense, sweet Beatrice?
BEATRICE	You have stayed me in a happy hour, I was about to protest I loved you.
BENEDICK	And do it with all thy heart.
BEATRICE	I love you with so much of my heart, that none is left to protest. (271–276)

Benedick has navigated his way into her heart, provoking her reciprocal declaration of love, beyond her customary habit of 'protest'. One might think that Shakespeare's navigation of feeling between these erstwhile antagonists into a mutual declaration of love might have ended there. But if he is acutely aware of the power of language to harness human creativity, he also knows the capacity of conventional language to be not only an engine for emotional expression but also a trap. And Benedick, who has shown remarkable care and sensitivity up to now, falls headlong into it. 'Come bid me do anything for thee' (277), he declares excitedly, resorting to the hyperbolic language of fantastical desire, in a direct appeal to Beatrice. Is this a command, a request, or just mindless elation? Which lover believes that his beloved will take his request seriously and indeed command him to do *anything*?

Beatrice does. She takes him deadly seriously. 'Kill Claudio' (279), she responds. Beatrice's command, which takes his injunction, 'bid me do anything', at face value, also turns out to be a forceful rebuttal. She is commanding him to kill his best friend – to abandon his world of comfortable male companionship for the world of female solidarity and social weakness. Her lover responds with similarly hyperbolic bluster: 'Ha, not for the wide world' (280). His response, following the language of his earlier 'bid me do anything', rejects Beatrice in the conventional hyperbolic language of love, or in this case, the denial of her value for him. 'I wouldn't do it for the world', he says, 'and I certainly won't do it for you'. She responds with equal hyperbole, and rejection. 'You kill me to deny it, farewell' (281).

From now the tables of power are turned. Beatrice is fully in command, with a retreating and entreating Benedick. Finally trusting what Beatrice's 'soul' tells her rather than the call of his old companions, he declares his loyalty to her and her cousin. He tries the old, conventional oath of love one more time, before shifting from the uncertainties of perlocutionary navigation to the commitment of illocutionary promise, and is told to act rather than indulge in empty declarations:

BENEDICK	Tarry, good Beatrice, by this hand I love thee.
BEATRICE	Use it for my love some other way than swearing by it. (308–309)

Finally, the two navigate to a mutual accommodation. Benedick commits himself to challenging Claudio, and in doing so he commits himself to Beatrice in an illocutionary act that has the force of a promise: 'Enough, I am engaged' (312). The uncertainties and risks of passionate or perlocutionary utterances in this exchange, through which emotions and relationships have been tested and navigated, culminate in an illocutionary speech act: his pledge to her to be her 'friend' in her cousin's cause. And that pledge or promise is a commitment to action, to engage in the further, decisive and deadly, illocutionary act of the challenge, one that without words nonetheless has the power to transform Hero to wronged virgin and, in killing him, brand Claudio's accusations as malicious calumny. Having navigated the disorders of desire with Beatrice, Benedick commits himself to the 'order of the law'.

Illocutionary Speech Acts and the 'Order of the Law': *Richard II*

The order of the law, and its intimate connection with the performative force of illocutionary speech acts, is not only the vehicle but also the subject of much of *Richard II*. The first and third scenes of play are structured by performatives of power, authority, and formalised competition: two antagonists, Mowbray and Bullingbrook, accuse each other publicly of treason before their king, subsequently turning their accusations into the kind of challenge that Benedick undertakes on Hero's behalf. Their speeches are filled with accusations, challenges, and oaths, almost all of which are made in the first person singular, the grammatical form that is the customary, though not the sole, vehicle of illocutionary performatives:

> Besides I say, and will in battle prove
> …
> That all the treasons for these eighteen years
> …
> Fetch from false Mowbray their first head and spring.
> Further I say, and further will maintain
> Upon his bad life to make all this good,
> That he did plot the Duke of Gloucester's death.   (R2 1.1.92–100)

Such challenges are dramatically signalled by the throwing down of gages (gloves); picking up the challenger's gage means accepting the challenge. These staged actions show that illocutionary acts are not confined to speech. Their force may consist entirely in bodily action, like the biting of thumbs in the opening scene of *Romeo and Juliet* or the promised duel between Benedick and Claudio. The accusations and challenges of the antagonists occur within a set of formal, public circumstances, over which the king presides. He has the power of the imperative, of command. But that authority does not stem from the individual alone. It is derived from a whole fabric of what Shakespeare calls 'ceremony'. This is the long history of generally unquestioned practices, from the coronation ritual that inaugurates a king or queen – the words and actions of such a ceremony literally bring them and their authority into existence – to the constitutive capacity of such practices that enable the monarch to exercise such power.

Bullingbrook and Mowbray thus exercise their conventional rights of public challenge to air and prove their charges of treason against each other. The charge of treason is itself a product of ceremony. It is brought into being by the socially and politically endowed concept of royal sovereignty, and in the medieval world of *Richard II*, it is extended in a plethora of available performatives that include the accusation, the challenge, and the duel as a way of determining the truth. In this respect the feudal performatives are wholly different from modern convention: we do not assume that killing one's opponent in a formal duel proves anything factual in the real world. But that is exactly the assumption here: Bullingbrook asserts 'what I speak / My body shall make good upon this earth, / Or my divine soul answer it in heaven' and 'What my tongue speaks my right drawn sword may prove' (1.1.36–38, 46).

Richard stands above these actions as subject of dispute, court of appeal and arbiter of the rules of action. But he is also complicit in the dispute, having colluded with Mowbray in the death of Gloucester, and this complicity robs him of the authority to exercise his proper power even if this is never stated explicitly or publicly. In him lies the power to hear the dispute and to decide how it should be resolved. But the traditional trial by combat is merely a feint, and Richard's true power is exercised in his banishment of both Mowbray and Bullingbrook, an illocutionary act that belongs only to the king. He has the power and authority to transform the world of his subjects merely *in* the saying of certain words: 'such', as Bullingbrook observes bitterly, 'is the breath of kings' (1.3.214).

But just as the two scenes are saturated with examples of illocutionary speech acts – in the accusations, the challenges, the throwing down of gages, the royal commands – they also register the limits of even a king's power of speech. What strikes Bullingbrook is not so much the power of a king to banish him, but the arbitrariness of such power: and his capacity, on a whim, to reduce the length of the sentence: 'How long a time lies in one little word. / Four lagging winters and four wanton springs / End in a word' (1.3.212–214). Nevertheless, this is probably Shakespeare's most self-conscious reflection of the extraordinary power words have, in the appropriate circumstances, to control and transform the world of human experience.

Bullingbrook may wonder at 'how long a time lies in a little word', but Gaunt also reminds us and Richard of the limits of the king's breath – its lack of power. To Richard's feeble attempt at consolation, 'Why uncle, thou hast many years to live' (1.3.225), the old man responds,

> But not a minute, king, that thou canst give.
> Shorten my days thou canst with sullen sorrow,
> And pluck nights from me, but not lend a morrow.
> ...
> Thy word is current with him for my death,
> But dead thy kingdom cannot buy my breath. (1.3.226–231)

The limits to the king's power here are metaphysical – the mark of a difference between the divine and the human. Richard may be able to shorten human lives; he has no power to prolong them. There are, however, other limits to the king's speech that are more mundane, registered in signs of Richard's circumstantial impotence when, for example, he fails to command Mowbray and Bullingbrook to withdraw their challenges and needs to resort to hollow affirmations of his status:

> RICHARD   Rage must be withstood.
>   Give me his gage. Lions make leopards tame.
> MOWBRAY   Yea, but not change his spots. Take but my shame
>   And I resign my gage. (1.1.173–176)

Finally, Richard seems to concede the limits of his performative power even as he tries to distinguish between the authority of the imperative ('command') and the weakness of supplication ('sue'):

> We were not born to sue, but to command,
> Which, since we cannot do to make you friends,
> Be ready, as your lives shall answer it,
> At Coventry upon Saint Lambert's day.
> There shall your swords and lances arbitrate
> The swelling difference of your settled hate.
> Since we cannot atone you, we shall see
> Justice design the victor's chivalry.
> Lord Marshal, command our officers at arms
> Be ready to direct these home alarms. (196–205)

The caesura in the second line, which should cause the actor to pause slightly before 'to make you friends', suggests a more extensive lack of command, which is highlighted by his moving, in the final two lines, to a more secure order to those who will obey him, the Lord Marshal and his officers-at-arms.

Richard performs two further, fatal, illocutionary performatives: the transformation of the trial by combat into the banishment of both antagonists (which witnesses his general political insecurity) and his order to seize all of Gaunt's (and therefore all of Bullingbrook's) property upon the former's death. The rest of the play traces the stripping away of the king's illocutionary power, to the point at which he is forced into the transformative act of publicly giving up the crown to Bullingbrook, whereupon the illocutionary power of kingship passes to Bullingbrook, now King Henry IV. But as Richard loses illocutionary power he gains an immense amount of perlocutionary power: he controls emotion and theatrical effect in the abdication scene, reducing Bullingbrook to little more than a puppet, and in his final monologue in prison just before his death, he moves the audience to sympathy in an extraordinary effective and affective navigation of feeling.

Illocutionary vs. Perlocutionary: Seduction in *Richard III*

Is seduction an illocutionary or a perlocutionary act? Austin's criteria would suggest that it is the latter. Seduction requires a range of passionate utterances or the navigation of feeling in which the other person has to acquiesce willingly. The seductive purpose is usually concealed behind a series of perlocutionary utterances. It needs all the 'talent', 'imagination and virtuosity', and uncertainty of outcome that are part of the 'disorders of desire' rather than the 'order of the law' (Cavell 185). One can say 'I accuse you' or 'I challenge you' or 'I banish you', but not 'I seduce you'.

And yet, in Shakespeare's most famous and shocking scene of seduction, that of Richard Gloucester's of Anne in the second scene of *Richard II*, illocutionary acts predominate in the first part of the scene. The scene begins with a secure command from Anne: 'Set down, set down your honourable load' (*R3* 1.2.1). She then makes her state of mourning verbally explicit by calling upon Henry's ghost to witness her grief: 'Thou bloodless remnant of that royal blood: / Be it lawful that I invocate thy ghost / To hear the lamentations of poor Anne' (7–9), before pouring that grief, rage, and hatred into a reiterated curse of the man who killed her father-in-law and 'slaughtered son' (10):

> Oh, cursèd be the hand that made these holes,
> Cursed the heart that had the heart to do it,
> Cursed the blood that let this blood from hence. (1.2.14–16)

These are illocutionary acts. But they also express the most intense emotion, so that the dividing line between illocutionary act and passionate utterance becomes difficult to sustain.

The curious thing about this performance is that it seems to enact a further effect central to many of Shakespeare's other plays, but distant from our experience and beliefs: by cursing Richard, Anne seems implicitly to have conjured his presence before her. For he appears almost at once, countering her earlier commands with his own illocutionary imperatives and threats:

RICHARD	Stay, you that bear the corpse, and set it down.
ANNE	What black magician conjures up this fiend
	To stop devoted charitable deeds?
RICHARD	Villains, set down the corpse or, by Saint Paul,
	I'll make a corpse of him that disobeys.
GENTLEMAN	My lord, stand back and let the coffin pass.
RICHARD	Unmannered dog, stand thou when I command. (1.2.33–39)

We are confronted by an historical distance between ourselves and the illocutionary conventions of Shakespeare's time. We understand well enough what a curse is, but in a modern, secular world we are not especially likely to believe that there are proper felicity conditions for a curse. The same is true of a prophecy or a conjuration. Cursing, conjuring, and prophesying are illocutionary speech acts that have had their day: they remain in the language as attenuated leftovers from an earlier age more inclined to believe in supernatural forces and the power of language to invoke them.

If we examine the interchange between Anne and Richard we notice that Shakespeare tends to give Anne a greater proportion of illocutionary acts, especially those that are obsolete to us, whereas to Richard falls the preponderance of perlocutionary acts or emotives through which to navigate his seduction – his bringing her into a receptive state of mind and heart. Recall that illocutionary acts are finite – they exhaust themselves upon their taking effect. Say 'I promise', and you have promised. Say 'I do', and you are married. Raise your index finger and the batsman must walk. There is no more to say, by either party, except to engage in another, different illocutionary act, or a series of subsequent, perlocutionary engagements. But there is no end to a passionate engagement unless a line is drawn by one of the parties. A refusal is itself a part of such a passionate engagement. Anne attempts to draw a line under the engagement from the start – to rebuff Richard, take up her beloved corpse, and leave.

Anne's illocutionary acts are 'unhappy' in Austin's sense, whereas Richard slowly but inexorably, indeed like a spider trapping and enveloping a fly, shifts Anne into a position first of uncertainty and then acquiescence. Part of that entrapment is displayed in the way in which her curses turn against her: having cursed Richard as a poisonous toad, it is Anne who turns herself into a 'creeping venomed thing' (20), spitting at her victim in the wish that it were 'mortal poison' (150), willing her infecting eyes to turn to basilisks. And in cursing Richard's wife, she in fact curses herself: 'If ever he have wife, let her be made / More miserable by the death of him / Than I am made by my young lord and thee' (1.2.26–28). The interchange of passionate utterance between the two antagonists also shows the discovery or 'navigation' of emotion not ready-formed but also essentially unpredictable.

Part of the problem for Anne lies in her horrified fascination for Richard, which begins as a series of angry imprecations and curses exemplified by 'Foul devil' (50), and which moves through the decisive opening of an invitation, 'Vouchsafe, diffused infection of a man, / Of these known evils but to give me leave / By circumstance t' accuse thy cursèd self' (78–80), through the uncertain desire to understand Richard – 'I would I knew thy heart' (197) – to the hesitant qualification, 'To take is not to give' (190), and finally to the fatal emotional capitulation of 'With all my heart, and much it joys me, too' (223). She tries to draw a line under the conversation, but she can't, mesmerised as a mouse before a snake, first by her fascination with Richard as an object of horror, and then slowly constricted by the performative power of his language and the rebounding force of her own. She will finally be swallowed later in the play.

Two things about performatives are apparent from Richard's seduction of Anne. First, the distinction between the illocutionary and the perlocutionary based on their respective relation to emotion does not hold. Some illocutionary acts may carry as much emotional force as any passionate utterance. Second, the felicity conditions (and therefore the force) of some illocutionary acts may change historically, so that the most fearful and powerful of such acts at one time – curses, prophesies, conjuration – may be attenuated in a different moment in history and culture. Some of their buried potency may however be restored by fiction, which may make us feel their attraction or horror once again. Shakespeare's plays are especially effective in returning us to the appreciation of such uses of language, in part because the plot structure has the capacity to show the ironic effects of a curse, the predicted outcome of a prophecy, or the capacity to conjure something out of a 'little word'.

And that is what the theory of speech acts is all about: the conjuring, from nothing, of something that wasn't present in the world before, through the mere use of words. Austin, Cavell, and Reddy offer ways of understanding the interactive uses of language in Shakespeare, always between people, who use speech acts to exercise or thwart power, to navigate feeling, and to transform the world.

NOTES

1 In Shakespeare (and his contemporaries) there are two different uses of the second person singular pronoun: 'thou' (and its cognates, 'thee' and 'thy') and 'you'. 'You' is formal, used of someone usually above oneself in rank, whereas 'thou' is a mark of lower status, used by superiors to inferiors, or as a mark of intimacy or familiarity, between equals, friends, or lovers. This is complicated by both the fact that early modern English was tending towards the exclusive 'you' and an emotional register in terms of which 'thou' forms could express intimacy, anger, or contempt. See Jonathan Hope, *Shakespeare's Grammar* (London: The Arden Shakespeare, 2003), p. 77. For a discussion of the second-person pronoun in the Sonnets, see Andrew Gurr, '*You* and *Thou* in Shakespeare's Sonnets', *Essays in Criticism* 32.9 (1982): 9–25; and Lynne Magnusson, 'A Pragmatics for Interpreting Shakespeare's Sonnets 1 to 20: Dialogue Scripts and Erasmian Intertexts', *Methods in Historical Pragmatics: Approaches to Negotiated Meaning in Historical Contexts*, ed. Susan M. Fitzmaurice and Irma Taavitsainen (Berlin and New York: Mouton de Gruyter, 2007), pp. 167–184.

2 J. L. Austin, *How to Do Things with Words* (Oxford: Oxford University Press, 1975); Stanley Cavell, 'Performative and Passionate Utterance', *Philosophy the Day after Tomorrow* (Cambridge, MA: Belknap Press of Harvard University Press, 2006), pp. 155–191; and William M. Reddy, *The Navigation of Feeling: A Framework for the History of Emotions* (Cambridge: Cambridge University Press, 2001).

3 William M. Reddy offers a very similar notion to Cavell's passionate utterances in the form of what he calls 'emotives', which are performative insofar as they do not merely express an emotion that is fully formed before it is put into words but is rather created and navigated in the act of speaking: 'To speak about how one feels is, very often, to make an implicit offer or gift, to negotiate, to refuse, to initiate a plan or terminate it, to establish a tie or alter it.' Emotives are performative in a way that is distinct from illocutionary force and perlocutionary effect (Reddy, *Navigation*, pp. 100–101).

4

OLIVER MORGAN

Verse and Metre

Everyone knows that Shakespeare wrote iambic pentameter. This fact is familiar even to those who know little else about Shakespeare and nothing else about prosody. Like most things that everyone knows, however, it is only partly true. One person who may not have known it is William Shakespeare. The phrase appears nowhere in his works and was not used to describe them until long after his death.[1] Like any other Elizabethan schoolboy, Shakespeare would have learned Latin prosody at school – including the terms 'iamb' and 'pentameter' – but how far, if at all, he would have seen this prosody as applicable to the verse he wrote for the theatre as an adult is moot. The metrical system that early modern English poets inherited from their classical forebears did not describe the kind of poetry they wrote, or the kind of metre they used to write it. Latin verse is quantitative. Its organising principle is a binary distinction between short and long syllables, which are arranged into patterns to form the different metres. English verse, by Shakespeare's time, was accentual-syllabic. Both the number of stressed syllables (or 'accents') per line and the total number of syllables per line are structurally significant. Early modern English scholars lacked a coherent way of theorising this distinction. They could see that native verse was not like Latin verse and that it did not conform to the rules of prosody as they understood them. But exactly how this gap could be bridged – whether it was the poetry that needed to change or the theory – was an open question.[2] To make matters worse, whatever phonetic basis the short–long distinction may have had for the Romans had long since been lost. The Elizabethan schoolboy was taught, not to hear the difference between the two types of syllable, but to work out which were long and which were short using a complex set of rules. So the most important way in which English verse differed from Latin (at least as Shakespeare would have understood it) is that in English the metre was an audible reality, whereas in Latin it was an intellectual abstraction.

This is why (bizarre as it may now seem) many of the early English humanists – of the generation that established the system of education through which Shakespeare passed – did not regard the kind of verse written in their own language as verse at all. They were able to recognise that it rhymed, and that it observed 'number' or 'just measure' (i.e. that the right lines had the right number of syllables).[3] But in the absence of a quantitive prosody, they struggled to recognise a pattern internal to the line itself. Latin poetry was verse. English poetry was 'rude beggarly rhyming', 'words unmetrified', or 'lines of prose, with a rhyme in the end'.[4] And this verdict was often accepted by the poets themselves. George Gascoigne concedes that while 'our Poems may justly be called Rhymes' they 'cannot by any right challenge the name of a Verse' (Smith I, 50). Even Philip Sidney seems to have thought of English poetry as primarily syllabic, 'observing only number (with some regard of the accent)' (Smith I, 204). How Shakespeare thought of it we do not know. There is range of theoretical positions he might plausibly have taken, but it is equally plausible that he took no position at all – that he had no interest in theorising what was for him a fundamentally practical activity. We do not know, in other words, whether Shakespeare was a metrical Mozart or a metrical Louis Armstrong.

To the intellectual historian or the corpus linguist, this uncertainty is a problem. To the undergraduate struggling to identify a trochaic substitution in the third foot, it is more likely to come as a blessed relief. What we are dealing with here is not a closed metrical system, governed by known laws, and comprehensible only to those who have mastered its arcane terminology. We are dealing instead with an incomplete picture that might reasonably be filled out in a variety of ways. What is needed, therefore, is an approach to Shakespeare's versification that makes as few assumptions as possible about how the finished picture ought to look. It is not possible, of course, for any approach to make no assumptions. In order to be able to talk about metre at all we will need a basic descriptive vocabulary, and that vocabulary will reflect what we take to be the parameters of the writing. But the lighter the theoretical load, the better. We should be aiming, as it were, for Occam's prosody – a terminologically minimalist account of Shakespearean versification that seeks to embrace, rather than disguise, its uncertainties. This chapter is an attempt to provide one.

What, then, are the basic parameters of Shakespearean verse? Three of them seem hard to escape. First, that it is written in lines. Second, that these lines sometimes rhyme with each other. Third, that it is accentual-syllabic – both the number of syllables per line and the occurrence of stressed syllables within the line are metrically significant (although not always equally so). This leaves us with a metrical vocabulary of four indispensable terms: 'line', 'rhyme', 'syllable', and 'stress'. Everything else can be set to one side – including the metrical foot, its elaborate Greek typology, and (holiest of holies) the iambic pentameter. What follows will be structured around the four basic terms identified above, starting with the most obvious and recognisable feature of the verse (its arrangement into lines) and ending with the one that seems to cause the most trouble (the placement of stress within those lines). At each point, the aim is the same – to help the reader become more aware of formal distinctions in Shakespeare's writing (between verse and prose, rhymed and unrhymed verse, short and long lines, tighter and looser rhythms). Implicit in this approach is a further assumption, of a slightly different kind. Shakespearean drama is extremely mobile with regard to form. It does not consist, as the popular imagination supposes, of line after line of thumpingly sonorous iambic pentameter. Rather, it is Protean – constantly shifting its shape in response to changes in the dramatic temperature. Prose, blank verse, rhyming couplets, lyric, song – these are the gears through which the writing moves. Simply paying attention to which gear we are in at any given moment – and, above all, to the moments at which we move from one to another – is more than half the battle.

Verse and Prose

The easiest formal distinction to recognise when reading a Shakespeare play is that between verse and prose. Verse is written in lines, the length of which is determined by the poet. Each line ends, as it were, with a hard return. In prose the line-endings are a matter of typographical convenience rather than authorial choice – the text wraps automatically whenever it happens to run out of space. This difference can be seen at a glance. Lines of verse begin with a capital letter and usually end well short of the right-hand margin, leaving an undulating ribbon of white space down that side of the page. Prose, on the other hand, expands to fill the space available, with capitalisation only where grammar demands. The clarity of the distinction is obscured (as we shall see) when characters have speeches of fewer than ten syllables, but editors do their best to minimise such ambiguity. About one-quarter of Shakespeare's dramatic writing is in prose, although the proportion varies from play to play, from period to period, and from genre to genre – rising gradually to a peak in the late 1590s, and usually higher in comedy than in tragedy.[5]

In the early part of his career, Shakespeare's use of the two media is more or less conventional. The basic function of the distinction is to add an extra layer of sociolinguistic complexity to the world of the play. Verse tends to be spoken by higher status characters and on formal occasions.

Prose tends to be spoken by lower status characters and at moments of relaxation and informality. Verse is the medium of tragedy, nobility, and heroic action. Prose is the medium of servants, clowns, and comic sub-plots. From the mid-1590s, however, things become a little more complicated. In mature Shakespeare, as Russ McDonald has pointed out, 'the alternation between verse and prose is so frequent, so unschematic, and so skilful that is it is risky to generalize'.[6] Shakespeare becomes increasingly aware, in other words, of the dramatic potential of switching from one medium to the other. The essentially sociolinguistic function of the distinction in the early plays (with its clear hierarchy of forms) does not disappear, but it is gradually subordinated to the needs of the dramatic moment. Switches between verse and prose come to serve an ever-widening range of uses – so wide, in fact, that listing them is difficult.[7] What this means in practice is that we need to be aware of the *type* of thing that a change can signify, but alert to the possibility that it is being used in a way that we have not previously encountered.

Take, for example, Act 3, scene 1 of *Hamlet*. This scene contains some of Shakespeare's most celebrated verse ('To be, or not to be, that is the question') and – from the mouth of the same character – some of his most notorious prose ('Get thee to a nunnery!'). It can be divided into four sections. In the first, the king and his advisers lay a trap for Hamlet, designed to test if his love for Ophelia is the root of his madness. In the second, Hamlet enters and speaks the most famous soliloquy in English, seemingly unaware that Ophelia remains onstage or that Claudius and Polonius have withdrawn to watch their encounter. The third section is the so-called 'nunnery scene', in which Hamlet unleashes a bizarre misogynist rant, warning Ophelia to shun the society of men. The fourth is the aftermath of this outburst, in which Ophelia laments Hamlet's fractured state of mind, and the two old men emerge from behind an arras, scratching their heads at what they have just heard.

It would not have been difficult for Shakespeare to have written the scene entirely in verse. Nor would it have been inappropriate. These are noble characters engaged in high and serious drama. Verse is their natural medium. And it is possible that his first instinct was to do just that – the famously 'bad' first quarto of *Hamlet* has a version of the scene that never moves into prose. In the two best early texts of the play, however, while the rest of the scene is in verse, the confrontation between Hamlet and Ophelia takes place in prose. In the course of a few dozen lines, the Prince of Denmark goes from this:

> To be, or not to be, that is the question –
> Whether 'tis nobler in the mind to suffer

> The slings and arrows of outrageous fortune,
> Or to take arms against a sea of troubles,
> And by opposing end them.   (3.1.56–60)

to this:

> I have heard of your paintings too, well enough. God hath given you one face
> and you make yourselves another. You jig, you amble, and you lisp, you nick-
> name God's creatures, and make your wantonness your ignorance. Go to, I'll
> no more on't, it hath made me mad. I say we will have no mo marriages. Those
> that are married already, all but one shall live, the rest shall keep as they are.
> To a nunnery, go.   (3.1.137–143)

As soon as he has left the stage, Ophelia switches back into verse to lament the overthrow of Hamlet's noble mind.

What, then, does this change of metrical register add to the scene? The obvious answer is that it signals a loss of control. Hamlet loses his temper with Ophelia, and with it his ability to speak in verse. But characters in Shakespeare often lose their tempers, and rant magnificently, in blank verse. So the switch here is likely to be doing something more specific. Ophelia, we recall, has recently shunned Hamlet – starving him, at her father's instruction, of her company. In this context, the prose may imply a kind of aggressive intimacy – a refusal to contain himself within proper metrical bounds – in revenge for her sudden distance. His language is ragged, unbuttoned, and sexually loaded. It is as if Hamlet is metrically exposing himself to Ophelia, in much the same way that he seems to have done physically in her closet (2.1.73–82). And perhaps he is. But it is equally plausible that the switch into prose signals the reverse – not a spontaneous act of revenge but a calculated act of disguise. If the real Hamlet is the one who speaks verse to himself in private, then the prose in which he abuses Ophelia may be part of the 'antic disposition' he puts on in public (1.5.172). Much of Hamlet's more obviously antic behaviour – his baiting of Polonius (2.2.169–212), for example, or of Guildenstern (3.2.312–336) – is conducted in prose. And prose is often the medium of real madness in Shakespeare. Ophelia herself, when her mind unravels, will speak a chatty prose enlaced with 'snatches of old lauds' (4.7.177).

My point is not that the verse–prose distinction allows us to settle such questions (it does not) but that it plays into them. The same set of concerns that is central to the drama of the scene is also at work in the shape of the writing. Our sense of what Hamlet is up to here – whether he is mad or just pretending to be so, whether he really does love Ophelia, whether he knows her father is watching – is inflected by the fact that he drops into prose. But noticing this fact deepens rather than resolves such ambiguities. Not only do verse and prose not have fixed meanings in this play, the ambiguity about what they might mean is mined for its dramatic potential.

Rhyme

Similarly easy to identify, most of the time, is Shakespeare's use of rhyme – with the obvious caveat that English pronunciation has changed over the last four centuries. It is likely, for example, that *love–prove* was a full rhyme in Early Modern English (with both words pronounced roughly as we would now pronounce 'love').[8] A good critical edition can help with this, if we are willing to trawl through the footnotes, as can David Crystal's *Oxford Dictionary of Original Shakespearean Pronunciation*. Even without one, however, most of Shakespeare's rhymes are recognisable to a modern reader or audience (at least in the sense that we can hear when some sort of rhyme is intended). Distinguishing full from half rhyme is more difficult, but this is difficult even for a historical phonetician. That Shakespeare sometimes uses half rhyme is indisputable (Crystal xxiii–xxiv). How much he uses it is not clear.

Like prose, rhyme is less common than blank verse (around one-tenth of Shakespeare's total dramatic writing). Like prose, the proportions change over the course of his career, and vary from play to play.[9] But while Shakespeare's use of prose steadily increases over the first decade of his career, his use of rhyme does the opposite. Edmund Malone famously described him growing weary of the 'bondage' of rhyme, but the decline is not consistent and Shakespeare's use of rhyme becomes more targeted as it gets scarcer.[10] The early plays frequently contain what Lorna Flint has called 'rhyming episodes' – when the blank verse gives way to a sustained passage of couplets (Flint 80–83). Usually, these occur at moments of high dramatic tension, in much the same way that a film moves into slow motion. In mature Shakespeare, rhyme is both more flexible and more purposeful. When we come across a sustained passage of rhyme, it is probably doing something more specific than upping the dramatic ante.

Consider, for example, the opening scene of *Macbeth*:

Thunder and lightning. Enter three WITCHES

FIRST WITCH	When shall we three meet again?
	In thunder, lightning, or in rain?
SECOND WITCH	When the hurly-burly's done,
	When the battle's lost, and won.
THIRD WITCH	That will be ere the set of sun.
FIRST WITCH	Where the place?
SECOND WITCH	Upon the heath.

THIRD WITCH	There to meet with Macbeth.
FIRST WITCH	I come, Graymalkin.
SECOND WITCH	Paddock calls.
THIRD WITCH	Anon.
ALL	Fair is foul, and foul is fair,
	Hover through the fog and filthy air.

Exeunt   (1.1.1–13)

Part of what makes this scene so weird is that it is not clear whether the witches are reciting a spell or having a conversation. Some of what they say seems to be incantatory and formulaic ('Fair is foul, and foul is fair') while some of it springs from the communicative needs of the moment ('That will be ere set of sun'). All of it, however, rhymes, and the effect of the rhyme is to blur the distinction between these two kinds of utterance. The witches seem to know not just what will happen later on that day, but which words the next speaker will use. They can see the future at the micro level of the dialogue as well as at the macro level of the plot. And they can see it, in part, because it is inherent to the sounds of the words they use – words they inevitably *must* use – to describe it. Whom else could they meet on the 'heath' but 'Macbeth'? That is what the rhyme demands and that is what the plot delivers. Both the word and the event are preordained – at least, Shakespeare's use of rhyme here raises that possibility.

The capacity of rhyme to make what is said seem necessary or inevitable makes it particularly appropriate for characters who, like the witches, know more than ordinary mortals (fairies, ghosts, descending goddesses). Likewise for the kind of speech act that is in some way bound to – or binding upon – the future (spells, prophecies, ceremonies, curses, oaths). The 'bondage' of rhyme, in this sense, is a dramatic resource rather than a metrical straightjacket. It is common, too, in the mouths of characters who are bound to each other. The first words exchanged by Romeo and Juliet fall into the pattern of a sonnet – the metrical archetype of romantic love – as if their fate were written into the sound of their words (*Rom.* 1.5.92–105). But perhaps the most interesting use of rhyme in Shakespeare's plays is as a kind of garnish, sprinkled onto scenes or speeches that are otherwise in blank verse.

Consider, once again, the moment at which Hamlet appears to lose it with Ophelia:

OPHELIA	My lord, I have remembrances of yours
	That I have longèd long to re-deliver.
	I pray you now receive them.
HAMLET	No, not I,
	I never gave you aught.
OPHELIA	My honoured lord, you know right well you did,

And with them words of so sweet breath composed
As made the things more rich. Their perfume lost,
Take these again, for to the noble mind
Rich gifts wax poor when givers prove unkind.
There my lord.

HAMLET   Ha, ha, are you honest?   (3.1.93–103)

Almost the last thing she does before he switches into prose is to produce a rhyming couplet. It is as if Hamlet's rant (however we might choose to read it) is triggered by the chime of her words. Edward Dowden has suggested that Ophelia's 'sententious generalization, couched in rhyme, has an air of having been prepared', and thus that she may have 'rehearsed her part to Polonius'.[11] The couplet makes Ophelia sound as if she is reciting something because it is too aphoristically neat to be spontaneous. It also sounds suspiciously like her father, a man addicted to sententious generalisations. If Hamlet hears these lines the same way Dowden does, then the rhyme marks the moment at which Ophelia gives herself away – the moment he realises that she is acting under Polonius's instruction – and this is what triggers his outburst.

But it is equally possible that Hamlet hears something else in Ophelia's sudden use of rhyme. Reproaching her son in sententious couplets is characteristic of Gertrude, Hamlet's mother:

GERTRUDE   Do not forever with thy vailèd lids
             Seek for thy noble father in the dust.
             Thou know'st 'tis common, all that lives must die,
             Passing through nature to eternity.
HAMLET   Ay madam, it is common.
GERTRUDE   If it be,
             Why seems it so particular with thee?
HAMLET   Seems madam? nay it is, I know not seems.   (1.2.70–76)

This is not to suggest that she too has been coached. Gertrude's couplets invoke a different kind of recitation. They are part of a cultural script – the worn-out platitudes we offer to the bereaved, simultaneously true and comfortless. Coming from her they sound like hypocrisy, at least to Hamlet. Thus, two acts later, when Ophelia reproaches him in a similarly aphoristic couplet, she unwittingly sounds like his mother. What she gets in return is an outpouring of vitriol that is only partly meant for her. Hamlet does not like being told off by women, least of all in the smug complacency of rhyme. What the example demonstrates is a kind of double-jointedness in Shakespeare's use of rhyme. It can confer an air of timelessness and finality on what is said, or make it feel trite and rehearsed. It can cause something to sound 'sententious' in either sense of that word, or in both senses at once. Shakespeare is able to exploit this ambiguity dramatically. What sounds to Gertrude and Ophelia like the ring of indisputable truth, sounds to Hamlet like an empty chime – the reverberation of female hollowness. The rhyme embodies these two viewpoints without deciding between them.

Line Length

The third of our four indispensable metrical terms is the syllable. By counting syllables we can measure the length of a line. Shakespeare uses variations in line length with characteristic expressive subtlety, both within blank verse and to distinguish it from other metres. The witches, for example, speak not just in rhyme, but also in creepily symmetrical seven-syllable lines ('Fair is foul and foul is fair') – they have their own weird metre, distinct from the largely unrhymed, and largely decasyllabic, verse of the other characters in the play. As with rhyme, we will need at least some acquaintance with original pronunciation if we are to avoid mistakes when counting syllables. As we would expect, the syllabic value of many words has changed in the last four centuries. But Early Modern English also seems to have had a wider range of permissible options – standard ways in which words could be expanded or contracted (Wright 149–159). Exactly *how* wide is open to debate. Whether Shakespeare thought this or that line of verse had nine or eleven syllables is not always something we can determine. But it is not something that matters much either – at least not to the student whose concern is the dramatic function of metre, rather than the establishment of statistical norms. We can focus instead on those lines which are unambiguously short or unambiguously long. As well as being the easiest to spot, these are the lines that do the most meaningful dramatic work. The real question is what work they do.

According to Samuel Taylor Coleridge, 'Shakespeare never introduces a catalectic [i.e. short] line without intending an equivalent to the foot omitted, in the pauses, or the dwelling emphasis, or the diffused retardation.'[12] This is not quite true ('never' is a risky word when it comes to Shakespeare) but it is a useful starting point for thinking about line length. Coleridge seems to be speaking, primarily, of the kind of short line that occurs in the middle of a speech. Here, for example, is a section of Hamlet's 'rogue and peasant slave' soliloquy, with the syllable count to the right of each line and syllabically ambiguous words in bold:

> I should ha' fatted all the **region** kites   10–11
> With this slave's offal. Bloody, bawdy villain!   11

Remorseless, **treacherous**, **lecherous**, kindless villain!	11–13
Oh, **vengeance**!	3–4
Why, what an ass am I! This is most brave,	10
That I, the son of the dear **murdered**,	9–10
Prompted to my revenge by **heaven** and hell,	10–11
Must like a whore unpack my heart with words,	10
And fall a-cursing like a very drab	10 (2.2.532–49)

The short line marks the moment at which Hamlet seems to catch himself ranting and suddenly becomes conscious of the feebleness of his words. It suggests both a pause, in which he makes this realisation, and a dwelling emphasis on the word 'vengeance' (stretching it out to three full syllables). And, as so often in Shakespeare, the implied pause makes space in the line for an implied action. Here perhaps a gesture – slapping himself on the forehead, for example, in exasperation at his own stupidity. Notice, too, how the short line is preceded by a long one (how long depends on whether we give 'lecherous' and 'treacherous' three syllables each or two). Taken together, these two lines mime the process of Hamlet's thought – first bloated with impotent rage, then empty and ashamed.

Short lines become increasingly common in Shakespeare as his career progresses, particularly at the beginning and end of speeches, and can often have the effect of blurring the distinction between verse and prose.[13] Here, once again, is the exchange between Hamlet and Ophelia, this time from the moment he first notices her:

HAMLET	Soft you now,
	The fair Ophelia. – Nymph, in thy orisons
	Be all my sins remembered.
OPHELIA	Good my lord,
	How does your honour for this many a day?
HAMLET	I humbly thank you, well, well, well.
OPHELIA	My lord, I have remembrances of yours
	That I have longèd long to re-deliver.
	I pray you now receive them.
HAMLET	No, not I,
	I never gave you aught.
OPHELIA	My honoured lord, you know right well you did,
	And with them words of so sweet breath composed
	As made the things more rich. Their perfume lost,
	Take these again, for to the noble mind
	Rich gifts wax poor when givers prove unkind.
	There my lord.
HAMLET	Ha, ha, are you honest?
OPHELIA	My lord?

HAMLET	Are you fair?
OPHELIA	What means your lordship?
HAMLET	That if you be honest and fair, your honesty should admit no discourse to your beauty.
OPHELIA	Could beauty, my lord, have better commerce than with honesty? (3.1.88–110)

At least, this is the exchange as it is presented in Philip Edwards's New Cambridge Shakespeare edition. In Edwards's text, the switch from verse to prose can be located exactly – at line 103, when Hamlet asks Ophelia whether she is 'honest'. Ophelia's preceding speech, with its rhyming couplet, is unambiguously in verse, and the short line with which it concludes seems to leave space for action, most probably the return of Hamlet's gifts. What follows is something of a non sequitur, as Hamlet begins an aggressive line of interrogation about Ophelia's chastity. Dramatically and interactionally, something changes at line 103, so it would make sense if that were also the moment at which Hamlet switches into prose.

But the clarity of this distinction is editorial. To produce it, Edwards has had to rearrange the text, indenting what he takes to be the second half of shared lines and relineating when he runs out of syllables. Compare the second quarto:

> *Oph.* Good my Lord,
> How dooes your honour for this many a day?
>   *Ham.* I humbly thanke you well.
>   *Oph.* My Lord, I haue remembrances of yours
> That I haue longed long to redeliuer,
> I pray you now receiue them.
>   *Ham.* No, not I, I neuer gaue you ought.
>   *Oph.* My honor'd Lord, you know right well you did,
> And with them words of so sweet breath composd
> As made these things more rich,   (sig. G2v)

Without the indentation, both of Hamlet's lines are metrically ambiguous – they could be short lines of verse, or they could be prose. The precise moment of the switch is thus impossible to locate. Edwards assumes that if Ophelia is speaking verse then Hamlet must be speaking verse as well, but this need not be the case. It is possible, in the quarto text, that he speaks one while she speaks the other – that he speaks prose, in fact, from the beginning of their conversation. Ophelia's failure to respond in kind might thus be seen as a metrical enactment of her bafflement at Hamlet's behaviour. Alternatively, we might see it as further evidence (along with the rhyme) that she is following some sort of script. Or we might see it as deliberate, a refusal rather than a mistake. Ophelia attempts to bring Hamlet to his wonted way again by insisting that they speak as they used to do, in a dignified and courtly blank verse. Once again, the point is not that any particular reading of the lines is correct, but that the questions they raise are deeply implicated in the larger dramatic situation. By removing the ambiguity over when Hamlet moves into prose, Edwards deprives the reader of the opportunity to ask them.

Stress

The last and trickiest of our four indispensable terms is stress. A stressed syllable is one that, for whatever reason, sounds more prominent than the syllables around it. By paying attention to the distribution of stressed syllables, we can chart the rhythmical contour of a line verse. It is stress that gives the line its internal structure. The easiest way to understand its use in Shakespeare is as an extension of the principle that governs his larger metrical choices. The same thing that happens at the macro level of form happens at the micro level of the line itself. Sometimes it stiffens into an insistently regular alternation of stressed and unstressed syllables. Sometimes it slackens into something more fluid and speech-like. There is a continuum, in other words, between a self-consciously verse-like verse (consisting of regular iambic pentameters) and looser, more prose-like verse – between verse on its rhythmical high-horse, and verse that saunters casually along. Unlike the distinction between verse and prose, however, which can usually be seen on the page, the stiffening and slackening of the line has to be picked out by ear.

This is both easier than it sounds and harder. It is easier because any competent English speaker can hear the difference between a stressed and an unstressed syllable. Were this not the case they would be unable to distinguish between the verb 'record' ('I will record what you have said') and the noun 'record' ('A new world record!'). What makes it hard is precisely how familiar this process is. It is one thing to be able to hear the difference between two words, and another to be able to describe it in metrical terms. So the problem is not so much learning to hear stress as learning to become conscious of what we can already hear – of learning to scan words rather than simply to use them.

Exactly what stress is – whether the result of an increase in the volume or duration of the syllable, or a change in the pitch or sound of the vowel – is complicated, and need not concern us here.[14] The critic does not need to be able to define stress, only to recognise it. For polysyllabic words, this is relatively straightforward. They tend to have a fixed stress-pattern and when in doubt we can look this up – either in the OED, or, if we suspect the pronunciation may have shifted, in Crystal's dictionary. Monosyllabic words pose more of a problem. Not having any fixed internal stress, these are emphasised relative to other words in the same sentence. The most obvious reason for stressing one rather than another is grammatical. We tend to stress what linguists call 'notional' or 'lexical' words – nouns, main verbs, adjectives, numerals, most adverbs – but not to stress 'grammatical' or 'functional' words – articles, prepositions, particles, conjunctions, modal and auxiliary verbs. The distinction is not perfect, however, and grammar is not the only thing in play. As Marina Tarlinskaja has pointed out, 'even normally unstressed monosyllables may acquire strong stress in a particular context'.[15] We also have the question of metre. Should verse be read as though it were prose, allowing the metre to make itself audible without our assistance? Or should we attempt to draw the metre out? Should we, in W. K. Wimsatt's phrase, 'tilt' our reading of the lines in the direction of metrical regularity?[16] Linguists have struggled manfully to produce sets of rules that will resolve all potential ambiguities.[17] Such rules can help us to be more consistent, but they cannot eradicate subjectivity, and, even if they could, it is not clear that consistency should be the aim. To strive for consistency is to ignore the many hints the plays give us about how to per-form (and thus how to scan) particular lines or speeches – calling now for one approach and now for another. It is to treat them not as plays, but as a corpus of metrical data.

It is for this reason that I will be annotating Shakespeare's verse with three marks rather than the usual two. These are as follows:

- A forward slash '/' to signify a stressed syllable
- A lower case 'x' to signify an unstressed syllable
- A hyphen '-' to signify uncertainty

A syllable might be 'uncertain' for a variety of reasons – because the stress pattern of the word itself is ambiguous, because it seems to carry some intermediate or secondary degree of stress, or because the dramatic context suggests different ways of hearing the line. The point of this new mark is that it enables us to scan verse in such a way as to identify, rather than to conceal, its ambiguities. For the same reason, it is worth scanning line by line, or even sentence by sentence, rather than word by word – working from the most obvious features of the line to the most doubtful, rather than from left to right. We should begin, I am suggesting, by marking any unambiguously stressed syllables. Then we should mark any that are unam-biguously unstressed. Finally, we should return to the more dubious cases, resolving those we can and marking those we cannot resolve as uncertain.

What this leaves us with is a partial contour – like a piece of string pinned to the page at certain points, but free to take different shapes between those points. The critic's job is to work through the possible ways of joining the dots – not in the hope of arriving at a definitive answer, but in order to understand what difference it makes if we stress the line one way rather than another.

I want to look at two examples of how this works, one of which can be used to shed light on the other. The first is crude enough to constitute a kind of special metrical effect. It comes from the tavern scene in *The First Part of King Henry IV*, just after Hal has been summoned to meet his father. Naturally, the prince decides to prepare for this meeting with a drunken rehearsal in the pub:

PRINCE	Do thou stand for my father and examine me upon the particulars of my life.
FALSTAFF	Shall I? Content! This chair shall be my state, this dagger my sceptre, and this cushion my crown. [...] Give me a cup of sack to make my eyes look red, that it may be thought I have wept, for I must speak in passion, and I will do it in King Cambyses' vein.
PRINCE	Well, here is my leg.
FALSTAFF	And here is my speech. Stand aside, nobility.
HOSTESS	O Jesu, this is excellent sport, i'faith.
FALSTAFF	Weep not, sweet Queen, for trickling tears are vain.
HOSTESS	O the Father, how he holds his countenance!
FALSTAFF	For God's sake, lords, convey my tristful Queen, For tears do stop the floodgates of her eyes.
HOSTESS	O Jesu, he doth it as like one of these harlotry players as ever I see! (2.4.310–328)

Both the scene and the rehearsal take place in prose, but Falstaff improvises three lines of verse as part of an impersonation (instantly recognised by the Hostess) of a 'harlotry player'. If we pull those three lines out of the exchange, they can be scanned as follows:

```
                                            1 2 3 4 5 6 7 8 9 0
Weep not, sweet Queen, for trickling tears are vain.   / / - / x / x / - /
For God's sake, lords, convey my tristful Queen,   x / - / x / - / x /
For tears do stop the floodgates of her eyes.      x / - / x / - - x /
```

The parody is metrical as well as stylistic. Each line is exactly ten syllables long, and (with one exception) there is an unambiguous stress on each of the even-numbered syllables. The alternation between stress and unstress is not perfect, but that may be part of the joke. The first four syllables are all to some degree stressed, but it would not be difficult to put a greater relative stress on the second and fourth (Weep *not*, sweet *Queen*). The only real difficulty comes in the last line. But that, it seems to me, is precisely the point. These lines *ask* to be tilted – they call for a hammy rendition that forces them into a pentameter straightjacket. Falstaff's performance climaxes, in other words, with a semantically unmotivated stress on the word 'of' – 'For tears do stop the floodgates *of* her eyes'. Shakespeare's twin targets are the thumpingly monotonous verse of other dramatic poets, and the hammily sonorous delivery of other acting companies. For the joke to work, there has to be a contrast between his own verse and the verse he parodies, between his own troupe and the harlotry players imitated by Falstaff. The context guides us towards a scansion that is not inherent to the lines themselves.

The second example comes, once again, from *Hamlet*. It is the moment at which Hamlet confronts Laertes, Ophelia's brother, at her grave (5.1.213–224):

```
                                         1 2 3 4 5 6 7 8 9 0 1
LAERTES           Oh treble woe                      - / x /
   Fall ten times treble on that cursed head   / / / / x - - / x /
   Whose wicked deed thy most ingenious sense  - / x / - - x / x /
   Deprived thee of. Hold off the earth awhile x / - - - - x / x /
   Till I have caught her once more in mine arms. x / x / - - - - - /
   Now pile your dust upon the quick and dead  - / - / x / x / x /
   Till of this flat a mountain you have made  - - - / x / x - - /
   T'o'ertop old Pelion or the skyish head     x / - / x - x / x /
   Of blue Olympus.                            x / x / x
HAMLET           What is he whose grief              - - / - /
   Bears such an emphasis? whose phrase of sorrow / / x / x - - / x / x
   Conjures the wandering stars, and makes
       them stand                              / x x / x / x / - /
   Like wonder-wounded hearers?                - / x / x / x /
```

After a brief scuffle, the prince continues (5.1.236–251):

```
                                              1 2 3 4 5 6 7 8 9 0 1

I loved Ophelia; forty thousand brothers      - / x / x / x / x / x

Could not with all their quantity of love     - - x / - / x x x /

Make up my sum. What wilt thou do for her?     / / - / - - - / x -

Woo't weep, woo't fight, woo't fast, woo't
    tear thyself?                              x / x / x / x / - -

Woo't drink up eisel, eat a crocodile?         x / / / x / x / x /

I'll do't. Dost thou come here to whine,        - / - - - - x /

To outface me with leaping in her grave?       x / / - x / x - x /

Be buried quick with her, and so will I.        - / x / - - x / - /

And if thou prate of mountains, let them throw  x - / / x / x - - /

Millions of acres on us, till our ground,       / x x / x - - - - /

Singeing his pate against the burning zone,     / x x / x / x / x /

Make Ossa like a wart. Nay, and thou'lt mouth,  - / x - x / / - - /

I'll rant as well as thou.                      - / x / x /
```

Tonally, this exchange is hard to pin down. Both men, we must assume, feel genuine grief at Ophelia's death. But, from the moment Hamlet steps forward, they seem far more interested in each other than in the woman they claim to have loved. The scene is tragic, but it teeters on the edge of parody. In Hamlet's case, this is at least partially deliberate. Enraged by the pitch of Laertes's rhetoric, he mocks the young man's posturing and theatricality. What is less clear, however, is whether Shakespeare joins him in doing so – whether Laertes *is* ridiculous, or only *seems* so to Hamlet. And the prince's own behaviour is hardly above suspicion. There is a competitive edge to his outburst that stops it from being straightforwardly sarcastic. What does it mean for someone to grieve in these terms? Is Laertes's ranting really any different from Hamlet's – here or at any other point in the play? Does Hamlet, of all people, have a right to object? Is it simply in the nature of grief to be beyond the reach of words? All of these questions are alive in the rhythms of the verse. How we choose to scan that verse will depend upon how we answer them. And by choosing to scan it one way rather than another we implicitly *do* answer them, whether we realise it or not.

Like Falstaff's parody of a harlotry player, Laertes's lines are conspicuously regular and can be tilted to produce a 'drumming decasillabon'.[18] Just how far we tilt them will depend on how ridiculous we take him to be (Fall ten times treble *on* that cursèd head? Till *of* this flat a mountain you have made?) If Laertes is simply a foil for Hamlet, a stock revenger of the kind churned out by lesser playwrights for other theatrical companies, then his verse should sound as stagily iambic as possible – a metrical as well as a dramatic contrast with Hamlet's more lifelike syncopations. The brutal contraction of 'To overtop' from four syllables to two (spelt 'To'retop' in the second quarto) nudges us in this direction. A more restrained scansion, on the other hand, retaining what little metrical variation the lines afford, suggests a Laertes who is more the prince's counterpart than his stooge, and in whose cause we see the portraiture of Hamlet's own.

Something similar is true of the prince's response. How far we tilt it will depend on how metrically sarcastic we think he should sound, where exactly we locate his sarcasm, and how successfully we think he manages to distinguish his own voice from that of the stock revenger. When Hamlet describes how Laertes 'Conjures the wandering stars, and makes them stand / Like wonder-wounded hearers', for example, his words are performing what they describe – parodying the kind of language adopted by Laertes. It therefore makes sense to tilt them in the same direction (by making 'wandering' disyllabic, for example). It would even be possible, at a push, to pronounce 'conjure' with the stress on the second syllable. By bending the word out of shape Hamlet can mock not just Laertes's metre, but the lengths to which he will go in order to preserve it. The 'emphasis' borne by Laertes's grief thus becomes the emphasis borne, rhythmically, by his words – hammering down on every second syllable to bang his public grief-drum.

When, on the other hand, Hamlet claims to have loved Ophelia more than forty thousand brothers, he is presumably being sincere. And one way of drawing this contrast out is to scan the lines less insistently. To tilt them would be to implicate Hamlet, rhythmically, in the practice he is mocking. But perhaps Hamlet *is* implicated in the practice he is mocking. 'Forty thousand brothers' is both an un-ironic hyperbole and a perfect alternation of stressed and unstressed syllables. Much as he might like to, Hamlet cannot quite separate his own voice from Laertes's, rhythmically or rhetorically. Having heard the old familiar tune, as it were, he finds himself humming it. Such a reading would justify further tilting – enough to give us, for example, 'To outface *me* with leaping in her grave?', as though Laertes's display were entirely for Hamlet's benefit. The result is a scansion that brings the two characters closer together, undermining the contrast Hamlet tries to draw between them. Even the prince has a whiff of the 'harlotry player'.

Conclusion

So where does all this leave us? If we agree to discard the term 'iambic pentameter', with what do we replace it? The obvious answer is 'blank verse' – a phrase used by Hamlet in anticipation of the players (2.2.302), by Jaques in dismissal of young love (*AYLI* 4.1.25), and by Robert Greene in an attack on Shakespeare.[19] Shakespearean blank verse tends to have roughly ten syllables, three or four of which are unambiguously stressed, and two or three of which *could* be stressed if an actor were so inclined. His lines tend to start with an unstressed syllable and to finish with a stressed one. Within the line, the two kinds of syllable tend to alternate – sometimes perfectly, as in an iambic pentameter, but more often loosely, as in a ballad or a nursery rhyme. Little runs of two or three unstressed syllables are common, as are pairs or triplets of adjacent stresses. One lightens and quickens the verse, the other clots and thickens it. This is what gives Shakespeare's metre its elasticity and its famously speech-like quality, hovering on the edge of prose. Sometimes the verse stumbles and sometimes it struts. And whatever it can do with a straight face it can also do with a smirk or a raised eyebrow. Crucially, at the distance of four hundred years, there is always an element of uncertainty. Shakespeare's versification, like his language, is partially out of earshot. But it is doubtful that it was ever meant to be heard in just one way. These plays consistently make dramatic capital out of metrical ambiguities – so consistently that it is hard to see such moments as accidents. Our job as critics is to map the range of possibilities and see what difference they make. For the purposes of the non-specialist, this is all that needs to be said – and all of it can be said using the four basic terms of a minimalist prosody: line, rhyme, syllable, and stress.

NOTES

1 On the rise of the iambic pentameter and its consequences, see Eric Griffiths, 'On Lines and Grooves from Shakespeare to Tennyson', *Tennyson among the Poets: Bicentenary Essays,* ed. Robert Douglas-Fairhurst and Seamus Perry (Oxford: Oxford University Press, 2009), pp. 132–159. The current chapter is also heavily indebted to Griffiths's (hitherto) unpublished lectures on 'Regular Iambic Pentameter'.

2 The classic study of the development of Elizabethan prosodic theory is Derek Attridge, *Well-Weighed Syllables: Elizabethan Verse in Classical Metres* (London: Cambridge University Press, 1974).

3 Roger Ascham, 'Of Imitation' from *The Scholemaster* (1570), reproduced in *Elizabethan Critical Essays*, ed. G. Gregory Smith, 2 vols. (Oxford: Clarendon Press, 1904), I, p. 31. For ease of comprehension, I have modernised the spelling and letter-forms in all quotations from Smith.

4 Respectively, Ascham (Smith I, 29) and the anonymous writer of *The First Booke of the Preseruation of King Henry the Vij* (1599) as quoted in Smith (II, 377). The modernisation is again my own, including 'Rhyme' for 'Rythme'. These two words were not clearly distinguished in early modern English, so that either spelling could take either meaning. The same applies to the Gascoigne quotation that follows.

5 For a complete table of percentages see Brian Vickers, *The Artistry of Shakespeare's Prose* (London: Methuen, 1968), p. 433.

6 Russ McDonald, *Shakespeare and the Arts of Language* (Oxford: Oxford University Press, 2001), p. 114.

7 Brian Vickers makes a valiant attempt in 'Shakespeare's Use of Prose', *William Shakespeare: His World, His Work, His Influence* (New York: Scribner's, 1985), vol. 2, pp. 389–396.

8 David Crystal, *The Oxford Dictionary of Original Shakespearean Pronunciation* (Oxford: Oxford University Press, 2016), pp. xliii, 330.

9 For totals see Lorna Flint, *Shakespeare's Third Keyboard: The Significance of Rime in Shakespeare's Plays* (London: Associated University Presses, 2000), p. 13.

10 Edmond Malone (ed.), *The Plays and Poems of William Shakspeare* (London: J. Rivington & Sons, 1790), vol. 1, p. 294n.

11 Edward Dowden (ed.), *The Tragedy of Hamlet* (London: Methuen, 1899) 3.1.101n (p. 102).

12 Terence Hawkes (ed.), *Coleridge on Shakespeare* (London: Penguin, 1969), p. 164.

13 See George T. Wright, *Shakespeare's Metrical Art* (Berkeley: University of California Press, 1988), p. 119 for statistics.

14 For a more detailed discussion of this question see Derek Attridge, *The Rhythms of English Poetry* (London: Longman, 1982), pp. 62–66.

15 Marina Tarlinskaja, *Shakespeare's Verse: Iambic Pentameter and the Poet's Idiosyncrasies* (New York: Peter Lang, 1987), p. 32.

16 W. K. Wimsatt, 'The Rule and the Norm: Halle and Keyser on Chaucer's Meter', *College English* 31 (1970): 774–788, p. 785.

17 See, for example, Tarlinskaja, *Shakespeare's Verse*, pp. 31–39.

18 Thomas Nashe, from the preface to Robert Greene's *Menaphon* (1599), reproduced in Smith (I, 308).

19 Robert Greene, *Groat's Worth of Witte* (1592), ed. G. B. Harrison (London: The Bodley Head Quartos, 1923), pp. 45–46.

5

LYNNE MAGNUSSON

The Dynamics of Shakespearean Dialogue

At the heart of Shakespearean drama is the dialogic encounter. Whether as arresting as the clash of irreconcilable opponents or as seemingly mundane as the everyday conversation of acquaintances, the performed encounters of plays deploy language in a special manner that differs from discursive writing or narration. Hearing it as spoken utterance in the here and now and watching it unfold in turns as the social interaction of impersonated characters, audiences need no extensive rhetorical training to orient their interpretation to some of the special qualities of dramatic dialogue. We have been there ourselves. As conversationalists we regularly engage using 'I' and 'you' in the call and response of verbal exchange. As addressees and overhearers we constantly refine our practical interpretive skills. We anticipate structured responsive sequences such as question and answer, summons and response, comment and rejoinder:

ANTONIO	Will you stay no longer? Nor will you not that I go with you?	
SEBASTIAN	By your patience, no. My stars shine darkly	
	over me.	(*TN* 2.1.1–2)

BRUTUS	Get me a taper in my study, Lucius.	
	When it is lighted, come and call me here.	
LUCIUS	I will, my lord.	(*JC* 2.1.7–9)

CASSIUS	If I know this, know all the world besides,	
	That part of tyranny that I do bear	
	I can shake off at pleasure.	
CASCA	So can I.	
	So every bondman in his own hand bears	
	The power to cancel his captivity.	(*JC* 1.3.98–102)

Our structured expectation of sequence readily alerts us to register violations and interpret surprises. Hence the theatrical impact of Lear's thrice unanswered question, 'Who put my man i'th'stocks?' (*Lear* 2.4.175) or the jittery fearfulness communicated in the opening exchange of *Hamlet*, as the sentinels at Elsinore Castle mix up their expected question and answer roles:

BARNARDO   Who's there?
FRANCISCO   Nay answer me. Stand and unfold yourself.
BARNARDO   Long live the king!
FRANCISCO   Barnardo?
BARNARDO   He.   (*Ham.* 1.1.1–5)

We are also attuned to patterns of digressive sequencing that can arise with what conversation analysts call 'dispreferred' responses,[1] as where the imprisoned Clarence in *Richard III*, questioning his visitors, ends up answering his own question:

CLARENCE   Why look you pale?
                  Who sent you hither? Wherefore do you come?
SECOND MURDERER   To, to, to –
CLARENCE   To murder me?
BOTH MURDERERS   Ay, ay.   (*R3* 1.4.160–164)

Affect and intellect go together: we cannot separate the interlocutors' full-bodied emotional responses from their instantaneous mental processing of thwarted or surprised expectations.

Despite the regulated framing of spoken exchange in call and response turn-taking patterns, its improvisational progression can still be highly unpredictable, for conversations (even everyday ones) unfold as remarkably complex inferential processes. Even when rejoinders appear incoherent or random, listeners actively construct meaning. As Horatio says of Ophelia's mad speech in *Hamlet*, 'the unshapèd use of it doth move / The hearers to collection. They aim at it'.[2] Horatio's claim about the powerful inference-making faculties Ophelia's listeners bring to bear on 'half sense' (4.5.7) applies more widely to all verbal exchange. His comment may be negatively inflected in the specific situation – he suggests 'They ... botch the words up fit to their own thoughts' (9–10) – but it explicates the inferential half-creating that we all do constantly in conversation and that we bring as a practised interpretive skill to theatrical dialogue.[3] Shakespeare knew he could depend on this collaborative meaning-making in the take-up of dialogue, just as his character Iago depends on how easily he can trigger it in Othello. By offering minimal answers and seemingly empty echoing words like 'for aught I know' and 'Think, my lord?' (*Oth.* 3.3.105–106), the calculating Iago leaves it to Othello to infer 'Thou dost mean something' (109), awakening in the hero a deep vein of fear that his wife is unfaithful to him.

Of course, theatre audiences know that dramatic dialogue is not improvised talk, for the actors are repeating scripted performances representing the conversation of characters. Nonetheless, as themselves social actors in everyday life, audience members relate to the dialogue's close affinity (however elaborated or stylised) with their own lived experience of face-to-face encounter. At the same time, speakers' 'knowledge' is tacit and practical: the mind and body *'know more than we can tell'*.[4] This chapter aims to explicate some of the complex dynamics of social dialogue that are relevant to drama and to offer tools and resources for its articulate discussion. I show how Shakespeare's dialogic art draws upon practices common to conversation as described and codified in recent research on social interaction. Often it tidies, adapts, magnifies, or stylises these practices, and, at times, it offers reflexive commentary on their significance. We can also learn from cultural ethnography and social discourse theory how speech events are situated within and affect social and institutional contexts. Reading plays with an alertness to the microcosms of dialogic interaction can teach us about historical cultures and their habits of engagement. We must also be alert to the institution of the theatre itself. To that end, this chapter explores complex participant frameworks distinctive to theatre dialogue and considers how Shakespeare's dialogic experiments exploit theatrical paradigms.

The Potential Stakes of Dialogic Encounter

As the sociologist Erving Goffman made clear, social interaction and theatrical performance are akin. The approach of another person, offstage or on, puts potential performers on the alert: something could happen. 'But who comes here?' – Shakespeare's repeated marker of approach – primes theatre audiences for the eventfulness of speech encounters. The situation is affectively charged. It holds out possibility and risk – enough risk that remediating rituals are characteristically observed to offset potential trouble or flare-ups. When social performers exchange words, they don't just get down to an obvious business at hand, developing topics of relevance or pursuing deliberated agendas. They characteristically act to sustain creditable roles or what Goffman calls 'lines' of self-presentation for themselves and also to acknowledge and maintain (even if just provisionally for the space of the encounter) other participants' projected self-images.[5] This performance of mutual accommodation is easy enough to dismiss as superficial politeness, a 'glib and oily art, / To speak and purpose not' (*Lear* 1.1.219–220), but forms of conversational accommodation (however often strained or violated) ground, normalise, and sustain social relationships, and with them, civilised life. For example, as things go astray with civility in Shakespeare's *King Lear*, well-intentioned characters like the Earl of Kent test out alternative speech forms, reaching for some kind of more authentic truth-telling expression, pared of apparent flattery, seemingly more direct and ethical. Abandoning forms of address like 'Good my liege' and 'Royal Lear' for 'What wouldst thou do, *old man?*' (1.1.114, 133, 140, emphasis added), Kent, both angry and strategic in his word choice, seeks to avert Lear's rash action disinheriting Cordelia. But the medicine of plain speech does not cure, and Lear's tragic journey unfolds as a terrifying 'unselving' largely effected by how his ill-intentioned daughters and their servants withhold the normal goodwill of conversation. By experimenting with such dislocations of talk, Shakespeare reveals how integral intersubjective accommodation and acknowledgement are to one's basic experience of the self.

If sociology alerts us to the self-sustaining performativity of everyday dialogue, philosophy has often theorised its special importance. Emmanuel Levinas, for example, rooted his fundamental concept of *respons*-ibility in intersubjective dialogue, underscoring its centrality to self-formation and ethical action in the world. As Bettina Burgo lucidly articulates, for Levinas the 'origin of language ... is always response – a responding-to-another, that is, to her summons'. In this account, 'no event is as affectively disruptive for a consciousness holding sway in its world than the encounter with another person'. The 'I' responds, not necessarily to explicit imperatives in the speech of another but in an anticipatory manner, 'as if to a nebulous command'.[6] In B. C. Hutchens's words, '*before* anyone speaks, the very approach of the other person is akin to an imperative delivered up to the self: "You must ...".[7]

It is fascinating to see how the opening of *Antony and Cleopatra* dramatises encounter in a similar way, whereby the 'approach' of another person is already fraught with imperative demand, which calls upon the self for an accounting. The theatricality of the scene's encounters is heightened by a participant framework that includes two onstage observers, providing a surrogate for the offstage theatre viewers. Audience members are primed to be alert to Antony's situation by the critical judgement of Philo's opening speech, which condemns the play's hero for abandoning his formerly well-tempered military demeanour to 'cool a gipsy's lust' (*Ant.* 1.1.10). When Philo invites Demetrius to 'Take but good note' (11), Shakespeare is also prompting his audience's close attention to the 'ought-ness' of the unfolding relationships. Cleopatra's opening address to Antony is, indeed, an explicit imperative – 'If it be love indeed, tell me how much' (14) – although the actual imperative comes freighted (by 'if') so it could fairly be called a 'nebulous command'. She makes a complicated affective demand, requiring the performance of all-encompassing devotion. The web of obligation quickly becomes even more complicated with the entrance of a messenger signalling the approach and demand of another person, here a mediated encounter 'from Rome' (18). The messenger's prospective address is interrupted and entirely closed down, so we hear nothing explicit in this scene about its content, nor indeed is the sender definitively identified. This places the entire interest on what Levinas accents – what is made of an approach '*before* anyone speaks'. Cleopatra plays interference for Antony, projecting his anticipation of an angry summons from Fulvia or of Caesar's 'powerful mandate to you' to 'Do this, or this' (1.1.21–23). Cleopatra works not just to turn aside the messenger's explicit demand, but to get inside Antony's head, to translate his irritated expression 'Grates me! The sum' (19) into the full-blown 'You MUST' of his affective construal of the approach from Rome: 'You must not stay here longer' (1.1.28). Her strategies and immediate presence result in Antony's responding in the present moment to her performance demands, but when he next appears the psychic 'You MUST' reveals itself as Antony's explicit and repeated 'I MUST': 'These strong Egyptian fetters I must break' (1.2.112) – 'I must with haste from hence' – 'I must be gone' (1.3.129, 133).

The strange idea of dialogue as 'response' before demand recurs in *Antony and Cleopatra*. It is emphasised by the device of the frequent messenger, whose message is almost always forecast by the recipient before it is spoken, as played out here in Cleopatra's analysis of a messenger's syntax:

MESSENGER	But yet, madam –	
CLEOPATRA	I do not like 'But yet'; it does allay	
	The good precedence. Fie upon 'But yet'!	
	'But yet' is as a gaoler to bring forth	
	Some monstrous malefactor.	(2.5.50–54)

With this Levinasian response before (or without) spoken demand, Shakespeare constructs the particular psychologies of the lead characters and brings the lived experience of 'responsibility' into focus as a theme of *Antony and Cleopatra*. Of course it does not always work this way in natural conversation or in Shakespeare's dialogic invention, where we often delight in how characters respond to (and project) actual utterances. Nonetheless, while the anticipatory quality of the responsive utterance is far more various in its workings than Levinas's philosophy allows for, it is crucially important – and illuminated by Mikhail Bakhtin's more encompassing understanding. For Bakhtin, no word can 'escape the profound influence of the answering word that it anticipates. The word in living conversation is directly, blatantly oriented to a future answer-word: it provokes an answer, anticipates it, and structures itself in the answer's direction.'[8]

Turn-Taking and the Participant Framework

A number of interdisciplinary fields of study aimed at making social actors' practical knowledge of speech interaction explicit emerged in the later twentieth century. Conversation analysis concerned itself especially with the anticipation-driven alternation of speaking turns, while pragmatics and ethnography considered speech situations and how utterances work in their social contexts of use. This research offers valuable starting points for thinking about speech distribution in the represented conversation of dramatic dialogue and for pinpointing the differences between talk and theatre interaction. In analysing dialogue, it helps to consider first a basic but important dimension of context – that is, the 'participant framework'.[9] We need to ask not just 'who is speaking?' and 'to whom?' but 'who are the other participants?' and 'what are their roles in the ongoing discourse?' Unpacking these simple questions leads us to complicate the binary for- mula of 'speaker–listener alternation' in speech exchanges and can tell us a lot about the special configuration of the theatre situation. Indeed, the participant framework will almost invariably be affected by the genre or kind of speech event occurring – for example, the participant framework of a modern-day business meeting or a classroom would differ from an Elizabethan court scene or street conversation. In *The Merry Wives of Windsor*, when Shakespeare chooses to show a grammar-school lesson onstage, he removes it from the all-male classroom that is its usual setting onto a town street in Windsor, thus allowing for the presence of women and changing both the social composition and the participant framework of the dialogue. A conversation or more elaborate speech event often has multiple participants, not just a singular addresser and addressee: many of the others present may be actively vying to speak or at least potential speakers. Others may be overhearers, not 'part of the conversation', yet affected, responsive in mental and bodily or physiological ways even if constrained in some manner from actually speaking. In the twenty-first century, the rapid change to the new normal of cell-phone usage on the street made people especially alert to their status as the non-speaking participant: suddenly they were right there in the midst of a conversation, directly affected and often stirred up emotionally by its performance, active – often in spite of themselves – in inference-making, and effectively barred from speech participation. If there are a plurality of potential 'listener' roles in social exchange, so too with speaker roles. Each messenger in *Antony and Cleopatra*, for example, speaks for a non-present participant (the sender or author of the message). We have already seen how potently this absent addresser can affect the emotions and responses of immediate speech participants. And, of course, in the complex mimesis of theatre performance, answering the question 'who is speaking?' must encompass the functions of play-actor, character, and playwright. The defeated Egyptian queen's expressed fear of seeing '[s]ome squeaking Cleopatra boy my greatness' (5.2.219) explicitly reminds us of the ever-present doubling or layering of the speaker role on stage.

The opening scene of *Antony and Cleopatra* illustrates as usefully as any other how a scan of the participant framework can contribute to interpretation. We have discussed how an interrupted conversation between two Roman followers of Antony in Egypt, Philo and Demetrius, frames the scene. In its hushed interim, the two characters provide an onstage surrogate for the theatre audience.[10] The conversation or speech performance that interrupts Philo's and Demetrius's talk happens amidst a sizeable company, including Cleopatra's ladies, Charmian and Iras, and a train of other attendants, including *'eunuchs fanning her'* (1.1.9sd). We begin to see how relative social power as well as speech event framework may constrain participant roles in specific situations. We later discover that Charmian and Iras can be unstoppably loquacious in other circumstances while Mardian, the only 'eunuch' with a speaking role in the play, is invariably of few words. But in this scene all these attendants remain silent (or at least non-speaking, which does not entirely preclude significant sound-making), with Antony and Cleopatra's interchange taking priority. As we shall discuss further later, speech distribution in any situation helps us to parse a social scene – to intuit something of its cultural particularity and understand in experiential terms the cast of its power relations. In a play, we tease this out amidst a range of other factors, including our expectation that key actors will represent characters with large speaking parts and that dialogue must serve the expository needs of the unfolding story. In a representation of the great Cleopatra's court with Antony, a 'triple pillar of the world' (1.1.12) as her companion, it is unsurprising that their speech 'dominates' the scene. What is surprising is the constriction of a messenger's speech turn to six words, where the practical and historic conventions of the theatre would forecast a lengthy speech of narration. But we have already seen how this disrupted expectation is precisely the significant matter of the scene and the accomplishment of Shakespeare's art here, what permits the psychological dialogue of 'responsibility' and the emotional affect of obligation to be 'heard' above (or folded within) its outward interchange of words.

Conversation analysts drew attention to the traffic rules of speech exchange, that is, what foundational research by Harvey Sacks, Emanuel

A. Schegloff, and Gail Jefferson called a 'systematics' of 'turn-taking'.[11] Many people find it hard to see some of their rules as fresh knowledge, let alone imagine their productive application to theatre dialogue. But in making explicit one kind of structured expectation governing the response to and co-creation by participants of conversation, they are crucial to our understanding of the norms and departures in Shakespeare's dialogic invention. They begin with the very basic expectations that 'Speaker change recurs, or at least occurs' and 'Overwhelmingly, one party talks at a time' with only occasional overlaps upon transition from one 'turn' to the next (Sacks *et al.* 700). This applies to theatre, and may (as we shall see) be a helpful corrective to the idea that plays are made up of 'speeches' by important characters rather than interactive units ('turns'). They proceed to observations that 'turn order' and 'turn size' are 'not fixed, but var[y]' and, in addition, that length of conversation, 'what parties say', and 'relative distribution of turns' are not specified in advance (Sacks *et al.* 701). In a very fundamental way, of course, these rules simply cannot apply to plays. All the dialogue is pre-scripted or 'fixed'. Only to the limited extent that a script remains a dynamic text, susceptible to changes in rehearsal and improvisation in performance, does such variation obtain in the enactment of dialogue by stage players. What conversational analysts are seeking to illuminate with turn-taking rules is the surprising way that conversationalists cooperate and collaborate with one another as they improvise spoken discourse as relatively seamless dialogue. This 'cooperation' happens whether they are agreeing with each other or engaged in open confrontation. It is a basic premise, recognised in political negotiation when potential participants ask whether a 'conversation can happen'. The choreography that holds off chaos is aided by 'turn-allocation techniques' and practitioners' recognition of 'turn-constructional units' and 'transition-relevance places' (Sacks *et al.* 701, 703). Part of the practical skill of the real-life conversationalist is this listening for and recognising syntax in motion, not as we register periods or completed thoughts in written sentences but as we register provisional stopping places. These are the places where the conversational ball can be picked up, a collaborative transition of speakers managed without fuss, or can equally be not picked up, leaving the current speaker to frame a further 'turn-constructional unit'. In this way, spoken utterance framed as conversation is repeatedly 'cueing' potential next speakers, and the current speaker remains uncertain when such a cue will be taken up.

The application of turn-taking systematics to the theatrical context cannot be direct. Neither those on stage nor the non-speaking offstage audience members are listening with the particular energy required to compete for the floor and collaborate in quite this open-ended way. Good actors can make us think they don't know when their speech turns will end, although of course they do. It may, nonetheless, be worth comparing real-life turn allocation procedures to the theatrical system of turn allocation insofar as it is regulated by the historic 'cued parts' Simon Palfrey and Tiffany Stern have studied productively in their book, *Shakespeare in Parts*.[12] As hearers in real life respond rapidly to non-specific syntactic cues to take the floor and develop their own conversational thread, cued actors working with prepared 'parts' including only their own lines and two- to three-word cues must be super-alert to the rapid uptake of their speaking turns. Thus, the cued parts that support this listening-to-perform, beyond saving the cost of paper and labour by not multiplying play-copies, might be considered a technology that provides a reasonable simulacrum of conversation's tension and spontaneous energy.

Turn-allocation technique is another shared practical skill in talk for which conversation analysts specify available options: either the current speaker selects a next speaker or the next speaker self-selects. We are very familiar with traffic direction signals for turn allocation in Shakespeare's dialogue. When a current speaker selects, it is usually by means of direct address or a directive speech act or question. The Duke's one-word opening line in *Measure for Measure* can be heard as both direct address and directive:

DUKE	Escalus.	
ESCALUS	My lord.	(1.1.1–2)

The comedy of the grammar-lesson scene in *The Merry Wives* derives from its disorderly alternation of selected and self-selecting speakers, the pupil William reluctant and the housekeeper Mistress Quickly over-eager:

MISTRESS PAGE	Sir Hugh, my husband says my son profits nothing in the world at his book. I pray you, ask him some questions in his accidence.
EVANS	Come hither, William. Hold up your head. Come.
MISTRESS PAGE	Come on, sirrah. Hold up your head. Answer our master, be not afraid.
EVANS	William, how many numbers is in nouns?
WILLIAM	Two.
MISTRESS QUICKLY	Truly, I thought there had been one number more, because they say ''Od's nouns'.
EVANS	Peace your tattlings! – What is 'fair', William?

(*Wiv.* 4.1.11–21)

In the layered participant configuration of theatre, speech specifically 'selecting' next speaker is functional at many levels: it supplies actors' needs to come in on time, it supplies audience need to be oriented to what's happening and who's speaking, and it sustains the dramatic illusion of lifelike interaction. Shakespeare relies on audience members' practical recognition of turn-taking allocation strategies and shifts in addressee to create significant dramatic effects.

Consider Hermione's exit following her jealous and increasingly tyrannical husband Leontes's demand that she be taken away to prison and her own speech asserting her grief and integrity.

HERMIONE	... Beseech you all, my lords,
	With thoughts so qualified as your charities
	Shall best instruct you, measure me; and so
	The king's will be performed.
LEONTES	Shall I be heard?
HERMIONE	Who is't that goes with me? Beseech your highness
	My women may be with me, for you see
	My plight requires it. – Do not weep, good fools,
	There is no cause. When you shall know your mistress
	Has deserved prison, then abound in tears
	As I come out. This action I now go on
	Is for my better grace. – Adieu, my lord.
	I never wished to see you sorry; now
	I trust I shall. – My women, come, you have leave.
LEONTES	Go, do our bidding. Hence! [*Exeunt Queen, guarded, and ladies*]
	(*WT* 2.1.112–125)

The long dashes modern editors have introduced into play texts are very helpful as we try to construe the characters' turn-internal shifts in address. Even without turn alternation, we can see that Hermione's final extended 'speech' is very clearly 'dialogue'. It is not just that she turns from one group of characters to another in making her adieus. Here Leontes's 'Shall I be heard?' registers his outraged sense that the conversational 'floor' has shifted out from under him. But this is not due to any unruly speech behaviour or shouting going on amongst the gathered company of lords and ladies or because he is being denied access to the floor. Instead, the company has granted the floor to Hermione, and she holds it, not by demand, but with her gracious truth-telling and her inclusive manner of speaking. Indeed, she explicitly and obediently defers to 'the king's will'. The final speech is susceptible, like all good dialogue, to more than one interpretation in performance. We can read 'Who is't that goes with me?' as directly addressed to her women or to any attendant willing to stand up against the king. But it may be a richer interpretation to read the question as addressed to Leontes, as if he can still hear reason, and can comprehend the assumed view that a woman at an advanced stage of pregnancy will require support.

The question's end is obviously a 'transition-relevance place', and it invites Leontes's responding accommodation. Something 'happens' in the dialogic action between the question's end and Hermione's reframing her utterance as a speech act of request, supported by an explicit reason. What 'happens' is that the king does not take up the proffered turn and recover the conversational floor. The queen shifts address to comfort and fortify her ladies, not inviting their speech, for that would make them susceptible to the danger of Leontes's lingering threat constraining the floor that 'He who shall speak for her is afar off guilty / But that he speaks' (2.1.104–105). She switches back to address words of farewell to the king, creating another potential opening for Leontes to speak. Audience members, experts at conversational inference when things make half sense, are invited to interpret Hermione's final words, 'My women, come, you have leave'. Hermione's dignified dialogic choreography of her own constrained exit supports the praise Leontes had showered on her ability with speech at the play's outset (1.2.33), praise clearly well deserved. In the Sicilian court situation that has increasingly turned speaker self-selection into danger to life and limb, Hermione has begun to model the courage to speak in the face of tyranny, a heroism she will further display in the trial scene. After the birth in prison of Perdita and again after Hermione's 'death', Paulina, self-selecting, takes it up with a very different dialogic style that includes direct confrontation while also endeavouring the hard task – whether in language, life, or art – of trying to change and reform another person.

Linguistic Capital and the Politics of Turn-Taking

The rules that the conversation analysts set forth for turn-taking assumed equal access of all persons to the conversational floor. Far from this being the case in the dramatic world of Shakespeare's plays, attention to speech allocation and negotiated access to the conversational floor differentiates characters and offers rich insights into the moment-to-moment power relations obtaining in any scene. The theoretical sociologist Pierre Bourdieu, developing his ideas for an economic model of linguistic exchange, critiqued linguists and philosophers of language for treating language as if it were merely 'an instrument of communication or … of knowledge' and emphasised that it was also and fundamentally an 'instrument of power': 'A person speaks not only to be understood but also to be believed, obeyed, respected, distinguished.' Placing importance on the 'right to speech', he emphasised that where 'the linguist regards the *conditions for the establishment of communication* as already secured … in real situations, that is the essential question'.[13] While linguistics has moved on since Bourdieu wrote these words, they remain a wonderful key for opening up what 'is the essential question' in many Shakespearean scenes. Clearly, conversation analysts aimed precisely at studying the conditions for the establishment of communication, but, in Bourdieu's view, their construction of conversation in terms of democratic access also fell short:

> An adequate science of discourse must establish the laws which determine who (*de facto* and *de jure*) may speak, to whom, and how (for example, in a seminar, a man is infinitely more likely to speak than a woman). Among the most radical, surest, and best hidden censorships are those which exclude certain individuals from communication (*e.g.* by not inviting them to places where people speak with authority, or by putting them in places without speech). One does not speak to any Tom, Dick or Harry; any Tom, Dick or Harry does not take the floor. (Bourdieu 648–649)

Shakespeare's plays typically depict social life that is much more recognisably hierarchical than our modern world. Given the monarchic government of his time and Shakespeare's choice more often than not to depict the upper reaches of society, many of the plays feature scenes at a king's or a duke's or a high potentate's court. It may be to state the obvious, but these scenes are often king-centric, with the monarch the default speaker selector, doling out not only scarce favours but speech turns. In stark contrast to the disordered sequence of the sentinels' speech turns in *Hamlet* Act 1, scene 1, in the court scene of Act 1, scene 2 Claudius, the new king, doles out brief speech turns with marked emphasis in a carefully crafted series. Expending his rhetorical skill on this orderly choreography of court speech, first he solicits the speech turn of his ambassadors to Norway ('You, good Cornelius, and you, Voltemand'), next Laertes ('what is't Laertes? / You cannot speak of reason to the Dane / And lose your voice ... What wouldst thou have Laertes?'), and soon after the father and counsellor Polonius, to whom a favour of recognised service was being paid by Laertes's carefully articulated order of priority ('What says Polonius?').[14] While it is perfectly normal for a king to control speech order, we might almost say that Claudius's foregrounded speech allocation techniques are 'hypercorrect', a term sociolinguist William Labov applied to non-spontaneous or over-correct speech performance bespeaking insecure social status.[15] The unspoken background to Claudius's carefully arranged court performance is indeed the precariousness of his claim to legitimate authority. All this sets in relief the irregularity and disruptiveness of the next speech exchange:

CLAUDIUS   But now, my cousin Hamlet, and my son –
HAMLET   A little more than kin, and less than kind.

CLAUDIUS   How is it that the clouds still hang on you?
HAMLET   Not so, my lord, I am too much i'th' sun.

(Hibbard (ed.), 1.2.64–67)

I omit the Cambridge edition's demarcation of Hamlet's first remark as an aside (a textual addition that follows Theobald and most modern editors, but not in Q2 or F), and take the lead of Oxford editor George Hibbard, who suggests the 'barbed obscurity' of Hamlet's adapted proverb 'is intended to be heard by Claudius, to puzzle him, and to disturb him'.[16] Clearly, Hamlet interrupts Claudius, 'self-selecting', and I would infer that Claudius is thrown off his prepared speech plan when he responds with an abrupt question, instead of a weighty and kinglike speech such as the one he proceeds with twenty-one lines later, when he recovers the floor. Here, and in many court scenes which unravel dramatic conflict as dislocations of dialogue, Shakespeare can rely on his audience's recognition of the monarch-selector speech allocation default as a baseline to help them interpret surprising departures.

Bourdieu's insights into how 'the whole social person' is involved in the entry into speech and then how a person's utterance is received – how and whether it is heard, 'believed, obeyed, respected, distinguished' – are invaluable to understand what Shakespeare achieves in representing the complex human speech world in his plays. Armed with greater clarity about how interactive discourse is not democratic in its basic mechanisms, we can begin to read how social difference-making – in terms of gender, class, ethnicity, race, and other constructed categories – may be operating in the dynamics of speech exchange. Free speech is never free for everybody. Sometimes Shakespeare displays distinction-making through language use in blatant terms, as in his early play *Love's Labour's Lost* where 'hard' Latinate word and 'ink-horn' terms are deployed by educated pedants like Holofernes and Nathaniel and by socially aspiring characters like Armado and Berowne to boost their own self-worth and to keep the confounded country folk like Costard and Dull in their low social places. Bourdieu's insights help us to see what is subtler, the construction of social dynamics at work in the 'hidden censorships' of speech. Hidden censorship can involve exclusion from speech or from the place of speech; it can involve negative or differential valuations registered by how interlocutors receive the speech of particular groups.

We can see the mechanisms of 'hidden censorship' with some of Shakespeare's most admirable female characters. Consider Isabella's speech profile in *Measure for Measure*. If the commodity Bourdieu calls 'linguistic capital' were evaluated impartially by the male characters, she should be the one taking over as Vienna's governor at the play's end. As with Hermione in *The Winter's Tale*, with Isabella Shakespeare has created a female character richly gifted in 'reason and discourse' (*MM* 1.2.166). At the play's outset, it is, of course, Angelo who is praised for his talents and set up for testing as a potential leader by the men in government, but the verbal combat and fine-tuned argumentation of the two debating scenes between Isabella and Angelo display her powers as an easy match for his. How readily these scenes in modern performance can reach across history and speak to what are currently burning issues in our society! When Angelo abuses his position, pressing for Isabella's forced 'consent' to sexual violation, she declares that she will use her voice power to call him out:

> I will proclaim thee, Angelo, look for't.
> Sign me a present pardon for my brother,
> Or with an outstretched throat I'll tell the world aloud
> What man thou art.   (2.4.152–155)

Angelo responds as so many sexual predators have responded: 'Who will believe thee, Isabel?' (2.4.155). Isabella takes in this horrible truth – 'Did I tell this / Who would believe me?' She articulates as 'perilous mouths' the outrageous voice power of high-placed men who make the law 'curtsey to their will' even amidst the truth-telling of women's 'outstretched throat[s]' (2.4.172–173, 176, 154). Her use of tortured bodily synecdoche gives passionate expression to the repugnance of a sexual-assault survivor who is doubly violated by the forced internalisation of self-censoring speech constraints.

The play's acute assessment of the gender dynamics affecting Isabella's speech 'credit' is forecast and complicated by her own brother's characterisation of her rhetorical abilities, when Claudio, *en route* to prison, asks Lucio to seek her help:

>   in her youth
> There is a prone and speechless dialect
> Such as move men; beside, she hath prosperous art
> When she will play with reason and discourse,
> And well she can persuade.   (1.2.163–167)

In second place, he acknowledges her full possession and control of the 'prosperous art[s]' of language that Renaissance men so valued and endeavoured to cultivate through schooling; in first place, he positions a 'dialect' (physical? gestural? a construct of male gaze?) which it is clear from the play that Isabella neither controls nor intends. Shakespeare captures in Isabella the confusion so many intelligent and talented women over the centuries have experienced when they have fully mastered the masculine arts of logic and persuasion but are misheard, or heard not as they intend and deserve but as if they are speaking a different language. Bourdieu's further insight into the 'economics of linguistic exchange' theorises how long-term patterns of speech reception drill into human subjects a patterned anticipation of reception, a self-censorship which in turn affects their characteristic production of utterance, their linguistic 'habitus'. His analysis of anticipatory self-censorship offers a crucial insight into how oppressed individuals and groups can be subjugated by their interlocutors' casual habits of negative reception. We only encounter the young Isabella, and can really only speculate about how such a woman's orientation towards dialogue, her address to the world, might be affected in the long term. If, however, she seems to be growing into boldness as a self-selecting speaker in the scenes we have discussed (supported by initial promptings by Lucio), she finds herself, as the play moves towards the Duke's orchestrated finale, uncomfortably denied positioning as a speech initiator but instead highly regulated by the Duke in her speech turns. Shakespeare leaves his audience with a rich ambiguity in the much-discussed puzzle of Isabella's silence at the play's end, where the Duke lays the groundwork for an unheard future conversation about marriage, and we are left to project Isabella's response, to 'botch' it up 'fit to [our] own thoughts'.

Mistake-Making and the Mechanisms of Repair

As I begin to unpack and reflect – with the help of lessons I learn from Shakespeare's artful dialogue – on the collaborative mechanisms of the conversations that people from all walks of life manage every day, the complex co-creation of social dialogue seems to me truly a matter for wonderment. My wonder is partly at the alert inference-making that is happening so rapidly and apart from our conscious initiation of mental action, a part of what cognitive scientists may be slowly coming to understand and illuminate. But, as with the bittersweet regeneration at the end of *The Winter's Tale*, which allows for people's faults and age's imperfections, my wonder at sustained conversation is intensified by how it anticipates and functions amidst constant mistake-making. Taking error and mistake-making as givens, our social interaction incorporates repair and maintenance strategies at many different levels. One of the clearest proofs that people constantly manage risk in managing conversation, even in talk that seems on the face of it purely pleasurable, is the rich variety of inbuilt mechanisms for strategic repair. Mistakes happen all the time in rapid speech utterances, whether people are well-intentioned or not: people mistime initiation of their speech turns and interrupt, talk over each other; people muddle or mispronounce words; people misunderstand words spoken or misconstrue speech acts; people forget and get words and names wrong; people correct their interlocutors and cause a small sting of offence; people make hurtful assumptions, multiply small social blunders. All this possibility in social dialogue for things-going-awry is, of course, a gift for the playwright: one need never seek far for the seeds of comedic error or tragic conflict. Stylised in drama, mistake-making often makes for dazzling pun sequences.

But conversation is not only full of risk and mistake-making; it is remarkably forgiving. For all these disorders there are remedies at hand, and conversation's arts of repair are important elements of our tacit knowledge and practical performance skills. Given the many kinds of inadvertent mistake-making we fall into and repair in talk, researchers coming at social interaction from different disciplines have highlighted many different mechanisms of repair. I will briefly consider two types: the dynamics of repair arising within the systematics of turn-taking as codi-fied by the conversation analysts and the ongoing 'face-work' repair that Goffman studied in social interaction, whose linguistic strategies Penelope Brown and Stephen Levinson have minutely anatomised in their model of 'politeness'.[17]

Conversation analysts were alert to the remedying of turn-taking errors and violations, but quickly recognised that, in spontaneous conversations, mistakes and trouble-sources could crop up almost anywhere, raising 'problems involving misunderstanding, mishearing, non-hearing, and other interactional dilemmas'. Schegloff, Jefferson, and Sacks's important move was to classify correction strategies by initiator and repairer (including 'self-initiated/self-repair', 'other-initiated/self-repair', 'other-initiated/other repair', and 'self-initiated/other repair') and to establish 'the evidence for the preference of self-repair over other-repair'.[18] Clearly, the classification recognises that repair is not a matter of dispassionate error-spotting and correction. Anyone putting things right should be anticipating the poten-tial of correction itself to create an interactional dilemma and cause social trouble. The main idea of this preference organisation is 'face-saving'. It articulates a baseline expectation of what participants will likely find least and most injurious to their self-esteem.

A play's dialogue is 'composed' by the playwright and not readily sus-ceptible to the morass of trifling and inadvertent verbal slips that are con-stantly triggering repair work in improvised oral conversation. However, the mistake-proliferating nature of conversation makes for wonderful material for the comedic dramatist, who can entertain by letting verbal mistakes and miscomprehension spin out of control, transform word mistakes into fortuitous puns, highlight 'dispreferred' correction sequences, and invent endless surprising variations on the 'mistake and repair' norm. Our delight at such comic wordplay is closely associated with this structured expectation of 'mistake and repair', which we can regard as a significant sub-category of dialogue's patterned 'call and response' framework (like question and answer, command or request and uptake). The humour of the Latin lesson street scene in *The Merry Wives of Windsor* arises almost entirely from its extended play of mistake-making and correction. Its invented situation also features a clash between cultural 'scenes' of correction, for it brings the institutional culture of schoolroom learning through imperfect performance and masterful correction into play with the procedures of natural conversation.

EVANS	William, how many numbers is in nouns?
WILLIAM	Two.
MISTRESS QUICKLY	Truly, I thought there had been one number more, because they say "Od's nouns'.
EVANS	Peace your tattlings! – What is 'fair', William?
WILLIAM	*Pulcher.*
MISTRESS QUICKLY	Polecats? There are fairer things than polecats, sure.
EVANS	You are a very simplicity 'oman. I pray you peace. – ... And what is 'a stone', William?
WILLIAM	A pebble.
EVANS	No, it is *lapis*. I pray you remember it in your prain.
WILLIAM	*Lapis.*
EVANS	That is a good William. (*Wiv.* 4.1.17–32)

This highlights Evan's institutionally condoned mode of correction, the 'other-initiated/other repair' manner of the teacher's 'No, it is *lapis*', supplied together with an expectation that the pupil will repeat the corrected form. William's pupil 'habitus' is reinforced in the immediate moment by Evans's reassuring compliment, but the scene makes clear it is also reinforced for the longer term by the threat and fear of punishment ('you must be preeches' (4.1.66)). We can read Mistress Quickly's 'Truly, I thought there had been one more' as a contrastive style of correction belonging to natural conversation; while 'other-initiating', it creates an opening (however indecorously refused) for the initial speaker (either William or his master Evans) to 'self-repair', as does her 'Polecats? There are fairer things ..., sure.' Much of the comic fun of this dysfunctional conversation is in the persistent error-making of the error-correctors, both Evans and Mistress Quickly, and in how it activates audience members' own practice of error-spotting. The scene might well remind us of how we are all gentle (or not-so-gentle) editors of the ongoing conversations we participate in. It should also help us see another way that the wherewithal of drama resides in natural conversation.

Clearly, repair is not just about correcting errors. Schegloff identified it as 'a major resource in maintaining and restoring intersubjective or mutual understanding in interaction'.[19] We might add that the reparative frame-work of conversation supports the healthful 'normality' of everyday social life and, indeed, people's emotional comfort (or managing of discomfort) within their social identities. Shakespeare's art can exhibit repair on one occasion as a delightful trifle, on another occasion as absolutely integral to our being. Furthermore, his art is attuned to the potential likeness between the microcosms of offence and repair in dialogic exchange and the macrocosms of injury and reparation that are so often working out at plot level. While this is a recognisable rhythm of comedy, it is also crucial to our hopes and expectations in tragedy, however dysfunctional or con-trary the outcome may prove to be.[20] Consider the speech situation with which *The Tragedy of King Lear* opens, not the love test that people imme-diately think of but the quieter conversation among high-ranking courtiers that supplies not just our need for background information, but the play's first conversational dilemma. Three people enter the stage, and two of them are conversing when the Earl of Kent asks the Earl of Gloucester the question, 'Is not this your son, my lord?' (1.1.7). The question is an indirect invitation to the duke to introduce his son and include Edmond in the conversation (that is, an 'other-initiated' gentle prompting to 'self-repair' of exclusionary verbal behaviour). Gloucester's actual repair of this blunder comes more than ten lines later, and certainly takes an unusual (and indecorous) form, to which Kent responds with the grace of profuse civility:

GLOUCESTER	… there was good sport at his making, and the whoreson must be acknowledged. Do you know this noble gentleman, Edmond?
EDMOND	No, my lord.
GLOUCESTER	My lord of Kent; remember him hereafter as my honour-able friend.
EDMOND	My services to your lordship.
KENT	I must love you and sue to know you better.
EDMOND	Sir, I shall study deserving. (1.1.18–26)

Even more frequently than with question-and-answer or command-and-response, the mistake-and-repair adjacency pair can turn into a longer inter-ruption or extended series of speech turns, as in this episode, to renegotiate the normative goodwill or even keel of conversational progression. This digression (1.1.7–18), as Gloucester spins out the locker-room-like mas-culine talk glossing over his own sexual misdemeanours, whether out of embarrassment or sheer oblivious bad taste, proceeds with Kent offering brief gentle ambiguous redirections. He works to avoid either direct confrontation or full-voiced agreement with Gloucester's objectionable attitudes as he strives to ameliorate the accumulating insults to Edmond. In this way, using repair mechanisms to accommodate the different needs of his interlocutors, Kent illustrates what constitutes adept and graceful 'polite' speech, right before the catastrophe of Lear's larger 'mistake' leads him to drop politeness and test the ethical functionality of other more direct and confrontational speech styles. As Shakespeare manages so subtly to plant in audience members' minds Kent's normative instance of civility, he also plants a significant word that will recur later in the play with charged meaning: that is, the word 'acknowledgement'. What Gloucester specifically fails to do at the outset of this scene and Kent leads him to is the simple conversational act of 'acknowledgement'. What Kent says to Cordelia at their emotional reunion in Act 4, scene 7 when she asks 'O, thou good Kent, how shall I live and work / To match thy goodness?' is this: 'To be acknowledged, madam, is o'erpaid' (4.7.1–2, 4). Again, at the play's conclusion, what Kent (who has attended Lear disguised as Caius) solicits is his confused master's acknowledgement:

LEAR   This is a dull sight. Are you not Kent?
KENT   The same,
        Your servant Kent. Where is your servant Caius?
LEAR   He's a good fellow, I can tell you that.
        He'll strike and quickly too. He's dead and rotten.
KENT   No, my good lord, I am the very man – ...   (5.1.340–345)

While Lear finally recalls to mind and speaks the simplest basic phrase of acknowledgement – 'You are welcome hither' – Albany comments that 'He knows not what he says' (349–350, 355). The audience is left uncertain that Lear's speaking actually constitutes acknowledgement, the minimal intersubjective act of mutual recognition that the undemanding Kent craves for his service and as his self-fulfillment.[21] The interchange nonetheless strongly expresses our basic need for functional social conversation, to find ourselves in the responses of other people.

As I have developed the argument that social dialogue affords not only the medium but often a significant matter for Shakespearean drama, I have endeavoured to offer some explicit concepts and methods that can help students and teachers dig deeper into the dialogue of any play or scene and make its analysis an entry point to richer understanding. In truth, given everyone's status as conversational performers, one does not need a very complicated set of new tools. We come well-equipped, with our long experience of conversation, to be Shakespeare's responsive co-creators in dialogue.

NOTES

1 For an excellent summary of conversation analysts' on turn-taking, including preference organisation, see Gregory M. Matoesian, 'The Turn-Taking Model for Natural Conversation', *Reproducing Rape: Domination through Talk in the Courtroom* (Chicago: University of Chicago Press, 1993), pp. 72–97. See also Malcolm Coulthard, *An Introduction to Discourse Analysis*, 2nd edn (London: Routledge, 1985).

2 I quote by preference for this scene only from G. R. Hibbard (ed.), *Hamlet* (Oxford: Clarendon Press, 1987), whose text with Horatio as speaker is based on the First Folio, 4.5.8–9.

3 H. P. Grice's insight into the inferential logic of conversation ('Logic and Conversation', *Syntax and Semantics*, vol. 3, *Speech Acts*, ed. Peter Cole and Jerry L. Morgan (New York: Academic Press, 1975), pp. 41–58) played a foundational role in linguistic pragmatics. For a useful summary of Grice's key concept, how a cooperative principle structures expectation and inference-making, see Coulthard, *Discourse Analysis*, pp. 30–32.

4 Michael Polanyi, *The Tacit Dimension 1996* (Chicago: University of Chicago Press, 2009), p. 4.

5 Erving Goffman, *Interaction Ritual: Essays on Face-to-Face Behavior* (New York: Pantheon Books, 1982).

6 Bettina Bergo, 'Emmanuel Levinas', *The Stanford Encyclopedia of Philosophy* (Fall 2017 Edition), ed. Edward N. Zalta. https://plato.stanford.edu/archives/fall2017/entries/levinas/.

7 B. C. Hutchens, *Levinas: A Guide for the Perplexed* (New York: Continuum, 2004), p. 47.

8 M. M. Bakhtin, 'Discourse in the Novel', *The Dialogic Imagination: Four Essays*, ed. Michael Holquist (Austin: University of Texas Press, 1981), pp. 259–422; p. 280.

9 For a helpful account, see Vimala Herman, *Dramatic Discourse: Dialogue as Interaction in Plays* (London and New York: Routledge, 1995), pp. 30–37.

10 While we imagine audiences as 'hushed' in most theatres today, this was unlikely the norm for the early modern theatre. Shakespeare's onstage theatre audiences (e.g., in *Love's Labour's Lost* and *A Midsummer Night's Dream*) are often raucous. At times they interrupt and become direct participants in the dialogic discourse.

11 Harvey Sacks, Emanuel A. Schegloff, and Gail Jefferson, 'A Simplest Systematics for the Organization of Turn-Taking for Conversation', *Language* 50.4 (December 1974), pp. 696–735. Oliver Morgan's *Turn-Taking in Shakespeare* (Oxford: Oxford University Press, 2019) is devoted to this topic.

12 Simon Palfrey and Tiffany Stern, *Shakespeare in Parts* (Oxford: Oxford University Press, 2007).

13 Pierre Bourdieu, 'The Economics of Linguistic Exchanges', *Social Science Information* 16 (1977): 645–68, p. 648.

14 *Ham.* 1.2.34, 43–45, 50, 57. For an application of these principles to a reading of *Othello*, see Lynne Magnusson, '"Voice potential": Language and Symbolic Capital in *Othello*', *Shakespeare and Social Dialogue: Dramatic Language and Elizabethan Letters* (Cambridge: Cambridge University Press, 1999), pp. 175–194.

15 W. Labov, *Sociolinguistic Patterns* (Philadelphia: University of Pennsylvania Press, 1972).

16 Hibbard (ed.), *Hamlet*, p. 158, 1.2.65n.

17 Penelope Brown and Stephen C. Levinson, *Politeness: Some Universals in Language Usage* (Cambridge: Cambridge University Press, 1987). For an account of the politeness model as a resource for detailed analysis of the power dynamics of social relationships in moment-to-moment Shakespearean dialogue, see Magnusson, *Shakespeare and Social Dialogue*.

18 Matoesian, 'The Turn-Taking Model', p. 90. See also Emanuel A Schegloff, Gail Jefferson, and Harvey Sacks, 'The Preference for Self-Correction in the Organization of Repair in Conversation', *Language* 53.2 (June 1977): 361–382.

19 Quoted in Matoesian, 'The Turn-Taking Model', p. 90.

20 For an extended account, see Magnusson, 'The Pragmatics of Repair in *King Lear* and *Much Ado about Nothing*', *Shakespeare and Social Dialogue*, pp. 153–174.

21 See also Stanley Cavell's complex engagement with acknowledgement and with *King Lear* in *Must We Mean What We Say? A Book of Essays* (New York: Cambridge University Press, 1976), chapters 9 and 10.

6

RUTH MORSE

Figures of Speech at Work

Poetic diction is always performing semantic work, no matter how much it justifies itself by virtue of its visual or aural beauty.

Russ McDonald, *Shakespeare and the Arts of Language*[1]

If all philosophy has been a series of footnotes to Plato, Aristotle is the ultimate source of footnotes to rhetoric and poetics. Rhetoric was widely defined as the art of persuasion; poetics was much more complicated, and remains much more complicated. From the earliest collections of figures of speech in recognisable patterns of poetry and prose, his vocabulary for the analysis and criticism of oratory and writing has had unmatched influence in education. Rhetoric, the art of moving and persuading listeners and readers, itself became the subject, not just the method; works of reference offered categories and examples. Sometimes lists of figures resemble a tradition of geekishness, as if recognising and naming were analysis. Medieval masters created books in series whose titles began 'The Art of', such as *Ars rhetorica* (*Rhetoric*), *Ars scribendi* (*Writing*) or *epistolaris* (*Letter Writing*), *musica* (*Music*), *poetica* (*Poetry*), even *Ars moriendi* (*Dying*) – not a skill one would repeat. Such works consolidated a whole terrain of language-use in daily life as well as in poetry and prose. In that sense, by Shakespeare's day collections of the 'figures of speech' in English-language books had long since become part of the library – what we might now call self-help books – for those who aspired to learning, appreciating, and imitating images, tropes, and figures in their own speech and composition. The largest and most comprehensive of these is 'metaphor'. Peter Mack's chapter in this book deals with metaphor, and many other figures. In this chapter, I will move in a different, yet related, direction, beginning with the traditions of certain inherited scenes and the words or phrases which marked the ambitions of poets, playwrights, and historians who aspired to the heights of their classical forebears. Such scenes of shipwrecks, storms, and other painterly figures such as ecphrasis, which links description to sight, is another way of working. I shall deal at length with what Shakespeare did with figures, with metaphor, metonymy, and metalepsis, but also with single words which functioned across whole plays in, for instance, *Twelfth Night*, and, even more surprisingly, *The Second Part of King Henry IV*. For Shakespeare, metaphors and standard scenes were also tools in defining the ethical stances of his characters, as I shall show.

Shakespeare makes figurative language do work, often hidden work, first, in the speeches and speech habits of individual characters whose vocabulary enacts their social and ethical ideas, reveals their motives and beliefs, moving through and beyond 'characterisation'. Second, beyond individual vocabularies, the changes Shakespeare rings on figurative speech connect parallel structures and interpretations by repetition through clusters of words. The figures speak through speakers who may not know what contribution they make, and certainly do not know themselves. Neither of the soldiers, Macbeth or Othello, could have had an education in rhetoric, but many people in the listening audience recognised their eloquence and apparent familiarity with those figures of speech they could not have studied. The 'realism' of specific word or phrasal choices need not call attention to itself, even in bravura speeches, because it belongs to a long tradition of set piece scenes which recall – to some in the audience – extracts they memorised and imitated at school. Small bricks can sometimes be keys to the thematic structures of the plays, as in the Soothsayer's tiny scene with Charmian and Iras at the beginning of *Antony and Cleopatra*, with his ironic observations and the play's earliest mention of figs. Such apparent triviality looks like a superfluous comic distraction, but is Shakespeare's way of organising the world of the play with speeches that seem irrelevant and unconnected, but are *never* superfluous – though one is likely to understand that only in retrospect. Shakespeare's opening scenes often introduce ideas beyond our immediate grasp, as they set the world of the play. Shakespeare didn't invent the immortal tear-jerker in which a Magistrate finds the criminal in front of him is his son (usually his only son) facing a capital charge. Sir Philip Sidney used this in his *Arcadia* (to give a very old example), but he used such ancient scenes in order to explore fathers and sons in ways I will develop later in this chapter. Other examples included short inset compositions of 'praise of a beautiful place' (*locus amoenus*), the walled garden (*hortus conclusus*), 'the speech before the battle' (such as Elizabeth's supposed oration at Tilbury, before the Armada), and one frequent forensic argument that appears in dialogues about a decision: what was good and right to be done – or not. There are examples in Geoffrey of Monmouth's *History of the Kings of Britain*, compiled in the first half of the twelfth century from Geoffrey's reading, but also from his imagination. In one familiar scene, King Arthur asks his barons to advise him and they argue both sides of a case: whether or not a course of action is legitimate to be done. The flip side of this position is what comes later: the defence of a course taken.

Unlike what we would consider 'historical', i.e. true, rhetorical historiography presents itself as possible or plausible, and is an important part of this compositional terrain, not least in its importance for continuity. Not just in single words or short phrases, but in common places (*loci commune*), the figures are to be recognised, recycled, and mastered, playing their roles in descriptions of cities, or the moral achievements of great men, which writers studied in Suetonius's *Lives of the Caesars*, or other Roman historians, such as Tacitus. The figures are legible, but the rhetorical work they do contributes to authors' own views about the past, historians' habits which continued seamlessly into the early modern period.[2] In the course of Shakespeare's historical plays, he uses many of these inherited commonplaces, as well as their styles of composition, sometimes in verbatim quotation from North's Plutarch or Holinshed's compendium of earlier chronicles. He is making a claim to a kind of truth which can be both elegant and false. Readers often do not attend to the work of the rhetorical structures, except to recognise the familiar.

Metaphor is the broadest figure of speech, not always easy to define; or, perhaps, it is easy to define but hard to manipulate to take account of variety as well as the edges of composition, such as moments when metaphor seems indistinguishable from its poor relation, simile, or where its companion, metonymy, becomes metalepsis, when a word stands for a much larger idea. As one way to begin, consider metaphor as more respectable than, say, puns (always considered very low), not least because a good metaphor invites us to think with it about resemblance whereas puns are immediate and straightforward occasions for groaning. They are also often masculine in orientation, unfit for the company of ladies. If we think of Shakespeare's contemporary, John Donne, both Donne's poetry and prose are full of 'conceits', exercises in unusual or unexpected similarities, or comparisons signalled by 'like' or 'as' to invite us to see surprising relationships where none had hitherto appeared to exist. The similitudes of 'Metaphysical poetry' (which included prose) offered the appreciating reader difficult ideas, in which 'resemblance' was unusual and had to be excavated. Metaphors can be hard to grasp. Aristotle thought that what made 'simile' inferior to metaphor was its explicitness (Rhetoric 3.4.1406b), which offers the mind less to think about. For example, Shakespeare's Sonnet 130 declaims stoutly, 'My mistress' eyes are nothing like the sun' (1), and the jokes are immediately convincing and require no further thought. Nor does the voice speaking the sonnet invite examination, in a moment in which wit is just that. But there are other complexities. If my readers find this confusing, they are spot on: it *is* confusing. That is one of the ways that metaphors do their work.

As its title indicates, this chapter focuses on how Shakespeare's characters use well-known metaphors, resort to epic similes, and praise or blame in ways that tell us more about the character speaking than the character seems to know. Sometimes Shakespeare gives them words which, together, unconsciously influence their interlocutors, but also his audiences or readers by creating the world of a play. At the beginning of his career he assigned rhetorically rich – but perhaps tiresome – lines to his actors (such as Marcus orating while his mutilated niece is reduced to a picture of woe in *Titus Andronicus*), staking his claims by imitating the grandeur of his classical predecessors. In a word, the young Shakespeare showed off. Sometimes his comparisons are all his own invention, and it will matter in what follows that the differences between Early Modern vocabulary and our contemporary usage are clear. For example, the Latin words 'invenio' and 'inventio' can add to the confusion: they mean 'finding', in the sense of 'finding a subject' and constructing it in writing. Early Modern English 'invention' therefore meant 'discovery', 'construction', but it could also mean a plan of action. Where today we say 'imagination', meaning things we create in the mind, in Shakespeare's lifetime it usually referred to 'images' available to the mind, which were not necessarily original, but pictures seen in thought. When Shakespeare and his contemporaries spoke of 'fancy', they sometimes meant 'fantastical' or 'extravagant', but in Shakespeare 'fancy' more often means emotional inclination as, indeed, Shakespeare's characters say sixty-seven times. Above all, some of our presuppositions threaten to get in the way, such as our explicit evaluation of originality as the artist's greatest challenge; this was not something Shakespeare's age sought – it risked being fantastical. Lest anyone dismiss these resorts to imaginative and figurative writing as pretentious decoration, it should be remembered that from cracker-barrel philosophers to Monday-morning quarterbacks such metaphors are characteristic of ordinary speech as well as poetry and prose, including hard-boiled crime fiction, such as that written by Dashiell Hammett and Raymond Chandler as well as hosts of imitators in many languages.

However briefly, we must begin with school, where memorising Latin verse created a shared culture of literary reference. Boys lucky enough to be subjected to a great deal of rote learning, at a grammar school, were taught to recognise that which was to be admired, assuming mastery of a series of key texts and scenes by great authors, in clear and comprehensive categories, in Latin learned by heart. These were not exactly 'literary' skills, but they were important. Nor was there much that resembled our ideas of analysis or criticism: if the texts weren't to be admired, they wouldn't have been selected. At a more advanced stage, boys also learned the figures of speech, with their Latin names indicating their functions in order to manipulate them in their own writing. The desire to memorise these figures, perhaps surprisingly, links Hamlet to *Twelfth Night*'s Sir Andrew Aguecheek as they 'set down' in their notebooks what they have admired. Translated into English, these labels offered a technical jargon from which readers and potential writers could learn to spot, admire, and, perhaps, imitate the skills of the ancients. Beyond such fine-grain reading lay recognition of larger units. In theory, the first skill was appreciating the metaphorical figure and its cultivation of similarities as well as the contiguities central to metonymy, which used a part for a whole, such as Northumberland's tasteless reaction to the news of his son's death,

> Ha? Again:
> Said he young Harry Percy's spur was cold?
> Of Hotspur, Coldspur? That rebellion
> Had met ill luck? (2H4, 1.1.48–51)

Such wordplay may seem tasteless or inappropriate, but when Northumberland reacts to his servant's metonym, 'spur' (for body), metalepsis 'cold' (for 'dead'), 'ill luck' (for 'defeat'), he puns on Hotspur's nickname. This is the beginning of one of Northumberland's extravagant losses of control. Like his father the Earl, Northumberland's son Percy never learned the second skill, the *controlled* use of metaphors (often a trap for the less-well educated), as he shows in *The First Part of King Henry IV*. Or, perhaps, the confused and grieving father is in shock. But perhaps, on the contrary, Northumberland's self-serving speeches give us reason to judge him harshly. I shall return to this question of vocabulary, action, and ethical judgement below. In such scenes a great deal more is happening on stage than just the words we hear. Other characters are present in ways we may struggle to imagine when reading.

This is not the place to assess the theoretical – or, at least, more abstract – attempts to create a morphology of metaphor. Historically, scholars have identified the writers and compilers of the guides to this technical language, and have often listed different kinds of metaphor or metonymy. Like the naming and classification of the units of metre in poetry, these exercises in recognition can be helpful in articulating what the metaphor or metonymy is doing – the 'semantic work' of this chapter's epigraph. But quotations extracted from Shakespeare to indicate his participation in this world of words inevitably escape questions of who is speaking them, to whom, at what point in a play. One important reason to be sceptical about systems is that often metaphor leans towards something else, and that something else slips through our fingers.[3] Words are not always stable, especially when we play with them and upon them – as Feste knows and tells Cesario in *Twelfth Night* (3.1).

Shakespeare used metaphor and metonymy to describe the linguistic terrain of early modern England from London to the countryside, with tastes of Britain's other nations. The four captains of *Henry V* have a scene of three or four minutes in which their discussion involves the idea of 'nation', buttressed by their recognisable accents: Jamie (Scotland), Ffluellen (Wales), MacMorris (Ireland), and Gower (England). Shakespeare thickens the texture by endowing his characters with metaphors appropriate to their age and status, education, and experience, and especially their experience at this point in the play. The bickering of the four captains offers a parallel to the angry discussion of the gentry and nobility of Henry's army.

In the next section, I turn to a brief look at two sonnets, slightly segregated, because they offer a different kind of appreciation from the physical activity of the stage, raising questions about who their speakers or *personae* are. The rest of the chapter is theatrical in focus: I begin with *Twelfth Night* and, finally, move back to *The Second Part of King Henry IV*.

Poems for Private Reading

> Images and metaphors may be grouped together with rhyme, metre, puns, and other such verbal features essential to poetry. Some of these features are known as tropes, from the Latin word for 'turn', since they turn a word away from its literal or everyday meaning, turn it to some extra-literal or figurative task.[4]
>
> Russ McDonald

The epigraph to this section suggests how difficult it is to isolate images and metaphors as they join the forces of 'verbal features essential to poetry'. Shakespeare uses 'like', 'as', and, in the Sonnets, 'like as' to cue metaphors in Sonnets 60 and 118, where he begins, 'Like as', announcing that there will be an extended comparison through metaphor.[5] Elsewhere he 'compares' a variety of things, including comparison itself, as he famously does in Sonnet 130. By contrast, in Shakespeare's more serious Sonnet 60, ideas of the sea, and of passing time, ring changes on his persona's love for the young man. At heart (a simile), whether addressing mistress or friend, the sonnets are constantly engaged with mutability. Nor is the poem's persona reticent about warning of the transience of physical beauty.

> Like as the waves make towards the pebbled shore,
> So do our minutes hasten to their end,

Each changing place with that which goes before,
In sequent toil all forwards do contend.
Nativity, once in the main of light,
Crawls to maturity, wherewith being crown'd,
Crookèd eclipses 'gainst his glory fight,
And Time that gave doth now his gift confound.
Time doth transfix the flourish set on youth,
And delves the parallels in beauty's brow,
Feeds on the rarities of nature's truth,
And nothing stands but for his scythe to mow:
And yet to times in hope my verse shall stand,
Praising thy worth, despite his cruel hand.   (Sonnet 60)

This poem is a fine example of change in Nature. Its movement is slightly tangential, as the waves' ebb and flow become first a metaphor for the cycle of human life and then a metalepsis for Time's visible power over human life. Each wave appears to slide back under the next-arriving one, as the poem's lines also seem to do. Like Donne's verse, this sonnet is intentionally difficult, and insists that its readers pay close attention. Though the first quatrain owes much to Ovid's *Metamorphoses*, there is sequence – like the waves – the gifts of birth and youth, time passing, the span of human life, which suddenly seems to exist only that Father Time with his scythe should mow them all down, as the inexorable ageing which destroys beauty, the cycles of nature, including its malignant miasmas and diseases. All are ripe for destruction, because all that lives must die.[6] There is hope that the *praise* of the young man's worth will withstand Time's changes, though neither the young man nor the poet will, and all must remember that '*verba volent, scripta manent*': words spoken fly away but writing remains. In the sonnet is a tightly compressed grievance less cynical and more accepting than Jacques's looser 'ages of man' monologue in Act 2, scene 7 of *As You Like It*. Its closing metonymy offers the 'cruel hand' for once-generous Time and sums up the poem's clear-eyed acceptance of Time's gifts and retractions. This section of Shakespeare's Sonnets reminds us that the poems are more (to indulge a metalepsis) like snapshots that refer to philosophical ideas (and classical poets such as Horace) than they resemble the active multiplicity and evolution of stage characters. Inevitably, though, they all share the figures of speech.

The reading mind is working hard, but one is tempted to ask if it is not working too hard. William Empson, that closest of close readers, uses these lines as the first example on the first page of *Seven Types of Ambiguity*:[7] sometimes we all over-read, as in Sonnet 73 where the persona speaks to his interlocutor:

That time of year thou mayst in me behold
When yellow leaves, or none, or few, do hang
Upon those boughs which shake against the cold,
Bare ruined choirs, where late the sweet birds sang. (1–4)

It is fair enough to say, crudely, 'autumn is like age', but then do the shaking boughs equate with human 'shivering' or old-age palsy? Ideas we test and discard can be as important in our experience as ideas we retain, and, given that a rickety old man would be ridiculous in this context, the fourth line quickly transforms branches to abbey or monastery ruins in stone (both metaphor and metonymy), and the sweet birds to the monks or nuns singing. Or does it? If we make a similar mistake and decide the leaves are hairs left on a balding pate, we catch ourselves seriously over-reading, because what I. A. Richards named the 'vehicle' (the word that fulfils the link, the imaginative similarity, 'yellow leaves', 'bough', or 'bird' in this quatrain) would be wrong in tone for 'the tenor' (the word or phrase that triggers the metaphor, here 'behold in me'). A tree has dignity that an imaginary palsied bald man usually lacks; dynamically, ruins are a commonplace for passing time, and have been since Horace. There are other pitfalls (the 'ashes of his youth' in line 10 can be misread if one does not know that Modern English 'its' replaced genitive 'his'). What is certain is that in the mind's ear the birds remain birds, the boughs boughs; there are other such commonplaces later on, when 'night' is both sleep and death. What is also certain is that we are reading a series of metaphors of similarity and memory. This is not all that is going on in the sonnet, of course, but it gives a glimpse of process, not static equivalence. Above all, reading a good poem is not a puzzle to be solved, and there is no simple decoding algorithm which makes reading Shakespeare easy. By contrast, in the theatre the actors' bodies, their movements and expressions, guide us to an understanding of what they mean, even if we have trouble with what they say.

How Happy?

Wherefore, sweet-heart? what's your metaphor?
(Sir Andrew Aguecheek, TN 1.3.131)

Early modern drama is full of characters who admire rhetorical flourish but cannot master it for themselves. But, then, in a culture of increasing social mobility, one finds many men (especially) depicted, commonplace books in hand, recording phrases that impressed them, or making notes to themselves about how to be more like the well-born and well-educated. And so did the educated, even if their reactions were to note well and remember. Poor Sir Andrew Aguecheek seems not to have had the important experience of good schooling or the advantages of learning the skills of courteous manners, and he copes by taking down good phrases he can use later, or elsewhere. So, of course, does Hamlet, in a rather more complex style, but still suitable for a student. Early modern drama, as Indira Ghose has recently shown, was a school for good manners and fine phrasing that offered its audiences examples both to emulate and to avoid.[8] It may seem easy to mock, but the exchange of quotations or learned tags is still with us, as we create fellow-feeling with others who know the same poems or phrases we do, and so also is variously coded control of the English language in different places, circumstances, or groups.

Twelfth Night opens upon a love-sick aristocrat in Illyria (wherever one imagines that to be). Orsino's enviable talents with wordplay show him at the acme of the courtier's skills – though as the Duke he is usually the focus of other men's courtliness, not counting his failure in courting Olivia. He emerges from such earlier plays as *Love's Labour's Lost*, in which the four young men are constantly playing with their wits in order to impress each other – while the ladies in their sights are rather less taken with their showing off. Orsino's court is a civilised place where music plays. The play's opening fourteen lines are all his (the italics are all mine):

> If *music be the food of love*, play on;
> Give me excess of it, that, surfeiting,
> The appetite may sicken and so die.
> That strain again, it had a *dying fall*;
> O it came o'er my ear *like the sweet sound*
> *That breathes* upon a bank of violets,
> Stealing and giving odour. Enough; no more.
> 'Tis not so sweet now as it was before.
> O spirit of love, how quick and fresh art thou,
> That notwithstanding thy capacity,
> Receiveth *as the sea*. Nought enters there,
> Of what validity and pitch soe'er,
> But falls into *abatement and low price*,
> Even in a minute. So full of shapes is *fancy*,
> That it alone is high *fantastical*.   (*TN* 1.1.1–14, emphasis added)

This is metaphor-heavy musing. 'Music' here is the first tenor, and its vehicle is love's 'food'; the consequences of over-eating make us feel ill and spoil our appetite (now 'music' threatens to become the vehicle as well, a metaphor's metaphor). In four lines, Shakespeare conveys a sense of the duke's dilemma, his great, even ostentatious, sensitivity to love (and music), and his fear of losing music's magical ability to assuage our griefs. The sweet sound that breathes may seem odd, but it is a metonym which substitutes the effect for the cause, as Orsino allows himself to be overwhelmed, as the best lovers (that's male lovers) must be. Shortly afterwards the sea becomes a measure of overwhelming power (nothing new here). Are we at the limit of Orsino's inventio? In the next act Orsino returns to the sea with a larger claim for the great power of his love: 'But mine is all *as* hungry *as the sea*, / And can digest as much' (2.4.101–102, emphasis added). This is not far from Juliet's claim in her own first throes of love:

> My bounty is *as* boundless *as the sea*,
> My love *as* deep; the more I give to thee,
> The more I have, for both are infinite. (*Rom.* 2.2.133–135, emphasis added)

Here 'bounty' is the tenor and the 'boundless sea' the vehicle. In addition, of course, the sound of 'bounty' and 'boundless' make the sea all the more encompassing, though not the 'infinite' resource Juliet imagines. By italicising the 'like' and 'as' markers I call attention to the signals for similitude which announce a metaphor. More important is the contrast between the Duke in Illyria and Juliet in Verona. Where he is self-obsessed and seems to want to overwhelm the sea, she is generous. His love is a literary conceit; hers is deep and unmeasurable with no hint of self-abnegation. It is, however, more fragile, in this different kind of play.

In *Twelfth Night*, Sebastian grieves for the sister the waves took from him, as his twin begins by hoping her brother was not drowned but saved. Neither thinks of the sea as metaphor or symbol; it is too real for that. 'Real', too, are the uses of pestilence and plague, various forms of illness much darker than one might expect in one of the Happy Comedies. Like the Soothsayer scene mentioned at the beginning of this chapter, the world of play is full of incidences or references to disease and death. One might also pause to consider how it is possible to think of imaginary people having a grip on reality, but we are accustomed to the theatre's creation of conviction, our suspension of belief. The actor's body will tell us how serious Juliet is and spare her from ridicule. When Olivia asks herself, 'Even so quickly may one catch the plague?' (*TN* 1.5.583), she is unaware of participating in a metaphor which is also a metalepsis ('plague' stands for a complex idea of love as an affliction) as well as a contribution to the dark shadows of loss and illness which permeate Illyria. The idea of contagion has been there from the beginning, when Orsino adds it to his thoughts about the sea, risk, danger, calling himself hunter and hunted, like Acteon, transformed by Diana into a hart pursued by his own dogs when he accidentally stumbled on Diana bathing (also from Metamorphoses III.138ff.).

> O, when mine eyes did see Olivia first,
> Methought she purged the air of pestilence!
> That instant was I turn'd into a hart;
> And my desires, like fell and cruel hounds,
> E'er since pursue me. (*TN* 1.1.19–23)

In quick succession, Olivia is a prophylactic against plague, while in seeing her once Orsino is condemned to suffer like Acteon. He is sick with love, and disease and death prowl through this first speech, doing that semantic work referred to in this chapter's epigraph. Here the pun on line 21 ambitiously suggests tragedy. Part of that work is to plant seeds of imagery from the outset that will infuse the whole play to come. It passes by us in less than a minute, locating the setting, the self-important poseur, the importance of music, the ever-present risk of early death, and the overwhelming powers of Nature, of love, and of the sea. Metaphor here sets the stage while supplying warnings that the duke cannot hear, any more than he will hear and understand Feste's songs, which function as external commentary on the internal action. Orsino is eloquent, but limited, and falls into received ideas in Act 2, scene 4, as he converses with Cesario while music plays, or, rather, gives a little lecture on how to choose a beloved who will be younger than her lover: 'For women are *as roses*, whose fair flower / Being once displayed, doth fall that very hour' (2.4.40–41). Although he does not know it, he is already learning to outstrip his love-sick yearnings from the example of his page's devoted service, as the play adds a thread of male friendship where it is unexpected (because there is too great a difference in their ages and status for equality in the loving bond). Shakespeare offers a second chance for this exchange of male friendship between Sebastian and Antonio (one of Shakespeare's names to conjure with).

One might argue that the figures of speech in this first scene come so thick and fast that the stage tradition of reversing the first two scenes makes it easier for the audience to understand what's going on in the play with less effort, less attention to the semantic work. But one can never give too much attention. Additionally, the reversal allows the possibility of audience recognition: confirmed theatregoers (and readers) expect that the separated will be reunited, as in *Comedy of Errors* or the pastiche *A Funny Thing Happened on the Way to the Forum*, the Broadway musical of 1962. When the shipwrecked Viola enters with the other survivors, among them the well-read and rather courtly captain of the ship, there is an offer of hope with another metaphor. He saw her brother bind himself to a mast, 'where, *like* Arion on the dolphin's back, / I saw him hold acquaintance with the waves / So long as I could see' (*TN* 1.2.15–17).

The introductory scenes continue with the balancing group who inhabit Olivia's house, from the recently bereaved lady herself (who has also lost her brother), to her paired steward and chambermaid (i.e. companion, not a servant), as well as paired parasite and fool, her uncle (or cousin) Toby and his gull. Poor Sir Andrew, whose life has clearly been disadvantaged, despite his wealth, has to ask what Maria means because he cannot understand her metaphor, 'Bring your hand to the buttery-bar and let it drink' (1.2.68–69). Such coarse metaphors abound. By contrast, the next scene has the Duke say to his charming new courtier, 'thy small pipe/ Is *as* the maiden's organ, shrill and sound, / And all is semblative a woman's part' (1.4.32–34), where the duke is more right than he knows. The markers 'like' and 'as' do their work rather as young people today will say 'It was – like – a total surprise' without realising that they are creating something akin to a metaphor which suggests a possible event without offering it as true.

We know where we are, or we think we do, but there is another kind of speech at the beginning of Act 2, the homosocial and – in one case – homo-erotic affection between the other castaway and his rescuer. Their exchanges are largely in prose of an elevated, stylised formality, because the two men, though clearly not equals in rank, are equal in affection, as their brief con-versation, steadily at the formal 'you' not 'thou' level, tells us. We do not know where they are, but one of them, Sebastian, having recovered from his terrible time in the sea, is off to Orsino's court, to which the besotted Captain Antonio follows him. This sudden appearance of the lost twin is not a surprise. We never thought the siblings were going to remain apart. In a shift of place and character worthy of the best soaps, the elegant exchanges between Sebastian and Antonio are juxtaposed with churlish complaint, as Malvolio throws Olivia's ring back at Viola, who protects Olivia's reputa-tion by taking up the idea that the ring was a gift from Orsino – courtesy trumping ill will.

As if that change were not enough, a longer scene with Sir Toby and com-pany – or perhaps Feste and company including Sir Toby – offers another level of exchange. Toby's false speech reintroduces metaphor: 'A false con-clusion: I hate it as an unfilled can [i.e. container for drink]' (2.3.5). Feste, and then Maria, join them, only to be invaded by Malvolio, lying once again about what Olivia has or has not said or done. As revenge turns towards drunken pathos, Sir Toby offers one metaphor more in praise of Maria: 'She's a beagle, true bred, and one that adores me: what o' that?' (151), provoking Sir Andrew's startling reminiscence, 'I was adored once, too' (152), which returns to him a deal more humanity than he receives from his cozeners and torturers. If this were television, we would think of the need for 'beats' to end a scene.

One last pair of speeches, to show the unsurprising recognition token:

> VIOLA He named Sebastian: I my brother know
> Yet living in my glass; even such and so
> In favour was my brother, and he went
> Still [i.e. always] in this fashion, colour, ornament,
> For him I imitate: O, if it prove,
> Tempests are kind and *salt waves fresh* in love.
>
> (3.4.330–335, emphasis added)

Fashion, colour, ornament: Viola's imitations owe something to rhetorical tropes that link clothes to social status and taste.

Vice versa, but equally delicate:

> SEBASTIAN Do I stand there? I never had a brother;
> Nor can there be that deity in my nature,
> Of here and everywhere. I had a sister,
> Whom the *blind waves* and surges have devoured.
> Of charity, what kin are you to me?
> What countryman? what name? what
> parentage? (5.1.210–215, emphasis added)

In creating the world of Illyria, Shakespeare gives the twins paired approaches to their apparent losses. Viola not only offers herself as her brother in her mirrored reflection, but she reverses the savage force of storms and the ocean waves that must be salt in her own surge of optimism and hopeful love. Sebastian, less optimistic than his sister, continues to believe her devoured by the blind waves. More learned than she, he completes her reflection on reflection by reaching for the philosophical axiom that no person or thing can be in two places at once, which was, as he recognises, an axiom modified by medieval Christian thinkers. In a play which early introduced misplaced devotion to the dead, the last scene invokes charity as Sebastian tastes the possibility that Viola is alive.[9]

Tongues and Fires

At certain crucial moments in many of the plays the attentive mind begins to perceive a distinct semantic coherence among images. Such aggregation of related figures is one of Shakespeare's preferred means of securing the thematic or emotional effect of a speech or episode.

Russ McDonald, *Shakespeare and the Arts of Language*, 72–73

This part of the chapter offers a slightly different approach, returning to *The Second Part of King Henry IV*, adding to metaphor and metonymy some complications beyond simile and metalepsis. I shall look more closely at an additional thread in my claims for the ethical status and function of certain figures as ornaments that are also keys to the world of a play, its themes, and judgements. That is, Shakespeare uses metaphor and metonymy as a matter of course, and he also interweaves certain key words which function without calling attention to themselves. In *The Second Part of King Henry IV*, Shakespeare's warp depends upon the straightforward idea of 'unquiet time' (1.2.119); his weft, however, introduces, embroiders, and continuously repeats motifs of 'fire' and 'blood', which begin from the Induction. The words' values depend upon who uses which words to whom at what particular moments in the play. That includes ambiguous promises which range from Falstaff's obfuscations to Prince John's shocking oath-breaking.

Let me begin with some apparently straightforward metaphors, and a reference to an imaginary figure, usually depicted in clothes covered with tongues. *The Second Part of King Henry IV* opens with an Induction, a scene-setting introduction that leads us in to what follows. The first speech is not by a human being at all, but by Rumour, a figure out of medieval and Renaissance allegory, as well as Morality Plays. In forty lines, Rumour stresses his omnipresence across the globe, in all the world's languages, and his specialty in false information; he speaks in formal blank verse, with a fine ear for rhetorical turns of phrase. A more malign figure than the Chorus in *Henry V* will be, he boasts of his power, emphasising the 'unquiet time' which recapitulates the rebellion against Henry IV in the previous play. Unusually in Shakespeare, he is an amoral figure because he is a label, an influence upon action rather than an actor. Speaking of himself, he shifts from the first to the third person,

> And who but Rumour, who but only I,
> Make fearful musters, and prepared defence,
> Whiles the big year, swoll'n with some other grief,
> Is thought with child by the stern tyrant War?
> And no such matter. Rumour is a pipe
> Blown by surmises, Jealousy's conjectures,
> And of so easy and so plain a stop
> That the blunt monster with uncounted heads,
> The still-discordant wav'ring multitude,
> Can play upon it. (Induction 11–20)

The unhappiness of a corporealised year, with its grief-swollen pregnancy, looks forward to other complex metaphors to come. The double metaphor of false information as a pipe, easily played by 'the blunt monster' that is 'the still-discordant wav'ring multitude' reminds us that misinformation is always within Rumour's reach. Both uses of 'still' in the Induction mean 'always' (4, 18), and Shakespeare emphasises the 'unquiet times' with the reference to musical discord. Rumour has no need to cultivate rumours: he is his own tongues, which will wag, and fabricate descriptions of entire battles lost and won by ungovernable soldiers, full of the news from Shrewsbury to Northumberland. This is a picture of unrest in which ordinary men and women threaten to become a rabble ('the blunt monster with uncounted heads') if only because the certainties of their lives now include civil war and a breakdown in order, largely created by rebellious barons, including clerics such as the Archbishop of York.

The Induction leads immediately into an illustration of Rumour's power. If Rumour's language is hard to follow, that is deliberate, as the thick metaphoric texture shifts from romance polysyllables to monosyllabic Anglo-Saxon English. It is also a perfect beginning for a play replete with extraordinary ordinary folk, from the tavern in London to the country life of Falstaff's victims to come. The following scene acts out what Rumour has described, exemplifying the strength of supposition and false news.[10] If we see 'fake news' news here it is well to remember Rumour's universality.

As the play proper gets under way, three messengers bring Rumour's harvest to the Earl of Northumberland who was – or perhaps was not – too sick to join his son, Hotspur, to fight the king. Lord Bardolph arrives with 'certain news' but he has had it at second hand, as has the next to arrive, Percy's servant, Travers, who has had news from a named source, but a contradictory account. Then, as the third messenger, Morton, arrives, Northumberland sees, rather than hears, the truth because he can read Morton's brow *'like to a title-leaf'* (1.1.60–61, emphasis added).[11] Morton, the truthful eyewitness messenger, cannot bear to say the words Northumberland readily puts in his mouth: 'If he be slain, / The tongue offends not that reports his death' (1.1.96–97). 'Tongue' here is a metonym for the man who speaks, using the part for the whole, so therefore also a simile. Morton, who dominates here (and enjoys additional lines in the Folio), has his share of both using the metonym and the simile; his speech belongs to the convention which has given historiography as well as the theatre scores of such messengers descriptive narrations by an eyewitness. Words such as 'fire' and 'blood' punctuate the scene, especially as Northumberland finally prepares himself for battle, and vengeance for the son he did not succour. In few, as Morton himself might say, the play's second beginning is a bravura scene of multiple points of view, overtaken by the man who has seen with his own eyes that which he has returned to tell. The value of eyewitness description was a key feature of medieval historiography. What becomes explicit is that Percy's soldiers were inhibited by the word 'rebellion', a metalepsis of breaking of an oath to one's immediate lord, to the king, and to God.

The strong sense of unease with which Rumour opens the play is partly fuelled by single-word metaphors which, in the course of the play, involve more than twenty lexical variants on 'fire'(9), including 'fiery' (2), 'fire-brand' (1), 'flame' (1), 'burns/t' (3/2), 'burning' (1). Additionally, they are accompanied by thirty-seven variants on 'blood' (23), as well as 'bloodied' (1), 'bloody' (8), 'bloody-faced' (1), 'bleed' (1), 'bleedeth' (1), 'bleeding' (1), 'bleeds' (1).[12] Opening scenes in Shakespeare often introduce ideas which become themes, though neither in the playhouse nor in the study do we usually remark them at first glance. How could we, when we do not yet know who or what is important? While the two clusters that I mention are striking, they are not the play's only thematic threads: time (unquiet or not), the sea, the often-remarked decrepitudes of illness and old age, and books, all have work to do. In this extraordinary historical play Shakespeare takes the conventions of history and makes them live. Throughout, the value of one's word rises and falls, from the histrionically lying Falstaff to the Machiavellian Prince John, both oath-breakers. In the range of fire from Bardolph's nose and Mistress Quickly's sea-coal fire, to descriptions of human temperament, to wholesale destruction, we are constantly aware of the rich variety of metaphoric language. It builds a world of loyalty and repudiation in unquiet times in which, from affairs of state to Sun Tzu-like war negotiations, supposedly dependable values such as keeping one's word no longer guarantee anything.

In the exchanges between Northumberland and Morton we hear historiographically derived discussions in the structures of a 'defence of a course taken' and then 'what is good to be done'. Northumberland allows himself to express his passionate personal grief in an exaggerated rant, and has to be pulled back by his followers (some of this is repeated by his daughter-in-law in Act 2, scene 3). Key concepts such as honour and keeping one's word are to the fore, and the stream of metaphors is obvious.

NORTHUMBERLAND   Let heaven kiss earth! Now let not Nature's hand
    Keep the wild flood confin'd! Let order die!
    And let this world *no longer be a stage*
    To feed contention in a ling'ring act;
    But let one spirit of the first-born Cain
    Reign in all bosoms, that, each heart being set
    On bloody courses, *the rude scene may end*,
    And darkness be the burier of the dead!

LORD BARDOLPH   This strained passion doth you wrong, my lord.

MORTON   Sweet earl, divorce not wisdom from your honour;
The lives of all your loving complices
Lean on your health; the which, if you give o'er
To stormy passion, must perforce decay.
You *cast th'event of war*, my noble lord,
And summ'd the account of chance, before you said,
'Let us make head'. It was your presurmise
That in the *dole of blows* your son might drop. (1.1.153–169)

Morton is circumspect and tactful here. Northumberland's call for universal disorder sounds remarkably like a man denying that any of this is his fault, but by circumlocution with metaphors he keeps his own responsibility at arm's length – something that two scenes later his daughter-in-law will not tolerate. That Shakespeare used this kind of tirade for other characters tells us something about his arsenal of figures: Northumberland's rant is not unlike the curses of other men who blame Nature, the land itself, or Fortune, as Suffolk does in 2 *Henry VI*, Act 3, scene 2, or, indeed, Richard II on his return from Ireland, blaming his land for his own faults. These men, including rebellious bishops, do not face up to their moral bankruptcy. They prevaricate over the sources of the 'unquiet time' they have themselves created. As often in Shakespeare, the last line of Morton's speech here moves to Anglo-Saxon monosyllables, especially indicating the charitable distribution of blows (rather than alms) in a 'dole' (1.1.169). *The Second Part of King Henry IV* is rich in ornamental solutions to the needs of the structure, the characters, and the words they weave into a world spoken by the play's characters without knowing what they create.

Conclusion

In conclusion, it is always worth remembering that one of Shakespeare's most important sources was Shakespeare, who recycles words, phrases, and ideas from earlier plays and poems. Rumour's country pipe might remind some readers of Hamlet's when he berates Rosencrantz and Guildenstern. Attitudes to land, stewardship, and ownership reappear throughout the corpus, testing and judging certain characters' sense of ethical responsibility, or lack of it. Orsino himself insists that property is nothing compared to his love for Olivia when he condemns 'quantity of dirty lands' (2.4.78) into the 'abatement and low price' of his first speech, quoted above. In *Richard II*, John of Gaunt, on his deathbed, praises the land of England and condemns his nephew for treating his kingdom like a saleable farm; in Henry V the Duke of Burgundy uses similar ideas for the lands of France. Both men describe a particularly blessed land, temperate and fruitful, and remarkably similar, since the descriptions reach back to the *locus amoenus* with which I began. The commonplaces, like the figures of speech, share a pedigree that goes back at least to Rome, and Rome's Greece. In this chapter, I have tried to show how the rhetorical heritage which Shakespeare imitates and embroiders, appealed to his audiences while offering them the occasion to think hard about what the figures of speech are doing, what they tell us, and why they matter. Additionally, I have stretched my brief to invite thoughts about how the repetition of single-word themes helps create the world of a particular play. Characters speak their lines, but do not know that the plays also speak through them. It makes the theatre feel more intense, more real than reality, and it insists that we do not just stand – or sit – there, but that we learn to listen with open ears.[13]

NOTES

1 Russ McDonald, *Shakespeare and the Arts of Language* (Oxford: Oxford University Press, 2001), p. 56. Russ McDonald was to have written this chapter; it is offered in his memory.

2 Such imitations could be dangerous for their authors: Sir John Hayward (c. 1564–1627) wrote a *Life and raigne of King Henrie the IIII* (1599), dedicated to the Earl of Essex, for which he was interrogated by the Star Chamber and imprisoned until the Queen's death. Francis Bacon is reputed to have reported to Elizabeth, who instructed him to examine the book for treason, that he found no treason, but that Hayward had feloniously cribbed numerous sentences from Tacitus. See *The first and second parts of John Hayward's 'The life and raigne of King Henrie IIII'*, ed. J. J. Manning, Camden 4th ser., 42 (London: Royal Historical Society, 1991).

3 For a wonderfully comic place to look, see the conversation while driving between Robin Penrose, a highly educated, but precariously employed, academic and a businessman she is 'shadowing' for several weeks, Vic Wilcox, in David Lodge's novel *Nice Work* (London: Secker and Warburg, 1988), Part 4, chapter 2.

4 McDonald, *Arts of Language*, p. 54.

5 Shakespeare uses 'compare' repeatedly in the Sonnets, as the persona invokes true or false comparisons, as can be seen in Sonnets 18, 21, 32, 35, 90, 130, and 142; without mentioning 'metaphor', they offer examples of resemblance or similitude. One might also consider his use of key commonplaces in the Sonnets, such as the way Sonnet 32 combines 'fortune', 'compare', and 'Time'.

6 See Stephen Booth's ground-breaking edition *Shakespeare's Sonnets* (New Haven: Yale University Press, 1977), pp. 239–241.

7 William Empson, *Seven Types of Ambiguity* (London: Chatto & Windus, 1930).

8 See her 'Sprezzatura and Cultural Capital in *The Merchant of Venice*', *The Shakespearean International Yearbook 17: Special Section: Shakespeare and Value*, ed. Simon Haines, gen. eds. Tom Bishop and Alexa Joubin (London: Routledge, 2018), pp. 62–73.

9 While Sebastian speaks once of love, it is Antonio's, not his own (2.1.613).

10 One way of clarifying Rumour's position outside morality is to juxtapose him with Orwell's 'alternative facts' in 1984. Recent use of such terms should not prevent us from remembering their provenance. Powerful people – especially politicians who are lying – can be unethical and, indeed, immoral; but the participants in 'Chinese whispers' who repeat in good faith news they have heard are mistaken because there is no sense of deliberate distortion.

11 Differences between the Quarto and additions registered in the Folio suggest that Shakespeare expanded Morton's role precisely where there are speeches out of long traditions (2.170–180 and 189–209). Morton is the voice of sense, but he combines the role of Nuncius (messenger), as well as an adviser who raises and reminds Northumberland of his acquiescence in the policy agreed upon in the previous discussions of rebellion against the king. His speeches comprehend not only a recapitulation of previous events but also turn the discussion from 'defence of a course taken' to 'what is to be done, and is it good to be done?'

12 Because of the textual variants in the various editions of this play, the keyword counts are more fluid than they would be with a single-text play. I include 'dead' metaphors.

13 More than my usual thanks are due to Stefan Collini, Peter Mack, and Robert Watson for their careful reading of this chapter.

PART II

Shaping Contexts

7

PETER MACK

Approaching Shakespeare
through Rhetoric

Rhetoric aimed to teach pupils how to argue persuasively and how to analyse other people's speeches and writing in order to understand what they were saying, to reply to them effectively, and, at times, to learn from their use of language. Rhetoric provides readers with a flexible set of categories for understanding acts of communication, texts, and performances.[1] Rhetorical theory presents one key idea – that one must think about one's relationship to the audience, the audience's view of the question, and the best means of persuading them – and hundreds of individual doctrines about, for example, self-presentation, the arousal of emotions, effective argument, the formation of elegant and memorable sentences, and the use of voice and gesture. Shakespeare and his audience would first have encountered the precepts of rhetoric at grammar school, and their grammar-school training would have influenced the way in which his audience responded to subsequent encounters with rhetorical teaching at university or through their private reading.[2] In this chapter, I shall describe the rhetorical training which pupils received at Elizabethan grammar schools. Then I shall show how the rhetorical skills and knowledge which pupils acquired can be applied to understanding Elizabethan play-texts, giving as examples analyses of some passages from Shakespeare.

Elizabethan grammar schools, many of which had been founded in the first half of the sixteenth century, pursued a reasonably standardised curriculum based on three main elements: a thorough knowledge of the Latin language, a reading course in the main genres of classical Latin literature, and a series of composition exercises. These exercises were based on three popular textbooks of the sixteenth century: Erasmus's letter writing manual, *De conscribendis epistolis*, Aphthonius's book of writing exercises, the *Progymnasmata*, and Erasmus's manual on rewriting and amplification, *De copia*. Pupils would also have had access to a list of the figures of rhetoric, such as Peter Schade's *De schematibus et tropis*.[3]

The main aim of the grammar school was to teach the pupils to read, write, and speak Latin. Latin was the language of international intellectual communication. Anyone who had a good knowledge of Latin could read the important books in any subject and could study at any university in Europe. Pupils, who entered the grammar school around eight years old, already able to read and write in English, began by learning the Latin grammar by heart and exercising on it by varying compact moralising sentences from 'Cato's' *Distichs* and *Sententiae pueriles*. Then they moved on to schoolboy Latin dialogues, intended to provide them with vocabulary for Latin conversation, Latin translations of Aesop's moral fables and to the short, easy letters from Cicero's *Ad Familiares*, books 13 and 14. Even when they moved on to more literary texts a good part of their time was devoted to learning new vocabulary and constructions.

In their later years at grammar school, pupils followed a fairly consistent course in the best examples of the major genres of Latin literature: Terence for comedy; Virgil's *Eclogues* and Horace for lyric poetry; Cicero's letters and some of his moral philosophy, especially *De officiis*; Virgil's *Aeneid* for epic; Ovid's *Metamorphoses* for mythology; and Caesar or Sallust for history. Teachers were expected to provide introductions to each of the texts studied and to go through sections of the text sentence by sentence four times: first construing the text and providing a Latin paraphrase; then word by word discussing vocabulary, etymology, and unusual constructions; third, rhetorically picking out figures of rhetoric, elegant expressions, *sententiae*, proverbs, histories, fables, and comparisons; and finally ethically pointing out moral axioms, exemplary stories, and the moral teaching provided by the text.[4] Pupils were also expected to attend the sermons in their parish church and to be questioned about them by the teachers. While the younger pupils were asked to record moral axioms from the sermon, more advanced pupils were expected to analyse the division and exposition of the Bible text and to reconstruct the ways in which the principal arguments, proofs, and examples fitted together.[5]

The students' writing exercises, which were the third part of the curriculum, were often based on reusing elements from their reading. Thus, the earliest writing exercises were letters, at first reusing the phrases and structures of Cicero's letters to his wife and daughter in letters to members of their own families, later drawing on the instructions of a manual of letter-writing, such as Erasmus's *De conscribendis epistolis*. Letter-writing manuals provided recipes and arguments for writing letters for many purposes important in sixteenth-century social life, such as encouraging, persuading, consoling, requesting help, recommending a friend, giving advice, providing information, giving thanks, congratulating, and offering assistance. They also gave practical advice on a number of more general rhetorical topics, such as the way in which one should think about one's relationship to the recipient before writing, the appropriate style to employ depending on the subject-matter and the addressee, self-presentation, ways of persuading someone of the rightness and advantages of the course of action one advocates, and when and how to arouse emotions in a recipient. The textbooks also provided phrases which might be helpful in particular types of letter, suitable lines of argument, worked examples, and suggestions for ancient and Renaissance models which the student might imitate. The textbook combined approaches to thinking about writing with practical assistance in writing letters.[6]

Aphthonius's *Progymnasmata* are a fourth-century Greek series of fourteen writing exercises, which provide a definition of the form, a division into different sub-types, a recipe for the content of the form and one or more examples.[7] They were translated into Latin by Rudolph Agricola (1444–85) and provided with a commentary and further examples by Reinhard Lorichius (1510–64), whose version was first published in 1542 and was widely reprinted over the next 150 years.[8] The *Progymnasmata* provide students with rules and models for composing fourteen genres: fable, narrative, *chreia*, maxim, confutation, proof, commonplace, praise, vituperation, comparison, speech for a character, description, thesis, and proposal for a law. Thus, for example a *chreia* is an elaboration of a saying or a deed of a famous person, which employs the following topics: praise of the person involved, paraphrase of the saying (or narrative of the action), cause, contrary, parallel (or similar), example, testimony, and conclusion.[9] The book expands the range of structures available to the student. Some of the exercises, such as narrative, confutation, proof, comparison, speech for a character and description, train pupils in writing components which could be incorporated in longer texts; others look like shorter versions of kinds of oration (e.g. praise, vituperation, proposal for a law) or preparations for writing school essays (thesis). The exercises combine a focus on invention, using topics (such as cause, contrary, similar, example, and testimony), with providing a forum for the reuse and elaboration of material taken from the pupils' reading.

De copia was Erasmus's most successful rhetoric textbook with 169 editions between 1512 and 1597 (and a further sixteen seventeenth-century editions). It aimed to teach pupils ways of varying a pre-existing text. The first book, on *copia* of words, proposes twenty methods of varying individual words (such as antonomasia (replacing a noun with a descriptive phrase), metaphor, allegory, metonymy, synecdoche (part for whole or vice versa)) or the form of the sentence, mostly based on the tropes of rhetoric.[10] This section culminates in a demonstration of 148 ways of rephrasing the useful sentence 'your letters pleased me greatly', followed by 202 ways of carrying out the more difficult assignment of varying the sentence 'always, as long as I live, I shall remember you'.[11] These demonstrations are intentionally virtuosic, showing students what can be achieved by playing with the resources of language. The remaining 173 chapters of the first book provide the pupil with multiple ways of expressing frequently occurring ideas or of connecting clauses or sentences. The second book, on *copia* of things, begins with eleven methods of varying a text based on thinking further on what is implied in the words. These methods are linked to the topics of invention. For example, method 1 involves exploring the more detailed implications lying behind a summary phrase like 'he completed a comprehensive course of education'; method 2 examines the actions leading up to an outcome; method 3 directs attention to the causes of an event; method 4 to the circumstances which accompany an event and the effects it has. By finding more material, the student is enabled to make a fuller and richer statement about the matter at issue.[12] Alongside his focus on the topics of invention and on narrative, Erasmus devotes attention to further elements of content in a text, such as descriptions, moral axioms, proverbs, comparisons, and examples.

De copia includes a description of the way to make commonplace books, another staple of grammar school education. The commonplace book was intended as a way of collecting material from one's reading in Latin literature in such a way as to keep the material ready for reuse in one's own compositions. It was a blank exercise book with headings at the top of each page, such as war, peace, friendship, justice, temperance, mercy, idleness, hypocrisy, and courage. The pupil would copy into the book particularly striking phrases or stories appropriate to the subject named. This seems to be what Hamlet has in mind when on the battlements he says, 'My tables – meet it is I set it down / That one may smile, and smile, and be a villain' (*Ham.* 1.5.107–108). This technique of compiling commonplace books encourages a special habit of reading. As one reads one must be continually asking oneself whether a particular phrase or story is striking enough that one might want to reuse it and, if so, under which heading should it go? This suggests that as well as reading (or listening to) a text in a linear way, Elizabethan readers could file material away under different headings and make comparisons between what was said about, for example, nature or justice, at different moments in a text.[13]

Some Rhetorical Themes related to Grammar School Training and to Plays

Thinking about Your Audience

The guiding idea of rhetoric is that whenever one writes one must think about one's audience and about what one aims to achieve through speaking to them, what they already think about the issues on which you will address them, what arguments are most likely to appeal to that audience, what emotions one might want to arouse in them and how one should present oneself. Within the grammar school syllabus, the injunction to think about the audience comes across most clearly in letter-writing, for example in Erasmus's instruction in *De conscribendis epistolis* that before one thinks about arguments, style, and models, one should reflect on one's relationship to the person addressed in relation to the thing which one aims to bring about by writing the letter. For Erasmus, everything else in the letter will suggest itself easily as long as one thinks about the person being addressed and about the best way to present oneself to that person.[14] Because the recipient of a letter is so clearly defined and is often well-known to the writer, considerations of audience always come to the fore in composing letters.

This guiding idea relates to theatre in a very complex way since it applies both to the thinking of each character in addressing someone on stage and to the thinking of the writer about the offstage audience. For example when we are watching or reading *Hamlet*, Act 3, scene 1, lines 88–143, we need to consider what Hamlet aims to convey to Ophelia and how he reacts to her responses, how Ophelia responds to him, knowing that she is being watched by her father and the king, how Claudius and Polonius understand what they are seeing and the information which Shakespeare intends to convey to, and the emotional response he wishes to evoke in, the offstage audience. Thinking about audiences is essential to working out what happens in a scene and the effect of that scene on the offstage audience.

Self-Presentation, Emotion, and Pleasure

Self-presentation is closely related to the speaker's understanding of the audience. Aristotle understands self-presentation (along with emotion and argument) as one of the three factors which the orator can use to persuade an audience.[15] The letter-writing manuals suggest ways in which the writer can remind the addressee of their previous good relations and give assurances of future gratitude. They argue that the position the writer should adopt will depend on the previous relationship with the addressee and on what they want to achieve. Characters in plays will often adapt their words to a particular interlocutor in ways which reveal that character's thought processes and plans. Both audience and onstage characters will often assess the truth and significance of a narrative on the basis of their understanding of the speaker's self-presentation.

The arousal of emotion, which is a central topic of Aristotle's *Rhetoric*,[16] had been restricted by the Roman rhetoric manuals to the concluding section of the speech but was reinvigorated by Renaissance rhetorical theorists. Erasmus considers the use of emotion in his account of the letter of exhortation and considers responses to emotion in his careful and nuanced discussion of letters of consolation.[17] Speeches in plays often arouse emotions. Plays aim both to portray characters' emotions convincingly and to arouse emotions in the audience. In both cases, the writer is dependent on the skill of the actor but must provide situations and words which an actor can work with. Observing the means by which emotions are aroused is an essential part of attending to dramatic technique. Rhetorical theories about emotions both help writers to incite them and guide readers in ways of thinking about plays.

Giving pleasure has long been understood as one of the aims of speaking. Poetry aims to teach and delight. Pleasing was one of the chief motivations of ceremonial or epideictic rhetoric (the rhetoric of praise and blame), which received renewed attention in the Renaissance. In *De oratore* Cicero defined the aims of rhetoric as to teach, to move, and to please.[18] Rudolph Agricola used this triad as one of the structuring elements of his *De inventione dialectica* (1479) and devoted four chapters to analysing the ways in which writers use style and subject matter to please audiences.[19] In letters in his account of demonstrative letters, Erasmus mentions descriptions of places and the use of suitable but surprising vocabulary as sources of pleasure.[20] The teaching of *De copia* in relation to ways of altering one's expression in order to provide variety is evidently related to pleasing, especially in the extravagant examples. Within the narrative of a play characters often seek to please and divert their friends, while the writer's overall aim is often to give pleasure to the audience, especially in comedies. Audiences often take delight in the lifelike way in which actions are presented or in the extravagance of language and ideas. Thinking about the ways in which characters and writers provide pleasure to their audiences helps us understand how plays work.

The Use of Reading: Coriolanus

Grammar school education placed considerable emphasis on pupils' reusing their reading in their own writing. This was the principal aim of the commonplace book. Some of the elementary letter-writing exercises were based on the words and situations of Cicero's letters, while later on pupils would be asked to write letters appropriate to a character in one of the poems or histories they were reading. Several of the *Progymnasmata* exercises provided students with forms of writing in which to place moral axioms and narratives taken from their reading. The doctrine of imitation which was implicit in Erasmus's provision of model letters required students to write new texts in dialogue with earlier texts which they hoped to draw on and surpass. Like other Renaissance writers, playwrights used their reading as sources of narratives and phrases. Sometimes they alluded to, or copied, incidents from classical poetry, especially Ovid and Virgil. Sometimes they borrowed exemplary stories which their characters tell. Very often the content of particular speeches may be based on ancient history or a previous play. All this can be connected with the ways in which Erasmus in book 2 of *De copia* suggests that sentences can be rewritten by thinking about the circumstances and employing the topics of invention. Playwrights also typically base their plays on existing short stories, romances, histories, or plays, restructuring them to give more effective scenes and to emphasise different aspects, as well as to achieve a particular overall effect. This large-scale reuse of reading is therefore closely related to the structuring of a complete text.

Shakespeare constructed the plot of *Coriolanus* from his reading of Plutarch's *Life of Coriolanus*. He was particularly taken by the climactic scene between Coriolanus and Volumnia in Act 5, scene 3, which in places he takes word by word from North's translation of Plutarch, whereas at other moments he elaborates Plutarch's words and makes them more concrete.[21] He simplifies Plutarch's historical narrative considerably, shaping it into a sequence of two rises and two falls, doubling the inherited pattern of tragedy. Coriolanus rises to great military eminence in Act 1, but fails in his attempt to become consul and is banished from Rome in Acts 2 and 3. From the status of a beggarly outcast, he rises through Acts 4 and 5 to the victorious command of the Volscian army, with the city of Rome at his mercy. In the final scenes of Act 5, he makes peace with Rome and is attacked and assassinated on his return to Corioles.

In the middle section of the play, Shakespeare more or less invents four great scenes (2.3 to 3.3), which show us the political machinations by which the plebeians eventually reject Coriolanus's candidacy, Coriolanus's emotional reaction to that rejection, the attempts of the more moderate senators to avoid civil war, Volumnia's persuasion of Coriolanus to conceal his true feelings and display contrition, and the failure of that diplomatic pretence under the taunts of the tribunes. Shakespeare here presents us with the machinations of politics, as people manage conflicts verbally to achieve goals while minimising violent conflict within the city. Coriolanus is isolated and destroyed for saying directly what most Elizabethan councillors believed about the changeability of the ordinary people and the dangers of divided power in the state. We also see extreme language and strong personalities, especially Volumnia, determined to remould Coriolanus in order to salvage his position in the city.

The latter part of the plot, copying Plutarch again, focuses on Coriolanus's dilemma and his fate. After resisting the appeals of his friends, Coriolanus gives way to the sometimes vicious arguments of his mother, knowing that he is putting his own life in danger. The play shows us that Coriolanus is unsuited to civil conversation and life in the city, as Plutarch said. Comparison shows us that the other characters are better adapted to political life and more adept at advancing their own interests but at the end Coriolanus, for all his unattractive arrogance, is the only character in the play who knowingly sacrifices himself to protect his family.

Disposition and Structure

Disposition (deciding the best order for one's material) has from the time of Aristotle and throughout the classical and medieval periods been regarded as one of the five skills of the orator.[22] In the classical manuals of rhetoric, however, the dominance of the four-part oration, and the fact that the lengthy section on invention was organised in relation to these four parts, meant that disposition played only a small role, restricted to occasions on which one might vary the expected order (exordium, narration, arguments in favour and refutation of opposing arguments, conclusion) or omit one of the parts. Renaissance theorists, especially Agricola, had given a more important role to disposition, arguing that rather than assuming the four-part oration as the norm for all acts of communication, one should determine the form of a work by thinking about all the material one proposed to employ, the aim and situation of the particular text, and the general principles of ordering.[23] Both the letter-writing manual and the *Progymnasmata* provided grammar school pupils with a range of generic forms outside the four-part oration. Some letter-writing manuals even suggest that apart from the salutation and farewell, each letter should be organised solely on the basis of what the writer aims to achieve in the light of the relationship between writer and addressee.[24] This awareness of a wide range of possible forms and the need to choose and adapt among them would also have been reinforced by pupils' study of a range of genres of Latin literature.

In analysing plays, we have to consider structure at several different levels: the speech or sequence of dialogue; the scene and its subsections;

the sequence of scenes; and the play as a whole. These different levels of structure will employ different adaptations of rhetorical principles. While a long speech may be analysed in terms drawn from a letter or from a four-part oration, individual scenes will tend to be organised around actions and around three-part sequences of preparation, action, and reaction. The beginnings of plays will need to seize the audience's attention and to introduce the key ideas and characters of the play, while their endings will often involve a response to (which may include a denial of) the expectations of different genres: reacting to a death, arranging a marriage, or proclaiming a new ruler.

Argument and Narrative

Argument was assured a central place in rhetorical theory when Aristotle proclaimed that it would be the larger of the two central parts of the oration.[25] Even though logic as such was not studied in the grammar school, the school writing exercises involved some practice in using the topics of invention and in constructing arguments. Pupils' analyses of sermons would have given them practice in observing the way in which Bible texts could be divided, analysed, and applied, and the way that arguments could be developed. To support their reading of lyric poems and speeches from epics pupils would have heard their teachers outline arguments and inferences. As readers, we may notice how characters argue overtly and how other things they say or do serve argument. In confrontations, we will want to decide which participant has made the most effective and the most honest arguments. We may try to put together the arguments which characters make and the outcomes which the play gives them in order to draw wider argumentative conclusions from the play as a whole, to see the play as a contribution to an argument within its society. Renaissance rhetorical theory informs us that the key move in analysing the hidden argumentative structures of a text is to identify the question which is being addressed and to appreciate, in a *De copia*-like way, the underlying questions which lurk beneath the words of the overt questions.[26] Identifying the overt and implied questions is of crucial importance to readers in understanding the contributions of different speakers and the sometimes complex arguments which may emerge from the play as a whole.

Narrative is central to human culture, essential to playwriting and of great importance to orators. Grammar school pupils observed narrative in their reading of Latin literature, collected stories in their commonplace books and practised writing narratives through the *Progymnasmata*. The exercise of the fable forced them to engage with the connection between narrative and moral teaching. Rhetorical theory provides a number of suggestions about ways to make narratives convincing in themselves and ways of inflecting them for particular persuasive purposes.[27] Narrative analysis within plays is concerned at the local level with understanding the stories characters tell, the reasons for telling them and the effect which their stories have on both the on- and off-stage audience. At the higher level it will be concerned with the implications of the overall narrative of the play, of the choices made in relation to presenting certain parts of the narrative onstage while narrating other parts, and of the meaning of the changes of emphasis which the playwright makes in adapting the inherited story. Renaissance rhetorical theory also invites us to contemplate the different persuasive effects of narrative as opposed to argument and the impact of narrative on the offstage audience.

Character and Description

Grammar school pupils learned about constructing a character through words from their reading of epics and comedies, from the doctrine of self-presentation, and from the *Progymnasmata* exercise of *ethopoeia* (speech for a character), which was closely related to the exercise of writing a letter appropriate to the situation of a fictional or historical personage. Character could be constructed through choice of style, through the arguments made and stories told, through judgement of actions, through character description, and through hints and narratives about a character's earlier life. All these techniques are useful to dramatists. Readers must focus also on the way in which character is revealed through dramatised interactions with other persons. They may learn a great deal from discrepancies between what we are told by favourable or hostile observers and what as an audience we see for ourselves.

Description was among the features of writing which *De copia* emphasised, in addition to argument and narrative. It was also among the *Progymnasmata* exercises.[28] Speakers in plays will often give descriptions which may have strong effects in persuading and delighting an audience. While rhetoric manuals emphasised the pleasure to be given by accurate descriptions, the figure of *enargeia*, a description so vivid as to appear to bring something to life, was thought to be a source of particular emotional power in writing.[29] Because the concept of a picture being brought to life is actualised in the performance of a scene, *enargeia* can be a fruitful notion for thinking about plays. It also invites readers to think about the differences in effect between physically presenting and verbally describing a person or an action, and the choices a writer may make between the two. For example the idea seems to illuminate Shakespeare's choices at the end of *The Winter's Tale*, first to describe rather than enact the earlier moments of the reconciliation, and second to bring the statue to life as the climax of the conclusion.

Examples and Comparisons: The First Part of King Henry IV, 3.2

In *De copia*, Erasmus also gives a good deal of space to the collection and use of examples, for instance of heroic figures or admirable deeds, and to the uses of comparisons.[30] Both exemplary figures and comparisons can be used to serve the purposes of argument but they can also have independent effects on interlocutors and audience. For example, the evocation of exemplary figures can fill listeners with the hope of emulation, while comparisons may clarify the nature of a particular achievement or serve to make one element of the comparison seem greater. Both ideas are also helpful to readers in thinking about the larger effects of plays, since they can sometimes ask themselves how much they regard a particular figure as worthy of being followed or they can find that the outcome of a play invites them to compare the success or the worthiness of the speeches, actions, and choices of different characters. In thinking about the overall meaning of a play, comparisons can be as valuable in clarifying differences as in inviting the audience to side with one person or another.

King Henry begins his attack on Hal by enumerating his failings (*1H4* 3.2.29–38). Then he makes the comparison with his own behaviour in the previous reign. If Henry had been so often seen in the streets and had kept such bad company he would never have become king. Henry paints an elaborate picture of the rareness of his public appearances and the amazement with which people greeted him. He attributes his success to careful management of his public image ('Thus did I keep my person fresh and new … And won by rareness such solemnity' (55–59)). Then he makes the contrast with King Richard, depicting his foolish behaviour in the streets, courting popularity (60–84). The double contrast between himself and his son and himself and King Richard leads Henry to make explicit the similarity between Richard and Hal ('As thou are to this hour was Richard then' (94)) which logically leads to the more surprising parallel between Hotspur and Henry himself. Henry lovingly details Hotspur's military victories (96–117), as if he wants part of Hotspur's soldierly achievements to thereby accrue to himself. Henry uses description, comparison, and exemplary figures from the recent past to build an accusation of treachery on the basis of the distance Hal has fallen.

Hal protests at the accusation but counters it not with comparison or argument but with a picture ('I will redeem all this on Percy's head, / And in the closing of some glorious day / Be bold to tell you that I am your son' (132–134)) of a sunset after a battle in which Hal will have defeated Hotspur. Hal responds to the unsatisfied desire for glory which motivated Henry's elaboration of Hotspur's deeds with a fictional description (ecphrasis) of his own future military apotheosis. Hal intuits that Henry unconsciously wants his son not so much to repeat his own strategy as to perform the deeds he cannot. Then he turns to his father's more calculating side with an explanation of his own strategy of image management, centred on a sequence of accounting terms ('exchange', 'factor', 'engross', 'account', 'render', 'reckoning' (145–152)). When Hal tells Henry that Hotspur is merely a device to amplify Hal's own honour (142–152), Henry is persuaded because Hal has understood how to speak his own language of calculation and comparison and to fulfil his hidden wishes. Hal's crucial winning of his father's lost trust is a consequence of his deep understanding of his father's words and character.

Proverbs and Axioms: Polonius in Hamlet, 1.3.55–81

Proverbs and moral axioms were central features of grammar school education. Students learned them by heart as models for syntax and for grammatical varying. They collected them from their reading and employed them in *Progymnasmata* exercises. *De copia* discusses the ways in which they can be used to enhance the dignity of a text, while Erasmus's highly successful *Adagia* collected and explained proverbs from classical literature and showed how they could be used for interpretation, persuasion, moral teaching, and to acquire distinction in style.[31] Observation of the extent to which, and the motives for which, a character or an author uses axioms and proverbs can provide readers with illuminating insights. Renaissance readers would also have collected proverbs and axioms from plays for use as a moral guide and to decorate their own compositions. Sometimes plays seem to invite us to contrast different axioms and proverbs used by the characters; sometimes a character tries to use a proverb to understand or generalise experience only to discover the inadequacy of the point of view expressed. Both for the characters and for readers, proverbs and axioms are tools which stimulate and enable thinking.

Polonius's first long speech is a second farewell to Laertes, urging him to hurry to the ship to catch the favourable wind while simultaneously delaying him with a long series of precepts to remember. The speech portrays Polonius as fussy, conventional, self-contradictory (rushing and delaying), and anxious to maintain position and control. It is bland and snobbish, the miscellany of an accomplished courtier, but it also serves to convey a kind of love between father and children which the children will bring out in their response: he goes on saying these endless, embarrassing, unnecessary things but his children can see through that to love him and what lies under his words. When we remember this scene later in the play, we may decide that Polonius didn't entirely deserve the love which his children continued to show him. We already know that his bland commonplaces are a cover for the corruption of the court; later we will see him spying on both children and betraying Ophelia to secure his position with the king. But we may also remember the words and think about them independently of the effect of the speech: 'Give thy thoughts no tongue' (59), grapple true friends to you with hoops of steel, 'to thine own self be true' (79). An audience can use principles like these to reflect on the behaviour of Laertes and Hamlet, as well as to judge Polonius himself. And they can use the stories of Ophelia, Laertes, and Hamlet to reflect on the truth and falsehood in moral (or puerile) sentences like these, familiar to them in Latin from their grammar school days. More than a few of Polonius's words we shall store away for reuse, perhaps with some ambivalence.

Style and Amplification: Hamlet's First Soliloquy

Style is one of the five skills of the orator. In rhetoric, style has four main aspects: use of clear grammatical structures and vocabulary suited to subject-matter, occasion and audience; the doctrine of three levels of style (high or grand, middle, and low or humble); the doctrine of ornamentation using the tropes and figures; and the construction of periodic sentences and prose rhythm.[32] In the grammar school reading of Latin texts, most attention was paid to commenting on vocabulary and identifying uses of the figures and tropes. Renaissance writers produced handbooks of the figures and tropes and teachers' notebooks suggest that pupils may have been made to learn at least a basic list by heart. This learning would support and be reinforced by the teacher's identification of figures used by Roman writers.[33] Modern readers sometimes find the long lists of figures of rhetoric formalistic and unnecessary. Their use is that they help readers identify formal features of language in a range of texts and compare the ways in which different writers use these techniques. Like the names humans have given to birds, the names of the figures are useful because they help readers notice what is happening, in this case how a particular technique is employed by a writer in a specific situation and for a purpose. The figures are probably not necessary in discussing passages from classical or Renaissance literature but they are a great help to someone who is hoping to learn how to use the resources of language by observing and comparing the different ways in which great writers use particular techniques. An appendix to this volume lists and defines the figures and tropes most frequently used by Shakespeare and his contemporaries. (See also the short list of figures on which the appendix is based in my *Rhetoric's Questions, Reading and Interpretation*, pp. 79–84.)

Amplification is the process by which, using a variety of rhetorical and logical techniques, writers make a passage stand out as particularly rich or emotionally forceful.[34] In Renaissance school commentaries and manuscript annotations to school classical texts, *amplificatio* is one of the most frequently found annotations. It makes sense that pupils would be trained to notice worked up passages and to ask themselves how and with what aim a writer has applied amplification to one passage, making it stand out from its neighbours. *De copia* could be regarded as a textbook in amplification which also makes a point about the value of brevity. Sometimes a writer may wish to flatter an audience by making an important point glancingly or by allusion rather than by developing it fully, as if to imply that the audience, like the writer, understands such things already and does not need further prompting. Amplification may seek to overwhelm an audience, or in a play to present a character who is overwhelmed. Brevity draws on the dramatist's favourite resource of implying that the offstage audience knows more and understands better than the characters on stage. The questions to ask about amplification are always where, how, and for what purpose. As with other stage events, the choice of a character or a writer to amplify may provide the audience with new ways of understanding the act of communication and the story of which it is part.

Shakespeare constructs Hamlet's first soliloquy (1.2.129–159) out of three elements which he leaves the reader to connect: a wish to die (129–132), a statement of the corruption of the world (132–137), and a history of his family (137–159). The last and longest section is a copious rewriting of a single sentence: within a month of my father's death, my mother married my uncle. Copia of things directs Hamlet to compare Claudius and his father ('Hyperion to a satyr' (140)) and to paint pictures of his parents' marriage ('he might not beteem the winds of heaven / Visit her face too roughly' (141–142); 'she would hang on him / As if increase of appetite had grown / By what it fed on' (144–145)). Copia of words prompts his interjections and axioms ('Must I remember?' (143); 'a beast that wants discourse of reason / Would have mourn'd longer' (150–151); 'frailty, thy name is woman' (146)) and his amplification of the issue of time, but the underlying sentence is still clearly visible among the elaboration ('within a month' (145, 153) 'she (149) ... married with my uncle (151)'). The amplification presents to the audience Hamlet's obsession with his mother's rapid remarriage and the chasm of difference between the two brothers. Although there is no grammatical connection, the implication must be that the violence of Hamlet's rejection of the world ('an unweeded garden that grows to seed ... things rank and gross in nature / Possess it merely'), which later seems to underlie his attack on Ophelia, is caused by his response to his mother's actions. But Shakespeare puts the audience in the position of having to connect the different elements and provide the explanations. Placing his strong desire for oblivion and the disgust at the world first, and apparently unmotivated, enhances the reader's sense of the strange disproportionateness of Hamlet's thought and behaviour, as if we see him from outside and inside almost simultaneously. We are made aware of the gap between the admittedly troubling events and Hamlet's response to them. We see that the links we make are at best our own conjectural attempts to make sense of chaotic emotional reactions. From the opening words and Hamlet's complete (if exaggerated) rejection of the world, we need the sense that this is his lowest point. What Horatio and the Ghost are about to tell him will give him a reason for continuing to struggle and a chance to reach a better equilibrium.

My aim in this chapter has been to build a bridge between the rhetorical principles and doctrines taught in Elizabethan grammar schools and approaches to reading Shakespeare's plays. While stylistic analyses are likely to remain the most frequent way of using rhetorical ideas to analyse Shakespeare, I would urge students and scholars to acknowledge the way rhetorical training shaped Shakespeare's procedures of writing and rewriting. Rhetorical theory helps us understand the way a dramatist set about writing a play on the basis of a pre-existing narrative, the organisation of the play at different levels, the self-presentation of characters, the arousal of emotion and the giving of pleasure, the ways in which characters and authors use argument, narrative, character-portrayal, description, comparisons, axioms, and proverbs.

NOTES

1 Peter Mack, *Rhetoric's Questions, Reading and Interpretation* (London: Palgrave, 2017).
2 Some other recent studies of Elizabethan rhetoric have focused more on English language resources (Quentin Skinner, *Forensic Shakespeare* (Oxford: Oxford University Press, 2014)) or on university training in rhetoric and dialectic (Lorna Hutson, *Circumstantial Shakespeare* (Oxford: Oxford University Press, 2015)).
3 John Brinsley, *Ludus Literarius* (London, 1612), ed. E. T. Campagnac (Liverpool: University of Liverpool Press, 1917); T. W. Baldwin, *Shakspere's Small Latine and Lesse Greeke*, 2 vols. (Urbana: University of Illinois Press, 1944); Peter Mack, *Elizabethan Rhetoric* (Cambridge: Cambridge University Press, 2002), pp. 11–47; 'Rhetorical Training in the Elizabethan Grammar School', *The Oxford Handbook of the Age of Shakespeare*, ed. R. Malcom Smuts (Oxford: Oxford University Press, 2016), pp. 200–212.

4   William Lily, *Brevissima institutio* (London, 1573), STC 15616, sig. H5r-v; Mack, *Elizabethan Rhetoric*, pp. 14–16.

5   Baldwin, *Shakspere's Small Latine*, p. 346; Brinsley, *Ludus Literarius*, p. 255; Mack, *Elizabethan Rhetoric*, p. 45.

6   Erasmus, *De conscribendis epistolis*, ed. J. C. Margolin, in Erasmus, *Opera omnia*, I-2 (Amsterdam: North Holland, 1971), pp. 205–579, trans. C. Fantazzi, *Collected Works of Erasmus*, 25 (Toronto: University of Toronto Press, 1985); Peter Mack, *A History of Renaissance Rhetoric* (Oxford: Oxford University Press, 2011), pp. 90–96, 228–256.

7   G. A. Kennedy, *Progymnasmata: Greek Textbooks of Prose Composition and Rhetoric* (Atlanta: Society of Biblical Literature, 2003), pp. 89–127.

8   L. Green and J. Murphy list 159 editions of Aphthonius printed between 1520 and 1700 in *Renaissance Rhetoric Short-Title Catalogue 1460–1700* (Aldershot: Ashgate, 2006), pp. 27–32.

9   Aphthonius, *Progymnasmata* (London, 1575), STC 700.3, sigs C8r-D2r. See M. Kraus, 'Progymnasmata, Gymnasmata', *Historisches Wörterbuch der Rhetorik*, 7, ed. Gert Ueding (Tübingen: De Gruyter, 2005), pp. 159–191; M. Kraus, 'Aphthonius and the Progymnasmata in Rhetorical Theory and Practice', *Sizing up Rhetoric*, ed. David Zarefsky and Elizabeth Benacka (Long Grove: Waveland Press, 2008), pp. 52–67.

10 Erasmus, *De copia*, ed. Betty Knott, *Opera omnia*, I-6 (Amsterdam: North Holland, 1988), pp. 38–76, trans. Betty Knott, *Collected Works of Erasmus*, 24 (Toronto: University of Toronto Press, 1978), pp. 307–348; J. Chomarat, *Grammaire et rhétorique chez Erasme* (Paris: Les Belles Lettres, 1981), vol. 2, pp. 712–761; Mack, *History*, pp. 31, 80–88.

11 Erasmus, *De copia*, pp. 76–90, trans. Knott, pp. 348–364.

12 Erasmus, *De copia*, pp. 197–230, trans. Knott, pp. 572–606.

13 Erasmus, *De copia*, pp. 258–269, trans. Knott, pp. 635–648; A. Moss, *Printed Commonplace-Books and the Structuring of Renaissance Thought* (Oxford: Oxford University Press, 1996); Mack, *Elizabethan Rhetoric*, pp. 43–45.

14 Erasmus, *De conscribendis epistolis*, p. 316, trans. Fantazzi, p. 74.

15 Aristotle, *Rhetoric*, 1356a1–21.

16 Aristotle, *Rhetoric*, 1378a21–88b30.

17 Erasmus, *De conscribendis epistolis*, pp. 324–329, trans. Fantazzi, pp. 79–85.

18 Cicero, *De oratore*, 2.27.115.

19 Agricola, *De inventione dialectica* (Cologne, 1539, repr. Nieuwkoop: De Graaf, 1967), III.4–7, pp. 394–411.

20 Erasmus, *De conscribendis epistolis*, pp. 513–516, trans. Fantazzi, pp. 205–207.

21 Peter Mack, *Reading and Rhetoric in Montaigne and Shakespeare* (London: Bloomsbury, 2010), pp. 74–79; T. J. B Spencer (ed.), *Shakespeare's Plutarch* (Harmondsworth: Penguin, 1964); Kenneth Muir, *The Sources of Shakespeare's Plays* (London: Routledge, 1977); full text of Plutarch's 'Life of Coriolanus' is also in Philip Brockbank's Arden edition of *Coriolanus* (London: Methuen, 1976).

22 Aristotle, *Rhetoric*, 1414a30–20b5, *Rhetorica ad Herennium*, II.9.16–10.18; Cicero, *De oratore*, II.307–332.

23 Agricola, *De inventione dialectica*, pp. 412–450; Peter Mack, *Renaissance Argument* (Leiden: Brill, 1993), pp. 218–226.

24 Mack, *History*, pp. 247–249, 254–256.

25 Aristotle, *Rhetoric*, 1414a30–b5.

26 Agricola, *De inventione dialectica*, pp. 355–362, 247–252; Mack, *Renaissance Argument*, pp. 226–239.

27 Quintilian, *Institutio oratoria*, IV.2; Agricola, *De inventione dialectica*, pp. 258–264, 296–306.

28 Erasmus, *De copia*, pp. 202–215, trans. Knott, pp. 577–580; Kennedy, *Progymnasmata*, pp. 117–120.

29 *Rhetorica ad Herennium*, IV.39.51, 55.68–69; Quintilian, *Institutio oratoria*, VIII.3.61–72.

30 Erasmus, *De copia*, pp. 232–248, trans. Knott, pp. 606–626.

31 Erasmus, *De copia*, pp. 248–254, trans. Knott, pp. 626–630; *Adagia*, in Erasmus, *Opera omnia*, II-1 (Amsterdam: North Holland, 1993), pp. 46–68, trans. Margaret Mann Phillips, in William Barker, *The Adages of Erasmus* (Toronto: University of Toronto Press, 2001), pp. 4–20; Mack, *Elizabethan Rhetoric*, pp. 32–35; Mary Thomas Crane, *Framing Authority* (Princeton: Princeton University Press, 1993).

32 Aristotle, *Rhetoric*, 1404b1–13a35; *Rhetorica ad Herennium*, IV, Cicero, *De oratore*, III.149–212, Quintilian, *Institutio oratoria*, VIII-IX.

33 Mack, *History*, pp. 208–227; *Elizabethan Rhetoric*, pp. 45–46.

34 Quintilian, *Institutio oratoria*, VIII.4, Agricola, *De inventione dialectica*, pp. 400–411.

8

JAMES SIEMON

Shakespeare and Social Languages

When Prince Hal boasts that he 'can drink with any tinker in his own language' (*1H4* 2.4.15–16), he is claiming to have mastered what might be termed a sociolect – 'a variety of a language used by a particular social class or group' (*OED*) – along with its associated behaviours. He claims knowledge of a sub-set of English employed by speakers whose identity and whose verbal 'lect' is not defined by region, national origin, or even profession, but by their social position and a shared vocabulary that constitutes their 'own language'. Taken out of context, Hal's claim to speak the language of 'any tinker' might appear to suggest that he had mastered a specialised English belonging to a specific trade or occupation. Some of Shakespeare's characters do speak languages shaped by their occupations and offices, as we shall see. However, Hal does not here refer to an occupational language specific to people who work on metal; in fact his term is meant as an insult to low-status common people in general. Though he prides himself on having won the hearts of his commoner companions, his name for them classifies them and their 'language' under a term that has nothing to do with actual occupation.

Hal may be accurate in the lexicon and behaviour that he attributes to his drinking companions. He says they distinguish themselves by using special terms like 'dyeing scarlet' for drinking or 'Corinthian' for a good companion and by performing rituals like crying 'hem' while drinking; but he also says that they radically violate Elizabethan social norms of deference when they swear ludicrously inappropriate brotherhood with their Prince and even address him as 'a good boy' (*1H4* 2.4.5–16). In ballad and fiction, there is a popular tradition of commoners who comically impress their king with their blunt manner (e.g. the merry tanner in 'The Tanner of Tamworth' or Jack the weaver from Thomas Deloney's *Jack of Newberry*), but such breaches of social decorum as Hal mentions would have resulted in severe punishment for actual Elizabethan commoners. Hal neither rewards nor punishes his companions; instead, following neither generic fictional nor actual legal standards, he appropriates their language and behaviour for his own future uses. And he classifies them. Surprisingly, even Francis, a hard-working bonded apprentice, already started on the long path towards London citizenship, gets lumped together by Hal with shiftless rogues, beggars, and vagabonds.[1]

Francis may be a 'loggerhead' – i.e. stupid – but he is no 'tinker'. Nor from Hal's own report is Francis's vocabulary limited to a constricted occupational language. If Francis proves unable onstage to speak 'other English in his life than "Eight shillings and sixpence", and "You are welcome", with this shrill addition, "Anon, anon, sir!"' (*1H4* 2.4.19–21), that is because he is forced into a situation that reduces him to such a narrowly occupational range of utterances. This case illustrates a frequently observed sociolinguistic phenomenon: different social languages and their speakers are usually interpreted, evaluated, and classified by those who belong to a socially dominant group and thus get to do the classifying.[2] This observation should be kept in mind when considering representations of and judgements upon different social languages and their speakers, whether in Shakespeare's plays or in the writings of his early modern contemporaries.

Hal's off-handed classification, lumping together vastly different people and their languages into one crude sort, stands out sharply by its contrast with the subtle differentiation of many social languages in Shakespeare's second historical tetralogy, where speakers occupy a broad swath of occupations, with different status and power, and often speak accordingly. Examples ranging from the bottom through the top of the social order include (among others): the rough and ready trade talk of labouring carriers (*1H4* 2.1); the specialised terminology of thieves employed among highwaymen (*1H4* 1.2.86; 2.2.40); the terms of horticultural practice articulated by a nameless Gardener (*King Richard II* 3.4); the clichés of Puritan piety laughably deployed by Falstaff in jests and vituperation (*1H4* 1.2.71–75 and *The Second Part of King Henry IV* 2.4.259–260); the legal phrasings shared by Justice Shallow and his servingman Davy (*2H4* 5.1) and the same mangled by the Hostess (*2H4* 2.1.22–27); the martial terms of arms and honour spoken by 'noble Percy', even in his sleep (*1H4* 1.3, 2.3.44–51); and the quasi-biblical language of sacred authority and hierarchy shared by John of Gaunt, the Bishop of Carlisle, King Richard II, and his Queen (*R2* 1.2.37–41; 4.1.115–149; 3.2.4–62; 3.4.72–80). This brief list drawn from a few plays only begins to suggest the rich variety of social languages to be found in Shakespeare's works. Elsewhere, for example, characters use languages specific to fashionable swordsmen (*Romeo and Juliet*), affected courtiers (*As You Like It*), sonneteering lovers (*As You Like It*), pedantic schoolmasters (*Love's Labour's Lost*), as well as doctors (*The Merry Wives of Windsor*), sailors (*The Tempest*), and many others. Before exploring a few examples in greater depth, and suggesting some of the ways in which they may signal important differences and conflicts, as well as agreements and alliances among characters, it is worth specifying what this chapter is – and is not – talking about.

Dialect vs. Social Dialect

In one respect, Shakespeare's second historical tetralogy is atypical because it represents certain aspects of linguistic differentiation that the playwright largely eschews in other plays. The first and second parts of *Henry IV*, and *King Henry V*, are unusual in the attention paid to speakers whose language may be defined by their 'nation' – characters who speak actual Welsh (*1H4* 3.1.193–206) or French (*H5* 3.5), or who speak English that appears phonologically and syntactically to represent their Welsh, Irish, or Scots accents (*H5* 3.3). With a few notable exceptions – e.g. Parson Evans and Doctor Caius in *Merry Wives of Windsor*, the disguised Edgar in *King Lear* – Shakespeare generally avoids differentiating speakers by accents national or regional. This may seem surprising, given the range of English accents and dialects noted by contemporary English observers, but Shakespeare's inattention to such differences is not unusual among Elizabethan dramatists. Although there are many examples of dramatic characters with foreign accents on the early modern English stage (e.g. in William Haughton's *Englishmen for My Money*; John Marston's *The Dutch Courtesan*; Thomas Dekker's *Shoemaker's Holiday* and many more), and despite the fact that actors themselves surely must have retained some regional accents, surviving play-texts evidence very few attempts to render such accents. However, this is not to say that characters whose lines display no markers of regional (or foreign) accents always sound the same as one another – or always sound different from one another, either. Their sociolinguistic differences and similarities appear primarily in word choice, in *lexis* rather than in sound, structure, or syntax, though syntactic features and formulae, such as repetition or antithesis, may also register sociolinguistic significance.

Shakespeare's characters exist within verbal environments where differing English sociolects interact with and interpenetrate one another in complex ways – even within the utterances of individual speakers, whose language may shift vocabulary and usage according to circumstance. In Hal's speech about drinking with tinkers, for example, the same prince who elsewhere mocks the martial talk and honour-obsessed speech of Hotspur, 'the king of honour', shifts briefly into Hotspur's sociolect when he employs a military term for battle in lecturing his companion Poins about losing 'honour' by missing the 'action' of the drinking bout: 'thou hast lost much honour that thou wert not with me in this action' (*1H4* 2.4.16–17). This is a joke, of course, but a joke that opens onto complexities in Shakespeare's rendering of social languages; for one thing, Hal's application of honour and battle language to his tavern indulgence mocks martial language from the inside, not openly attacking it or its users, but slighting it by employing it sarcastically, by speaking with what the twentieth-century Russian analyst of speech behaviour M. M. Bakhtin would call a 'sideward glance'.[3] It would be useful to consider Shakespeare's socially multi-lingual characters and plays by way of suggestive responses to Shakespeare's lexis by the great eighteenth-century lexicographer, Samuel Johnson, and also to introduce some related aspects of Bakthin's account of 'multi-languagedness'.

Multi-Languaged Shakespeare

As early as the mid-eighteenth century, Doctor Johnson recognised that English readers could no longer fully understand the vocabulary of Shakespeare's plays. Johnson attributes Shakespeare's 'obscurity' to three causes.[4] First, '[e]very age has its modes of speech', Johnson writes, and phraseology produced by 'fashion', but in Shakespeare's day English itself was intermingled and confused 'with dead and with foreign languages, with obsoleteness and innovation' (Johnson 269–270). Johnson's observation about the 'flood' of Latin loan words and of new terms adapting Latin originals in the period has been upheld by linguists.[5] Second, 'in [Shakespeare's] age, above all others, experiments were made upon our language, which distorted its combinations, and disturbed its uniformity' (Johnson 270).[6] And finally, Shakespeare was so interested in portraying 'the manners of the world then passing before him', that he makes 'more allusions than other poets to the traditions and superstitions of the vulgar' (Johnson 270).

Doctor Johnson's historical claims are specific to Shakespeare's time and Shakespeare's works, but the factors he enumerates as posing challenges to understanding Shakespeare resemble the elements of 'socio-linguistic speech diversity and multi-languagedness' that M. M. Bakhtin has claimed to be present within 'any single national language'.[7] Bakhtin's suggestive list of the kinds of social 'languages' or 'social dialects' present within any national language at any time offers useful prompts for a consideration of Shakespeare's own multi-languagedness:

> The internal stratification of any single national language into social dialects, characteristic group behavior, professional jargons, generic languages, languages of generations and age groups, tendentious languages, languages of authorities, of various circles and of passing fashions, languages that serve the

specific sociopolitical purposes of the day, even of the hour (each day has its own slogan, its own vocabulary, its own emphases)[.] (Bakhtin, *Dialogic*, 263)

Crucially, these many sub-languages that Bakhtin claims to inhabit any national language do not simply exist separately side by side or stand one above another in a *single* 'internal stratification'; instead they interact and clash. Not only do such social languages respond to one another, but they also overlap, combine, and compete in complex forms of socially inflected usage and language behaviour to constitute the conflictual vitality of living language that Bakhtin calls social *heteroglossia*.[8]

From the many social languages inhabiting Shakespeare's English, this chapter will take up a sampling and provide brief examples from the plays: languages of the era, languages of fashion, languages of authorities and their counter-languages, and professional languages. While examples from only a few works will have to suffice, these few are meant to suggest the dynamic importance of multi-languagedness in many other plays where the words and usage of characters often signify, impose, affirm, or repudiate social identities while registering pervasive tensions and conflicts of status.

Courtly and Pedantic vs. Commonly Received

Early modern commentators claim to find differences between Northern and Southern English, between courtly or urbane London speech and 'outlandish' rustic English, or between pompously affected 'inkhorn' English and a general, commonly understood 'King's English'; in addition, many popular narratives refer to a language of thieves called 'canting'.[9] That said, Paula Blank notes that Shakespeare and his fellow early modern dramatists offer 'no full-scale portraits of lower-class urban dialects'.[10] Nor with a few significant exceptions – e.g. Richard Brome's *The Northern Lass* and Ben Jonson's *Tale of a Tub*[11] – do Shakespeare and his contemporary dramatists emphasise regional dialects even when there was opportunity to represent them: not among clowns or muddling speakers like the Constables Dull (*Love's Labour's Lost*) and Dogberry (*Much Ado About Nothing*) or Elbow (*Measure for Measure*), nor even with country shepherds and shepherdesses.[12] Thus, when the 'courtier' Touchstone makes fun of the language used by the humble shepherd William, the joke concerns differences in their socially defined vocabularies. Touchstone translates his supposedly courtly words and phrases into other English words and phrases that he presumes a shepherd would understand – with none of the differences in syntax, endings, or phonology typical of actual dialects:

[Y]ou clown, abandon, which is in the vulgar 'leave', the society, which in the boorish is 'company', of this female, which in the common is 'woman': which together is 'abandon the society of this female'; or, clown, thou perishest or, to thy better understanding, 'diest', or, to wit, 'I kill thee', 'make thee away', 'translate thy life into death[.]'   (*AYLI* 5.2.42–46)

Touchstone laboriously – and ridiculously – explains that *abandon the society of this female or you perish* means *leave the company of this woman or you die*, rendering each term 'in' an idiom that he calls vulgar, boorish, or common and that he presumes will befit a lowly shepherd.

Touchstone intends to mock the shepherd, but the joke is really on the condescending courtly translator, for the play here as elsewhere makes fun of courtiers and their self-identified sociolect, as well as the disdain that courtiers express not only towards 'boorish' – i.e. coarse, uncultured – language but towards 'common' or 'vulgar' – i.e. clearly understandable and generally used – English, what the Elizabethan rhetorician Thomas Wilson calls 'speak[ing] as is commonly receiued'.[13] In sum, a court fool ('Clowne' in Folio Speech Prefix), offers another 'clown', a lowly forest-born shepherd, terms mostly Latinate, mostly polysyllabic, and, in the case of 'abandon', an upscale synonym for 'leave'.[14] And Touchstone proceeds laughably from there, piling on multiple synonyms and phrases the way *Monty Python*'s John Cleese hilariously iterates fourteen ways to say that his parrot is dead.[15]

While the fool Touchstone claims foolishly – as George Puttenham's *Arte of Poesy* asserts seriously – that English spoken at court is inherently superior to rural English, his language lesson in fact offers a version of a joke about the pretensions of the speaker himself that Shakespeare also makes in another play that relentlessly mocks linguistic affectations. No courtier but a 'schoolmaster', Holofernes lectures the aptly named Constable Dull of *Love's Labour's Lost* in odd and heavily Latinate English mixed with Latin. Holofernes opens with a non-standard use of 'intimation' (to mean 'interjection') and follows up with other pompous terms: 'Most barbarous intimation! Yet a kind of insinuation, as it were, *in via*, in way, of explication, *facere*, as it were, replication, or rather *ostentare*, to show, as it were, his inclination' (*LLL* 4.2.12–14). Holofernes here illustrates a linguistic abuse called 'inkhornism' that Elizabethan critics claimed to be widespread across all social strata. Thomas Wilson attacked contemporaries – including speakers both rural and urban, learned and unlearned – for affecting an ink-horn English in attempting to 'Latin their tongues'; and Richard Mulcaster mocked the use of 'strange and pompous terms' where perfectly understandable alternatives already existed (Wilson, *Rhetorique*, 162; Barber, *English Language*, 159).

Languages of the Hour or the Circle

No character in the forest of Arden speaks 'rustic' English, nor is any other character in *Love's Labour's Lost* so obviously obsessed with showing off inkhorn language as Holofernes. However, *As You Like It* does represent other socially distinctive forms of English signalled by vocabulary and phrasing specific to a time period: Bakhtin's category of the language of the day or hour.

Again, Shakespeare makes Touchstone the speaker, and again dramatises a disjunction of languages that resembles a linguistic clash in another play. When Touchstone explains at great length the 'lie seven times removed' (*AYLI* 5.4.62) to a duke and his attending gentlemen, he lectures courtly individuals who would be already well-informed in traditional codes of honour and chivalry. Touchstone assumes the authority to lecture his superiors by virtue of his fluency in brand new terms and phrasing that had only recently become available to Englishmen in Vincent Saviolo's 1595 book on rapier fencing and duelling.[16] Saviolo, who addresses 'Gentlemen or Caualiers' (Saviolo sig. V2r) – a group identity vague enough to be claimed or aspired to by virtually anyone with the means and inclination to purchase a rapier – popularised technical terms of duelling. But significantly his book also enumerates multiple and intricate ways for a true man of honour to give, respond to, and avoid verbal challenges or 'lies' along with basic grammatical principles to be observed in order to avoid the linguistic mistakes that typify the utterances of the 'common sort' who bungle duelling terms and phrasing when they attempt to use them (sig. T2r-v). It is his command of this fashionable new language that empowers Touchstone's laughable lecture to his superiors.

This language of the hour also appears in *Romeo and Juliet*, and there Mercutio employs it to mock the faddish linguistic pretensions of duellists. 'Ah, the immortal "passado", the "punto reverso", the "hay"!' (*Rom.* 2.4.23), Mercutio says, invoking the new terms sarcastically, before rounding on Tybalt with a string of insults directed at him and his sub-group: 'The pox of such antic, lisping, affecting phantasimes, these new tuners of accent!' (25–26). Mercutio then concludes with a string of exclamations that evidently mimics the phrases that typify their social language: '"By Jesu, a very good blade! a very tall man! a very good whore!"' (*Rom.* 2.4.26–27). This part of Mercutio's mockery is not exactly directed to faddish vocabulary per se, since it employs no words specific to Saviolo's duelling terminology. In such a case, it is impossible to recover the precise manner in which these otherwise common phrases are 'accent[ed]' by Mercutio: does he 'lisp' fashionably when speaking? What this example should make clear, though, is that even straightforward English phrases like 'a very good blade' could be recognised and called out – at the right time and under the right circumstances – as identifiably belonging to a social language of a certain hour.

In its Elizabethan context the language here mocked by Mercutio is also identifiable as belonging to a certain group. Using Saviolo's terms not only set those in the know about the 'new form' apart from those who were not yet abreast of current fashion, but this usage divided Englishmen according to different schools concerning weaponry and its uses. Saviolo and the circle of 'Rapier-men' who followed his 'outlandish' teachings were mocked for their foreign weapons, their school techniques, and their terminology by a group of competitors, the English 'Masters of Defence' who taught and championed what George Silver called 'their own ancient weapons' of sword and buckler.[17]

Generic Languages

There are other social languages in the plays that belong to fashionable English circulating in Shakespeare's day but were not quite as immediate to the moment or identified with a particular group of people as was the duellists' jargon. When it comes to expressions of erotic passion, for example, plays such as *As You Like It*, *Romeo and Juliet*, and *Love's Labour's Lost* contain characters who, as lovers, employ a generic vocabulary and figures of speech identifiably derived from the sixteenth-century English tradition of Petrarchan sonneteering. With its stylised representation of the male lover who occupies 'the social position of the deferential suitor' and who religiously suffers the sometimes 'cruel' disdain of a deified beloved, with its agonised vocabulary of tears, sighs, pains, imprisonment, and 'wounds invisible' (*AYLI* 3.6.30), with its stock of oxymorons, and its praises of the beloved's individual features according to the blazon tradition, the language spoken by Orlando and Silvius in *As You Like It* shares characteristics with that of Romeo, when he speaks in the 'numbers that Petrarch flowed in' (*Rom.* 2.4.34–35).[18]

That actual Elizabethan courtiers used this heavily stylised language in their writing and recorded discourse signals its potentially high social status (see Marotti, '"Love"'). Yet Shakespeare joins many of his contemporaries in mocking Petrarchan language for its easily stereotyped limitations and its users for a tendency to emotional self-indulgence. Tellingly, Rosalind strives to wean Orlando away from employing such language and chastises the shepherd Silvius for taking its poetic excesses for reality (*AYLI* 3.6.49–56). In *Titus Andronicus*, similar language is rendered grotesque when the physically violated Lavinia is addressed in a Petrarchan blazon (*Tit.* 2.4.11–32).

In *Love's Labour's Lost*, Berowne descants about 'heavenly Rosaline' and compares himself to a 'vassal' who is 'blinded by' a 'majesty' in her that oxymoronically makes 'black fair' (*LLL* 4.3.215–252); but he is finally shamed into renouncing such 'spruce affectation' (*LLL* 5.2.407).

A related, but somewhat different, treatment of an identifiably Elizabethan social language appears in the plays' deployment of another highly stylised language known as euphuism. Euphuism, taking its name from Euphues, a character in prose works by John Lyly (*Euphues: An Anatomy of Wit* (1578) and *Euphues and His England* (1580)), may itself have been derived from elements of educated humanist discourse, especially the deployment of copious similes, often drawn from natural history; however, it became a recognisable spoken and written language of the Elizabethan era generally, and was often associated with courtly circles in particular.[19] Edward Blount, writing in 1632, credits Lyly for having invented a 'new English' which was so appealing to courtiers that in Lyly's day 'that Beautie in Court, which could not Parley Euphuisme, was as litle regarded as shee which now there, speakes not French'.[20] In its simplest forms, euphuism typically strings together lists of exaggerated proverbial or natural similes in antithetical pairings, playing up similarities of sound and syntax to create extended series of often far-fetched comparisons and contrasts, likenesses and disjunctions that are treated as if they illustrate logical ideas. For an atypically brief example: 'The foule Toade hathe a fayre stoane in his head, the fine goulde is founde in the filthy earth, the sweete kernell lyeth in the hard shell.'[21] Here a negatively characterised natural creature, a *foul* toad, is treated as a container that, according to proverb lore, contains an opposing positive object, a *fair* stone; the toad is then paralleled by another negative container, the *filthy* earth, with its own alliterative positive, *fine* gold to be *found*, within it; and finally, there is one further parallel in the *hard* shell containing its own positive, a *sweet* kernel. This accretion of supposed parallel examples is meant to imply that nature itself supports a general logical principle: good things come in forbidding packages. Lyly does this sort of thing with maddening frequency and at prodigious length.

By the time Shakespeare gets hold of this fashionable language, it had been around for at least a decade, and the plays treat it in a variety of ways. Characters who are clearly not courtly slip into euphuism with and sometimes for comical effect: an illiterate messenger speaks to himself, unintentionally garbling a passage from Lyly (*Rom.* 1.2.38–43); Falstaff, the debauched knight, deploys euphuism's natural similes, verbal antitheses, and alliterations in a joking tavern impersonation of King Henry lecturing Prince Hal (*1H4* 2.4.329–344). But Portia, the wealthy heiress, employs euphuistic language to her waiting woman with no hint of parody

(*The Merchant of Venice* 1.2.11–22; cf. Bond, *Lyly* 1.153). One of Shakespeare's more extended and complex treatments of euphuism appears in *Much Ado about Nothing*.

In *Much Ado*, as Claire McEachern has demonstrated, euphuism constitutes a 'sociolect' that 'signals relations of a courtly class of persons, and is the means by which they display their membership in this class, and also the means by which others display their aspirations to the fashionable company'.[22] Thus subordinate but aspiring characters such as a nameless Messenger appear capable of imitating their betters in speaking euphuistically. The Messenger praises Claudio as having 'borne himself beyond the promise of his age, doing in the figure of a lamb the feats of a lion. He hath indeed better bettered expectation than you must expect of me to tell you how' (1.1.11–13). McEachern points out differences in the ways that different speakers employ euphuism: socially subordinate men are actually 'the most slavish speakers of the idiom' and their excessive observation of its characteristic terms and uses invites contempt from higher-status characters, as for example, when Don Pedro dismisses ornate wordplay from the subordinate Balthazar with 'these are very crotchets that he speaks' (*Ado* 2.3.48). A similar instance occurs when a lower-status female speaker, the maid Margaret, offers a densely patterned speech that occasions Beatrice's dismissive query: 'What pace is this that thy tongue keeps?' (*Ado* 3.4.69).

Yet among the characters with power and high positions, the most impressive speakers who 'parley Euphues' are aggressive improvisers rather than formulaic imitators. Above all others, Beatrice and Benedick 'animate its forms, chiefly by means of aggressive appropriations and inversions of the meaning of the speech of others' (McEachern 73). So, for example, when Benedick is asked by Claudio to evaluate Claudio's beloved Hero, Benedick responds with highly patterned phrases that directly echo a passage in Lyly's *Euphues*, but that twist and turn back upon themselves with unexpected, seemingly unpredictable wit: 'Why i'faith, methinks she's too low for a high praise, too brown for a fair praise, and too little for a great praise. Only this commendation I can afford her, that were she other than she is, she were unhandsome, and being no other, but as she is – I do not like her' (*Ado* 1.1.126–130).[23] Similarly, when Benedick queries Beatrice about whether she does not find his expressions of love to be 'strange', Beatrice responds by picking up his words and handling them with her own agile improvisation. His lines to her – 'I do love nothing in the world so well as you, is not that strange?' – are answered by playful turns of his terms: 'As strange as the thing I know not: it were as possible for me to say, I loved nothing so well as you, but believe me not, and yet I lie not, I confess nothing, nor I deny nothing' (*Ado* 4.1.261–263). In repeating his 'so well as' and his 'nothing', Beatrice manages to echo Benedick's evasive admission of 'love' while just as carefully preserving deniability.

Languages of Authorities and Resistance

Scholars have long recognised passages in Shakespeare that employ a long-lived, early modern official language which assumed the universal pervasiveness of divinely ordained ranks and degrees and the especially sacred nature of the monarch and monarchical office. Analogies between order and subordination in the kingdom and similar relationships both among and within the ranks of beings spiritual (from God to angels to humans to demons) or natural (among planets, animals, plants, minerals, etc.) informed a rich metaphorical lexicon.[24] It could be and frequently was applied at every level of society, from high-level pronouncements of church and state to advice about home and family, or within official discourses employed by schools and universities, courts, parishes and civic bodies. Such language assumes particular prominence in its specifically Christian form in *King Richard II*, where it informs speeches about kingship by King Richard, the Bishop of Carlisle, and Richard's Queen; and it also appears central to a lengthy sequence of more generally philosophical discussions of all kinds of 'degree' in the classical setting of *Troilus and Cressida*.

While such officially approved languages presume to be universal, they are of course inherently social, claiming divine and natural authorisation to condemn or silence any challengers to those holding power and office. It is to be understood as implying or sometimes directly making attacks upon the impudence of the 'wavering commons' (*R2* 2.2.128), the 'many-headed multitude' (*Cor.* 2.3.14), the 'giddy multitude' (*2H4* 4.2.21), the 'common herd' (*JC* 1.2.256), 'the blunt monster with uncounted heads, / The still discordant wav'ring multitude' (*2H4* Induction 18–19). Echoes of languages that challenge the hegemony of languages of order and degree are evident in Shakespearean echoes of at least two historically existing and, in one case, widely reported (though probably largely fictional) oppositional languages. These three languages, one derived from an amalgam of English and German revolts, another from English advocates of political 'commonwealth', and the third from literary depictions of underworld 'canting', are registered in Shakespeare's plays, though as always, in different ways.

Probably the least dramatically central of these oppositional languages in Shakespeare is canting or 'peddler's French'. Canting language appears in treatments by contemporary writers in forms that are sufficiently different from ordinarily used English and so evidently designed to be incomprehensible to the majority of English speakers as to constitute what has been called an 'anti-language'.[25] Whether such argot ever was actually spoken by underworld populations, the non-standard vocabulary and usage attributed to it by popular writers appear in early modern dramas such as Ben Jonson's *Gypsies Metamorphosed*, Thomas Dekker and Thomas Middleton's *Roaring Girl*, Beaumont and Fletcher's *The Beggars' Bush*, and Richard Brome's *The Jovial Crew*.[26] But as S. Musgrove points out, Shakespeare makes sparing and allusive use of canting terms. Some examples are words like 'purchase' (for booty) and 'setter' (for lookout) in tavern and thieving scenes of *Henry IV, Part 1* (2.1.74, 2.2.40); and 'prig' (for thief) and 'doxy' (for whore) are used by the cheating pickpocket in *The Winter's Tale* (4.3.2, 4.3.91).[27] Interestingly, though taken to be an underworld alternative to common English, canting appears in contemporary accounts to share aspects of the pervasive assumptions about order and degree that ground official languages of church and kingdom. Although Thomas Dekker claims that contemporary thieves, vagabonds, and cheats embody 'a base disorder in their living and in their Manners' and though he depicts their curses in the name of the devil rather than prayer in the name of God, he nevertheless represents the canting population as internally organised into a society of twenty-seven 'Ranks' ranging from 'Kinchin Coes' to 'Rufflers or Upright men, which are the highest degree amongst them'.[28] Dekker also claims that they 'observe ... Method in their speech' (Dekker, *Lantern* 253).

By contrast, the language that Shakespeare amalgamates from a verbal tradition that follows on from the English Peasant's Revolt of 1381 and unrest in sixteenth-century Münster suggests a social order turned upside down. The most dramatic Shakespearean representation of this language appears in the scenes of Jack Cade's rebellion in *Henry VI, Part 2*, where Cade proclaims 'liberty' to mean murdering every lord and gentleman, and announces 'then are we in order when we are most out of order' (2H6 4.2.158–160; 164). While Cade does long to crown himself king, he addresses his band of rebellious craftsmen as 'Fellow kings' (2H6 4.2.140). Furthermore, Shakespeare has Cade unhistorically adapt radically egalitarian slogans shared by John Ball in 1381 and the 'Anabaptist' John of Leiden in 1525 to claim 'all the realm shall be in common' (2H6 4.2.56–57) as well as Ball's widely echoed counterblast to the biblically based language that enjoined commoners to accept subjugation to their betters by lineage: 'Adam was a gardener' (2H6 4.2.113).

Among their rebellious slogans, Cade's 'handicraftsmen' adopt sixteenth-century phrases that expressed resentment at the loss of an imaginary 'merry world' of social equality that has been unjustly destroyed by the rise of 'gentlemen' (2H6 4.2.6–7).[29] But they, too, like their leader also borrow terms from Tudor theologians and counsellors who wrote about 'the commonwealth' and even from the official *Homilies*. Of course, they manage to radically misappropriate biblically derived language even when the words remain. So, the Pauline injunction to 'labour' that the *Homilies* render as 'every one ... to walk uprightly in his own calling' gets twisted into revolutionary sloganeering: '[It] is said, "Labour in thy vocation": which is as much to say, as let the magistrates be labouring men; and therefore should we be magistrates' (2H6 4.2.11–13).[30] Such easily measured distortion, however, is only one form of Shakespearean usage. Consider the garden scene of *King Richard II* and the storm scene that opens *The Tempest* in both of which a labourer's language contrasts positively with the language of royal authority and its demands for deference.

The Gardener in Act 3, scene 4 of *King Richard II* employs gardening terminology, but nothing he says differs from what a reformer or a humanist writer might say in horticultural metaphors about cultivating a child, ordering a church, or as the Gardener says, governing a 'commonwealth' (*R2* 3.4.35). Each of his gardening terms – from 'caterpillars' to 'weeds' to 'fruits of duty' to 'crown' – betrays a thoughtfulness that simultaneously applies to factors plausibly horticultural as well as politically appropriate to the 'sea-walled garden' of England.[31] The interesting effect is to re-enforce the authority of the outspoken labourer with the authority conveyed by a widely circulating public discourse. Furthermore, when he responds to the Queen's angry biblically inflected vituperation, the Gardener shows no sign of the humble timorousness thought appropriate to his station. Remaining calmly unfazed despite being rebuked for his 'harsh rude tongue' and called 'old Adam's likeness', he sticks to his point with dignity and precisely measured argument despite her royal anger. His final promise to plant symbolically resonant 'rue' clearly concludes in the language of literate allegory rather than within the limits of a functional language of horticulturalists (*R2* 3.4.72–107). A related point could be made concerning Friar Laurence's allegorically inflected herb-gathering in *Romeo and Juliet*: his herbs might be intended for medicinal purposes, but his reflections go beyond usage narrowly specific to working herbalists to invoke 'grace' and 'rude will' (*Rom.* 2.4.1–30). In fact, his lexicon and his argument are virtually the same as those invoked by the Homilies when discussing the 'temper[ing]' of 'Christian liberty' in order to remain 'moderate' in terms of the diverse 'necessary uses' of 'herbs, trees, and sundry fruits' and their attending smells, tastes, delights – and dangers.[32]

By contrast the Mariners who open *The Tempest* in their storm-driven vessel accompanied by a king, noblemen, and labourers make no reference to the obviously germane allegory of the Ship of State. Instead of echoing humanist or religious commonplaces like the Gardener, the Boatswain speaks in a language that is intensely trade-specific. Furthermore, he counters the attempts of the noblemen to put him in the labouring man's accustomed social place with words well-sorted to his trade as well as para-linguistic signals of his resistance to aristocratic hegemony. And here too, as in the case of the Gardener of *Richard II*, there is no effective reduction of the outspoken working man to laughable self-contradiction or to silenced acquiescence. These scenes offer direct contrast to the comic trivialisation and ultimate silencing of the Cobbler who dares to speak up in the opening scene of *Julius Caesar* or to the silencing of the Citizens who open *Coriolanus*. The aristocrats may mock the Boatswain, but his language and manner are no joking matters.

Shakespeare's *The Tempest* opens with a series of shouted commands and hostile exchanges between the sailors and the aristocrats. To one another, the seamen employ the terminology and succinct commanding usage of early modern nautical labour: 'Down with the topmast! Yare, lower, lower! Bring her to try with main-course' and 'Lay her a-hold, a-hold; set her two courses. Off to sea again; lay her off!' (*Temp.* 1.1.30–31, 42–43). Shakespeare's sailors accurately speak like sailors, but the nobles appear incapable of understanding what the sailors are saying or doing. Instead, they try to assert their accustomed superiority, rail at the Boatswain as a 'blasphemous ... dog' for his failure to respond to them with the deference demanded by their superior rank, and threaten him with hanging. The play's courtiers, that is, speak and act like early modern noblemen by demanding respect regardless of the situation and their own lack of expertise; they are unable to make sense of the Boatswain's utterance as anything but 'noise' expressive of 'insolen[ce]' towards their authority. In turn, the Boatswain mocks them precisely for the hollowness of their own utterances in this nautical emergency. He answers their invocation of royal sanctity, demands for deference, threats to hang him, and hollow use of imperative forms treating him as their inferior or an animal, with: 'What cares these roarers for the name of king' (*Temp.* 1.1.15–16). He rounds on the blustering courtiers with a sarcastic challenge to their offices: 'You are a councillor; if you can command these elements to silence ... use your authority' (*Temp.* 1.1.18–20).

With this short scene we see a world in which a shared national language, English, may be employed differently by speakers who differ socially. Sometimes the differences amount to something no more substantial than fashion or affectation. Often a single character will shift his or her language to signal aspiration to, mockery of, or acquiescence to another's language. Servants ape their betters, swordsmen mock duellists, lovers reluctantly unlearn their formulaic linguistic models. This can be comical. At other times, differences between speakers suggest deeper tensions within the body politic as different forms of language embody different, even opposing, sources of and conceptions of authority. This can be serious. A sailor or a gardener's speech, for example, might register the limits of the very language that grounded the nation's official pronouncements on order and degree. There is a lot at stake here, and there is much more to be said about the many languages that struggle with one another, sometimes agreeing and often conflicting, but pervasively informing Shakespeare's multi-languaged English.

NOTES

1 *OED* 'tinker', n. 1b; cf. Thomas Overbury, *Sir Thomas Ouerburie His Wife with New Elegies* (London, 1611), 'Tinker'.

2 See Walt Wolfram, 'Social Varieties of American English', *Language in the USA: Themes for the Twenty-First Century*, ed. Edward Ferguson and John R. Rockford (Cambridge: Cambridge University Press, 2004), pp. 58–75; pp. 59–60.

3 See M. M. Bakhtin, *Problems of Dostoevsky's Poetics*, trans. Caryl Emerson (Minneapolis: University of Minnesota Press, 1984), p. 201; cf. Pam Morris (ed.), *The Bakhtin Reader: Selected Writings of Bakhtin, Medvedev and Voloshinov* (London: Edward Arnold, 1994), pp. 108, 111.

4 Samuel Johnson, 'Proposals for an Edition of Shakespeare (1756)', *William Shakespeare: The Critical Heritage, Vol. 4, 1753–1765*, ed. Brian Vickers (London: Routledge, 2000), pp. 268–273; p. 269. Johnson citations from this edition.

5 Charles Barber, *The English Language: A Historical Introduction*, 2nd edn (Cambridge: Cambridge University Press, 2012), p. 188.

6 It is unclear what 'experiments' Johnson means; Catherine Nicholson suggests Lyly's ornate prose, Spenser's odd diction, Marlowe's thundering verse (*Uncommon Tongues: Eloquence and Eccentricity in the English Renaissance* (Philadelphia: University of Pennsylvania Press, 2014), p. 164). But compare Barber, *English Language*, pp. 188–189 on attempts to coin new words, as in Ralph Lever's innovations like 'endsay' for 'conclusion' or 'naysay' for 'negation', etc.

7 M. M. Bakhtin, *The Dialogic Imagination: Four Essays*, ed. Michael Holquist, trans. Caryl Emerson and Michael Holquist (Austin: University of Texas Press, 1981), pp. 326, 263.

8 Bakhtin, *Dialogic Imagination*, p. 291; cf. Morris, *Bakhtin Reader*, pp. 115, 248–249.

9 Among other commentators, see George Puttenham, *The Art of English Poesy*, ed. Frank Whigham and Wayne A. Rebhorn (Ithaca: Cornell University Press, 2007), pp. 228–230; Thomas Wilson, *Wilson's Arte of Rhetorique 1560*, ed. G. H. Mair (Oxford: Clarendon Press, 1909), pp. 162–165.

10 Paula Blank, *Broken English: Dialects and the Politics of Language in Renaissance Writings* (London: Routledge, 1996), p. 40; cf. Jonathan Hope, *Shakespeare and Language: Reason, Eloquence and Artifice in the Renaissance* (London: Arden, 2010), p. 99.

11 On Brome, see Julie Sanders's Introduction to *The Northern Lass* at Richard Brome Online: www.hrionline.ac.uk/brome/viewOriginal.jsp?play=NL&type=CRIT.
   On Ben Jonson's *Tale of a Tub*, see Manfred Görlach, 'Regional and Social Variation', *The Cambridge History of the English Language, Vol. 3: 1476–1776*, ed. Roger Lass (Cambridge University Press, 2006), pp. 459–538; p. 510.

12 See N. F. Blake, *Non-Standard Language in English Literature* (London: Deutsch, 1981), p. 81; also Görlach, 'Regional and Social Variation', p. 508.

13 Wilson, *Wilson's Arte of Rhetorique 1560*, p. 162.

14 Robert Cawdrey, *A Table Alphabeticall of Hard Usual English Words* (1604), ed. Robert A. Peters (Gainesville: Scholars' Facsimiles, 1966), sig. B1r.

15 For the dead parrot sketch, see: http://montypython.50webs.com/scripts/Series_1/53.htm.

16 Vincentio Saviolo, *Vincentio Saviolo his Practise* (London, 1595).

17 George Silver, *Paradoxes of Defence* (London, 1599), sig. B1r; see Joan Ozark Holmer, '"Draw, if you be Men": Saviolo's Significance for *Romeo and Juliet*', *Shakespeare Quarterly* 45.2 (1994): 163–189.

18 On the lover's stylised language and attitudes, see, among many others, the excellent account by Arthur Marotti, '"Love is not Love": Elizabethan Sonnet Sequences and the Social Order', *ELH* 49.2 (1982): 396–428, p. 413.

19 On Lyly's relation to humanism, see e.g. Mike Pincombe, *Elizabethan Humanism: Literature and Learning in the Later Sixteenth Century* (London: Routledge, 2013), pp. 107–124, 148–150.

20 John Lyly, *Sixe Court Comedies Often Presented and Acted before Queene Elizabeth*, ed. Edward Blount (London, 1632), 'To the Reader'.

21 *The Complete Works of John Lyly*, ed. R. W. Bond (Oxford: Clarendon Press, 1902), vol. 1, p. 202.

22 William Shakespeare, *Much Ado About Nothing*, ed. Claire McEachern (London: Arden, 2006), p. 71.

23 For the relevant passage, see Lyly, *Complete Works*, vol. 2, p. 60.

24 The critical literature is vast, but for a brief recent account of the 'great chain of meaning', see David Rollison, *A Commonwealth of the People* (Cambridge: Cambridge University Press, 2010), pp. 181–184.

25 On anti-languages, see M. A. K. Halliday, 'Anti-Languages', *American Anthropologist* 78.3 (1976): 570–584; Lee Beier, 'Anti-Language or Jargon? Canting in the English Underworld in the Sixteenth and Seventeenth Centuries', *Languages and Jargons: Contributions to a Social History of Language*, ed. Peter Burke and Roy Porter (Cambridge: Polity Press, 1995), pp. 64–101.

26 See, e.g., Ben Jonson, *The Gypsies Metamorphosed (1621)*, pp. 21–25; James Knowles (ed.), *The Cambridge Edition of the Works of Ben Jonson Online* (2015); Middleton and Dekker, *The Roaring Girle* (1611), sig. K4r; Francis Beaumont and John Fletcher, *The Beggars Bush* (1661), sig. C2v; Richard Brome, *A Jovial Crew* (1652), sig. F3r.

27 S. Musgrove, 'Thieves' Cant in *King Lear*', *English Studies* 62.1 (1981): 5–13.

28 Thomas Dekker, *Lantern and Candlelight* (1609), in Barbara Hodgdon (ed.), *The First Part of King Henry the Fourth* (Boston: Bedford, 1997), pp. 250–257; p. 253.

29 On the relationship of the language here to Robert Kett's Norfolk Rebellion of 1549, see Richard Knowles (ed.), *King Henry VI, Part Two* (London: Arden, 1999), 4.2.8n.

30 See *Certain Sermons or Homilies* (Oxford: Oxford University Press, 1840), pp. 459–460.

31 Similar uses of gardening metaphors to talk about order are pervasive, see e.g. Thomas Elyot, *The Boke Named the Gouernour* (1531), ed. H. H. S. Croft (London: Kegan Paul, 1883), Bk 1. Section 4; Henry Brinklow, *Complaynt of Roderyck Mors*, ed. J. M. Cowper (London: EETS, 1874), p. 55; Thomas Dekker, *The Seven Deadly Sinnes of London* (London, 1606), p. 28.

32 See *Certain Sermons or Homilies*, pp. 274–275.

New Technologies

9

Digital Approaches to Shakespeare's Language

There has never been a more exciting time to be working on Shakespeare's language. If you have an internet connection, fire it up. Follow the advice in this chapter, and today you could be making genuine discoveries about the context and the substance of what Shakespeare wrote:

- compare the language of one play to that of all the others to reveal the words Shakespeare falls in love with, and those he avoids, at different points in his career;
- test the claim that Shakespeare invented hundreds of words, and improve the *Oxford English Dictionary*;
- correct and expand notes in scholarly editions, and add them where they are missing;
- improve our sense of how Shakespeare fits in the print culture of his time and how he compares to other writers.

All of this is possible now and constitutes the first major benefit of digital approaches to Shakespeare. They enable us to do what literary studies has traditionally done – contextualise, historicise, debate meanings and textual cruces, search for repeated ideas and motifs within and between texts – using a more extensive evidence base than previous students could have believed possible, and with more flexible and (mostly) more reliable tools and searches.

For most of us, doing what we have always done, only more thoroughly, more reliably, and faster, should be sufficient to justify the relatively gentle learning curve required to use the set of tools and methods I will outline in the first part of this chapter. All of the sites and tools I introduce are open-access, and the instructions and links here should enable academics and their students to use them to make discoveries.

There is, though, a second reason to be interested in digital tools and approaches: with more complex analytic tools and visualization techniques, and an admittedly much steeper learning curve, we can approach Shakespeare, early modern literature, and early modern print culture in ways impossible before. Drawing on methods developed in corpus linguistics, data visualisation, and statistics, we can attempt to 'read' authors, genres, even cultures, in ways fundamentally different to previous literary or cultural studies. The key conceptual shift between the two types of digital work is that the first tends to begin with, and remain with or return to, a single word, phrase, text, or author at a single point in time, while the second typically considers larger objects of study (genres, text types, concepts) over much greater spans of time.[1]

This chapter begins with the first type of digital work and shifts in its later stages into the second (though like all scholarly distinctions, the closer you get to the dividing line, the more blurred the point of transition becomes). My aim is to show you in some detail how to do what might be termed 'basic' digital analysis and give some sense of the excitement of the more ambitious analytic techniques. But do not be misled by the term 'basic': used properly, the most straightforward techniques and searches can produce very significant insights. I begin with digital editions of Shakespeare's texts, and tools to explore them, then move on to tools that allow us to get beyond Shakespeare to early modern print culture as a whole. I end with a look beyond what it is possible to introduce in a single chapter, to models of large-scale cultural and linguistic analysis, and to the research questions we are only just being able to formulate, and which the next generation of humanities researchers will investigate.

Doing What We've Always Done, Only Better: Digital Shakespeare as Image and Text

One of the fundamental, and most useful, affordances of the digital is the easy access it gives us to Shakespeare's texts. This access comes in two ways: access to high quality images of early printed editions, and access to transcribed and edited versions of those texts. It is worth thinking about this shift from digital image files to transcribed text files, because it introduces us to the history of digital Shakespeare, and shows us something about the potential, and limitations, of the digital.

In the past, if you wanted to work on the earliest texts of Shakespeare, you had to be in a place with a rare books library. Editors of Shakespeare, and scholars of early modern literature, travelled the world to consult early copies. In the late 1930s, fears of impending bombing prompted the initiation of a project which was to lead to the digital revolution in early modern studies we are currently living through. An American team began photographing early modern books in libraries throughout the UK as a way of preserving them. After the war, this project became a company, University Microfilms, who made the page images of early modern books (eventually over 130,000 books) available to universities and libraries all over the world (at a cost).[2] Several generations of early modern scholars (mine perhaps the last) grew up spooling through reels of microfilm to read the books we were studying. In many ways, the availability of these microfilms was an advance similar to the first stage of digital advances: it allowed scholars to do what they had traditionally done (read old books) more easily and more thoroughly.

Of course, there were drawbacks to these microfilmed images: they were not always very easy to read (either because the printing of the books themselves was problematic, or because the images were unclear); in most cases, only one copy of each edition of a book was imaged (even though different copies of the 'same' early modern book often vary due to alterations during printing, binding, or subsequently); and the images were not searchable in themselves, except by the human eye. If you were looking for material on a research topic (the representation of 'snakes', for example) you had to rely on title searches in library catalogues, mentions in other scholarly literature, or hunches. There was no way to search the text of all of these books, except by reading them.[3]

Images of old books can be very useful indeed if you are doing detailed textual work, but it is digital *texts*, fully searchable by word or phrase, that really make a difference to studying Shakespeare's language. For example, imagine you are reading *Titus Andronicus*, and you come across this self-description by Aaron:

> What signifies my deadly-standing eye,
> My silence, and my cloudy melancholy,
> My fleece of woolly hair that now uncurls
> Even as an adder when she doth unroll
> To do some fatal execution?   (*Tit.* 2.3.32–36)

There are many words we might be interested in here, but let's focus on 'adder'. What does this word mean? A look in the paper, or electronic, *OED* can tell us the current meaning, and give us a sense of past shifts (if any), and that is always a good place to start. But we can go beyond that general description and ask ourselves 'Does this word have any particular resonances for Shakespeare?', 'Does he use it frequently elsewhere?', 'Is it significant in this play rather than others?'. Given scholarly interest in Shakespeare's representations of race, this passage, and the precise implications of this word, are important if we want to understand the range of Shakespearean responses to physical otherness. It makes sense at this point to ask if Shakespeare uses the word elsewhere in his plays, and if he does, if the implications there match or contrast with this passage (for example, does he use it in relation to hair, or race, or threat anywhere else?).

There are various ways you could answer this question, and they do not have to be digital. For instance, you could physically read through Shakespeare's complete works, looking for other instances of the word. No doubt this would be a commendable thing to do in itself, but as a practical search strategy it has flaws: it would take a long time; and you might well miss an instance (it is easy to get distracted by other amazing things when you read Shakespeare looking for linguistic examples, as I know well). Alternatively, you could consult a paper concordance: a book listing all the words Shakespeare uses, arranged in alphabetical order. Concordances are very useful things indeed, but the chances are you do not have one at home, or on the train, or bus, or in the classroom. There are also restrictions on the kind of searches you can do with a concordance.

So the best way to answer your question is to use an electronic text of Shakespeare, and search it using concordancing software. There are several dedicated sites, using different texts of Shakespeare, that will allow you to do just this (see 'Digital Resources'), but my go-to site for searching Shakespeare is *WordHoard*, which is not just a very good concordance program, but also able to do powerful statistical analysis. Here is how to answer our 'adder' question using *WordHoard*:

1. Go to http://Wordhoard.northwestern.edu/userman/index.html.
2. Click on 'Download and Run WordHoard'.
3. At this point *WordHoard* should download, and you will be prompted to allow your computer to run the relevant files and connect to its public site. If you don't have the necessary permissions to do this on your machine, use *Open Source Shakespeare* instead, or download *AntConc* and your own set of Shakespeare files.
4. In the 'Table of Contents' window select 'Shakespeare'.
5. From the menu options at the top of the screen select the pull-down menu 'Find'.
6. Select 'Find Words', select: 'Corpus is ' > 'Shakespeare'
   'Lemma is ' > 'adder'
7. Click 'Complete' (which will identify 'adder' as a noun) and then 'Find'.
8. A 'Search Results' window will open up, with a list of every text containing the lemma 'adder'. You can expand each result to see the context by clicking on the triangle at the left of the result – clicking on the search term in the result will open the full text in a window below for more detailed study.

At this point you are in a position to go back to traditional literary close-reading in order to assess Shakespeare's use of 'adder', both in his work generally, and specifically in *Titus*. Interesting as it would be to do that here, space is limited, so I want to address a technical distinction which is very important in doing linguistic searches. You may have noted that at step 6 above we told *WordHoard* to search for 'lemma' – what does this mean? We began with an apparently simple question, 'How many times does Shakespeare use the word "adder"?'. *WordHoard* gives us the answer twenty. But if you try this search in *Open Source Shakespeare*, or on the *Folger Digital Texts* using *AntConc*, you may well get a different number. How can this be?

Like many apparently simple questions in linguistic and digital ana-lysis, our question turns out to be less than straightforward – and digital searching requires above all that we pose our questions in ways that are entirely straightforward and unambiguous. What do we mean by the *word* 'adder' here? Shakespeare uses the word 'adder' in four different forms:

It is the bright day that brings forth the **adder** (singular; *JC* 2.1.14)

Wool of bat and tongue of dog, / **Adder's** fork and blindworm's sting (possessive; *Mac.* 4.1.15–16)

my two schoolfellows, Whom I will trust as I will **adders** fanged (plural; *Ham.* 3.4.203–204)

How she longed to eat **adders'** heads and toads carbonadoed (plural possessive; *WT* 4.4.264)

Common sense might tell us that these are all the 'same' word, but computers don't have common sense, and to a concordancing program these are four different strings of characters. So searches for the string <adder> may not return all of the forms, or they might return other words containing this string, such as *ladder* (which is what the 'Text Search' box on the front page of *Open Source Shakespeare* does). *WordHoard* returned all of the forms because we told it to search for 'lemma', the term linguists use to refer to all of the possible forms of a word. Lemma searches can be very useful: search the lemma 'be', and you get 'be', 'am', 'is', 'was' and so on. But sometimes, we might only be interested in a single form of a word: maybe we only want to see singular 'adder', or just present tense third person 'is', in which case, we need to tell the software we are using to do this.

If you do any kind of digital, or analogue searching for 'words', it is important to know the distinction between 'lemma' and 'word', and frame your search accordingly. But there are other reasons why running the 'same' search for 'adder' on different platforms can produce different results. First, and perhaps most straightforward, when we use these different search engines to search what we think of as the works of 'Shakespeare', we are actually searching different sets of texts, and texts that have been prepared differently. The text behind *WordHoard* is different to the text behind *Open Source Shakespeare*, and the *Folger Digital Texts* are different again. Sometimes the Sonnets and poems are included, sometimes not. Some 'complete' works include *The Two Noble Kinsmen*, some do not. Different editions of the text underlie these engines, and different things have been done to the texts in terms of modernisation and editorial conventions. It is up to us to be aware of these differences and their potential effects on our search results.

So, we now know how many times the lemma 'adder' appears in 'Shakespeare' according to *WordHoard*: twenty. But what does knowing this number tell us? There are many possible questions: is twenty a lot? Not very many? Does Shakespeare use this word more than his contemporaries? Does it appear only in certain plays (for example the Roman ones) or in certain contexts (associated with danger?). Notice that some of these questions could be answered digitally, and some need to be answered by human reading. To compare Shakespeare to his contemporaries, we would need to count the instances of 'adder' in the 1,244 plays of the *Visualizing English Print* extended early modern drama corpus. To get a sense of the contexts in which Shakespeare uses the word, we need a human to read the twenty instances of the lemma in Shakespeare.

There is also a more fundamental theoretical question to be asked here, which as far as I know has not been answered satisfactorily by literary or linguistic scholars: what does knowing the frequency of a word tell us about that word's meaning or significance? Common sense might suggest to us that the more frequent a word is, the more important it is to the meaning of a text; but the most frequent words in texts are those which seem to carry very little of the unique meanings of that text (they are words like 'the', 'and', 'if', and so on). How about if we exclude this type of word (function words) from our analysis, and only look at content words (nouns, adjectives, verbs)? Traditional literary scholarship often makes claims about the frequency of content words in texts without specifying the threshold that triggers a word as being 'frequent', and arguing instead for the importance of a word to the meaning of a text via traditional literary reading.[4] There are some interesting psychological questions here: how many times does an unusual word have to be repeated before human readers 'notice' it? Do we pick up on repetition subconsciously at low rates, and then become conscious of it at higher ones (for example, does the second use of an unusual word go under the radar, while the third is highly salient?). I can't begin to answer these questions in this chapter – but you as a student of literature and reading could.

There are statistical techniques which attempt to address some of these concerns about making inferences from the frequencies of words in texts. The statistical tests themselves cannot make inferences about texts of course, but there are tests that attempt to give us better bases for making inferences than simple frequency counts. The test that I have found most useful in this regard is *log-likelihood*.[5] Log-likelihood works by comparing one text by an author (the analysis text) to a larger sample of work by the same author (the reference text). It takes each word in the analysis text, computes its frequency, and then compares that score with the frequency score for the word in the larger reference sample. Effectively it asks for each word in a text, 'Is the author's use of this word in line with their normal use, or is it *more* or *less* frequent than we would expect?'. So, for every word in a text, a log-likelihood analysis tells us if the author is using it 'normally' (in which case we'll probably ignore it), or above or below their 'normal' rate (in which case we might become interested in it).

To run a log-likelihood analysis of Shakespeare in *WordHoard*, follow the following steps (I'm going to analyse *Titus Andronicus*):

1. Open and run *WordHoard*: http://wordhoard.northwestern.edu/userman/index.html.
2. In the 'Table of Contents' window select 'Shakespeare'.
3. From the menu options at the top of the screen select the pull-down menu 'Analysis'.
4. Select 'Compare Many Word Forms'.
5. In the 'Compare multiple word form frequencies' window make the following selections (or retain if they are pre-selected):
   - Word form: Lemma
   - Analysis Text: Open the list of plays and select *Titus Andronicus*
   - Reference Text: Select the folder 'Shakespeare'
   - Minimum Count: 5 (this sets a threshold for the minimum number of times a word must appear in the corpus as a whole)
   - Minimum Works: 1 (this sets a threshold for the minimum number of texts a word must appear in)
   - Report Percents As: Parts Per Ten Thousand (this gives an normalised frequency for each word, telling us how many occurrences there are in every 10,000 words – this allows us to reliably compare the frequency scores in texts of different lengths).

Check boxes: Select all of these:
   - Mark significant log-likelihood values (*WordHoard* marks significant values with up to four stars)
   - Adjust chi-square for number of comparisons

- Filter out proper names (for most analyses it makes sense to filter out proper names, as they are highly play-specific)
- Show word classes for all words (turns on *WordHoard* part of speech tags).

6. Click 'OK'.
7. The analysis will run and numerical data will appear in a new window, with words arranged in descending order of significance (i.e. the words at the top of the list are those which deviate most from Shakespeare's normal usage – either up or down).
8. At this stage you can either read the *WordHoard* spreadsheet (see Hope and Witmore, 'Language of *Macbeth*'),
9. or generate a visualization of this data by clicking 'Cloud' (bottom right of the window). This generates a word-cloud of the data: the larger a word is, the larger the shift away from Shakespeare's normal usage; black words are overused; grey ones underused.

Log-likelihood analyses are very good ways of seeding traditional literary essays on texts, since they identify words for further discussion. Note, however, that not all words that show up are equally interesting in terms of analysis. Here are the top words from *Titus* (in decreasing order of the strength of effect):

> Words markedly more frequent in *Titus:*
> emperor, empress, son, thy, rape (n), tribune, tear (n), revenge (n), roman, hand, brother, and, moor, pit, grandsire, brethren, bury, dishonour (v), thou, justice, sorrow, boy, deed, pigeon, plead, barbarous, hue, lovely, murder (n), hole, these, sign, ravish, mother, witness (v), surprise, gracious, careful, this, kneel, nephew, ease, let, fly (n), aunt
> Words markedly less frequent in *Titus:*
> be, he, sir, you, of, king, which, love (n), it, most

In *Titus*, a set of words associated with the classical setting ('empress', 'tribune', 'roman') feature very highly as overused compared to Shakespeare's work as a whole. This is hardly surprising, given the setting of the play, and obvious findings like this rarely suggest any literary questions worth pursuing (unless there's something to be made of 'empress' on gender grounds). The grim subject matter of the play is confirmed by the very strong rise in the frequency of the noun 'rape' and decline in the use of 'love' as a noun; but again, this does not tell us anything we did not know about the play, so isn't likely to be productive of further work. Perhaps more fruitful are the kinship terms that are raised in frequency ('son', 'brother', 'grandsire', 'brethren', 'mother', 'nephew', 'aunt'); and perhaps even more interesting are the shifts in pronouns: 'thou' is raised, while 'you' is lowered, and 'he' is also reduced. Most intriguing of all (to me at least) is the finding that the verb *to be* is significantly lowered in *Titus*. What could be producing this strong effect? I have no idea – which suggests that this would be a very good starting point for work on the language of the play.

Running a log-likelihood analysis is an excellent first step when starting work on any play; and it allows students to begin working with the language of a play right from the start, especially if they are directed towards the function words (pronouns, determiners, verb *to be*), and especially if they have the word-class tags turned on.[6]

Not Just Better, But Different: Changing the Scale and Scope of Literary Studies

So far, I have introduced digital techniques and tools that allow us to work with Shakespeare's texts more powerfully and efficiently, but which effectively simply improve on or speed up methods literary scholars are used to applying. However, we are now living through a revolution in the study of early modern culture. This revolution is thanks to the latest manifestation of the photographs of rare books an American group began taking in the late 1930s. These photographs were first transformed into microfilm, and then into digital image files to constitute *Early English Books Online (EEBO)*. The images had the affordances of that medium: they could be distributed easily anywhere with an internet connection, but, like the microfilm images before, they could not be searched for words.

Recent years have seen the transcription of over 60,000 of the 130,000 *EEBO* texts by the *Text Creation Partnership* to produce the *EEBO-TCP* corpus. The availability of these texts in fully searchable form does not only allow us to do traditional things faster and more effectively; it also opens up the possibility of asking entirely new questions about cultural shifts over time, and the nature of literary culture. The precise point at which the increased scale of data sets like *EEBO-TCP* changes fundamentally what we are doing is arguable: a single individual can have an excellent knowledge of the works of one writer (such as Shakespeare), so perhaps digital tools are only ever a convenient prosthesis here. But once we go beyond Shakespeare's thirty-eight plays, and start to work on early modern drama as a whole, we quickly get to a stage where our object of study is larger than any one person could 'read' and retain, even over a lifetime. There are 1,244 dramatic texts in the extended *Visualizing English Print (VEP)* drama corpus: I doubt any single person has ever read them all. But once those texts are transcribed, we can 'read' them using text analysis software, enabling us to make comparisons across the whole corpus. Where before we constructed literary arguments on tiny samples of texts, using quotations we assume (but cannot prove) to be exemplary, now we can accurately describe 'the whole' of early modern drama – and make claims about historical and generic shifts which are informed by almost every extant printed text.

For example, in work with Anupam Basu and Mike Gleicher, Michael Witmore and I have shown that generic differences are visible across the corpus of plays (with comedies and tragedies showing distinct linguistic fingerprints).[7] This is very early work, and is likely to be refined by other scholars in the future, but it does suggest, perhaps surprisingly, that attributes of texts we might consider to be high-level interpretations (for example, generic identity) have objective linguistic correlates at the relatively low levels accessible to computer searching. This raises extremely interesting questions about the nature of genre, both in abstract theoretical terms (what *is* genre?), and in specific historical instances.[8]

A key point for scholars to consider here is the question of the *proxy*. This is a topic likely to drive literary research in the area for some time to come. Simply put, digital work is constrained by the very practical issue of what we are able to count, which is rarely the same as what we want to research. In looking at genre, for example, we can't directly count 'tragedy' or 'comedy' in texts: there is nothing a piece of software can recognise. So we count things we hope act as proxies for the higher level features. The work referenced in note 7 counts a set of around one hundred linguistic features identified by the program *Docuscope*, to see if any groups of those features correlate with human assignments of plays to generic groups. These linguistic features then become our proxies for 'genre'.[9]

It will be important for literary scholars to think about the use of proxies, and the way we move from them to assumed higher-level features of texts: as a discipline we ought to be well-prepared to analyse this kind of shift. A constant danger is that we forget that our results are not directly on the thing we want to study, but on a proxy for it. And it is notable that here literary digital work tends to depart from linguistic corpus work, since linguistic corpus work tends not to treat the things it counts as proxies. Linguists really are interested in the frequencies of 'the' in a corpus in and of themselves. Literary digital scholars are more likely to be making inferences about those frequencies in terms of higher-level shifts in conceptualisation (assuming, for instance, that an increased rate of 'the' is a proxy for increased information content, or objectivity).

So what does it mean to have access to 60,000 early modern texts? *EEBO-TCP* enables us to track words and phrases through thousands of texts, and across time, like a super-charged version of the *OED* entries which try to give a sense of the historical development of a word's meanings. If we find a word or phrase in Shakespeare that seems obscure (or even one we think we understand), we can look to see how other writers used it. This is what scholarly editors traditionally do: they will often gloss a word or phrase in Shakespeare with a citation from elsewhere in Shakespeare, or from another writer from the period. Before *EEBO-TCP*, spotting these parallel uses involved much searching through paper concordances, previous editions, and luck. Now we can search 60,000 books from the period in seconds. But, of course, you can only do this if you have access to the texts, and to a search engine. The good news is that everyone, in theory, has access to about half of the texts (*EEBO-TCP* phase 1) and these could be searched, given a decent laptop, with *AntConc*. The even better news is that you don't need to download *EEBO-TCP* or *AntConc*: you can access all the *EEBO-TCP* texts via one of the most useful early modern websites: *Early Print*.

Early Print was developed as a tool to study spellings in the *EEBO-TCP* data. Its *EEBO N-gram Browser* will allow you to compare the frequencies of different spellings of the same word across the whole of the *EEBO-TCP* data set ('loue' vs. 'love' for example). This turns out to be even more fascinating than you might imagine, and Basu's work on spelling shifts is likely to revolutionise accounts of the standardisation of spelling in English. Probably more relevant to literary scholars, however, is *Early Print's EEBO-TCP Key Words in Context* search function. This allows you to search for a word or phrase in the 60,000 *EEBO-TCP* texts, and see the results in key word in context format: a single line from the text with your search term highlighted in the middle. You can also see the date, author, and title of each text – an extremely useful feature. One fascinating use of *Early Print*, excellent for showing students how to do genuine research, is to check claims in academic articles and popular websites that Shakespeare invented a certain word. Such claims are very common (at one time he was regularly cited as the first user of over 3,000 words), but they almost all turn out to be false when we look in *EEBO-TCP* for earlier uses of these words.

My paper 'Who Invented "Gloomy"? Lies People Want to Believe about Shakespeare' is a detailed study of this use of *Early Print*,[10] but here is a new example to show the value of the site. David Crystal is a rightly celebrated scholar of the English language, and Shakespeare in particular, and in a series of brief articles for *Around the Globe*, the magazine produced by Shakespeare's Globe Theatre in London, he looks at 'Williamisms' – his term for the words Shakespeare is claimed to have invented. One such notable word is 'sheeted', as used by Horatio in *Hamlet* when he describes the portents and disruptions that attended the fall of Julius Caesar:

> The graves stood tenantless and the sheeted dead
> Did squeak and gibber in the Roman streets.   (*Ham.* 1.1.115–116)

Crystal notes, 'Shakespeare would use *sheet* as a verb again (in *Ant.* 1.4.65, "when snow the pasture sheets"), but his use of *sheeted* here is original'.[11] Crystal's claim seems very plausible: surely this kind of noun-verb conversion is typical of Shakespeare's linguistic creativity, the kind of brilliant innovation only a truly great writer could come up with. Certainly, the *OED* has Shakespeare's use as the first citation, dated to 1604. But we can now test this claim using *Early Print*, as follows:

1. Go to https://earlyprint.wustl.edu/.
2. Scroll down to find the link to 'EEBO-TCP Key Words in Context' on the right of the page and click on it.
3. In the query boxes, 'Regularized spellings' should already be selected as 'Corpus' (if it isn't, select it now).
4. In 'Search Pattern' enter 'sheeted'.
5. Leave other fields blank, and click 'View Words'.
6. The first result of your search should look like this:
   A03032 1598   NOT SPECIFIED   The riddles of Heraclitus and Dem ... made his heart full soar To set them in a sheet, alas why should it be, They had been **sheeted** now.

Immediately we can see that the first result is from 1598, pre-dating Shakespeare's use of the word in *Hamlet*. The preceding number, A03032, tells us that this result is found in TCP text number A03032. 'Not Specified' appears where the author's name should be, letting us know that this is an anonymous text, and the title is *The riddles of Heraclitus and Dem* ... (the title is truncated to save space). In this case, it is quite hard from the context given to understand how the word is being used, so it would be wise for us to check the full text. If you happen to have a download of all of the TCP files, you can do that by searching for A03032, and doing a simple word search on the file. Alternatively, within *Early Print*, you can click on the TCP file number, and this will take you to the text record at the main TCP site:

https://quod.lib.umich.edu/cgi/t/text/text-idx?c=eebo;idno=A03032

Because this text is part of TCP phase 1, the whole text is available on this site. Click on 'View entire text' (right-hand side of your screen) to see it. At this point, depending on your browser, you should be able to use your pull-down 'Edit' menu to 'Find' or 'Search' the file for 'sheeted' – which you will find in riddle 35.

Riddle 35 turns out to be a rather racy poem, telling the story of an officer who is having an affair with a married woman (patching the husband's coat, as the poem has it). While visiting his mistress, the officer posts a sentry, to warn him in case the husband comes back early; but the sentry falls asleep, and the husband catches the couple naked in bed. Before all their neighbours, the husband accuses his wife of adultery, but contrary to expectations, she is not ashamed. Instead, she points out that he has been stealing his neighbours' corn, and asks for a divorce.

The husband is abashed, and refuses to instigate divorce proceedings, because this would result in the couple being paraded in church, clad only in sheets, as a punishment for their crime. This is where 'sheeted' appears – as part of a rather good joke:

> it made his hart full sore
> To set them in a sheete, alas why should it bee,
> They had been sheeted now three howers and somwhat more.

In other words, the husband did not want to cause the couple to be sheeted (punished in church) given that they had just been sheeted (in bed) for three hours. They all kiss and make up.

So *Early Print* can enable us to go beyond the *OED*, and reject claims about Shakespeare's word-coining. It can do this because it effectively allows us to recreate the searches done by the original readers for the dictionary in the nineteenth century, but in our recreated searches we read far more texts than they could and do so more systematically (though not perfectly).[12] But *Early Print*, and other digital tools, enable us to do more than simply improve on what we have been doing for hundreds of years. Scaling-up allows us to 'read' culture in-depth in a way impossible before today. I will end this chapter with two examples of this – one focusing on a single word, and one, much more complex, on tracking 'discourse'.

My first example concerns the word 'sequent', which is a word Shakespeare seems particularly, and peculiarly, fond of. In the *VEP* corpus of core drama, the word appears seven times, and all of these instances are in plays by Shakespeare. No other dramatist in the period uses the word. Shakespeare does not invent this word – it is well-established in the language before his birth – but for some reason, he is fond of it, and it marks his language out. So where did Shakespeare get this word from?

We can use *Early Print* to get a picture of the movement of 'sequent' through early modern print culture, and to get a sense of its associated meanings and connotations by seeing the types of text it occurs in. To do this for 'sequent' (or any other word), simply repeat the key word in context search outlined above, using 'sequent' as the search term. This search finds

367 instances of the word in *EEBO-TCP*, with many books using the term multiple times. Reading through the results in key word in context format makes something very clear: in by far the majority of cases, 'sequent' is being used as a bibliographical reference term, where the reader is referred to a numbered line or section of a work, and the following ('sequent') sections. For example,

> A68172 1566   Heskyns, Thomas. The parliament of Chryste auouchi …
> Chrystes words: This is my body, be not figurative. Lib. 2 cap. 42. 43. 44. &
> **sequent**.

Strikingly, almost every use of 'sequent' in an English book before Shakespeare's first use of it in 1598 (*Love's Labour's Lost*) is in this sense, and almost every text that uses the term is a religious polemic like that of Heskyns. The one exception stands out in the *Early Print* key word in context lists because it is the only recorded use of 'sequent' in continuous prose, and as a full adjective rather than a bibliographical convention. In fact, there are two uses of 'sequent' in this previously unseen way in the same text:

> A08452 1585   Ocland, Christopher The valiant actes and victorious
> As though in fight the **sequent** day, should bring his fall [i.e.fatal] end
> And in the **sequent** spring, the surging flood with navy vast …

Ocland's *Valiant actes* is a now little-known text that perhaps deserves more attention from Shakespeareans, and early modern scholars more generally. It is a translation by John Sharrock of a Latin poem written by Christopher Ocland. The Latin poem is a long, jingoistic, celebration of the victories of the English, which was prescribed for teaching in all English schools in the late 1580s (though we do not know how effective this prescription was). Sharrock's translation is presumably a crib – perhaps for teachers rather than pupils. I can't prove it of course, but Sharrock's translation of Ocland looks a better bet for Shakespeare's source of 'sequent' than the interminable works of religious controversy that account for all but two of the pre-Shakespeare instances that survive (it is notable that none of the Shakespearean uses of 'sequent' make any play on the technical bibliographical sense). Shakespeare was an avid reader of British history in search of material for plays. It may be that other rare words in Ocland will turn up in his plays. Here we see how digital tools allow us to 'read' the progress of a word through print culture, assessing its likely resonances at the time, and identifying possible sources for the sense in which Shakespeare comes to use it; and we also see a common side-effect of large-scale digital searches: neglected works come suddenly into the limelight alongside canonical texts.

If we can follow one word through the print record using *Early Print*, it is now also possible to attempt to follow groups of words, using more complex statistical techniques that look at semantic and collocational associations between groups of words to establish themes or concepts. Several projects have been investigating ways of doing this, and one recent paper demonstrates some of the exciting potential of the techniques, as well as some of the current limitations.[13] The study I will end with, Jaehoon Lee *et al.* in the *Journal of Cultural Analytics*, gives some sense of the ambition and potential of digital approaches to culture. The researchers ask a much more complex version of my 'sequent' question, seeking to identify word clusters to do with the concepts of 'Moor' and otherness in the periods before and after the writing of *Othello*. Their aim is to situate Shakespeare's use of these terms in the discourse of his own period (something many traditional literary studies have attempted to do, using necessarily highly selective evidence from contemporary texts). The paper uses two statistical techniques: topic modelling and word2vec. Briefly put, both techniques attempt to identify groups of words that can be seen to appear together regularly across a number of texts. Using the whole of *EEBO-TCP*, it is possible to identify 'topics' or associated word-fields, that correspond to what we might call 'the discourse of X'. The paper intriguingly, and controversially, suggests that the language associated with 'Moor' in *Othello* is more closely aligned to the discourse of trade found in travel and economic works, than to the language surrounding Moorish characters in other plays. Other playwrights use word-groups that associate 'Moor' with race and otherness; Shakespeare seems to ignore this discourse tradition.

Jaehoon Lee *et al.* would be the first to admit that their techniques are still in development, and their conclusions must be taken as preliminary, but the ambition of their paper, 'reading' discourses across thousands of texts shifting in real time, gives a sense of what may be possible in the future. Historicisation has long been an aim of literary and historical studies: I grew up as a scholar in a period dominated by New Historicism, a literary and historical method that prototypically matched one canonical text with one non-canonical one to produce a 'reading' of text and culture. We are now entering a period where it will be possible to historicise texts against tens of thousands of non-canonical texts: if we begin with the desire to speak with the dead, we must learn first to listen to the unread.

Digital Resources

AntConc (Laurence Anthony, Waseda University)
www.laurenceanthony.net/software/antconc/

General-purpose concordance program. There is extensive support for *AntConc* available on the web. For an excellent starter lesson, see Heather Froehlich, 2015, 'Corpus Analysis with *AntConc*': https://programminghistorian.org/lessons/corpus-analysis-with-antconc

Early English Books Online-Text Creation Partnership (EEBO-TCP)
www.textcreationpartnership.org/tcp-eebo/
Homepage for the project, with download links.

Early Print (Anupam Basu with Steve Pentecost, Douglas Knox, and Joseph Loewenstein, Washington University, St Louis)
https://earlyprint.wustl.edu/
This site gives access to the entire *EEBO-TCP* corpus. Other sites which enable you to search *EEBO-TCP* (unlike *Early Print*, these may involve registration/subscription):
Lancaster CQPWeb https://cqpweb.lancs.ac.uk/
Mark Davies *Corpus* https://corpus.byu.edu/
JISC Historical Texts http://historicaltexts.jisc.ac.uk/ (UK only)

Visualising English Print (VEP) (Mike Gleicher *et al.*, Wisconsin-Madison University, Strathclyde University, Folger Shakespeare Library)
http://graphics.cs.wisc.edu/WP/vep/
Downloadable, curated corpora of Shakespeare (multiple versions and formats), early modern drama, early modern scientific texts, and others. Includes a customisable on-line tagger (*Ubiquity*).

WordHoard (Martin Mueller and Philip R. 'Pib' Burns, Northwestern University)
http://wordhoard.northwestern.edu/userman/index.html
A deeply tagged corpus of Shakespeare. Allows for complex statistical analysis (e.g. log-likelihood) and simpler word searches. Excellent supporting documentation.
Other sites enabling you to search different versions of the Shakespeare corpus:
Folger Digital Texts www.folgerdigitaltexts.org/
Open Source Shakespeare www.opensourceshakespeare.org/

NOTES

1 See Ted Underwood, *Why Literary Periods Mattered: Historical Contrast and the Prestige of English Studies* (Stanford: Stanford University Press, 2013), especially chapter 6, 'Digital Humanities and the Future of Literary History', pp. 157–175.

2 See Erica Zimmer and Meaghan Brown *et al.* (eds.), 'History of Early English Books Online', *Folgerpedia*, https://folgerpedia.folger.edu/History_of_Early_English_Books_Online.

3 See Ian Gadd, 'The Use and Misuse of *Early English Books Online*', *Literature Compass* 6.3 (2009): 680–692.

4 See the discussion of Frank Kermode's comments on 'blood' in *Macbeth* in Jonathan Hope and Michael Witmore, 'The Language of *Macbeth*', *Macbeth: The State of Play*, ed. Ann Thompson (London, Bloomsbury, 2014), pp. 183–208. Pre-print downloadable at http://winedarksea.org/?page_id=1990.

5 For a good introduction to log-likelihood, see the *WordHoard* documentation at http://WordHoard.northwestern.edu/userman/analysis-comparewords.html.
     Michael Witmore and I discuss this test in more detail in 'The Language of *Macbeth*'.

6 Another interesting *WordHoard* feature, which can combine well with log-likelihood analysis, is 'Track Word Form Over Time'. This allows you to compare Shakespeare's use of a word or lemma across his career.

7 See Anupam Basu, Jonathan Hope, and Michael Witmore, 'The Professional and Linguistic Communities of Early Modern Dramatists', *Community-Making in Early Stuart Theatres: Stage and Audience*, ed. Roger D. Sell, Helen Wilcox, and Anthony W. Johnson (London: Routledge, 2014), pp. 63–94; Michael Witmore, Jonathan Hope, and Michael Gleicher, 'Digital Approaches to the Language of Shakespearean Tragedy', *The Oxford Handbook of Shakespearean Tragedy*, ed. Michael Neill and David Schalkwyk (Oxford: Oxford University Press, 2016), pp. 316–335; Jonathan Hope and Michael Witmore, 'The Hundredth Psalm to the Tune of "Green Sleeves": Digital Approaches to the Language of Genre', *Shakespeare Quarterly* 61.3 (2010): 357–390.

8 For a radical questioning of the notion of 'genre' in the period, see Andy Kesson, 'Was Comedy a Genre in English Early Modern Drama?', *British Journal of Aesthetics* 54.2 (2014): 213–225.

9 Recent work in literary modernism has explored the creation of proxies for such high-level concepts as the influence of the haiku on English-language poetry and 'stream of consciousness'. See Hoyt Long and Richard Jean So, 'Literary Pattern Recognition: Modernism between Close Reading and Machine Learning', *Critical Inquiry* 42 (Winter 2016): 235–267; Hoyt Long and Richard Jean So, 'Turbulent Flow: A Computational Model of World Literature', *Modern Language Quarterly* 77.3 (September 2016): 345–367.

10 Jonathan Hope, 'Who Invented "Gloomy"? Lies People Want to Believe about Shakespeare', *Memoria di Shakespeare* 3 (2016): 21–45. Open access at: http://ojs.uniroma1.it/index.php/MemShakespeare/article/view/14167/13898.

11 David Crystal, 'Citing Scripture for My Purpose', *Around the Globe* 48 (2011): 20–21. PDF available from www.davidcrystal.com/books-and-articles/shakespeare.

12 If you search for 'sheeted' in *Early Print*, you may be surprised to see that your results do not contain Shakespeare's use of 'sheeted'. Nothing has gone wrong. The explanation is that while TCP contains two texts of *Hamlet*, the first quarto and the first folio, neither of these texts has the 'sheeted' passage, which is only present in Q2, the second quarto – a reminder not to treat TCP, or any data set, as 'complete'.

13 See, for example, the Linguistic DNA project: www.linguisticdna.org/. The paper I discuss is James Jaehoon Lee, Blaine Greteman, Jason Lee, and David Eichmann, 'Linked Reading: Digital Historicism and Early Modern Discourses of Race around Shakespeare's *Othello*', *Journal of Cultural Analytics* (2018). Open access at: http://culturalanalytics.org/2018/01/linked-reading-digital-historicism-and-early-modern-discourses-of-race-around-shakespeares-othello.

10

HUGH CRAIG

Authorship, Computers, and Comparative Style

The beginning of Macbeth's soliloquy in Act 2, scene 1 is one of the most recognisable passages in the canon. 'Is this a dagger which I see before me, / The handle toward my hand? Come, let me clutch thee' (*Mac.* 2.1.33–34). The words may be familiar but they still have some secrets. On first inspection, what stands out in the first of these lines is the word 'dagger' itself, and the main verb 'see', and then after that the pronoun 'I'. The words which make up the rest of the line – 'is', 'this', 'a', 'which', 'before', and 'me' – have a grammatical function but are near-invisible. They have a meaning, and are duly processed, but barely impinge on the consciousness of a listener or reader. Yet one of them, the relative pronoun 'which', is by some lights an important element in Shakespeare's style. Shakespeare's characters use it more often than the norm for the dialogue of his day. It is one of a bundle of similar words – words with a grammatical function rather than a meaning in the usual sense – which together can be used to make a quantitative model of Shakespeare's style, a skeletal representation of his characteristic language use at the level of syntax and construction.

The higher frequency of 'which' in Shakespeare passages reflects a style in which precision is marked, to the extent that relative clauses are included, and are headed by a relative pronoun rather than leaving it understood.[1] A translation of this passage into modern English begins 'Is this a dagger I see in front of me', losing a little of the cadence of the original even before the change to the last phrase.[2] As it happens, 'which' is important in the prosody of the line, bearing a stress which completes the third iambic foot. This is the heaviest stress in the line in Antony Sher's performance of this passage.[3]

After the speech Macbeth exits and Lady Macbeth enters for a soliloquy of her own: 'That which hath made them drunk, hath made me bold' (2.2.1). There is another relative 'which' in this line, and two instances of 'hath', which is another marker of Shakespeare passages as opposed to those of his peers. Macbeth returns and has a fraught exchange with Lady Macbeth including his account of the killing of Duncan: 'There's one did laugh in's sleep, and one cried "Murder!", / That they did wake each other' (2.2.25–26). In this pair of lines there are two instances of 'did', another inconspicuous word which Shakespeare favours, and an instance of one more such word, 'that' as a conjunction.

Stylometry and Shakespeare's Style

These so-called 'function' words, 'which' as a relative, 'hath', 'did' and 'that' as a conjunction, are not the usual materials for a stylistic analysis but they are certainly characteristic of Shakespeare – that much can be shown empirically – and they do yield some indications of larger stylistic structures which make intuitive sense. They are readily countable and are one of the staples of stylometric studies using computation to determine what is distinctive about an author's style, in order either to describe that style, or to determine whether a part or the whole of a work was written by that author.

Stylometric analysis is the quantitative study of linguistic style. In recent work, it is computer-assisted, and it is most often used for authorship attribution in the case of disputed or anonymous plays. This chapter will demonstrate a method called Linear Discriminant Analysis which can compare large numbers of texts by different playwrights, on the basis of counts of a set of individual words, and can be used to reveal what is distinctive about their style in general or about their use of pre-selected elements of language. Illustrating this process should help readers towards an understanding of how stylometric analysis can discriminate between one writer's work and another's. But rather than offering a full-blown case-study of attribution methods, this chapter will aim at something a little different. I will explore how this computational 'distant reading' method, which arrays texts and text segments with quantitative tools, can generate material for a novel kind of comparative 'close reading' that can help us see new things in both Shakespearean and non-Shakespearean text segments.

Our interest is in what is distinctive about Shakespeare's style, but in a quantitative study this can only be established by comparison with the style of others. My control set for this purpose is a collection of 146 plays written for professional companies, first performed between 1580 and 1619, and all confidently attributed to authors or pairs or teams of authors other than Shakespeare.[4] My Shakespeare set is the twenty-eight plays which are usually accepted as Shakespeare's unassisted work, and then the portions of seven collaborative plays, the parts of them which are identified by the *New Oxford Shakespeare* as Shakespeare's.[5] The full corpus is thus 181 plays: 28

wholly by Shakespeare, the Shakespeare portions of 7 others, and 146 plays by other writers.

I started with a set of 225 taken from the class of function words already mentioned. Some of these words include quite different grammatical functions – 'no' as an adjective, as in 'no cause', and 'no' as an exclamation, for example. This and eighteen others, including two already mentioned, 'which' as relative and interrogative, and 'that' as conjunction, demonstrative and relative, were tagged to separate these homographs. This expanded the list to 254 function words and function word homographs. I then found the 100 most common of these function-word forms in my corpus. There are 26,962 different words in my Shakespeare sample, and 49,322 in my sample of plays by others first performed in the years 1580 to 1619, so using just 100 is a severe restriction. However, these words account for more than half of all the running words in the plays.[6] They are markers of the infrastructure of discourse, forming the grammatical frames of sentences. Their frequencies – relative abundances or scarcities – are a remarkable source of information about changes and contrasts in style, one which is often overlooked because these are words which do not have obvious meaning in themselves, but rather a less obvious structural function. Moreover, they are better candidates than words with more obvious meaning like 'lord' and 'love' when we wish to put passages with different settings, genres, plot material, and situations on the same footing. At one end of the range in the chosen 100 words are some extremely common words like 'the', which on average constitutes around 3 per cent of the total of words, so we expect around 15 instances in a 500-word segment. At the other end are the merely regular, as with 'thus', on average 0.1 per cent of the words, so that we expect one instance in every other segment.

As a first step, Linear Discriminant Analysis standardises all the word counts so that each individual count is expressed as a difference from the overall average for that word.[7] The absolute frequency of the word is thus eliminated as a factor, and the comparatively rare word 'thus' potentially contributes as much as the commonest word, 'the', to the analysis. For this reason, it is preferable to limit the disparity in overall frequency and use just 100 words. In addition, a smaller variable set is easier to interpret.

As units of analysis, I chose text segments 500 words long, rather than full plays or larger units like acts. 500-word segments are convenient because more often than not the chosen section falls within a scene or even within a single exchange between a stable set of characters, making it easier to understand what is going on in stylistic terms. These segments are long enough to bring a rudimentary mixture of styles, however, so that the more extreme idiosyncrasies are balanced out. I take words 1 to 500, 501 to

1,000, and so on, ignoring act and scene boundaries, excluding prefatory matter, headings and stage directions, and including any residue of dialogue in the last segment. The 181-play corpus yields 6,955 segments in all, 1,403 from the Shakespeare group and 5,552 from the group of plays by others.

Using smaller segments in this way highlights variation within an author's work as well as the patterns that persist through all or almost all of it. Authors have styles, in these terms a characteristic profile of consistent relatively heavy or light use of given words. This is what makes attribution work possible, allowing the researcher to check the profile of a new work against the author's established profile and make a judgement about whether the disputed work fits or not. At the same time authors vary in their writing style. They may have an early or a late style, a comic or a tragic style, or a new style in imitation of some other writer. With quantitative methods we can place some segments close to a writer's overall norm and others at the extreme of their departure from it. This variation places a limit on how certain we can be about an attribution. Fortunately, we can establish empirically from a given canon what are the bounds of this variation. Based on the author's performance elsewhere, it is possible to declare, for instance, that a disputed work departs from an author's core profile so markedly that it is unlikely to be his or hers.

Linear Discriminant Analysis works by giving each word-variable from 'the' to 'thus' a weighting, so that some contribute strongly to the result and some hardly at all. The rule for arriving at the weightings is that together they should provide the best possible separation between the two sets of samples. The procedure also calculates a score for each segment by multiplying each standardised word count for the segment by its weighting and then adding these products together.

To help understand the model in stylistic terms, there are various avenues. The words with the largest weightings in the positive and negative direction help reveal the structures that are more or less common in the two groups of plays. We can consider what a markedly heavy or light use of a given word implies about the characteristic style of the author. Another strategy is to examine the outliers among the segments. They are examples of the stylistic contrast taken to extremes and thus should make its characteristics more obvious. We read these sections of the plays, characterise their style, and generalise this to the overall contrast in styles presented by the Linear Discriminant Function. We can also identify which words made the most difference with each segment and look at them in context.

The Linear Discriminant Function is a way to isolate what is specifically Shakespearean about the dialogue of the plays. These are tendencies within a shared language. All 100 words are known to all the writers and they will

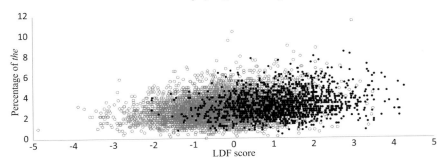

Figure 1 500-word segments of Shakespeare plays and of plays by others: Linear Discriminant Function scores and percentage counts of the word 'the'.

use all of them at some time, but at different rates of regularity and frequency. We identify the segments as Group 1, Shakespeare, and Group 2, non-Shakespeare, and instruct the procedure to define a composite variable that best distinguishes between the groups, so that as many Shakespeare segments as possible have higher scores than as many non-Shakespeare segments as possible.

Results

Figure 1 shows the segments' scores on the function (horizontal axis) set against their percentage counts of the word 'the' (vertical axis), to provide a point of reference and scatter the points for easier visualisation.

There are a group of Shakespeare segments at the Shakespeare end and a group of non-Shakespeare segments at the non-Shakespeare end, and then progressively more mixed groupings towards the middle. Shakespeare segments, the black circles, appear generally to the right of the non-Shakespeare segments, the grey circles. Nevertheless, there is a considerable overlap. Non-Shakespeare segments can have high scores on the function and Shakespeare segments can have low scores. There is a bias in Shakespeare towards a certain kind of discourse, or a mixture of certain kinds of discourse, for whatever reason, but no absolute distinction. The discriminant function, as already discussed, is constructed in such a way as to maximise the difference in scores between Shakespeare segments and the rest, and the chart shows that a strong, but not overwhelming, result has been achieved.

Looking at the vertical axis, Shakespeare is evidently a little higher on 'the', which is the most common word in the corpus, and (as discussed later)

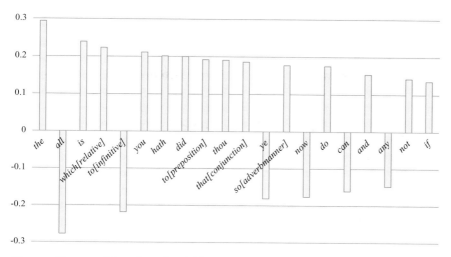

Figure 2 Top 20 weights of word-variables in a Linear Discriminant Function based on 100 function words, with Shakespeare play segments as Group 1, non-Shakespeare play segments as Group 2. Positive weightings are the words favoured by the Shakespeare segments.

the most heavily weighted Shakespeare marker in the function. Figure 1 shows that frequencies of this word have a higher centre of gravity, as it were, in Shakespeare.

Figure 2 shows the twenty words with the strongest weighting, positive – where Shakespeare is a frequent user – and negative – where he tends to avoid the word.

We can see some broader patterns in the words singled out by the analysis. 'Hath', 'thou', and 'that' as a conjunction are all forms that were in retreat at the time, and become progressively rarer in the play texts over the years. 'Hath' was being replaced by 'has', 'thou' by 'you', and 'that' as a conjunction was increasingly omitted.[8] 'Did' is weighted positively, indicating that Shakespeare uses more of this form relatively. Its commonest use in the plays is in the older 'unregulated' form of positive declaratives, as in 'I did consent, / And often did beguile her of her tears' (*Oth.* 1.3.154–155), rather than 'beguiled her'.[9] Shakespeare's frequent recurrence to this word again indicates that his language is old-fashioned. The very common word 'you' is positively weighted, as well as the word 'thou', and this indicates that Shakespeare uses more of the second person pronouns generally. (Admittedly, 'ye' is negatively weighted, but this is a much rarer form.) 'All', 'now', 'can', and 'any' are words used most often in the plays for emphasis and as filler words, rather than bearing any syntactic weight. They may well make dialogue more verisimilar. Shakespeare has fewer of these.

'The' and Shakespeare's Style

The definite article 'the' is the word-variable with the strongest weighting in the function. We can examine segments with very high and very low counts of this word to help understand what the variations in incidence mean in terms of style.[10] Figure 1 shows that there is a segment – by one of the non-Shakespeare authors, as it happens – in which instances of 'the' make 11.4 per cent of all the words, 57 out of 500. This is the seventeenth segment of Thomas Heywood's tragedy *The Rape of Lucrece*.[11] This segment includes a song defining what sort of man goes to what sort of tavern – the 'man of war' goes to 'The Drum', and so on.[12] Songs are not constrained by any requirement to resemble speech, so can take language patterns to extremes, as in this case. There are thirty-three instances of 'the' in the twenty-two lines of the song which are included in the segment. This is followed by a report of what has happened to Prince Sextus, with reference to 'the messenger' and 'the proud king'.[13] In this case insistent external reference brings an abundance of instances.

The same is true of a song in John Marston's comedy *Jack Drum's Entertainment* celebrating 'the hogshead, the barrel, the kilderkin, the firkin' and so on.[14] They are invoked as entities everyone will recognise. In Ben Jonson plays, Puritans are heavy users of 'the'. The article calls on a shared circle of meaning and affiliation. In *The Alchemist*, Tribulation Wholesome declares that 'These chastisements are common to the Saints, / And such rebukes we of the Separation must bear.'[15] In *Bartholomew Fair*, Zeal-of-the-Land Busy says to his followers as they pass by the stalls, 'Look not toward them, hearken not: the place is Smithfield, or the field of Smiths, the grove of hobby-horses and trinkets, the wares are the wares of devils. And the whole fair is the shop of Satan!'[16]

As You Like It has one segment scoring very high on 'the', in large part the result of the frequent recourse to this word in Touchstone's catalogue of the causes of quarrels.

> I will name you the degrees: the first, the retort courteous; the second, the quip modest; the third, the reply churlish; the fourth, the reproof valiant; the fifth, the countercheck quarrelsome; the sixth, the lie with circumstance; the seventh, the lie direct.　　　　　　　　　　　　　　　　(5.4.79–83)[17]

Other Shakespeare segments with high scores bring us closer to understanding the relationship between style and variations in incidence of 'the'. One is from *The Winter's Tale*. In this segment Cleomenes and Dion share impressions of the setting of the oracle and its pronouncement, and of the likely consequences of their report at the Bohemian court. This is unusual in that they are comparing notes rather than informing each other.

Thus they can refer to common knowledge via 'the' – 'the burst / And the ear-deaf'ning voice o'th'oracle' (3.1.8–9).[18]

Ariel's exchange with Prospero about the storm in *The Tempest* includes many instances of 'the' in closed, directed discussion of a shared topic. They talk of 'the foaming brine' (1.2.211) and 'the rest o'th'fleet' (1.2.226). The definite article here adds to a sense of downrightness and precise specification. This is not a speculative or introductory discourse but a view from *in medias res*. Menenius's fable of the belly in *Coriolanus* also has a concentration of instances of 'the', since characters in the story do not have proper names but are referred to as 'the belly', 'the arm', 'the tongue', and so on (1.1.80, 99, 100).

Figure 1 also shows that it is possible for a playwright to write 500 words of dialogue with no instances at all of 'the', but also how rare this is, occurring just once in 6,955 segments, in the fifteenth segment of George Chapman's comedy *The Gentleman Usher*.[19] Prince Vincentio is playing on the vanity of Bassiolo, the gentleman usher of the title. The discourse is reflexive, focusing on the nature of the exchange they are having, including the question of what Bassiolo should call Vincentio, and has no recourse to the kind of specification which brings the definite article.

Other segments with low counts give more insight into the kinds of discourse which tend to have very little recourse to 'the'. The discussion of love early in Act 5 of Thomas Dekker's comedy *Old Fortunatus* is not anchored to detail but has illustrations lightly touched in. Instead of the definite article, there are plurals with no article, indefinite articles, or generic singulars with no article:

> He's mad, whose eyes on painted cheeks do dote,
> O Galloway; such read beauty's book by rote.
> He's mad, that pines for want of a gay flower,
> Which fades when grief doth blast, or sickness lower,
> Which heat doth wither, and white age's frost
> Nips dead …[20]

Discourse about people, rather than things concrete or abstract, also can produce segments with very few instances. In the twenty-second segment of John Fletcher's comedy *Monsieur Thomas*, Sebastian and his daughter Dorothy discuss Dorothy's brother Thomas. Sebastian despises Thomas for being pious and going to bed early.[21] In Sebastian's speech of fourteen lines, there are no instances of 'the', but negatives, indefinite articles, and pronouns. This is a casual, questioning, speculative portrait. The main reference is through pronouns.

> Thou liest, thou hast marred him,
> Thou, and thy prayer books: I do disclaim him:

Did not I take him singing yesternight
A godly ballad, to a godly tune too,
And had a catechism in his pocket, Damsel,
One of your dear disciples, I perceive it.
When did he ride abroad since he came over.
What tavern has he used to? what things done
That shows a man, and mettle?   (3.2.6–14)

Shakespeare does have one segment with as low as 0.4 per cent, or two instances – the twentieth segment of *A Midsummer Night's Dream* (3.2.254–312). This is highly unusual for Shakespeare. It is exceptionally free of reference to shared knowledge of absent entities. The exchange between Hermia, Helena, Lysander, and Demetrius is directly personal, by turns insulting, placatory, angry, and indignant.

Shakespeare uses the word 'the' more often than his peers. Passages with unusually high concentrations of this word often give a heavy, dark impression. They may have songs that are simple, bold, and repetitive, or narratives with a high degree of specification. Passages with low concentrations, on the other hand, have fewer references outside the here and now arena of interaction, often because of the intensity of the immediate relationship, or fevered attention to a crisis.

Shakespeare's Neglect of 'All'

Shakespeare evidently uses the word 'all' less often than his peers. The weighting of this word in the Linear Discriminant Function is negative, and in overall strength second only to 'the' (Figure 2). Shakespeare does use 'all' sometimes – the lowest count for one of his plays is still just 0.25 per cent, in *Twelfth Night*, where there are 49 instances among the almost 20,000 words spoken – but he consistently underuses it by comparison with his contemporaries. His highest count is 0.72 per cent for the parts of *Timon of Athens* deemed to be by Shakespeare.[22] This is an outlier, and the next highest is just under 0.6 per cent, for *Taming of the Shrew*, which would be only a middling count for a non-Shakespeare play. There are 77 non-Shakespeare plays in the set of 146 non-Shakespeare plays with higher counts than *Shrew*. The count for *Twelfth Night* is lower than for any of the non-Shakespeare plays, even though, with four times as many plays in this set, they have more opportunities to range lower (and higher).

George Chapman is an especially high user of this word.[23] The two highest non-Shakespeare plays are his *Byron's Conspiracy* (highest) and *Revenge of Bussy* (second highest). He uses it to amplify the grand rhetoric of his tragic heroes. Laffin, in *Byron's Conspiracy*, has a list of deeds he says he can perform for the king, ending with the promise to make

> Midday turn midnight; to dissolve all laws
> Of nature, and of order, argue power
> Able to work all, I can make all good,
> And all this tell the King.[24]

Passages with high concentrations of 'all' appear in comedies as well. Frederick, in John Fletcher's play *The Chances*, comments that

> men say gold
> Does all, engages all, works through all dangers:
> Now I say beauty can do more: The King's exchequer,
> Nor all his wealthy Indies, could not draw me
> Through half those miseries this piece of pleasure
> Might make me leap into: we are all like sea-cards,
> All our endeavours and our motions,
> (As they do to the north) still point at beauty.   (1.10.48–55)

Shakespeare does less of this. He writes long stretches of dialogue without a single instance. There are four successive 500-word segments of *Romeo and Juliet* with zero counts (2.3.89–2.5.38). This encompasses exchanges between Mercutio and Benvolio, Romeo's entrance, the encounter with the Nurse and Peter and the first part of the scene in which Nurse returns to Juliet. There is banter, led by Mercutio, the Nurse's expostulations, and Juliet's lament, a wide range of styles, but not the recourse to summary, generalisation, or sweeping statement that would bring one or more instances of 'all'.

Shakespeare's dialogue has relatively frequent recourse to 'the', and uses 'all' less than the run of his contemporaries. The first suggests his writing is more concrete, and the second that he is less prone to filler words and to sweeping generalisations.

Segments from the Least Shakespearean End of the Spectrum

The styles of the segments which appear at either extreme of the Linear Discriminant Function provide a second avenue for understanding the differences between Shakespeare's writing and that of his contemporaries that the procedure has identified. They are passages displaying the characteristics that differentiate Shakespeare's style from that of his peers with special sharpness and consistency. Focusing on whole segments also reminds us that within the Shakespeare segments there is a range from highly characteristic – adhering closely and consistently to the overall Shakespeare

Table 1 *Segments scoring lowest on the Linear Discriminant Function*

Author	Play	Segment #	Act, scene and lines[*]	Linear Discriminant Function score	Date[**]	Genre[**]
Fletcher, John	*Humorous Lieutenant*	39	4.5.45 to 4.6.5	−4.88	1619	Tragicomedy
Middleton, Thomas	*Mad World My Masters*	1	1.1.1–54	−3.87	1608	Comedy
Fletcher, John	*Loyal Subject*	30	3.4.46 to 4.5.33	−3.73	1618	Tragicomedy
Middleton, Thomas	*Trick to Catch the Old One*	31	4.4.239–302	−3.58	1605	Comedy
Fletcher, John	*Valentinian*	15	2.4.33 to 2.5.68	−3.52	1614	Tragedy

[*] Lineation as in Bowers (Fletcher plays) and *Thomas Middleton: The Collected Works*, ed. Gary Taylor and John Lavagnino (Oxford: Clarendon Press, 2007) (Middleton plays).
[**] Date of first performance and genre from *DEEP: Database of Early English Playbooks*.

norms – to aberrant – passages written by Shakespeare but on this occasion, for whatever reason, unlike his usual style. Here I will concentrate on the extremes across the full corpus to bring out the contrast most fully.

Table 1 lists the five lowest-scoring segments, those with the greatest concentration of features the procedure has identified as unlike Shakespeare.

Just two authors are represented, with two plays from the 1615 to 1619 half-decade, one from the 1610 to 1614 half-decade, and two from the 1605 to 1609 half-decade. Given the eight decades available over the span 1580 to 1619, there is a bias towards later plays here. The history genre is not represented, but all the three other main genres are.

The dramatic material in these passages singled out as remote in style from Shakespeare is diverse. The *Humorous Lieutenant* segment covers an interview between Celia, the disguised daughter of King Seleucus, and the lascivious old King Antigonus. This is a high-stakes scene with soaring rhetoric and bold pronouncements. The segment from *Mad World My Masters* is the opening of the play, an extravagant rant from the dissolute Follywit, punctuated by admiring joshing from his companions, entirely prose, a series of tavern sallies. The *Loyal Subject* segment covers Theodor's bawdy presentation of two of his sisters to the evil royal counsellor Boroskie and two other unsavoury courtiers, and then four comic songs sung by soldiers from a disbanded army. The segment from *A Trick to Catch the Old One* comprises the merchant Hoard finalising a deal with the young Witgood's creditors, Witgood's document undoing his supposed pre-contract to the supposed rich widow Hoard has just married, and the aftermath of the tying up of these legal and financial matters. The *Valentinian* segment covers the attempted seduction of Lucina by various panders to the Emperor, involving elaborate flatteries, courtly Petrarchan discourse, and two sensuous songs designed to prepare Lucina for acquiescence.

Sifting through the various styles a contradiction appears. There is no shortage of extravagant, emphatic, colourful speeches, but the syntax is plain, on the whole, with many parallel, simple constructions. In the *Humorous Lieutenant* passage, both Celia and Antigonus ask repeated rhetorical questions. Celia addresses the threat from the king thus:

> Nay say you had your will, say you had ravished me,
> Performed your lust, what had you purchased by it?
> What honour won, do you know who dwells above sir,
> And what they have prepared for men turned devils?
> Did you never hear their thunder? start and tremble,
> Death sitting on your blood, when their fires visit us?
> Will nothing wring you then do you think? sit hard here?   (4.5.66–72)

The paired clauses 'say you had your will, say you had ravished me' create patterning without elaborate syntax. Antigonus responds, 'Lust, how I hate thee now? and love this sweetness? / Will ye be my Queen? can that price purchase ye?' (4.5.77–78). These are short, independent clauses, creating a jagged effect.

Overall the *Humorous Lieutenant* passage is scrappy, swaggering, and hyperbolic. Its sweeping, soaring, unanchored rhetoric, modish and stylish, brings numerous instances of 'now', 'all', and 'can', and few or no instances of relative 'which', 'that' as a conjunction, and 'if'.

The *Mad World* exchange is set in the tavern rather than the court and is extravagant in a different way. Yet its sentences are also simple in syntax. Follywit's playful *jeux d'esprit* are usually generalisations. They are loose and paratactic; commentary, not argument; sweeping and emphatic; and present-oriented. Three function words which help form the counter-Shakespearean style identified by the analysis, 'all', 'can', and 'now', all appear in this extract:

> Mass, that was well found out: all drunkards may lawfully say, they drink
> within measure by that trick. And now I am put i'th'mind of a trick. Can you
> keep your countenance, villains? Yet I am a fool to ask that, for how can they
> keep their countenance that have lost their credits?   (1.1.29–34)

Follywit is generalising and commenting rather than specifying or adding detail.

There are songs in two of these very low-scoring segments. This time these songs have simple syntax and frequent recourse to phatic vocabulary. Here is the fourth soldier's song from the *Loyal Subject* segment:

> Have ye any cracked maidenheads, to new leach or mend?
> Have ye any old maidenheads to sell or to change?
> Bring 'em to me, with a little pretty gin
> I'll clout 'em, I'll mend 'em, I'll knock in a pin,
> Shall make 'em as good maids again,
> As ever they have been. (3.5.33–38)

The song in the *Valentinian* segment is pastoral and courtly:[25]

> Roses blushing as they blow,
> And enticing men to pull,
> Lilies whiter than the snow,
> Woodbines of sweet honey full:
> All love's emblems and all cry,
> Ladies, if not plucked we die. (2.5.9–14)

The segment from *A Trick to Catch the Old One* stands out an example of a less adorned, more workaday style. It presents a discourse of commerce and negotiation, including a legal document. It is prosaic and matter-of-fact. The focus is on inert material objects and arrangements rather than on emotional and imaginative elements. The dialogue creates a disenchanted, verisimilar present which is both material and disembodied.

We can calculate which word-variables contribute most to the low score of a given segment. Fletcher uses the second-person pronoun form 'ye' extensively in his three segments in the group, and this is much the most important factor in bringing these segments to the lower end of the array created by the Linear Discriminant Function. This was a rare form by 1600. Even without the benefit of digital text and computer counts, Cyrus Hoy noticed that Fletcher was exceptional among his contemporaries in his heavy use of 'ye'. Hoy found it the best Fletcher marker in his attribution studies.[26] High scores of 'can', 'all', and 'now', and low scores of 'is', are important contributors to the placement of segments of both authors. The first three are used to add emphasis, as already noted. Low counts of 'is' imply a lesser focus on the immediate present of the onstage world.

Segments at the High End of the Spectrum

We can also examine the styles of the segments which score highest on the function, those that are at the Shakespeare extreme of the spectrum from

Table 2 *Segments scoring highest on the Linear Discriminant Function*

Author	Play	Segment #	Act, scene and lines (NOS)	Linear Discriminant Function score	Date*	Genre*
Shakespeare, William	*Winter's Tale*	15	2.3.68–123	4.26	1609	Tragicomedy
Shakespeare, William	*Tempest*	6	1.2.242–304	4.15	1611	Comedy
Shakespeare, William	*Antony and Cleopatra*	10	2.1.52–2.2.67	4.14	1606	Tragedy
Shakespeare, William	*All's Well That Ends Well*	17	2.3.159–213	4.12	1603	Comedy
Shakespeare, William	*Macbeth (Shakespeare sections)*	9	2.1.34–2.2.31	4.11	1606	Tragedy

* Date of first performance and genre from *DEEP: Database of Early English Playbooks*.

Shakespeare to non-Shakespeare styles that it has defined. Table 2 gives the details for the five with highest scores.

As with the lowest-scoring segments, the three main genres apart from history plays are represented. They are all seventeenth-century plays, from the middle or late parts of Shakespeare's writing career. The average date (1607 exactly) is lower than for the lowest-scoring plays in Table 1 (just under 1613), but the contrast is not extreme, and does not indicate that date is the predominant contributing factor. Comparing the furthest ends of the spectrum, as given in Tables 1 and 2, we see a mature Shakespeare style, crossing a range of genres, contrasting with a style of his younger contemporaries in a similar genre range, in a date range staggered a little later.

A passage from *The Winter's Tale* has the highest score of all. It covers part of Act 2, scene 3, in which Paulina brings in the baby princess, whereupon Leontes rejects the child, demands that Antigonus control his wife, and orders the baby and her mother to be burnt. There is intense, closely-woven dialogue, with much circumstantial detail, and a high degree of personal interaction, reflected in abundant 'thou' forms.

The segment's high score comes firstly from its five instances of 'which' as a relative, implying syntactic complexity. The next largest contributor is its twenty-five instances of 'the', following from a style of close focus on particularities:

> Although the print be little, the whole matter
> And copy of the father – eye, nose, lip,

> The trick of's frown, his forehead, nay, the valley,
> The pretty dimples of his chin and cheek, his smiles,
> The very mould and frame of hand, nail, finger. (2.3.98–102)

Then there are four instances of 'so' as an adverb of manner, used for anaphora, reinforcing a close interlinking of argument. Leontes mocks Antigonus, 'He dreads his wife' (2.3.79). Paulina responds, 'So I would you did' (2.3.80).

The segment from *The Tempest* includes Prospero's speeches reminding Ariel of the captivity Prospero had rescued him from. Once again this is a markedly intense interaction. Prospero is emphatic, insistent, and personal. The focus is on the past, with dense circumstantial detail. The passage is brought to the Shakespeare end of the stylistic spectrum by high frequencies of 'did', 'thou', 'thee', and 'which' as a relative, and an absence of the word 'all'. Six of the seven instances of 'did' are as an auxiliary rather than a main verb, as when Prospero asks Ariel if he has forgotten 'From what a torment I did free thee' (1.2.251). This reflects both the subject matter, i.e. past events, and Shakespeare's use of the older form of the past tense – 'I did free thee' rather than 'I freed thee'. Prospero and Ariel address each other as 'thou' and 'thee' and never as 'you', a consistency which is unusual even for Shakespeare. There are five instances of relative 'which', accompanying a style of precision and careful detail. Prospero says Sycorax imprisoned Ariel 'Into a cloven pine, within which rift / Imprisoned thou didst painfully remain / A dozen years; within which space she died, / And left thee there' (1.2.277–280). One in seven Shakespeare segments have no instances of 'all', compared to one in twelve of the non-Shakespeare segments, and this extract from *The Tempest* is one of them.

The segment from *Antony and Cleopatra* covers the last couple of lines of Act 2, scene 1 and then the first quarter of Act 2, scene 2. After a preliminary exchange between Lepidus and Enobarbus, Antony and Caesar enter, embrace and then have a robust exchange about Antony's time in Egypt with Cleopatra. The speeches focus on the past, with six instances of 'did', five of them in the old-fashioned past tense forms as in the segment from *The Tempest*. There is a close personal emphasis, with twenty-four instances of 'you'.

The syntax is knotty, giving a sinewy, compressed effect. There are thirteen instances of 'not', a marker of close argument, and again no instances of the generalising 'all'. Here is Caesar's response to the charge that he took innocent doings of Antony's amiss, and concerned himself with matters which were none of his business:

> I must be laughed at
> If or for nothing or a little, I

> Should say myself offended, and with you
> Chiefly i'th'world; more laughed at that I should
> Once name you derogately, when to sound your name
> It not concerned me.   (2.2.36–41)

The segment from *All's Well that Ends Well* starts with Bertram's acceptance of Helen at the King's angry insistence, and then includes the first part of the sharp quarrel between Lafeu and Paroles. The style is punning, abstruse, and contorted:

> I find that she, which late
> Was in my nobler thoughts most base, is now
> The praisèd of the king, who so ennobled,
> Is as 'twere born so.   (2.3.162–165)

The quarrel starts with short plain sentences – 'Do you hear, monsieur? A word with you' (2.3.176) – but soon becomes demanding for the listener on and off stage, muscularly witty and hard to follow: 'I have now found thee. When I lose thee again I care not; yet art thou good for nothing but taking up, and that thou'rt scarce worth' (2.3.193–195).

The *Macbeth* segment starts a few lines after the beginning of the soliloquy at the end of Act 2, scene 1, just after the line which first mentions the dagger, already quoted, and ends with Macbeth aghast at the memory of being unable to say 'Amen' just after the murder in the next scene. Macbeth in the soliloquy addresses the dagger, the earth, and Duncan as 'thou', and this word is unusually frequent in the segment as a whole, along with other older forms like 'hath', past tenses with 'did', and 'that' as a conjunction.

It includes twenty-seven instances of 'the', and this is the largest contributor to the segment's high score on the function.[27] The focus is myopically close. There is claustrophobic particularity rather than generality.

MACBETH   I have done the deed. Didst thou not hear a noise?
LADY MACBETH   I heard the owl scream and the crickets cry. (2.2.14–15)

The segment is one of intense interaction and specification. There is a narrative of past events and an old-fashioned slant to the choice of grammatical forms.

Here and in the other segments just discussed we are not focused on a late or even on a mature style, rather these passages are singled out by the analysis as prototypical of Shakespeare's dialogue overall, encompassing all thirty-five plays and parts of plays. It is worth recalling also that this is a view of style refracted through frequencies of just 100 very common words, though, as already mentioned, given the abundance of these words, this encompasses more than half of the running total of words in the corpus.

Differences within Plays

One further way to interpret the contrast of styles defined by the linear discriminant function is to examine segments within a play with widely disparate scores. The largest difference in any non-Shakespeare play happens to be between the segment of *The Humorous Lieutenant* already discussed and a second segment from this play, the forty-second, spanning Act 4, scene 8, lines 61–114. In this segment the King's son Demetrius, who is in love with Celia, interrogates her about her time with his father. She plays up the story of this episode to make Demetrius jealous. The longest speeches are Demetrius's, lamenting Celia's supposed fall from innocence (4.8.80–84, 86–92, and 103–113). The main difference from the low-scoring passage is particularity, and the intensity of the interpersonal interaction. Demetrius addresses Celia as 'thou'. There is some description and narrative, bringing with them instances of 'did' and 'there'. He presses her for details of her time with the king. The passage also has a low count of 'to' as an infinitive particle, which is an anti-Shakespeare marker (Figure 2), and helps push this segment to the Shakespeare end of the function.

This comparison adds weight to the interpretation of the Shakespearean style as closely engaged and dense, and opposed to an anti-Shakespearean style which is hyperbolic and sweeping. Celia's extravagant celebration of her freedom is anti-Shakespearean. By contrast, the chapter-and-verse detail of her supposed seduction, and Demetrius's accusing lament at it, brings Fletcher close to the Shakespearean style for once.

The within-play segment pair with the greatest disparity in the Shakespeare sub-corpus is in *Troilus and Cressida*. The third segment scores high, 4.02, around seventh overall. It covers Act 1, scene 2, lines 8–66, a passage in which Pandarus, Cressida, and Alexander discuss Hector and Ajax. There is metaphoric description, with convoluted clarifications of relationships, witty sallies, and wordplay. The twenty-third segment, on the other hand, is towards the non-Shakespearean end of the function, with a score of 1.87, the fourth lowest for Shakespeare. It is one of the group of four black dots at the extreme left-hand end of the Shakespeare cluster in Figure 1. This segment covers 3.1.67–133. Helen, Pandarus, and Paris exchange banter and there is a song. The dialogue is markedly repetitive. Speeches are mostly very short, with simple syntax. The style is plain, if stylishly so. The Shakespeare style is dense and highly wrought, while the anti-Shakespeare style within this Shakespeare play is witty in a different way, slangy, slapdash, conspicuously lazy, with one character picking up another's terms and repeating them. Shakespeare is capable on occasions of writing in a style quite unlike his regular self. We are dealing with overlapping ranges, as Figure 1 illustrates, rather than absolute distinctions. Two truths are evident: there are a number of tendencies which differentiate Shakespeare's style from that of his contemporaries; and at times Shakespeare can write passages in which these tendencies are hardly evident at all.

Conclusion

The question, 'What is distinctive about the language of Shakespeare's plays?', may not have been asked before in such literal and mechanical terms, but it does seem an obvious one, given Shakespeare's extraordinary status. In answering this question, quantitative work can only be comparative, which makes it an uncomfortable fit with mainstream criticism. Few among the continuing flood of readings of individual Shakespeare plays approach them by direct comparison with the work of his peers. At the same time, this also constitutes one of the strengths of the method, since it deploys an explicit standard of comparison, rather than analysing Shakespeare with an intuitive background norm of dramatic language in general, or comparing particular parts of Shakespeare to other parts of his work. A quantitative analysis also treats all comers equally. A venerated, much-debated passage is given exactly the same importance as a scene from a play which is only a name even to specialists. This gives a distorted result, from one point of view, but also brings a fresh perspective.

The stylometric treatment of Shakespeare's language offers a firm point of reference. If we define Shakespeare's style as the pattern of use of these words, in these play segments, compared with this statistical procedure with this set of segments, by these other playwrights, we get this result. Some claims about Shakespeare's style are immediately put in doubt. There is nothing in the analysis to support the idea that he is an innovator in terms of grammatical forms, for instance. There are many archaic words among the Shakespeare markers. There is also no universal essential Shakespeare style. We have some central tendencies, but there is striking variation, as we can see in the segment from *Troilus and Cressida* discussed above.

It is hard to know what Shakespeareans would expect to emerge in a contrast between the dialogue style of Shakespeare plays and the styles of a collection of plays by his peers, especially if we cast the comparison in terms of the patterns of use of very common words. However, we might speculate that some would expect Shakespeare's style defined in this way to turn out to be extravagantly figurative, recalling favourite passages of this kind. Others might have guessed that Shakespeare's dialogue would emerge as unusually attentive to capturing the cadence of everyday exchanges. In the event Shakespeare's style in these terms is neither of these things. It is old-fashioned; concrete and particular in focus; entangled and complex in construction; and its syntax is pointed and foregrounded. It avoids generalisation, hyperbole, and filler words. It is at the opposite end of a spectrum from modern, verisimilar, generalising, and casual styles.

NOTES

1 'Who' and 'that' are also possible ways of marking the relative in Early Modern English. See Jonathan Hope, *The Authorship of Shakespeare's Plays: A Sociolinguistic Study* (Cambridge: Cambridge University Press, 1994), pp. 27–31. Hope shows that Shakespeare has the highest use of relative 'which' among the six dramatists he examines (Graph 3.10, p. 53).

2 SparkNotes, *No Fear Shakespeare*, *Macbeth*, Act 2, Scene 1, Page 2, http://nfs .sparknotes.com/macbeth/page_50.html (accessed 10 August 2017).

3 Illuminations Media, 'Macbeth – Antony Sher – "Is this a dagger … ?"', *YouTube*, www.youtube.com/watch?v=CXzBR3knsPs (accessed 10 August 2017).

4 The texts in the corpus are my own set of specially prepared machine-readable versions. The quotations in the chapter and the act, scene, and line numbers in Tables 1 and 2 and in the text refer to New Cambridge Shakespeare editions. For dates of first performance, and company of first performance, I rely on *DEEP: Database of Early English Playbooks*, ed. Alan B. Farmer and Zachary Lesser (created 2007; accessed 14 July 2017), http://deep.sas.upenn.edu. Lists of the 254 function words and homographs, the 100 most common function word forms, and of the plays, appear in the Supplementary Materials for this chapter, which can be found at www.newcastle.edu.au/research-and-innovation/centre/ education-arts/cllc/publications.

5 I did not include in the Shakespeare set the putative Shakespeare portions of the three parts of *Henry VI* or of *Arden of Faversham* or *Edward III*, nor the likely Shakespeare additions to *The Spanish Tragedy* or *Sir Thomas More*.

6 1.8 million out of 3.5 million. See Supplementary Materials for tables showing counts of all the words in the two sub-corpora and of the 100 most common function words in the full corpus.

7 The procedure is to find the average for a word across the full corpus, and its standard deviation, and express each individual word count as the difference from the mean divided by the standard deviation. This standardised score is also known as a z-score. See Hugh Craig and Brett Greatley-Hirsch, *Style, Computers, and Early Modern Drama* (Cambridge: Cambridge University Press, 2017), p. 45.

8 See Hugh Craig, 'Shakespeare's Style, Shakespeare's England', *Fashioning England and the English: Literature, Nation, Gender*, ed. Rahel Orgis and Matthias Heim (London: Palgrave Macmillan, 2018), pp. 71–95.

9 For Shakespeare and the auxiliary 'do', see Hope, *Authorship*, pp. 11–26. Hope considers that Shakespeare is anomalous among his peers in adhering to the '"old fashioned"' grammatical forms involving auxiliary 'do' (p. 20). 'Did' is also used in the modern, 'regulated' form of interrogatives, with 'Did she come?' replacing 'Came she?', and so on, but these interrogative uses are only a small

proportion of the instances overall. Figure 2 shows that 'do' is also positively weighted, thus more common in Shakespeare, but uses of this word are more varied, so interpretation is more difficult.

10 For further discussion of the stylistics of the passages from *The Rape of Lucrece*, *As You Like It*, and *The Gentleman Usher* quoted below, see Hugh Craig and Brett Greatley-Hirsch, *Style, Computers, and Early Modern Drama* (Cambridge: Cambridge University Press, 2017), pp. 150–151. Jonathan Hope and Michael Witmore discuss the stylistic implications of a particularly heavy incidence of 'the' in *Macbeth* compared to other Shakespeare plays in 'The Language of *Macbeth*', '*Macbeth*': *The State of Play*, ed. Ann Thompson (London: Bloomsbury, 2014), pp. 183–208.

11 Thomas Heywood, *The Rape of Lucrece*, ed. Allan Holaday (Urbana: University of Illinois Press, 1950), pp. 81–83. Lines 1152–1225.

12 Lines 1152–1171; these items at line 1155. Spelling has been modernised.

13 Lines 1188, 1189. Spelling has been modernised.

14 John Marston, *Jack Drum's Entertainment*, in *The Plays of John Marston*, ed. H. Harvey Wood (Edinburgh: Oliver and Boyd, 1934–9), vol. 3, pp. 238–239. Spelling has been modernised.

15 Ben Jonson, *The Alchemist*, 3.1.1–2. Jonson plays are quoted from *Ben Jonson*, ed. C. H. Herford and P. and E. Simpson (Oxford: Clarendon Press, 1925–52). Spelling is modernised.

16 Jonson, *Bartholomew Fair*, 3.2.39–42.

17 This is from the forty-first segment of the play, comprising 5.4.39–86.

18 This is from the seventeenth segment of the play, comprising 2.3.183–3.2.18.

19 George Chapman, *The Gentleman Usher*, in *The Works of George Chapman: Plays*, ed. Richard Herne Shepherd (London: Chatto & Windus, 1874), pp. 90–91 (3.1).

20 Thomas Dekker, *Old Fortunatus*, *The Dramatic Works of Thomas Dekker*, ed. Fredson Bowers (Cambridge: Cambridge University Press, 1953–61), vol. 1, p. 82 (5.1.43–48). Spelling has been modernised. This is from the fifteenth segment, 5.1.39–98.

21 Fletcher plays are quoted here and below from *The Dramatic Works in the Beaumont and Fletcher Canon*, ed. Fredson Bowers (Cambridge: Cambridge University Press, 1966–96). Sebastian's full speech runs to 3.2.19. Spelling has been modernised. The segment runs from 3.1.373 to 3.2.21.

22 This may indicate that further work is needed on the division of *Timon* between Shakespeare and Middleton. Alternatively, on this occasion, Shakespeare may have departed from his usual practice and adopted an unusually sweeping, generalising rhetoric bringing with it a concentration of instances of 'all'.

23 As noted by Brian Vickers, *Shakespeare, 'A Lover's Complaint', and John Davies of Hereford* (Cambridge: Cambridge University Press, 2007), Tables 6.2 and 6.3, and p. 239. There is further discussion of rates of use of 'all' in various poets in Hugh Craig, 'Shakespeare, John Davies of Hereford, and "A Lover's Complaint"', *Shakespeare Quarterly* 63 (2012): 147–174, esp. pp. 171–172.

24 George Chapman, *Byron's Conspiracy*, in *The Plays of George Chapman: The Tragedies With Sir Gyles Goosecappe; A Critical Edition*, ed. Allan Holaday

(Cambridge: D. S. Brewer, 1987), p. 294 (3.1.125–28). Spelling has been modernised.

25 The segment covers 2.4.34 to 2.5.68.

26 Cyrus Hoy, 'The Shares of Fletcher and His Collaborators in the Beaumont and Fletcher Canon (I)', *Studies in Bibliography* 8 (1956): 129–146.

27 See Hope and Witmore, 'The Language of *Macbeth*'.

11

AMY COOK AND SETH FREY

Reading in Time: Cognitive Dynamics and the Literary Experience of Shakespeare

Critics and scholars specialise in analysing poetic experience. But writers and readers are human animals, and there must be a framework that can apprehend both poetic experience and daily experience, a scaffolding for thought, language, and experience that is used one way to structure our experiences of life, and another for our experiences of poetry. The continuity of art and life, of verse and everyday language use, is an unacknowledged premise of the cognitive turn in the humanities. The study of linguistic processing – and the embodied and embedded thinking that it reflects and shapes – potentially offers a tremendous tool to those of us wanting to both understand text and performance and understand the mind through them. Working against centuries of Cartesian dualism, contemporary cognitive science does not separate body from mind or privilege thinking over feeling. Its openness to imagination, creativity, and the body is part of what makes cognitive linguistics an exciting match for Shakespeare. This chapter, a collaboration across the disciplines, will use cognitive linguistics and cognitive dynamics to attend to the small words that structure basic literary thoughts, and the small moments that structure basic literary experiences, in Shakespeare's poetry. Following the work of Lynne Magnusson and Sylvia Adamson, we begin by privileging Shakespeare's small words. Using conceptual integration theory (or blending) and metaphor theory, along with recent research in cognitive science, we will explore the metaphoric scaffolding set up by often-neglected words like 'in', 'on', and 'from'. These words indicate conceptual metaphors at work that may escape critical attention but that organise a set of meanings. We then move from meaning to experience, suggesting how cognitive approaches might extend our understanding of the dynamic experience of reading Shakespeare's poetry as this process has been previously modelled by literary critics like Bruce R. Smith and Stephen Booth. We conclude by demonstrating how an attention to language – to sense and nonsense – can enrich the experience of reading Shakespeare.

189

The Scaffolding of Poetic Thought

Adamson has argued for the importance of attending to 'small words' like 'shall', 'its', and 'you' in Shakespeare's language. By keeping alert to these often-neglected words, we can avoid 'pitfalls' to comprehension due to language change since Shakespeare's day, and we can also discover 'pleasures' in the writer's grammatical choices from a 'different repertoire of options' than we have today.[1] Possessive 'its', she reminds us, did not exist during Shakespeare's time so Shakespeare would have referred to something as 'his' even if he wasn't trying to personify it, as with 'love' or 'the star' in Sonnet 116: 'It [love] is the star to every wand'ring bark, / Whose worth's unknown, although *his* heighth be taken' (lines 7–8). The difference between calling someone 'you' or 'thou' was a choice 'filled with complex social and emotional significance'.[2] At the start of *As You Like It*, when Oliver initially addresses his brother Orlando as 'you' it registers, however grudgingly, their comparable status as brothers. As a violent quarrel develops, we can read in Oliver's shift to 'thou' address – 'Wilt thou lay hands on me, villain' (1.1.52) – a register of anger and contempt.

Magnusson extended this argument to analyse the use of modal verbs such as 'would' and 'might' to create 'Shakespeare's language of possibility'. Turning from the fireworks generated by the thematic words like 'liberty' or 'constancy' in *Julius Caesar*, Magnusson analyses the rich work done by 'shall' and 'will' in Caesar and Calpurnia's scene about whether or not Caesar will go to the capital the day he is murdered (3.2). The whole scene about what he's going to do becomes interesting because it's about potential action and agency. '"Caesar **shall** forth" construes the future as "bound to happen", the remarkable third person formulation giving it the force of a decree. Nonetheless, this unmoved mover's vacillation, registered by the shift from the magisterial third person "shall" to first person "will", triggers self-analysis.'[3] Though small, these words do tremendous work in a sentence, shifting the stance, the expectation, the structure, and as such they deserve the kind of 'slow reading' Magnusson suggests. The small words we want to attend to in this essay are the ones that make visible the workings of metaphor.

Cognitive linguistics, with its insistence on embodiment and scale of evidence similar to literary theory (both look at comprehended text to understand something behind or beyond the words spoken or written), provided an interesting lens through which to ask questions about Shakespeare's less visible metaphors. Consider the mirror metaphor in *Hamlet*: 'the purpose of playing, whose end both at the first and now, was and is, to hold as 'twere the mirror up to nature; to show virtue her own feature, scorn her own image, and the very age and body of the time his form and pressure'

(*Ham.* 3.2.17–20). As many times as we have heard Hamlet's advice to the players quoted, no one mentions that it doesn't make sense. Hamlet wants a 'mirror' that will expose Claudius's (and later Gertrude's) guilt. He wants a mirror that will not only reflect but also editorialise. How can one mirror do all those things? In *Shakespearean Neuroplay*, Amy Cook pulls apart the poetry to argue that the networks of meanings evoked and primed in the process of understanding the text are then part of the scaffolding of larger thematic threads throughout the play. The mirror Hamlet holds up to nature at the centre of the play is not an actual mirror. This is not the mirror we use to check our blind spot or correct our lipstick: this mirror is capable of reflecting impartially and also anatomising or expanding. The purpose of playing is not just strict duplication or precise mimetic representation. Indeed, the play Hamlet has performed for the king is 'something *like*' the murder of his father (2.5.548, emphasis added): it is a slightly edited, amended, or distorted reflection that allows the audience to see virtue's or vice's 'feature'. Through examining *how* audiences have understood this creative image, rather than what they have understood, Cook found a web of evoked sources (convex mirror, political tracts, the use of glass in scientific instruments, and the small flat glass mirrors newly available from Italy) tied together. Understanding 'the purpose of playing' evokes a number of tools for vision that do different things.[4]

This is only helpful to see, of course, if seeing it allows us to ask new questions about the poetry or to perceive new angles in the performance. Cognitive linguistics – and especially cognitive metaphor studies – has produced some influential works on Shakespeare that invite us to see major plays from fresh perspectives. Donald Freeman's work on *Macbeth* views the play as being tightly constructed around the image-schemata of PATH and CONTAINER. Cognitive linguists understand such image-schemata to structure not just literary language but, importantly, our everyday language and perception. Freeman notes that the metaphoric structure that provides the scaffolding for Shakespeare's play then becomes the metaphoric structure for critics who have written about the play; the conceptual scaffolding afforded by the metaphors becomes contagious.[5] Also writing on *Macbeth*, Raphael Lyne explains and connects theories of rhetoric and contemporary cognitive science in order to explore how the two may be harnessed together to depict Shakespeare's characters as thinking with and through their language. In this regard he discusses Macbeth's famous simile:

> And pity, like a naked newborn babe
> Striding the blast, or heaven's cherubin horsed

> Upon the sightless couriers of the air,
> Shall blow the horrid deed in every eye,
> That tears shall drown the wind.   (1.7.21–25)

Lyne is interested in how moments of rhetorical failure are often the most exciting in unfolding thought process, as here where the conflicting and arresting image shows Macbeth unable to find the words to compel restraint.[6]

We can illustrate how Shakespeare's small words and cognitive metaphor work together in the opening scene of *As You Like It*. Orlando explains to his servant that he is angry at his brother, Oliver: 'As I remember, Adam, it was upon this fashion bequeathed me by will but poor a thousand crowns, and, as thou say'st, charged my brother, on his blessing, to breed me well: and there begins my sadness' (1.1.1–3). There is historical and contextual information we may need – we need to know that 'crowns' are monetary units, and some basics about inheritance and primogeniture – but perusal rewards us with meaning: Orlando was given consideration in his father's will, but things have not gone well since his death. This is basic exposition and could be cut without Shakespeare scholars decrying the loss of critical poetry. And yet how Shakespeare introduces the idea of the problematic transference of money, breeding, blessing, suggests a possible conceptual scaffolding for the play as a whole.

Language *works* on an audience: because how we speak is how we think, one can shape the other.[7] The bequeathing 'by will' evokes the conduit metaphor that is operational in such phrases as 'he got his point across' or 'her feelings came through loud and clear'. This conceptual metaphor structures how we think about something as being packaged and sent from one person to another and then being 'unpacked' once 'received'. In Orlando's complaint, the will is a conduit for his money, the means by which the money is assured. Legally, the will does have this kind of power; it can compel the transfer of money, even though it will require an agent of the estate to deliver the crowns. The breeding, however, required a promise made 'on his blessing' and locating the charge 'on' or 'by' a blessing does not have legal or actual agency to affect anything. In the very next scene, Touchstone points out a critical challenge to intangible things like 'honour' or 'blessing' with his funny lesson about the knight who could not swear on his honour because he had none. If you do not have the thing 'by' which you have the power to swear, it means nothing.[8] A will is a legal document with the authority to ensure transfer; a blessing is not legally reliable. Orlando's sadness begins 'there', at that moment when his father told Oliver (his oldest son and heir) that he should see to Orlando's upbringing, on his blessing, which he clearly does not have. 'There' is the kind of deictic that often necessitates physical pointing on stage.[9] In this case, though, there is nowhere to point: Orlando's 'there' makes clear his 'sadness' is a journey, one with a beginning located at the moment his brother was asked to breed him well and did not, and ends when Rosalind 'gives' herself to Orlando. The interplay of small words and conceptual metaphors helps establish the scaffolding for this play that starts with a circuitous discussion of how material and immaterial things did and did not transfer successfully and ends with four weddings completing the comedy's property transfer.

The linguistic work is not just semantic but physical. Language comprehension can be a full-bodied affair. As George Lakoff and Mark Johnson, the initiators of cognitive metaphor studies, pointed out years ago, the metaphors we use to describe many of the abstract experiences in life – from falling in love to blowing our top – come from concrete, physical experiences in our body. The language does not wholly define our thinking on love or anger, but it does constrain our thinking. For example, if we talk about a debate in terms of the ARGUMENT IS WAR metaphor – 'My example penetrated her defenses and destroyed her side', 'his position was weak', 'Mine eye and heart are at a mortal war' (Shakespeare's Sonnets 46.1) – we are not going to view the experience as positive or productive unless we 'win'. And this is not just how we speak about arguments, this is how we experience them: 'The language of argument is not poetic, fanciful, or rhetorical, but rather literal. We talk about arguments that way because we conceive of them that way – and we act according to the way we conceive of things.'[10] Another culture might talk about argument in terms of a dance – wherein through mutual interest and collaboration, people come together to respond to a prompt, creating something new in the process of disagreement.

There are other mechanisms at work that make the verse require the physical body. The body is a medium through which abstract concepts get situated into the conceptual structure on which the verse is built. For example, time is an abstract concept that seems to require metaphoric conceptualisation in terms of physical motion. In English, time is both something we move over and something that moves over us, which is why it is simultaneously possible that 'the holidays are careening toward us' and that 'we are moving quickly toward the holidays'. This can lead to some ambiguity: if one is told that 'Next Wednesday's meeting has been moved backward two days', does she put the meeting in her calendar for Monday or Friday? If she imagines herself moving through time, then she is more likely to think that moving the meeting backward will mean Monday. If she thinks that time is moving towards her, facing her, she is more likely to say the meeting will be on Friday, two days further back. This ambiguous question has provided researchers with a clever experiment opportunity: how might the conceptualisation vary depending on the person's physical relationship to space? Lera Boroditsky and Michael Ramscar found that if they asked subjects to imagine moving towards an object before asking the question, the subjects would be more likely to say that the meeting was moved to Friday. Subjects asked to imagine themselves moving away from an object prior to being asked the question were more likely to answer that the meeting was moved to Monday. What this demonstrates is that the perceived meaning of the sentence depends on the structuring metaphor used to understand time. It also shows that our experience with or imagination of moving impacts our conceptual ideas about moving. In other words, abstract or fictive motion (e.g. 'the meeting was moved', 'the highway races over the railroad tracks', 'the tattoo runs along her spine') is not so abstract, as it actually accesses our motor cortex in the processing of the sentence.[11] Language can literally move us.

Shakespeare uses *As You Like It* to celebrate these ambiguities of time, which come up thirty-five times in the play. Celia reports that she 'willingly could waste my time in' the forest (2.4.88), conceiving of time as a commodity, something that can be spent, wasted, or lost. This is picked up in the long discussion about time between Orlando and Rosalind, when Orlando fails to 'keep' his time with Rosalind. Time as commodity or treasure, wasted or kept, is one metaphoric schema explored in the play. Another more 'literary' metaphor, associating time with legal accounting, is voiced by Rosalind: 'Well, Time is the old justice that examines all such offenders; and let Time try' (4.1.160–161). But what predominates are indeed the metaphors of physical motion, elaborated extensively in Rosalind's tutorial for Orlando:

ORLANDO	You should ask me what time o' day. There's no clock in the forest.
ROSALIND	Then there is no true lover in the forest, else sighing every minute and groaning every hour would detect the lazy foot of time as well as a clock.
ORLANDO	And why not the swift foot of time? Had not that been as proper?
ROSALIND	By no means, sir. Time travels in divers paces with divers persons. I'll tell you who time ambles withal, who time trots withal, who time gallops withal, and who he stand still withal.

(3.2.254–274)

Here, as the metaphors start to develop, time appears to be personified as a separate moving figure, lazy or slow-footed. But then it becomes the physical carrier that moves or propels 'divers persons' along on their various life journeys, figured specifically (by the use of 'ambles', 'trots', 'gallops', and 'stands still') as the most common of carriers in Shakespeare's day, the horse. Thus, time is clearly figured as physical movement, not in an abstract way but in a way associated with the physical actualities of the world in which Shakespeare and his audience members would have characteristically experienced journeying movement.

As a Shakespeare critic grounded in phenomenology, which emphasises sense experience from a first-person point of view, Bruce R. Smith's influential Shakespeare criticism has tended to scaffold Shakespeare on the body and attend to the under-examined 'phenomena' such as 'emotions, reading, watching and listening in the theater'. He reminds us that 'Books, at least when they are being read, always exist within coordinates of space, time, and a human body.'[12] Cognitive criticism that emphasises how Shakespeare deploys metaphorical scaffolding to construct cognitive processes as deeply physical experiences develop a closely related critical approach.

The Scaffolding of Poetic Experience

As Smith's phenomenological criticism foregrounds the physicality of reading Shakespeare, Stephen Booth's innovative mid-twentieth-century close reading of Shakespeare's Sonnets and dramatic poetry rejects the attention on disguised or submerged meaning that has been of interest to many Shakespeare scholars in favour of the power of the nonsense on the surface. Yet, in both scholars' work on the reading experience of Shakespeare's poetry, we find striking consonances with the cognitive science of language processing dynamics. Both base their analyses on a fast, frugal, and parallel processing of language; on the inextricable interactions of all levels of language; and on the continuity of language with consciousness. This leads us to ask a number of questions: Do we most love the poem at the end, when the story has unfolded and the rich associations have been made, or do we, fractal-like, reach mini-realisations, and experience more pleasure in the process? How much of our appreciation of verse is in the act of reading it? How might we actually test the thoughts as they come while reading?

Phenomenology has provided a smart bridge between Shakespeare and the cognitive sciences. Although they involve different sources of evidence and methods of interpretation, phenomenology and cognitive science both understand that there is no separating the experience of the world from the bodies in which we experience it, and each sees the mind at its most active when it is in the struggle to understand. Through nonsense, through an ability 'to let us understand something that does not make sense as if it did make sense', the work is able to 'free us from the limits of the human mind'.[13] Indeed, this comprehension of the incomprehensible makes up our mind as it evades our limits: 'the feats of comprehension enabled by the phenomena I talk about here are not so much performed for their audiences as by them'.[14] For Booth, Shakespeare's language evokes expectations for paths that it chronically fails to follow. This element of the phenomenon is likely to be jettisoned if the goal is to come to a 'reading' of the sonnet or play, but if the goal is to understand the dynamic nature of the comprehension of the work in real time, such an experience becomes central.

Booth's reports tell a very complex story about Shakespeare's work, invoking a range of mental manoeuvres. The reader starts reading a poem and is promptly confounded. A basic need for comprehension makes him or her grasp at whatever threads seem to offer meaning. Experiencing this process of grasping deepens the reader's appreciation of some grasping that is being described in the verse at that moment (as with Macbeth's pity-as-babe simile). All of this – the entanglement, the grasping, and the parallel – is happening subliminally so as not to take attention away from the work. These are not processes that cognitive scientists have traditionally been equipped to study. Some of them are not even documented. But in recent years cognitive scientists have started developing the vocabulary necessary to translate between Booth's insights and the language of cognitive dynamics.

Cognitive dynamics is an umbrella term covering dynamic varieties of cognitive psychology, psycholinguistics, and cognitive linguistics – all within cognitive science. Dynamic cognitive linguistics introduces a change in focus from structure to process, opening the door to the empirical study of phenomenology with models and tools that understand language processing in terms of the continuously unfolding course of cognitive processes.[15] Dynamic cognitive science favours the view that the mind is continuous with a physical body in an external, possibly social, environment. It breaks completely with historical approaches in the sciences of mind, which have imposed upon language the temporal and conceptual constraints of computer engineering, and divided syntax and semantics into serially arranged self-contained processing units that initiate when reading has completed, and work in isolation before reporting to consciousness with an interpretation. Dynamic cognitive science can give us new tools for approaching the phenomena of poetic experience, which begin at the beginning of the poem, not at the end, and provide us with meaning, feeling, and the feeling of understanding, even when the sentences frustrate our actual understanding.

An attention to the conceptual metaphors undergirding the language at the start of *As You Like It* rewards the reader with new questions to ask about the play, such as, where else does it challenge the transference of material and non-material goods? (The multiple felicitous and infelicitous marriages is one clear place to turn.) Similarly, thinking with Booth's attention to nonsense and a cognitive dynamic approach to reading offers a lens through which to perceive the start of *Twelfth Night*. Lovesick Orsino begins the play calling for music:

> If music be the food of love, play on;
> Give me excess of it, that, surfeiting,
> The appetite may sicken and so die.
> That strain again, it had a dying fall;
> O it came o'er my ear like the sweet sound,
> That breathes upon a bank of violets,
> Stealing and giving odour. Enough; no more.
> 'Tis not so sweet now as it was before.
> O spirit of love, how quick and fresh art thou,
> That, notwithstanding thy capacity,
> Receiveth as the sea. Nought enters there,
> Of what validity and pitch soe'er,
> But falls into abatement and low price
> Even in a minute. So full of shapes is fancy,
> That it alone is high fantastical. (1.1.1–15)

Reading this poetry, silently or aloud, invites the body to ebb and flow with the rhythm. The first line is regular, moving us forward on the back of the five 'ta dums'; the second injects variety with an opening trochee, then returns to the regular beat. The duke's speech is itself musical. And yet, the rhythm and musicality mask the 'precious nonsense' of its argument.

Booth points out many of the ways that the speech is incoherent. For example, music both nourishes love and then works as a kind of binge therapy, killing what it nourishes. Despite beginning with the MUSIC IS FOOD OF LOVE metaphor, the topic changes to the spirit of love, which, despite having endless capacity like the sea does, seems to be the graveyard of value. Booth's point is that this beautiful incoherence is critical: 'But no parachute to rationality will effectively make this exchange logical or – and this is vital – make it *feel illogical* as it is heard or make it feel in need of explication ... We do not notice what Orsino says; we hear what he must be saying. We listen to nonsense as if it were sense' (140). What this accurately presumes is our need to feel like we understand; close attention to the sound and sense of the language allows us to ask a different question: what is gained by this misdirection? For Booth, it is the phenomenon of these failures, these contradictions, that generate the wit and wonder of the play as a whole: 'active but casual failures – if they are so gentle as not to become the focus of our attention – put minds that perceive them under stress – but under stresses with which those minds can cope without strenuous effort, stresses that are real but ultimately inefficient' (165). This is the kind of claim that cognitive dynamicists study.

In verse, mechanisms like idiom and simple association may offer subtle hints that bring attention to plausible parses. But the hints that Shakespeare leaves in Orsino's monologue offer only dubious assistance: they don't seem to be about keeping readers on track logically. The words feel like they belong together – 'food of love', 'quick and fresh' – but what follows undercuts the sense we had made of the phrase the first time through. How is sound sweet? Is it 'stealing' as a way of moving – as in furtively – or stealing as in taking? Readers do not proceed in steps that were completed, but more often in steps that were only begun. This is where the dynamics of reading – or listening – is central; we experience the meaning of a sentence in chunks, in time, and a premium is placed on making whatever kind of sense is necessary to move on. Literary experiences are not different in kind from language experiences: both may 'happen' above or below the level of conscious awareness.

Despite the myriad individuating factors that necessarily influence the experience of Shakespeare's verse, you don't have to be a literary critic (or a neuroscientist – or an Elizabethan) to experience the meanings that a critic unpacks. Ultimately, the experience we, and Booth, are observing – of trying to understand language – is a relatively narrow type of human experience, but one that is rich enough to help us connect to Shakespeare's characters and to illustrate the continuity of language with thought. This is the way that dynamicists understand sentence comprehension as something that happens in time and that necessarily forms expectations, makes assumptions, and integrates 'context ... continuously as a statement is unfolding' to maintain 'the fullest possible interpretation at each moment in time'.[16] Booth, Smith, and cognitive dynamicists are attempting to describe how understanding develops from syllable to syllable. Their theories share a picture of the brain as desperate for understanding, grasping ever more indiscriminately the longer it goes unsated. What an attention to the metaphors and pleasures in Shakespeare's language unveils is the underappreciated value of being misled or misguided into assumptions of understanding.

What Cognitive Dynamics Can Do for Shakespeare's Language

Cognitive dynamics and a phenomenologically guided reading of Shakespeare's language share a focus on the phenomenon of verse experience. But dynamic cognitive science, as an empirically driven branch of cognitive science, advances itself through the dialogue between testable models and laboratory experiments. Cognitive processes cast measurable shadows through the actions of the body. Whether a shadow obscures or reveals information about its owner depends on the position of the light. A good psychological experiment looks at a cognitive phenomenon from the right angle. Dynamicists study the fifty-millisecond lag in responding to this or that version of a sentence, or the flicker of a subject's eye at this versus that word. A few concepts in cognitive dynamics are particularly relevant to our dynamic account of Shakespeare. The research on priming and expectation dynamics will introduce the psychological processes that Shakespeare's language keeps so busy.

Normally, if you are shown an arrangement of letters (e.g. 'heart' or 'floor' or 'dgrhh'), it will take you some small amount of time to determine if they constitute a word or nonsense. But if, just before seeing those letters, you are flashed a word like 'BODY', you will identify semantically related words, like 'heart', more quickly. 'BODY' primes 'heart'. Primes have a short life-span (typically less than half a second). Cognitive scientists identify associative priming and expectation as separable processes operating on different timescales. When a concept is activated (by being read, heard, thought of, and so on) it instantly and automatically primes associated concepts to be activated in turn.[17] By contrast, an expected concept wasn't activated by a related concept, but by some higher-level cognitive process. Expectation is understood as a slower top-down process that can override automatic priming.[18] In other words, mention of 'Jaws' is less likely to make me think of the shark if it comes from my dentist. To build upon our test above, in which you are identifying words and non-words, imagine that the environment has now built in an artificial expectation: in this particular identification test, 'BODY' tends to be followed by words in a different semantic network, such as those associated with buildings. They are semantically unrelated, but if they co-occur reliably, you will nonetheless develop an expectation for building words after 'BODY'. James Neely, an early dynamicist, developed this scheme to prove that association (BODY:heart) and expectation (BODY:door) are different constructs that operate over different timescales. While associations work in the blink of an eye (about 300 ms) expectations work within a lagging window of 700 to 2,000 ms.[19] Expectations are slower but stronger than associations.

Reading 'body', 'door', and 'dgrhh' is not the same as reading poetry. How can these studies be adapted to inform language experience in less controlled and abstract domains? The first few lines of a play or a poem are particularly well-suited to testing a hypothesis about the act of literary experience. Being at the beginning, readers' expectations about the plot and the narrative are less likely to obscure the more local effects that we are interested in. Shakespeare's long poem, *Venus and Adonis*, for example, begins:

> Even as the sun with purple-coloured face
> Had tane his last leave of the weeping morn,
> Rose-cheeked Adonis hied him to the chase;
> Hunting he loved, but love he laughed to scorn.
>   Sick-thoughted Venus makes amain unto him,
>   And like a bold-faced suitor gins to woo him.

This densely woven stanza introduces many of the thematic conflicts that will later emerge in the poem. Adonis is a great hunter; Venus embodies love. But the poem has reversed these roles by lines five to six, presenting the female as the masculine 'bold-faced suitor' wooing the coy youth; soon this masculine love-goddess will be plucking the hunter from his horse. Literary critics have understood this poem as a whole from within different contexts (historical, allegorical, moral, etc.); but a close cognitive dynamic approach tests the way Shakespeare manipulates the reader's assumptions as early as the first line.

The poem opens with a sun in the 'morn' even as the reader is primed (by 'Even', 'purple-coloured face', and 'last leave') to expect an evening sun. After being primed by 'morn', the rising-sun concept gets a moment's reinforcement from 'rose' before the appearance of 'cheeked' consigns it to modify a new subject. This forces the reader to abandon the verb interpretation – to rise – immediately before it is resurrected in 'Adonis'. (Adonis – Adawnis – phonetically invokes the rising sun.) Shakespeare deftly guides readers towards one interpretation and then turns them about-face, twice, playfully withholding the thematic interpretation of rise until the right moment. That we don't notice it in the moment makes it no less dizzying. This is a neat account of flouting expectations, but does it have any psychological reality or is it more symptomatic of critical apophenia, seeing patterns that are not there? By the end of the second line, there are already at least three testable questions:

1. Are readers generally expecting an evening sun more than a rising sun before 'weeping morn'?
2. Does the first word 'Even' really prime the concept evening?
3. If expectations mature in time, can a well-timed performative modification amplify priming effects? Specifically, can a dramatic pause amplify the priming effect of evening? Does different timing modulate the reader's shift from an evening to a morning sun?

There are ways we can ask these questions in a laboratory setting. Does that make the poem more or less engaging, erotic, and important? No, but the mere existence of three testable questions about poetic experience means that literary interpretation can be a science, and cognitive science an art.

Cook has written about her chronic misunderstanding of the start of *Richard III*, noticing that the line 'Now is the winter of our discontent' made her anticipate and assume a dark and miserable start to the play – winter being the most cold of the discontent – only to realise later in the sentence that Richard meant the end of a year of discontent.[20] On the level of the syntax she was wrong, but on the level of the play and the character she was right: for Richard, peace is a negative and fighting brings power and pleasure. This, perhaps, is just an idiosyncratic reading on her part: others perhaps anticipated summer as soon as Richard mentioned winter. We could conduct an experiment to find out, but we could start by questioning the value of the confusion in interpreting the rest of the play. Does this interpretive false start prepare us for a play where language slips from sense, where questioning our initial read on a phrase or an event is useful? We can move on with a shallow read of the phrase 'winter of our discontent' and understand enough about the situation by the end of the soliloquy, or we can be stopped short by 'made glorious summer' and return for a deeper read of the language that fooled us the first time. Our point is not that experiments are necessary, but rather that questioning how we make sense – and fail to make sense – of the poetry is a fruitful avenue of research, both into the mind of the reader and the meaning of the language.

Authors can intentionally decouple their audiences from a work; difficult words, sentences, or ideas can break the rhythm and give readers time to reason more deeply 'offline'. With tricks like these, writers can use semantic context and sentence structure to predispose their readers to the deep or shallow read. Applied to the study of literary experience, an understanding of depth of processing allows us to understand how writers take their audiences for rides. It may be that readers that have been induced to start reading shallowly are suddenly open to suggestion – and that reading through nonsense without comment makes readers unwitting participants in that nonsense. The craft of poetry, and the beauty of Shakespeare's verse, is in orchestrating these conspiracies while keeping them just below the surface of conscious comprehension. Readers and listeners are so enchanted by the scenery, and so lulled by the rhythm, that they don't realise that they have been thrown.

This doesn't stop us from loving the experience of Shakespeare's language; in fact, many of us insist that the pleasure in the language only increases. Why should this be so? Why don't we prefer far more simple, clear, logical, literal language? The cognitive scientists generally assume that sentences are comprehensible. But Shakespeare frustrates this, as Booth notices the tension in the poetry between the seeming comprehensibility and actual incomprehensibility. The metre keeps moving us forward, pressuring us to keep our reading rate relatively constant, preventing us from dwelling for insight on murky bits. Reading one of Shakespeare's complex and misleading sentences, we may become ensnared and stop comprehending the verse at anything but the level of the current word and its immediate neighbours. But, being entrained, we don't notice and we don't stop. In Shakespearean verse, the opaque syntax, the esoteric or fabricated vocabulary, the counterintuitive imagery, and the momentum of the reader's voluntary entrainment to the metre collectively intercede in the reader's attempt at sentence-, quatrain-, and sonnet-level meaning. Readers are forced to abandon it, so they resign themselves instead to a steady current of serial word-ideas and mental imagery. Traditionally, teachers point students to footnotes and glossaries and the promise of an expert reading – of no-fear Shakespeare – but without some of the fear, some of the confusion, the precious nonsense in the poetry, Shakespeare isn't Shakespeare.

NOTES

1   Sylvia Adamson, 'Understanding Shakespeare's Grammar: A Study in Small Words', *Reading Shakespeare's Dramatic Language: A Guide*, ed. Sylvia Adamson, Lynette Hunter, Lynne Magnusson, Ann Thompson, and Katie Wales (London: Arden Shakespeare, 2001), pp. 210–236; p. 211.

2   Adamson, 'Understanding Shakespeare's Grammar', p. 227.

3   Magnusson, 'Shakespeare and the Language of Possibility', A Folger Shakespeare Library podcast: Shakespeare's Birthday Lecture 2015, 16 April 2015. folgerpedia.folger.edu. p. 16.

4   Amy Cook, *Shakespearean Neuroplay: Reinvigorating the Study of Dramatic Texts and Performance Through Cognitive Science* (New York: Palgrave Macmillan, 2010).

5   Donald Freeman, '"Catch[ing] the Nearest Way": *Macbeth* and Cognitive Metaphor', *Journal of Pragmatics* 24 (1995): 689–708.

6   Raphael Lyne, *Shakespeare, Rhetoric and Cognition* (Cambridge: Cambridge University Press, 2011). See also Mary Thomas Crane's important study, *Shakespeare's Brain: Reading with Cognitive Theory* (Princeton: Princeton University Press, 2001).

7   See Lyne's *Shakespeare, Rhetoric and Cognition*, which makes the argument that the characters' minds are seen at work in their use of rhetoric and metaphor. Mary Thomas Crane's *Shakespeare's Brain* makes the argument that close attention to the language of the plays reveals things about Shakespeare's brain – or at least the historical moment it was in.

8   And as Feste jokes with Viola in *Twelfth Night*, one can live 'by' the church, in terms of location – one's house is near the physical structure of the church – or one can live by the church – the church provides the method by which one lives. To laugh at this exchange one must switch from one meaning to the

other – what Seana Coulson calls a semantic leap in *Semantic Leaps: Frame-Shifting and Conceptual Blending in Meaning Construction* (Cambridge, MA: MIT Press, 2001).

9 On such deictics, see Bruce Smith, *Phenomenal Shakespeare* (Chichester: Wiley-Blackwell, 2010), pp. 62–63; and Farah Karim Cooper, *The Hand on the Shakespearean Stage: Gesture, Touch and the Spectacle of Dismemberment* (London: Arden, 2016).

10 George Lakoff and Mark Johnson, *Metaphors We Live By* (Chicago and London: University of Chicago Press, 1980), pp. 5–6.

11 Lera Boroditsky and Michael Ramscar, 'The Roles of Body and Mind in Abstract Thought', *Psychological Science* 13.2 (2002): 185–189. For a strong overview of current research in cognitive linguistics, see Benjamin K. Bergen, *Louder Than Words: The New Science of How the Mind Makes Meaning* (New York: Basic Books, 2006); for a specific argument about abstract motion, see Teenie Matlock, 'Abstract Motion is no Longer Abstract', *Language and Cognition* 2.2 (2010): 243–260.

12 Smith, *Phenomenal Shakespeare*, pp. xv–xvi, 45.

13 Stephen Booth, *Precious Nonsense: The Gettysburg Address, Ben Jonson's Epitaphs on his Children, and Twelfth Night* (Berkeley: University of California Press, 1998), p. 5.

14 Booth, *Precious Nonsense*, p. 12.

15 For representative work see Jeffrey Elman, 'Finding Structure in Time', *Cognitive Science* 14.1 (1990): 179–211; Thomas A. Farmer, Sarah E. Anderson, and Michael J. Spivey, 'Gradiency and Visual Context in Syntactic Garden-Paths', *Journal of Memory and Language* 57.4 (2007): 570–595; Walter Kintsch, 'The Role of Knowledge in Discourse Comprehension', *Psychological Review* 95.2 (1988): 163–182; Michael K. Tanenhaus, James Leiman, and Mark Seidenberg, 'Evidence for Multiple Stages in the Processing of Ambiguous Words in Syntactic Contexts', *Journal of Verbal Learning and Verbal Behavior* 18.4 (1979): 427–440.

16 Yuki Kamide, Gerry T. M. Altmann, and Sarah L. Haywood, 'The Time-Course of Prediction in Incremental Sentence Processing: Evidence from Anticipatory Eye Movements', *Journal of Memory and Language* 49.1 (2003): 133–156.

17 Allan M. Collins and Elizabeth F. Loftus, 'A Spreading Activation Theory of Semantic Processing', *Psychological Review* 82 (1975): 407–428.

18 Posner and Snyder, 1975, as cited by James Neely, 'Semantic Priming and Retrieval from Lexical Memory: Roles of Inhibitionless Spreading Activation and Limited-Capacity Attention', *Journal of Experimental Psychology: General* 106.3 (1977): 226–254.

19 Neely, 'Semantic Priming and Retrieval from Lexical Memory'.

20 Amy Cook, 'Interplay: The Method and Potential of a Cognitive Scientific Approach to Theatre', *Theatre Journal* 59 (2007): 579–594.

PART IV

Contemporary Sites
for Language Change

12

CAROL CHILLINGTON RUTTER

Writing for Actors: Language that Cues Performance

Hamlet, Prince of Denmark, does it. Likewise, Peter Quince, carpenter of Athens. They write for actors. And writing for actors, they tell us something about how the playwright who's written them writes for actors. Among those actors, it should never be forgotten, was the playwright himself. William Shakespeare began his theatrical career as an actor. Only later did he double the business of writing plays with the work of acting them.

Hamlet, of course, first *remembers* writing. Not because he's read it, like those 'Words, words, words' (*Ham.* 2.2.189) he mockingly quotes back to Polonius out of a book he's perusing. But because he's heard it. A speech. In an 'excellent play' (though to be honest, it 'pleased not the million' (2.2.399, 396–397)). The 'lines' – that is, the writing – contained 'no sallets' to make them 'savoury' (401). The 'matter in the phrase' – again, the writing – boasted no 'affectation' (402). The 'speech' Hamlet 'chiefly loved' was 'Aeneas' tale to Dido' where 'he speaks of Priam's slaughter' (404–406). It's a speech that, when the professional Player takes it up from the Prince, finally overwhelms the actor. It 'turn[s] his colour', puts 'tears in's eyes' (476–477). Or, alternatively, it does nothing of the sort. Rather, it *simulates* that emotional affect. It's a speech the professional Player has so thoroughly mastered that he can use it to master the reactions of his audience. His speech, that is, performs an imitation of those very actions that so impress his spectators as 'real', its evidence the artificially constructed but persuasive 'forms' (namely, 'Tears in his eyes', 'A broken voice') 'suiting' his 'conceit' (507–509). In any case, it's a speech that, standing as the feigning double of Hamlet's real 'Tears … distraction … passion', will shortly launch a tumultuous reaction, the Player's 'call' triggering in Hamlet a 'response', another speech: 'O, what a rogue' (502). By then, however, it will already have prompted other writing, writing conceived as 'speech', because before he dismissed the Player, Hamlet put it to him that he 'could for a need study a speech of some dozen or sixteen lines, which I would set down and insert in't, could [he] not?' (493–495).

With those 'dozen or sixteen lines' Hamlet enters *The Murder of Gonzago* as writer, adapter, reviser – and as what a later theatre will call a 'director'. He hasn't just given the players new writing, a new speech. He's 'pronounced it' to them (3.2.1). He's taught them how to speak it. With this, Hamlet the Dane momentarily shades into Quince the Carpenter (and his sidekick, Bottom the Weaver).

That Quince, borrowing from Ovid, is the writer of *Pyramus and Thisbe* may be granted. That Bottom thinks the play needs doctoring is indisputable: 'There are things in this comedy ... that will never please' (*MND* 3.1.8–9). They might be remedied by cuts (cut the sword, cut the killing). Or as Bottom proposes, the opposite. Additions. More writing. To be produced to order, it appears, by Quince, on instructions from the actors ('Write me a prologue'; 'in eight and six'; 'No ... eight and eight' (13, 18–20)). Writing begets writing. Between rehearsal and performance, three new prologues are written (and Quince's 'original' prologue is substantially altered), creating three new speaking parts (and cutting three others), adding significantly more new 'matter' to this play than Hamlet added to *Gonzago*.

What do we learn from these vignettes? First I think we see something of the immediacy of exchange between playwright and players and the push and shove of its dynamic. The play is an active work of collaboration; the script (literally, 'something written', *OED*1) is not fixed, finished, and final but elastic, permissive of addition, revision, wholesale redesign and reconceptualising, even of changed endings.[1] The 'matter' between playwright and player is writing, 'lines' 'set down' that they both conceive as 'speech'. Sometimes it's told, 'pronounced' to the players by the writer in a read-through.[2] Sometimes it's demanded by the players to satisfy 'some necessary question of the play' (*Ham.* 3.2.34).

Speeches are what Shakespeare writes. They're what *Hamlet*'s players speak, what actors on stage do. 'Talk' – like Aeneas' to Dido – tells stories. 'Talk' speaks of other persons, times, places, happenings, tugging 'elsewhere' and 'else when' into the here and now. It conducts what Shakespeare learned to write as a pupil in the grammar school, in composition exercises teaching *narratio*. But it also produces what we think of as 'character effect', that is, what Shakespeare was trained in school to write as *ethopoeia*, the 'speech for a character' that literally 'pronounced' the character through the speech. Bottom demonstrates with some lines he's remembered from a previous gig. 'The raging rocks/And shivering shocks' is 'lofty' writing, writing for 'a tyrant', for 'Ercles' vein' (*MND* 1.2.24–33). A lover, like Pyramus, is made of different stuff. 'A lover is more condoling' (33).

Writing, then, serves actors, not least to work affectively on audiences. Again, learning strategies in writing and speaking to address and move an audience was part of the core grammar school curriculum. (Some audiences will just get bored, like Polonius: 'This is too long' (*Ham.* 2.2.456); others will be so rapt that any interruption will drive them to threats of violence: 'It shall to th' barber's with your beard' (57).) Bottom is thinking of the audience when he warns them to 'look to their eyes'. The 'true performing' of his projected death as Pyramus will cause them to weep buckets of 'tears': 'I will move stones' (*MND* 1.2.19–20). But playwrights, too, use writing to get things done – like Hamlet, baiting a mousetrap with a dozen or sixteen lines.

If writing is work for the playwright – and there's a clue in the word that connects him to the shipwright, the wheelwright, to what is 'wrought' by hard graft – it is also work for the player. It requires 'study', the effort of learning lines: 'let me see', says Hamlet cudgeling his brain to stir from the limbeck of memory a 'speech' he 'heard ... once' (2.2.407, 395). He gets it wrong, ''Tis not so' (409), like poor little Flute in *A Midsummer Night's Dream* stumbling over 'Ninny's tomb' (*MND* 3.1.79). But he knows 'it begins with Pyrrhus' (*Ham.* 2.2.409). Thus, tracking Hamlet remembering, Shakespeare's writing (also) documents the actor's craft.

Where language, if by 'language' we mean 'word choice', comes in to all this is at the level, perhaps, of 'sallets' and 'savour[ies]', word choice registering the 'lofty' vs. the 'condoling' vs. the 'affected' vs. the 'greasy' (the latter Mistress Page's term in *Wiv.* 2.1.86). But 'language', a word Shakespeare uses only forty-three times across the canon of his plays, is always subsumed in 'speech', the activity of speaking. 'Speech' and 'speeches' are words that appear four times as often – while 'speak' and its cognates occur more than 1,400 times. (It appears impossible to talk about 'language' in Shakespeare as a separate category from 'speech': to wit, the director, Richard Eyre, writing that 'The life of his plays is in the language, not alongside it or underneath it'.[3] But in the next sentence: 'Feelings and thoughts are released at the moment of speech' (22/23). The scholar, Frank Kermode, wanting to take 'us back to the essence of Shakespeare – his words' because Shakespeare's 'use of language' is 'where the true power of his plays lies', is yet unable to talk about those words without considering how they 'register' in 'speech').[4]

Speech is prodigiously generative in Shakespeare. As the director Adam Smethurst puts it, 'Everything in Shakespeare comes out of the characters' mouths. They are by nature verbose. Modern plays are full of gaps, silences; you have to figure out what characters mean by what's unsaid. But Shakespeare's characters leave nothing unsaid – because Shakespeare gives it to them to say.'[5] Shakespeare's plays start talking before they've even begun. Actors enter mid-speech, mid-conversation (*Othello*, *As You Like It*, *King Lear*). They keep talking after the final line (*Merry Wives*, *Taming of the Shrew*, *Two Gentlemen of Verona*, *Winter's Tale*). Speech begets speech – because every speech is a script for an encounter, a 'call' antici-pating, even goading a 'response' (even when sometimes the object of the speech is to close off response). As Lynne Magnusson acutely observes, on Shakespeare's stage it is not the speech that is 'the unit of dramatic discourse' but '*the exchange*' (my italics).[6] It's evident that exchange occurs between characters, in dialogue. But it's also built into speeches themselves, speeches constructed dialogically as debates with the self that record decisions but that also discover interiority ('It must be by his death' (*JC* 2.1.10); 'I am settled' (*Mac.* 2.1.79)).

Does anyone ever get the last word in Shakespeare? Equally, to under-stand any speech in Shakespeare, can one start anywhere but with the one before?

'There's something in the writing'

In what follows, I offer close readings of a small sample of actorly writing under two broad headings.[7] I could go about this following Peter Mack's lead. In his Chapter 7 of this volume, he builds up a detailed account of the grammar school training in rhetoric that furnished William Shakespeare's mind, that equipped him between the ages of about seven to thirteen as reader, writer, and speaker with the 'techne' to 'wright' plays that every-where exhibit his pupil learning. Once we know the syllabus, we can see Shakespeare the adult poet-maker composing his writing out of a toolkit picked up 'in the grammar'.

But I want to start somewhere else, not with the writer, but the actor, with Bottom, sent home by Quince with a part in his hand to 'con ... by tomorrow night' (1.2.79–80), a part that, when he pitches up at the following day's rehearsal, he's seriously questioning: 'How answer you that?' (3.1.10). It's the actor probing the writing that interests me here. When actors like Hamlet's Player 'study' Shakespeare's lines, what do they find in them that cues their performance? When an actor like Simon Russell Beale muses 'There's something in the writing' as he tries to account for his Macbeth or Leontes or Richard; or when Antony Sher talks about 'learn[ing] from the writing'; or Harriet Walter about 'working through the words' and 'trust[ing]' Shakespeare's words because they 'do most of the job for you', what do they mean?[8]

Speaking Action

Armed with two further observations from Walter, that in Shakespeare, 'speeches are actions' and that in his time, 'language was nearer to action than it is now' (162), coupled to Lynne Magnusson's observation that 'the unit of theatrical discourse' in Shakespeare is 'the exchange', I begin with five short lines from *Antony and Cleopatra*:

CAESAR	Welcome to Rome.
ANTONY	Thank you.
CAESAR	Sit.
ANTONY	Sit, sir.
CAESAR	Nay, then. (2.2.30–34)

The backstory to this exchange is that threats of civil war in Italy have forced Antony, long absent from duty in Egypt where he's quite prepared to let 'the wide arch / Of the ranged [Roman] empire fall' as long as he can occupy the 'space' that is Cleopatra, to return to his imperial responsibilities in Rome (1.1.35–36). He's one of the triumvirs – the 'triple pillar[s] of the world' (1.1.12) who rule the empire from Asia in the east to Britain in the west. Here, summoned from a life the men in Rome have imagined as a continuous round of 'lascivious wassails' (1.4.57) that have transformed their 'plated Mars' (1.1.4) into a sex tool, 'the bellows and the fan / To cool a gipsy's lust' (9–10), Antony meets his estranged partners-in-power. These five lines stage the opening of their summit. They come on the heels of an emollient appeal from Lepidus, the third 'pillar'. He urges that as 'friends' they 'debate' their 'trivial difference' 'gently' (2.2.19–23) and 'Touch … the sourest points with sweetest terms' (26). That is, he sets up a diplomatic framework, a set of verbal criteria for the talks, but also loops discourse through himself, staving off the moment when Antony and Caesar address each other. (The one thinks of his companion in empire as a 'scarce-bearded' 'boy', the other mocks his elder as 'the old ruffian' (1.1.22, 4.1.4).) Antony responds in kind – *to Lepidus*: ''Tis spoken well' (2.2.27). And he offers a gesture of unity, signalled by 'Were we before our armies, and to fight, / I should do thus' (28–29), where 'thus' is perhaps an embrace (of Caesar? of Lepidus?) even as the hypothetical 'Were we' uneasily frames peace talks within the behaviours of warfare. An embrace is the show you put on in front of your soldiers to demonstrate that the generals are of one mind no matter what they've argued in their tent. Caesar, who has held back, silent, is the third to speak: 'Welcome to Rome.' The line does the business. Its courtesy is functional. It gives nothing away. Neither does Antony's response: 'Thank you.' The formalities are observed. But barely. Tight-lipped, the terseness enacts the relationship – and characterises it. (Earlier, in their separate scenes, they've never been lost for words.) Caesar issues an instruction. 'Sit.' An imperative, not an invitation. (Treating Antony like one of those 'boys' he earlier thought needed to be 'chid' for 'Pawn[ing] their experience' to their 'pleasure' (1.4.30–32)?) Antony revises the instruction. Does he correct what he hears as Caesar's insolence ('You meant to say, "Sit, *sir*"')? Or is he rebuffing Caesar, turning the imperative back on him barbed with courtesy, telling *him* 'Sit, sir'? How does 'Nay, then' function? A rebuff to a rebuff? A refusal to be instructed? A back-handed un-declaration of 'I know what you're up to and I'm not playing'? And what about the body language? Do either or both perform the act of sitting? Sitting *how*? Does one or other remain stubbornly standing? If so, do different levels between sitting and standing enact a power differential? (Notice: while the Cambridge editor marks '[*They sit*]' after line 34, there's no Shakespearean authority for that stage direction. It's an interpolation that closes off other options. And perhaps it should be removed, for no single performance is 'coded' or 'blueprinted' in Shakespeare's writing. The writing provides a framework. It gives actors performance choices. The choices they make will change the story told on stage.)

On a stage where the bodies are frozen in a tableau of suspense, these five lines give the action: manoeuvring, positioning, brinkmanship; a face-to-face showdown. They give the culture of relationships that's going to be put into hazard as the play proceeds, the 'pair of chops' that 'between them' will 'grind the one the other' to the ruin of the geopolitical order (3.5.11–13). Who's going to blink first? This writing laid out on the printed page (both in the 1623 Folio where *Antony and Cleopatra* is first published and in modern editions) formats a balance of power between the 'competitors'. For now, they're evenly matched.

Typography in *Macbeth* Act 2, scene 2 tells a different story. Lines printed staccato fashion in the Folio unravel down the page of a modern text. This is the scene of the offstage assassination of the sleeping king. Onstage, Lady Macbeth's lines cover the killing. She hears her husband's voice (off) ask 'Who's there? What ho?' (8) and she, alone on stage, cries,

> Alack, I am afraid they have awaked,
> And 'tis not done; th'attempt and not the deed
> Confounds us. Hark! I laid their daggers ready,
> He could not miss 'em. Had he not resembled
> My father as he slept, I had done't.   (9–13)

Five ideas rush across these five lines that tip headlong into each other across the iambic pentameter line endings. It's almost as if she's gulping for breath, hyper-alert to sight and sound; to almost stupid practicalities ('I laid their daggers ready') alongside urgent politics ('attempt … the deed'). But then the mind that has so far been fixed on the efficient mechanics of the 'deed', the 'it' she can't name, is stunningly repositioned, hijacked by that non sequitur that zooms into her interiority ('My father'). A window onto an alternative existential space opens, then slams shut as Macbeth enters and she anchors on the immediate, the familiar:

LADY MACBETH	My husband?
MACBETH	I have done the deed. Didst thou not hear a noise?
LADY MACBETH	I heard the owl scream and the crickets cry.
	Did not you speak?
MACBETH	When?
LADY MACBETH	Now.
MACBETH	As I descended?
LADY MACBETH	Ay.
MACBETH	Hark ... (13–21)

This writing produces speakers on fast-forward. It enacts fear, fear registered in the hyper-sensitivity to a world in the dead silence of two hours past midnight that is suddenly loud with screams, cries, noise. Fear registered in the string of questions. A world weirdly defamiliarised, unknowable. Jumpy. Nervous. It gives hearts racing, thumping across the monosyllables. Earlier Macbeth pondered the hypothetical 'If it were done when 'tis done' (1.7.1). Then, when murder was just a plan, he declared himself 'settled' to 'bend up / Each corporal agent' to the 'terrible feat' (79–80). Now the 'deed' *is* 'done'. The conspirators are perpetrators. And the writing shows nothing 'settled'. Earlier, husband and wife were so bound into each other's thinking that they finished each other's lines: see 1.7.30, 35, 45, 47, 59. Here, lines fly apart. The partnership is unravelling.

Macbeth (1606) comes well into the period of Shakespeare's mature playwriting. Early on, when he's still an apprentice, his writing feels as though it's been plagiarised from his school exercise books, its 'action' consisting of spinning out post-adolescent debates on pupil themes as if he's been tasked to compose a description, a comparison, an analogy cast as dialogue; to use a commonplace or proverb or to elaborate a particular trope. This writing is artful, literally artificial, crafted. It characterises *The Two Gentlemen of Verona* (1590–1), perhaps Shakespeare's first play,[9] one that opens as if conscious of its debts to the grammar school, mid-debate, with Valentine bidding his best mate Proteus farewell: 'Cease to persuade, my loving Proteus' (1.1.1). He's off to the court in Milan to seek manly adventure while love-sick Proteus hangs around Verona like some big girl's blouse, pining for Julia. Invoking a proverb ('Home-keeping youths have ever homely wits' (2)) Valentine ridicules his friend's willingness to 'wear out [his] youth with shapeless idleness', 'living dully sluggardised at home' (7–8): the hyperbole functions as mock advice. Saying his 'adieu', literally giving his soon-to-be-absent friend 'to God', prompts Proteus to cast himself in the role of protector, elevating himself to holy prophylactic:

> PROTEUS   If ever danger do environ thee,
>   Commend thy grievance to my holy prayers,
>   For I will be thy beadsman, Valentine.   (16–18)

'Beadsman', someone hired to say round-the-clock prayers for your soul. That's a bit much, isn't it? Particularly set against the name 'Valentine'. Does this writing make Proteus earnest? Priggish? Or simply silly? Whichever, it's the set-up that launches the lads into a sequence of one-liners, banter that's also barbed, competitive as it uses repetition, inversion, rhetorical questions, classical allusion, exaggeration and diminution, paronomasia, demonstration, to play upon words in a chain of witticisms where the action *is* the speaking:

> VALENTINE   And on a love-book pray for my success?
> PROTEUS   Upon some book I love I'll pray for thee.
> VALENTINE   That's on some shallow story of deep love –
>   How young Leander crossed the Hellespont.
> PROTEUS   That's a deep story of a deeper love.
>   For he was more than over shoes in love.
> VALENTINE   'Tis true; for you are over boots in love,
>   And yet you never swam the Hellespont.
> PROTEUS   Over boots? Nay, give me not the boots.
> VALENTINE   No, I will not; for it boots thee not.
> PROTEUS   What?
> VALENTINE   To be in love ...   (1.1.19–29)

The artfulness of this writing sits on its surface. These youths bandy words like today's lads kick footballs. Is the display dazzling? The polished rhetorical equipment of the gentleman? Or finally tedious? It speaks a kind of laddishness, as in *Romeo and Juliet* (2.4.40–75). But women are adept at it too: Julia interrogating Lucetta in *The Two Gentlemen of Verona* 1.2; Kate sparring with Petruchio in *The Taming of the Shrew* 2.1.190–257; the women of France managing their would-be suitors in *Love's Labour's Lost* 2.1.90–125; Queen Elizabeth out-pacing Richard III (*R3* 4.4.199–434). In *Twelfth Night* the reluctant ambassador-of-love to Olivia, Viola disguised as Cesario, is strung along with wordplay that she has initiated but that progressively trips up the messenger ('divinity', 'profanation', 'text', 'doctrine', 'chapter', 'heresy'). Finally she goes off text. She cuts through word-bandying to open a new, direct line of negotiation: 'Good madam, let me see your face' (1.5.188).

By the time he's written his way to *The Merry Wives of Windsor* (1597–8) Shakespeare is embedding school exercises in the fabric of the writing.

At the top of Act 2, scene 1 Mistress Page is reading a letter – a form of writing Shakespeare had practised hundreds of times at school following Erasmus's practical manual, *De conscribendis epistolis*, which gave dozens of examples to imitate: letters of advice, warning, invitation, encouragement; begging letters, apologies. In Mistress Pages's hands he makes a worn convention an explosive device.

Modern editions mark her entrance alone, 'with' a letter. Folio, however, gives something different, a group entrance, '*Enter Mistris Page, Mistris Ford, Master Page, Master Ford, Pistoll, Nim, Quickly, Host, Shallow*', as though at the top of the scene the stage is crowded with Windsor life passing across it, absorbed in various affairs before Mistress Page steps forward, reading:

> What, have I 'scaped love-letters in the holiday time of my
> beauty, and am now a subject for them? Let me see.   (2.1.1–2)

An entrance 'solo' begs a question: where has the letter come from? And how does she know it's a love letter before she's opened it? Folio's busy 'scrum' entrance allows for the letter's onstage delivery – and business to be performed to characterise that delivery. In what spectators have just seen, Pistol and Nim have refused the assignment. They're now on a revenge mission to 'out' Falstaff, the would-be seducer, to the husbands he plans to abuse. Meanwhile, little Robin has been made the fat knight's messenger boy. Is this messy scenario what is shaping up in Folio's group entrance? Are Falstaff's cashiered bully-boys now dogging Page and Ford? En route from A to B, is Mistress Page literally knocked off course, blind-sided by a letter secretly thrust into her hands by someone who disappears? Is her opening comment irony ('Of *course* it's not a love letter! I'm a middle-aged woman, not a green girl') that instantly rebounds? Is there something sad about this jesting-with-the-self? Is this a woman who, genuinely, has *never* received a love letter? Not even from Page wooing her in the 'holiday time' of her 'beauty'? What might this say of their relationship now? What does it say about the culture of female behaviour in Windsor that love-letters are something to be ''scaped'?

With 'Let me see', Mistress Page enters the letter, and what she's speaking as she begins reading is Falstaff – though of course, she doesn't know it yet. That's the beauty of the theatrical letter. It puts an absent person (and message) on stage, but ventriloquised by the reader who is not just voicing but interpreting the message. It produces dialogue in the form of soliloquy, allowing the audience (who in this case knows the identity of the writer) to measure the discrepancy between the reader and the matter read, the distance between the sender (as he imagines himself; in this case, the endlessly self-regarding, self-fantasising Falstaff) and the recipient, and to anticipate what's going to happen when the reader finds out what the audience already knows. Just as the letter subjects the reader to its communication, so the reader subjects *it* to comment:

> Let me see.
>
> 'Ask me no reason why I love you, for though Love use Reason for his precisian, he admits him not for his counsellor. You are not young, no more am I. Go to, then, there's sympathy. You are merry, so am I. Ha, ha, then, there's more sympathy. You love sack, and so do I. Would you desire better sympathy? Let it suffice thee, Mistress Page – at the least if the love of soldier can suffice – that I love thee. I will not say pity me – 'tis not a soldier-like phrase – but I say, love me. By me.
>
> > Thine own true knight.
> > By day or night
> > Or any kind of light,
> > With all his might,
> > For thee to fight,
>
> > > Jack Falstaff.'   (2–16)

Her reading finished, Mistress Page starts exclaiming on the writing – and writer:

> What a Herod of Jewry is this! O, wicked, wicked world! One that is well-nigh worn to pieces with age, to show himself a young gallant! What an unweighed behaviour hath this Flemish drunkard picked – with the devil's name – out of my conversation, that he dares in this manner assay me? Why, he hath not been thrice in my company. What should I say to him? I was then frugal of my mirth. Heaven forgive me! Why, I'll exhibit a bill in the parliament for the putting down of men. How shall I be revenged on him? For revenged I will be, as sure as his guts are made of puddings.
>
> > [*Enter* MISTRESS FORD]   (2.1.17–25)

The first thing to remark about this double speech, this speech-inside-a-speech, is that it's almost entirely in prose, which allows for an entirely different beat, rhythm, and pace to the speaking than blank verse, reined-in as it is by iambic pentameter. Prose works towards the 'period', the full stop (where Mistress Page takes a breath – or gasps) in sentences of various length and complexity of construction. The comic brilliance of the letter read aloud is that, delivering himself secretly in writing, Falstaff utterly exposes himself, and in ways he doesn't expect. A seduction letter? This would get F-minus in school. Erasmus's first principle of letter-writing was 'know your audience'. Falstaff clearly hasn't got a clue. Aiming to seduce, he insults ('You are not young'); to find 'sympathy', he's buffoonish ('Ha, ha'). Suggesting his love interest could be his drinking companion is hardly aphrodisiac. Positioning himself simultaneously as soldier and lover, bound together in the role of chivalric 'knight', he writes himself a fool in the jingle-jangle doggerel that signs him off: 'Jack Falstaff'. JACK FALSTAFF! The mystery writer named, the letter takes on a radically different reading. For Mistress Page, like an actor working through the writing, the contents discover themselves bit by bit (and the actor, who is in complete control of the pace of discovery, will find instructions about that discovery in the rhythms of the prose, not least by observing sentence structure and hitting full stops).

Her speech is a welter of colliding ideas: first, bemused? pained? surprised? beguiled? flattered? at being 'subject', middle-aged, to a 'love-letter[]'; bewildered by the letter's opening opacity, built on impenetrable antitheses ('Love' and 'Reason'; 'precision' and 'counselor'); increasingly perplexed by the letter's direction of travel, veering between the fantastic-ally artful and the hopelessly blunt; then sucker-punched by the signature. Was she momentarily fantasising 'a true knight' and a romantic flirtation in the autumn of her life? Not after she reads 'Jack Falstaff'. But just as he's exposed in the writing, so is she. Turning massive, hyperbolised indignation upon him, where the comedy value lies in the outsized-imagery ('Herod of Jewry') and the way such extremes of deluded self-image are poised against actuality ('worn to pieces with age'/'young gallant'; 'true knight'/'Falstaff') she instantly re-turns the gaze inwardly upon herself to examine her own behaviour. What's she done to provoke this letter? Has she been immodest? Too free with words, with welcome, with mirth? *Is it her fault?* The mis-ogynist lobby that regularly gets a voice in Shakespeare (from Angelo to Iago to Lear) would make any sexual fault 'naturally' the woman's. But just as instantly, Mistress Page turns her view outward again: proposing, outra-geously, to submit a private member's bill in parliament for the suppression of men. Because *they're* what's wrong with society. Cultural innovation ('putting down … men') explodes cultural cliché ('unweighed behaviour'). The unsolicited letter – that has performed Falstaff's work on the unsus-pecting recipient insofar as it has seduced her into reading it, and *to keep reading it* – has taken Mistress Page on a rollercoaster ride. Its action comes full circle: from imagination piqued to humiliation, a woman flattered to one realising she's been duped. If, to begin with, it tempted Mistress Page down a primrose path to dalliance, it ends setting her on the war-path – to revenge. And that project can get going right now, with '[*Enter* MISTRESS FORD]'.

Speaking Thought

If 'speeches are actions', as Walter says, one of the actions they perform is thinking. Soliloquies are first-person thinking-machines, studies of the self, arguments with the present, evaluators of alternatives, places for imagining an 'other'. (The term 'soliloquy', though, is a misnomer: no one on Shakespeare's stage ever 'talks' 'alone'. The audience is always there, listening.) As soliloquies tussle with the world observed, they reveal interiority. They reveal a self. But they also act upon the world. Soliloquies conduct 'some necessary question[s] of the play' (*Ham.* 3.2.34). They 'do' plot.

In *The Third Part of King Henry VI*, the pacifist king sits himself on a molehill, wearily retired from the indeterminate slaughter at Towton where both sides, 'tugging to be victors', are 'neither conqueror nor conquerèd' (2.5.11–12). He reflects wryly that his warrior Queen, at the front of his army, has 'chid' (17) him from the battle. She does better without him. He wishes he were dead, 'if God's good will were so' (19). It's not. Not yet. So, instead, he apostrophises 'O God' as he begins imagining another life, a 'happy life' (21), not King of England, but the king's anti-body, a shepherd. 'Life' (against the death he desires) provokes thoughts about the span of human time, which he amplifies by imagining his shepherd-self fashioning a clock, carving numbers on a dial, watching it to 'see the minutes how they run' (25), thoughts that are themselves fashioned by repetition across six lines ('How many hours ... How many days ...' (26–29)). Watching his clock, learning 'How many years a mortal man may live', he'd know how 'to divide the time' (29–30). Across eight lines that all begin 'So many hours must I ...' (31–38), he orders time ('tend my flock', 'take my rest') to reach the wished conclusion of a life finished, 'white hairs' brought 'unto a quiet grave' (40). He reflects: 'Ah, what a life were this! How sweet! How lovely!' (41). And that reflection prompts a comparison that he elaborates across the next fourteen lines, comparing the shepherd's 'homely' 'leather bottle' (47–48) to the king's 'curious' 'golden cup' (52–53), his life tending 'seely sheep' (43) to the king's, betrayed by 'subjects' treachery' (45); a 'sweet' (41) life against a life of 'care, mistrust and treason' (54).

This is early writing. It's contemporary with *The Two Gentlemen of Verona* and shows that play's same indebtedness to the classroom. King Henry needs fifty-four lines to elaborate his four big ideas that take him from war-reportage to the nihilistic core of his thinking – 'Would I were dead' (19) – out the other side to a meditation on kingship (a 'theme' that Shakespeare will re-write over and over across his whole career, putting it in the mouths of Richard II, Henry IV, Henry V, and even, grotesquely reiterated, Lear). Its status as rhetorical 'proof' is signalled: 'And to conclude' at line 47 brings him to a final two-part comparison, balancing an antithesis across eight lines. The craft of this writing, as in *Verona*, is visible on its surface. The repetition is almost stultifying. But as ethopoeia, paradoxically it's mesmerising: fifty-four measured lines give us a Henry paralysed, locked into an immobilising discourse that places him a million miles remote from his war-mongering barons, the only man in England who thinks like he does. (Shakespeare will do this better later, where the pressure of repetition will produce the paralysis of a fixated mind going mad: 'Methought I heard a voice cry "Sleep no more: / Macbeth does murder sleep" … sleep, / Sleep … / … Sleep … / … sleep … / … sleep … sleep …' (2.2.38–46).) King Henry's ineffectuality registers not just in his distance from the battle, stranded on that impromptu rustic throne, the molehill, or in the rhetorical tropes that anaesthetise the mind, but in the fact that he has no one to talk to but the audience.

When Helena, in *A Midsummer Night's Dream*, has no one to talk to but the audience, she's trying to make sense of her love life. The lad she's in love with has fallen for her best friend who's just confided that she and the lad who loves *her* are eloping. Tonight. The love-birds flap off. Helena watches them go. Then turns and speaks:

> How happy some o'er other some can be!
> Through Athens I am thought as fair as she.
> But what of that? Demetrius thinks not so;
> He will not know what all but he do know.
> And as he errs, doting on Hermia's eyes,
> So I, admiring of his qualities.
> Things base and vile, holding no quantity,
> Love can transpose to form and dignity.
> Love looks not with the eyes, but with the mind,
> And therefore is winged Cupid painted blind.
> Nor hath love's mind of any judgement taste;
> Wings, and no eyes, figure unheedy haste;
> And therefore is love said to be a child
> Because in choice he is so oft beguiled.
> As waggish boys in game themselves forswear,
> So the boy Love is perjured everywhere;
> For, ere Demetrius looked on Hermia's eyne,
> He hailed down oaths that he was only mine,
> And when this hail some heat from Hermia felt,
> So he dissolved, and showers of oaths did melt.
> I will go tell him of fair Hermia's flight:
> Then to the wood will he tomorrow night
> Pursue her; and for this intelligence,

If I have thanks it is a dear expense;
But herein mean I to enrich my pain,
To have his sight thither, and back again.   (1.1.226–251)

How is it that Demetrius doesn't love her anymore? How is it that *everyone* loves Hermia? Helena's opening line is a giveaway: 'How happy some o'er other some can be!' She's talking about herself and Hermia, but she can't, or won't, pronounce the names – a formal (ridiculous?) distancing of herself from her painful narrative, holding her aloof from the topic of her heart-ache. She starts by taking stock with that commonplace. Which produces a factual observation. Dismissed with a rhetorical question. *That* leads to another observation-as-fact. And another. Then a comparison. Another commonplace ('Things base and vile'). Another. Another; almost a string of proverbial 'knowledges' about how love works assembled as logical 'argu-ment' that brings her to a conclusion ('And therefore … Because … As … So … For … And … So') which the rhetorical structure, using example and analogy, demonstrates as truth. It's incontrovertible. And dismal: love is blind, mistaking, fooled, and false. Working things through, Helena has longer and longer thoughts: first, four end-stopped one-liners; then six end-stopped two-liners; then four lines that bring general 'truth' to roost on Helena's particular problem; followed by six lines that – with a huge gulp of breath – turn the speech, as radically as Mistress Page turns from reading to revenge.

The citations Helena uses here rhetorically to frame her discourse – the role of 'blind' 'Cupid', the operations of 'eyes' vs. 'mind', the transform-ational capacity of love ('things base and vile') – are going to return, embodied across the play: metaphors 'translated' into action. Eyes are going to be interfered with; a hard-handed 'mechanical' of Athens is going to be transformed into the beloved of the Fairy Queen – but with the head of an ass. Here, soliloquy plants the images that are going to produce the magic flowers gathered later in such abundance. But there's something else about the writing of this speech for the actor to catch hold of: the rhyming coup-lets. Everything Helena says is locked into the structure. She can't think beyond two lines. There's no space for free-wheeling speculation – for getting out of the box of received opinion ('Love looks not … And there-fore …'). There's something endearing about the flatness of Helena's misery. (That string of images that connects 'oaths' 'hailed down' to 'oaths' as 'hail' 'dissolved' by 'heat' into watery 'showers' is heart-rending and ludicrous in equal parts.) But there's also something irritating (or laughable) about Helena's rhetoric of stalemate – until line 246, where she kick-starts the future by moving from reaction to action. She hatches a plot. 'I will go tell him of fair Hermia's flight.' And for the first time, she is talking beyond the couplet: 'Then to the wood will he tomorrow night / Pursue her' – Helena is off. Sprung free by the writing.

What Shakespeare is doing in Helena's speech is as crafted (and crafty) as his writing for Henry VI, but, as with the development from *Verona* to *Windsor*, in *Dream* the art is not so attention-seeking. It's on the surface, but also submerged in the deep structure of the writing. And once again, it's the means of discovering character.

There is in Shakespeare one character who makes a career of talking not just to the audience (like Iago and hunchback Richard Gloucester) but *with* the audience: Hamlet. His first soliloquy – 'O, that this too too solid flesh … self-slaughter' (1.2.129–132) – might be a rewrite of Henry on the molehill that ends, like Henry's, in paralysis: 'But break my heart, for I must hold my tongue' (1.2.159). What's different is what happens in between, as, like Helena, he tries to make sense of his life in a tumult of thought prompted by his bewildered 'That it should come to this' (137), where he tries to explicate 'this', and can't, for another nineteen lines until he gets to 'She married' (156). The brokenness of the speech, its constant self-interruptions, interjections, exclamations, back-trackings are rhetorically rooted in his anguished cry 'Must I remember?' (143) as the writing tugs him into devastated memory even as he tries to talk himself out of it.

His second soliloquy parks the death-wish. (It will return later.) But not the self-loathing. He's had his soul-searing interview with the Ghost, his offstage silent-film encounter with Ophelia in her closet. He's wrong-footed Polonius ('What do you read, my lord?'; 'Words, words, words' (2.2.188–189)). His old school chums have turned up. The players have arrived, and they've responded to his command to 'give us a taste of your quality' (2.2.393). He wants that speech he heard once, Aeneas's tale to Dido 'where he speaks of / Priam's slaughter' (404–406): a tale, that is, of a father-king killed by a son revenging the death of his own father. When the First Player gets to Hecuba, to the old queen running 'barefoot up and down' (463), and, as she sees Pyrrhus 'mincing with his sword her husband's limbs' (473), letting out an 'instant burst of clamour' to make the gods weep, he has to break off. 'Look where he has not turned his colour, and has tears in's eyes', Polonius exclaims (477). The impromptu performance ended, the players exit to be 'bestowed' (480). The stage clears. Hamlet observes, 'Now I am alone' (501), and then, under the hyper-pressure of that 'Now', faces the crowd who's watching him, hardly 'alone'. What he needs to talk about is what he's just seen. He's struck by the paradox of acting. The player produces real effects out of fictional materials – 'nothing'. The first line operates as an implied comparison with the next seven lines, one sentence on one breath that bursts out of him, fixed on the actor's body. And what's it for? The half line at 510 says it all:

> O what a rogue and peasant slave am I!
> Is it not monstrous that this player here,
> But in a fiction, in a dream of passion,
> Could force his soul so to his own conceit
> That from her working all his visage wanned,
> Tears in his eyes, distraction in's aspect,
> A broken voice, and his whole function suiting
> With forms to his conceit? And all for nothing?
> For Hecuba! (2.2.501–10)

Saying 'nothing', Hamlet instantly revises himself. 'Nothing' (and this bears thinking about) becomes 'Hecuba' in the next short iambic pentameter line, short by six beats, which Hamlet takes as silence. Thinking. Is Trojan Hecuba 'nothing'? Or everything? Thoughts of the player's (real) responsibilities to (fictional) Hecuba turn Hamlet to comparison, a hypothetical 'What would he do', that analogises the player to the prince, who *should be acting*, but isn't:

> What's Hecuba to him, or he to Hecuba
> That he should weep for her? What would he do,
> Had he the motive and the cue for passion
> That I have? He would drown the stage with tears,
> And cleave the general ear with horrid speech,
> Make mad the guilty and appal the free,
> Confound the ignorant, and amaze indeed
> The very faculty of eyes and ears. (511–518)

The actor Hamlet imagines acting as his fantasy double is almost comically sensationalised. He 'out-Herods Herod' (3.2.11): 'drown', 'cleave', 'appal', 'amaze'. The agitation in his voice is registered by his longer and longer periods: half a line, one-and-a-half lines, two lines, five lines, pushing out ideas on bigger and bigger breaths. But the point of this hyperbolic activity, in Hamlet's conceit, is to contrast his own inability to act, to get in character, cast by his father-Ghost as 'Revenge'. The turn from outward observation to inward examination, like a film camera's shot/reverse shot, comes on the final two beats of the line, marked by 'Yet':

> Yet I,
> A dull and muddy-mettled rascal, peak
> Like a John-a-dreams, unpregnant of my cause,
> And can say nothing – no, not for a king,

Upon whose property and most dear life
A damned defeat was made.   (518–523)

The player's 'passion' puts 'John-a-dreams' in his abject place. The player's 'nothing' resonates with his own 'nothing', a 'nothing' that paradoxically creates something – 'For Hecuba' – while his own black hole of 'nothing' can do 'nothing – no, not' *for a king*. Hamlet's 'nothing' sobers him. Defeats him. The double-backed syntax registers the knot in his stomach. Then Hamlet cuts through to ask straight out:

> Am I a coward?
> Who calls me villain, breaks my pate across,
> Plucks off my beard and blows it in my face,
> Tweaks me by th'nose, gives me the lie i'th'throat
> As deep as to the lungs? Who does me this?
> Ha, 'swounds, I should take it, for it cannot be
> But I am pigeon-livered and lack gall
> To make oppression bitter, or ere this
> I should ha' fatted all the region kites
> With this slave's offal. Bloody, bawdy villain!
> Remorseless, treacherous, lecherous, kindless villain!
> Oh, vengeance!   (523–534)

Taking on the audience, he gives them permission through his rhetorical questions to voice what they're thinking of him, rolling out the 'character' of the coward in the actions that humiliatingly demonstrate him a craven (his beard plucked, nose tweaked, head cracked, called a villain and a liar: a damning catalogue to set alongside the qualities of the passionate player). The up-front challenge 'Who does me this?' explodes in 'Ha': not a word, but a sound, like the 'Fie' and 'Foh' that are coming, bigger than language or what can be alleviated by language, a pressure gauge that releases Hamlet's steam, deflates him to 'I should take it', which begins another journey of thought that produces another comparison between himself ('pigeon-livered') and the part he should be acting. It's a part he tries on, rehearses in speech. Mouthing words, he makes himself the revenger, fatting 'the region's kites' with 'this 'slave's' – that is, Claudius's – 'offal', an image that turns his uncle-king to human trash; spewing out violent images like vomit fermented in his sick stomach and curdled soul, climaxing with 'Oh, vengeance!' where, like reaching 'For Hecuba', he stops. Thinks. Bluster doesn't suit him:

> Why, what an ass am I! This is most brave,
> That I, the son of the dear murderèd,
> Prompted to my revenge by heaven and hell,
> Must like a whore unpack my heart with words,

> And fall a-cursing like a very drab,
> A scullion!
> Fie upon't, foh!   (535–541)

Now he's not just a rogue, a muddy-mettled rascal, a coward, he's a whore, all mouth. His only action, women's words – women having no recourse to power except through their tongues – makes them drabs, and Hamlet effeminate. Hamlet's next thoughts are too inchoate for articulation. 'Fie' and 'foh' clear Hamlet's mental room. All the 'words, words, words' up to this point have fashioned a space for a new thought to drop in. 'Fie' and 'foh' figure brain activity that launches innovation, lateral thinking attached to what started this whole thinking process off, now taking it in a new direction:

> About, my brains. Hum, I have heard
> That guilty creatures sitting at a play
> Have by the very cunning of the scene
> Been struck so to the soul, that presently
> They have proclaimed their malefactions;
> For murder, though it have no tongue, will speak
> With most miraculous organ.   (541–547)

Memory – what he's heard of theatrical affect – prompts action, paralysis kick-started into agency imaged in precise terms of forensic medical examination, the probe searching the suppurating wound of 'rotten' 'Denmark':

> I'll have these players
> Play something like the murder of my father
> Before my uncle. I'll observe his looks,
> I'll tent him to the quick. If a do blench,
> I know my course.   (547–551)

But one final consideration draws Hamlet back from fixed resolution:

> The spirit that I have seen
> May be the devil – and the devil hath power
> T'assume a pleasing shape. Yea, and perhaps,
> Out of my weakness and my melancholy,
> As he is very potent with such spirits,
> Abuses me to damn me.   (551–556)

It's a genuine fear. It comes out of a stunning, appalling self-diagnosis, admitting a mind diseased. There may be an antidote. Cure may lie in the creative imagination, fiction performing the recuperative operations of truth-telling:

> I'll have grounds
> More relative than this. The play's the thing
> Wherein I'll catch the conscience of the king.   (556–558)

In Hamlet's speech we see performed Harriet Walter's observation that for Shakespeare's audience, soliloquy didn't 'hold up the action, it *was* the action' (163). It performs struggle – live before spectators' eyes. It isn't premeditated; Hamlet doesn't know where it's going until he gets there. It's speech that *needs* speaking, and it stages the play's core paradox, that Hamlet works his way out of his inertia by the activity of thinking through speaking.

There is much more that Shakespeare's writing gives actors than can be demonstrated in these few samples. He writes mental systems crashing, speech breaking down, incoherence: Lear, Othello, Leontes, Lady Macbeth. He writes speech running out: Hotspur, Cleopatra dying, their last lines unfinished. He writes singing and dancing; conjurations and curses; theatrical cover stories, like Touchstone's vaudeville 'turn' at the end of *As You Like It* proving the 'quarrel' upon 'the seventh cause' (5.4.48) that gives Ganymede time to change costume into Rosalind. He writes speech that can only be interpreted in performance: Cleopatra's 'O' to Caesar's messenger at 3.13.57. There's always 'something in the writing'. But also, in Shakespeare, something beyond it. Another kind of language, for bodies in performance. ('Sit': how?) That, however, is subject matter for another essay.

NOTES

1   On the play as unfinished business, see Tiffany Stern, *Documents of Performance in Early Modern England* (Cambridge: Cambridge University Press, 2009), pp. 232–236.
2   See the Admiral's Men listening to their new play at the Sun in Fish Street on 13 March 1598, R. A. Foakes and R. T. Rickert, *Henslowe's Diary* (Cambridge: Cambridge University Press, 1968), p. 88.
3   Richard Eyre and Nicholas Wright, *Changing Stages* (London: Bloomsbury, 2000), pp. 22–23.
4   Frank Kermode, *Shakespeare's Language* (London: Penguin, 2000), pp. 14–17.
5   In conversation, 6 September 2016.
6   Lynne Magnusson, *Shakespeare and Social Dialogue* (Cambridge: Cambridge University Press, 1999), p. 4.
7   I am grateful to the following for conversation at various times about Shakespeare's writing for actors: Paapa Essiedu (on *Hamlet*), Phillip Breen (on *The Merry Wives of Windsor*), Barrie Rutter, Ben Fowler, Simon Russell Beale, Harriet Walter, Antony Sher, John Barton, and Cicely Berry. Their thoughts are the bones and muscle of this chapter.
8   Beale quoted in Carol Chillington Rutter, 'Simon Russell Beale', *The Routledge Companion to Actors' Shakespeare*, ed. John Russell Brown (London: Routledge, 2012), pp. 1–14; p. 9; Antony Sher, *Beside Myself* (London: Arrow Books, 2002), p. 163; Harriet Walter, *Other People's Shoes* (London: Nick Hern Books, 1999), pp. 155, 163.
9   For the dating of Shakespeare's works, I depend on Stanley Wells's 'Chronology' in the New Penguin Shakespeare volumes of individual plays.

13

DIRK DELABASTITA

Language and Translation

At first sight, it may seem odd for this *Cambridge Companion to Shakespeare's Language* to include a chapter on Shakespeare's language and translation. After all, a translation renders a text into *another* language; inasmuch as a translation of Shakespeare is a real translation, it will no longer be in Shakespeare's language. Multilingualism and translation are therefore issues that have nothing to do with the language of Shakespeare's works per se. The translations have been written afterwards and are essentially irrelevant to the English-language writer that Shakespeare is. Such is the widely accepted logic of monolingualism which prevailed until not so long ago, not just in Anglophone public perceptions of Shakespeare but also in Shakespearean scholarship. The study of multilingual or translated Shakespeare was seen as 'an interesting and harmless occupation for researchers abroad',[1] while the Anglo-American critical establishment was devoting itself to the real thing in English. There were surely deeper motives to this logic, such as a lingering Romantic belief in natural genius and absolute originality as supreme aesthetic values. More than a century and a half before the breakthrough of Romanticism, such a belief was already expressed in the laudatory poem by Leonard Digges which was included in John Benson's 1640 edition of the *Sonnets*:

> look through
> This whole book, thou shalt find he doth not borrow
> One phrase from Greeks, nor Latins imitate,
> Nor once from vulgar languages translate,
> ...   All that he doth write
> Is pure his own: plot, language exquisite.[2]

Moreover, from the eighteenth century onwards, Shakespeare was recast as the national poet of England at a time when English was turning into the hegemonic medium and unifying symbol of an expansive world empire. This process further strengthened the nexus between Shakespeare and the

English language, making it almost impossible to imagine him in a language other than his native tongue. Finally, at an admittedly more mundane level but no less tangibly, Shakespearean scholars in the English and American epicentres of academic criticism tended to have limited proficiency in foreign languages, which restricted their access to non-English source materials and made them loath to give much attention to the study of multilingual Shakespeare, a research area in which it would be hard, moreover, to stop more polyglot 'overseas' colleagues from taking control of things.

Not surprisingly, therefore, earlier publications on Shakespeare and his language usually remained silent on issues such as multilingualism and translation. More strangely perhaps, this situation did not alter when a new wave of 'alternative Shakespeares' swept over Shakespearean criticism in the 1980s and 1990s, despite many of these critical renewals heavily investing in themes such as 'language' and 'difference', and *themselves* representing 'translated' forms of Derrida, Foucault, and other French theorists. Other aspects of Shakespeare reception (criticism, film, the visual arts, stage versions, adaptations, anecdotes) were visible on their alternative critical radars but emphatically *not* translation.

This is not to say that Shakespearean translation was not being studied. It was, but in different and largely separate academic quarters. There is a long tradition of researching the international reception and translation of Shakespeare within fields such as comparative literature and theatre history. The oldest monograph of this type known to me, *Histoire de l'influence de Shakspeare sur le théatre français jusqu'à nos jours* (*History of Shakespeare's Influence on the French Theatre until Today*) by Albert Lacroix, goes back as far as 1856![3]

Much significant work on the topic has also been done in translation studies, an interdisciplinary field dealing with the different forms and functions of interlingual and intercultural communication, and combining theoretical, historical, and applied perspectives. Since its emergence from the 1960s and 1970s onwards this discipline has produced a range of new conceptual paradigms and methodological frameworks, which in several cases have ended up being tested on, or applied to, a corpus of Shakespeare translations. *BITRA*, an open-access online *Bibliography of Interpreting and Translation*, has no fewer than 1,128 entries responding to the search-term 'Shakespeare' (out of a total of 70,000 entries); the *Translation Studies Bibliography*, another online reference tool, lists 317 Shakespeare-related entries (out of a total of 28,000 entries).[4]

For the reasons indicated above, this growing body of research was more often than not overlooked or marginalised by 'official' Shakespearean criticism, but one is happy to note that something like a modest 'translational turn' has been occurring of late in Shakespeare studies, doubtless as a result of pressures exerted by wider social trends such as post-colonialism, post-nationalism, migration, internationalisation, and the digital revolution. 'Globalisation' is the catchword that springs to mind here to sum up the radical increase in the mobility not just of capital, decision power, and violence, but also of people, languages, and texts that these phenomena have entailed. The officially Anglophone countries – Shakespeare's own Britain included – are increasingly having to face the social and cultural realities of multilingualism and translation, while, conversely, the rapid spread abroad of English as a world language is enhancing rather than reducing the multilingualism of the traditionally 'non-Anglophone' countries. As a result of these processes, the space in which Shakespeare's texts are now circulating is less than ever defined by neatly separated nationalities and corresponding linguistic borderlines.

The volume *Shakespeare and the Language of Translation*, edited by Ton Hoenselaars in 2004, was a landmark in the discovery of the theme of translation by Anglo-American Shakespeare criticism.[5] The ground had been prepared a decade earlier by volumes such as *Foreign Shakespeare: Contemporary Performance*, edited by Dennis Kennedy, which played a big part in taking off the English-only blinkers (while admittedly devoting more attention to performance than to issues of language and translation as such).[6] Being published under the Arden imprint and by Cambridge University Press, respectively, these two books, among other publications,[7] were instrumental in moving multilingual Shakespeare towards the centre of Shakespearean scholarship.[8]

Much of the work on Shakespeare in other languages is currently being done under the banner of Global Shakespeare. A typical instance of this is the volume *Shakespeare beyond English: A Global Experiment* (2013), edited by Susan Bennett and Christie Carson,[9] which grew out of the 2012 Globe to Globe festival (itself part of the Cultural Olympiad) that saw the complete Shakespeare canon performed in three dozens of different languages in Shakespeare's very own London with or without English surtitles. Ton Hoenselaars and Alexa Huang coined the witty term 'boomerang Shakespeare' for this growing trend of Shakespeare in foreign garb becoming an 'import' product in England after having been chiefly an 'export' product for centuries.[10] The phenomenon is symbolic of today's globalised culture in which the 'world' status both of Shakespeare as a writer and of English as an international lingua franca is more than ever a complex affair involving tensions, negotiations, cohabitations, and hybridisations with other languages and cultural traditions. It is a globalised culture in which, more generally, translation is becoming something like a master metaphor epitomising our present human condition by evoking the search for a sense of self and belonging in a puzzling decentred world full of change and difference.

These developments have fostered an environment in which Shakespearean scholarship is joining theatre directors, audiences, authors, translators, publishers, and other cultural agents worldwide in their acknowledgement of the massive cultural relevance and creative power of Shakespeare and translation. One of the challenges awaiting scholars now is to overcome the disciplinary and, in many cases, the linguistic fragmentation that may prevent us from taking stock of relevant existing research in what are to us less familiar areas. Depending on the exact research questions one wishes to address, the study of Shakespeare translation will require different types of expertise in traditionally distinct fields and subfields such as linguistics (including stylistics), literary studies (including comparative literature), Renaissance studies, theatre history, media studies, and the digital humanities, to mention but those. Crucially, the list would be incomplete without translation studies, a field which has very much come into its own in the last four decades, as is demonstrated by its impressive research output and by the emergence of dedicated book series and international scholarly journals – all of which have been made easily accessible by means of the aforementioned bibliographical tools, as well via several excellent 'handbooks' and 'companions' now available.[11]

There is much to say about the many developments in translation studies and their applications to Shakespeare translation, or about the long and variegated history of the Shakespearean translations themselves. But this chapter will focus on the basic initial question of why students of Shakespeare and Shakespeare's language can benefit from discarding the notion of Shakespeare's exclusive linguistic Englishness and from finding out more about Shakespeare translations. More specifically, four reasons will be presented, with examples taken from the Sonnets and from *Hamlet*.

First, as a creative author, Shakespeare himself drew heavily on a large number of foreign literary and historical sources that came to him either in their original version or in an already translated form. This makes Shakespeare himself into a translator (occasionally) or at least an avid user of translations (systematically). Leonard Digges in the poem quoted above sketches the outline of the popular later picture of Shakespeare as a strictly original writer who is always a sender but never a receiver of influences. Shakespearean source criticism has shown this to be completely wrong. Being a voracious literary recycler, Shakespeare was a 'borrower' as much as he was to become a 'lender'. His texts are fully enmeshed in the multilingual network of intertextuality, which spanned all of Europe and its history.

Hamlet (1600?) provides a good example here, as one of Shakespeare's probable sources for the play was a French version (by François de Belleforest, included in the fifth volume of his *Histoires tragiques* (1570)) of a Latin version (by Saxo Grammaticus, *Historiae Danicae*, (1200?)) of an old Scandinavian legend. How exactly (i.e. how directly or indirectly) Shakespeare was indebted to this French source remains unclear, but there is no doubting his strong dependence on historical and literary sources, or the fact that the study of these sources is to a large extent a form of translation history.

A similar argument can be made for the Sonnets, even if these poems do not contain a 'story' for which a textual 'source' may be found. The number of their verbal echoes of foreign and translated authors (e.g., Ovid) also remains limited. In this case it is the very format of the poems that Shakespeare owed to translation, more specifically, to the efforts of the early-Tudor sonneteers Thomas Wyatt and Henry Howard, who had introduced and then slightly modified the genre into English through their translations and adaptations of Petrarch. Following the line from Wyatt and Howard to Shakespeare, we recognise a familiar pattern of *translatio* ('faithful' translation) leading to *imitatio* ('free' adaptation in the writer's own language) and *aemulatio* (trying to surpass your models), finally enabling what is believed to be fully 'original' composition to take place in the newly imported generic template.

Second, working in, and for, the cosmopolitan, multidialectal and multilingual city that London was, Shakespeare made clever use of the dramatic potential of interlinguistic gaps and translational effects in many of his plays. Shakespeare's recourse to a wide range of English accents, registers, and dialects is well-known and need not detain us here. It would not be hard to find suitable examples of Bakhtinian 'polyphony' in *Hamlet*, a play in which an amazing range of socially embedded 'voices' can be heard resonating. The play variously stages the discourses of power, diplomacy, hypocrisy, rhetoric, theatrical bombast, fashionable affectation, friendly banter, madness, bawdy, and so on. Such examples could count as instances of stylistic variation at the intralingual level. The latter adjective usefully reminds me of Roman Jakobson's often-quoted distinction between three types of translation:

1. Intralingual translation or *rewording* is an interpretation of verbal signs by means of other signs of the same language.
2. Interlingual translation or *translation proper* is an interpretation of verbal signs by means of some other language.
3. Intersemiotic translation or *transmutation* is an interpretation of verbal signs by means of signs of nonverbal sign systems.[12]

To dwell a moment longer on this tripartite distinction, the murder of Gonzago scene in *Hamlet* presents a nice instance of intersemiotic translation, as this play-within-the-play is preceded by a dumb show and is itself a theatrical 'transmutation' of the murder of the old king Hamlet by his brother. On the other hand, when it comes to interlingual translation, *Hamlet* does not contain any straightforward instances. In this respect the play can only serve here as an example *ex negativo*. Thus, the story of Gonzago which Hamlet commissions the players to perform in order to catch the conscience of the king, was originally 'written in very choice Italian' (3.2.238), but Shakespeare decided not to further pursue the potential line of intercultural and interlingual interest opened by this fleeting reference with its whiff of Renaissance exoticism. Nor did he exploit the dramatic interest in the language theme that the overall plot might plausibly have given rise to. Remember that the story takes place in Denmark, but also features a Norwegian Prince at war with Poland, has an actor recite a classically inspired speech about the fall of Troy, puts the hero on a trip to England, and sees its bright young men going to university in France (Paris) and in Germany (Wittenberg). While the play gets a great deal of dramatic mileage out of intralingual polyphony and intersemiotic translation, the potentially wide communicative gaps between the story's various different geo-linguistic settings and groups of characters are not exploited. They are papered over in what is essentially a multidialectal and multisemiotic but monolingual play. Admittedly, such linguistic homogenisation happens in many Renaissance plays, but surely not in all. Shakespeare's own notoriously polyglot play *Henry V* is by no means an exceptional case, indicating that the absence of heterolingualism (the use of 'other' languages) in *Hamlet* is not something that we can simply take for granted as a 'natural' state of affairs. Rather, it follows from an artistic design which was prompted by certain constraints and motivations, and which has certain consequences. The management of linguistic choices, including their narrative and ideological implications, has received a great deal of attention in recent research on multilingualism in English Renaissance drama,[13] as it has for other periods, too, and for other genres such as the novel and the cinema.

Third, we need to refer to the very basic reality that the majority of readers and theatregoers know the works of Shakespeare much better, or even exclusively, in translation rather than in their original versions. It is a sobering thought that the number-one position of English as a world language does not depend on its number of native speakers. 'Only' an estimated 350 million people speak English as a first language, roughly corresponding to a modest 5 per cent of the world population. This is significantly lower than the numbers for Spanish and especially Mandarin, and not that much higher than those for Hindi and Arabic. Where English does stand out is in its rapid worldwide spread as a second language. Exact statistics are diffi-cult to obtain, partly because opinions will vary about threshold levels of proficiency required for EFL (English as a foreign language) speakers to be included in the count. Be that as it may, while the command of English of these EFL speakers will usually suffice for everyday social, professional, or other utilitarian purposes, it is unlikely in a majority of cases to give them full semantic access to the Early Modern English of Shakespeare. Xiaolu Guo's 2007 novel *A Concise Chinese-English Dictionary for Lovers* provides an anecdotal but recognisable example here.[14] The novel tells the story – in the character's own flawed English – of a young Chinese woman spending a year in England to improve her linguistic skills. As she explains, everyone in China knows Shakespeare ('in our local government evening classes they telling everyones Shakespeare most famous person from Britain'), but trying to read his poems turns out to be an obstacle race. As she puts it, 'Shakespeare write bad English. For example, he says "Where go thou?". If I speak like that Mrs Margaret [her English teacher] will tell me wrongly.'

The difficulty of Shakespeare's English is in large part caused by the his-torical gap separating it from the language as it is spoken nowadays. In point of fact, this is even becoming an issue among native speakers *within* the Anglosphere. Debates have been had about whether the time has perhaps come to 'translate' Shakespeare into modern English, as certain groups of readers and theatregoers appear to feel alienated by the perceived difficulty and obsolescence of Shakespeare's language. Protagonists in these debates have included the linguists David Crystal (strongly opposed to the idea) and John McWhorter (very much in favour). The controversy flared up again in 2015 when the renowned Oregon Shakespeare Festival announced the launch of 'Play on! 36 playwrights translate Shakespeare', a large commissioning project aiming to have all of Shakespeare's dramatic works translated into contemporary English by a pair of one playwright and one dramaturg for each. *Hamlet* is to be translated by playwright Lisa Peterson and dramaturg Luan Schooler. Leading Shakespearean scholar James Shapiro was quick to condemn the whole project in an op-ed piece in the *New York Times* published 7 October 2015, attracting many further reactions. However, none of this controversy alters the fact that a high-profile cultural institu-tion such as the Oregon Shakespeare Festival took the step it did to have Shakespeare translated into English, and that it is even planning to stage some of these translations alongside its ongoing programme of productions in Shakespeare's original language. Another fact that remains is that in the past three decades the book market has effectively seen the arrival of a large number of modern-English translations of Shakespeare, some of them being

shoddily produced study aids, others showing higher levels of editorial pro-
fessionalism or indeed artistic ambition.[15] True, the established literary and
academic publishers or imprints very much hesitate to venture into this
market, with fear of credibility loss still outweighing the attractive prospect
of commercial success, but one wonders if the Oregon Shakespeare Festival
project could turn out to be a herald of change in this respect.

But it is, of course, the non-native speakers of English and, *a fortiori*,
those who have no English at all, who are most likely to have recourse to
translations of Shakespeare. Potentially at least, these two groups together
would amount to 95 per cent of the world population! Significantly, the
Index Translationum lists Shakespeare as the world's third most-translated
author ever.[16] This is an astonishing feat for a 'classic' writer, who has to
compete in the top five with writers representing commercially popular
genres such as the whodunit, sci-fi, children's books, and romance: Agatha
Christie (first), Jules Verne (second), Enid Blyton (fourth), and Barbara
Cartland (fifth). The *Index Translationum* lists 559 translations for *Hamlet*
alone, and this must count as a very conservative estimate, as the *Index*, for
all its merits, is neither up-to-date nor exhaustive. Nor does it tell us anything about the numbers of readers or spectators who have actually read the
translations or watched them in performance, or about the cultural prestige they have enjoyed (Shakespeare's great texts tend to attract the greatest
writers as translators). In his study of Dutch *Hamlets* between 1777 and
2001, Jan Willem Mathijssen mentions more than thirty Dutch-language
authors who have tried their hand at rendering the play in Dutch all or in
part; the list features some of the best-known writers in the language, such
as Willem Bilderdijk, Jacobus van Looy, Cees Buddingh', Harry Mulisch,
Hugo Claus, and Gerrit Komrij.[17]

In most countries the history of translating the Sonnets started at a much
later date than for *Hamlet* and the other plays. But once it took off, poets
and translators worldwide have lived up to the challenge with tremendous
gusto and creativity. A fine sample of this translation work is contained
in an anthology edited by Manfred Pfister and Jürgen Gutsch under the
title *William Shakespeare's Sonnets for the First Time Globally Reprinted: A
Quatercentenary Anthology 1609–2009*.[18] The volume has a radically multilingual design. We are all familiar with the kind of translation anthology
that brings poems by many authors and even from several source languages
together in one single target language. But this conventional model is here
turned inside out in a sweeping centrifugal movement, with a single source
text – a selection of Shakespeare's sonnets – appearing in more than sev-
enty different languages and even in different scripts – but strangely also
disappearing into them, as the English originals of the sonnets are not

reprinted and no back-translations into English are given. This anthology does not give multiple translations into a single target language that can serve as a reassuringly inclusive common denominator closing gaps between readers, texts, and languages. More uncomfortably, *Shakespeare's Sonnets Global* highlights translation as an uncompromising demonstration of the divisive reality of linguistic and cultural difference. The range of target languages goes from Afrikaans and Albanian to Ukrainian and Yiddish, and includes Sign Languages, Esperanto, Latin, and Klingon. A data disc which comes with the book includes a number of visual, spoken, and musical and filmic interpretations of some of the sonnets.

The countless non-English *Hamlets* and Sonnets we have briefly alluded to belong to the reception history of Shakespeare's works. Following cultural critics such as Aby Warburg and Walter Benjamin, we can refer to it metaphorically as the 'afterlife' of the artist and his creations. More than ever before, this afterlife now also includes Shakespeare on film, television, and digital media. The Shakespeare films by the likes of Laurence Olivier, Orson Welles, Franco Zeffirelli, Kenneth Branagh, Baz Luhrmann, and many more, or TV productions such as the *BBC Television Shakespeare* (1978–85) or *Shakespeare: the Animated Tales* (1992–4) have reached much larger audiences than the theatrical performances of their generation ever could. But here, too, we need to acknowledge the basic reality that these impacts in film theatres, on television, on DVD, and now increasingly through YouTube and other internet-based channels, have to a large extent occurred in non-Anglophone markets, and that the 'Shakespearean' dialogues that these foreign viewers are reading (in the subtitles) or hearing (in the dubbed versions) are not the Bard's own words but were really written by his audiovisual translators. AVT (Audiovisual Translation) is now one of the booming subfields in translation studies, providing tools and models for a much-needed study of AVT Shakespeares.[19] The study of Shakespeare on film is a thriving area within Shakespeare studies, but the fact that most of the films it covers were produced for or have been screened in a multilingual world constitutes a massive blind spot in it.[20] The neglect is deeply worrying inasmuch as nothing less is at stake than the access to Shakespeare's meanings for the larger part of the world's population in today's most popular and influential media.

To sum up my third main argument, we could say that a very significant part of Shakespeare's afterlife takes place outside the English language and involves some form or degree of translation. But before moving on to the next point, I want to underscore that the word 'life' in the compound 'afterlife' is no less operative than the prefix 'after-'. It is through our ulterior interpretations, rewritings, and re-enactments that Shakespeare's semiotic lifeblood flows. The performances, film versions, adaptations, critical discussions, and, yes, the translations enable Shakespeare's work to be more than just material objects gathering dust in archives and to 'survive' as meaningful texts.

A fourth and final point prompts us to highlight the special status of translations among all the interpretations, rewritings, and re-enactments that make up the afterlife of Shakespeare's work. Most manifestations of Shakespeare's afterlife *do* things with Shakespeare's texts, such as annotating, adapting, visualising, or interpreting them. Translations, on the other hand, tend to be entrusted with the more ambitious task of *being* or representing Shakespeare's texts in another language. We expect them to somehow capture the 'essence' of the original textual meanings and transpose it into the target language as faithfully, directly, and completely as possible, so that the translation can stand for the original.[21] Inasmuch as this is true, every Shakespeare translation has something 'essential' to say about its original.

What exactly constitutes the 'essence' of the original and how it should then be 'transposed' into its new context is, of course, impossible to determine in any absolute sense. For the sake of the argument, I have phrased the very questions in naively essentialist terms. Few would believe that a translation can ever convey the 'same' meanings as its original, or that such stable source-text meanings can even exist, to begin with. That is why translation theoreticians were quick to replace source-text/target-text *synonymy* (identity of meaning) as the distinctive feature of translations by the more cautious and more relationally defined notion of *equivalence*, be it equivalence in general terms or more specific variants of it, such as expressive equivalence (trying to render the original author's intentions with target-language means), dynamic equivalence (trying to activate the same effect as the source text), formal equivalence (copying the forms and features of the original text), referential equivalence (trying to render the same denotative meanings), and so forth and so on. But even with such specifications, the equivalence concept often remains vague and difficult to put to empirical use. How could one 'measure' equivalence of 'intention' or of 'effect' between a Shakespearean sonnet and its modern translation? Many translation scholars have therefore come to accept that equivalence, far from being a demonstrable objective reality, really operates in the realm of socially shared perceptions and beliefs. After all, both the translations and the originals are context-dependent and culturally specific, and thus characterised by an irreducible historicity which must foreground the idea of linguistic, cultural, and ideological difference between originals and translations. But then, if the translation is done in a way that matches the community's norms of translation, the members of that community will accept it as being an equivalent text and thus as a valid substitute. On that basis we shall be happy to say that we have read *Hamlet*, even if it was really a *translation* of the play not containing a single word that flowed from Shakespeare's pen.

The impossibility of objective equivalence – let alone identity – of meanings in translation is nicely demonstrated in 'Shakespeare in the Bush' (1966), an essay by anthropologist Laura Bohannan (1922–2002).[22] The essay takes the form of an allegorical narrative recounting the first-time introduction of *Hamlet* into a 'primitive' African culture. The story supposedly takes place in the 1950s or 1960s in a remote place where neither the English language nor Western civilisation has penetrated yet, namely, the Tiv culture, which forms an ethno-linguistic minority in what is now called Nigeria. The story is a lively and mildly humorous pseudo-autobiographical fictional narrative, which works symbolically to make a few serious points about culture and translation, about the cultural embeddedness of any interpretation, and about the ever-present danger of ethnocentrism. The story begins by setting out a universalistic theory of meaning which is then soon deconstructed. The author/narrator posits the basic universality of human experience, which creates the possibility of a universal understanding of the true substance of Shakespeare's plays anywhere and anytime, and thus the basic conditions for the translatability of their 'essence'. As a test case, the anthropologist decides to present *Hamlet* to the Tiv elders in what is from our perspective a triple form of translation: in terms of genre, the dramatic text, written to be performed, is now rendered as an oral narrative; linguistically, Shakespeare's English becomes Tiv (even if, in an interesting representational shortcut, the dialogues in Tiv are rendered as English in the story); culturally, unfamiliar Western concepts and customs are replaced by their supposed closest African equivalents. Shakespeare's 'castle' and 'king' are transculturated into 'homestead' and 'great chief'; Horatio is referred to as 'a man who knows things' (for 'scholar'); Polonius is killed while hiding behind a 'cloth' (for 'arras') in Gertrude's 'sleeping hut' (for 'closet'); swords become 'machetes' and the poisoned wine from the fifth act is transubstantiated into 'poisoned beer'. In this way, the narrator systematically offers what she calls 'tribal analogies', making surface-level accommodations to the target culture to get the 'essential' meaning of the story across. But despite her best efforts, her version of *Hamlet* falls completely flat. Her listeners keep interrupting her and throw her off-balance with their questions, objections, and alternative interpretations. Most unsettlingly of all, the listeners turn out to applaud the hasty marriage of Claudius and his widowed sister-in-law. According to the Tiv kinship rules, Claudius did absolutely the right thing to marry Gertrude, and with such commendable speed too!

True, Bohannan's story gives a hugely magnified picture of the challenges that attend Shakespeare translation between less remote source and target systems. But even between European languages the linguistic and cultural gaps are real enough. How to translate the blank verse in *Hamlet* if this is not a standard verse form in the target language (e.g. French), or if it was decided that maximum grammatical and semantic precision has to be the translator's overriding priority? What to do with a punning name like Fortinbras (French: 'strong [in] arm') in a target culture where the French subtext would not be understood? Should the *Hamlet* translation reflect the archaic patina that the play's language has acquired for native speakers of English today, or, rather, aim for the freshness it would have had for spectators when it was first performed in the Globe more than four centuries ago? How to deal with classical allusions in the play – such as those to Damon, Hecate, Hercules, Hyperion, Jove, Mars, Mercury, Niobe, and Pyrrhus – which tend to require an annotation for modern audiences regardless of language?

Translators can deal with these gaps in a variety of ways, depending on personal preference, on the dominant literary, theatrical, and translation norms in the receptor culture, and on the degree of individual power and agency that he or she believes to have in the social milieu that they are operating in. The multiple choices that the translators are facing will require them to position themselves on several continua, such as those between covert (creating at least an illusion of transparency and equivalence) and overt modes of translation (foregrounding the translator's presence and intervention), between source-oriented approaches (aiming for maximum reproduction of source-text features and thus 'bringing the reader or spectator to the source text') and target-oriented approaches (looking for stylistic, cultural, etc. analogues in the target language and culture, and thus 'bringing the text to the reader or spectator'), or between translating for the page (focus on textual features) and translating for the stage (prioritising speakability and performability according to target-culture theatrical conventions). These choices can be consistent with each other, or not, such as in the case of translators with a postmodern translation aesthetic who may sometimes be seen combining very literal strategies (to the point of simply copy-pasting phrases from the original) with extremes of creative adaptation in the same rendering.

The successful negotiation of all these differences requires high levels of empathy, creativity, technical skill, and sheer artistic talent from the translator. The outcome of these efforts will never be an exact copy of the original text, but it will constitute an intense and comprehensive engagement with the complex fullness and the historical specificity of the original as the translator attempts to grasp the artistic design of the text and to move it across multiple barriers of linguistic and cultural difference.

Looked at from researcher's angle, studying these negotiations and their results can yield important insights in two distinct but ultimately complementary ways. On the one hand, studying Shakespearean translations can help us understand the specificities of the target language and the historical dynamics of the target culture. After all, the translation of a historical text happens at the end of reception and on the terms (as well as *in* the terms) of the target culture. With a now hyper-canonised writer like Shakespeare, there is a lot that we learn from investigating when, by whom, how, why, via which intermediaries, through which media and institutional channels, he was introduced into other languages and cultures. Studying the history of the translations of *Hamlet* into (say) German takes us straight to the heart of German culture itself – to its struggles between conservative and progressive forces in the fields of language, literature, the theatre, and politics. The proverbial phrase 'Deutschland ist Hamlet' ('Germany is Hamlet') sums this up nicely.

On the other hand, the study of Shakespearean translations can also help us understand the Shakespearean source texts themselves in a new light. This is the line of approach to which mainstream Shakespearean scholarship will perhaps find it easiest to commit itself. The basic argument here is that translations constitute an extremely rich and historically varied corpus of explicit textual records of how the originals can be read and have been read. They can thus widen our sense of the original's semantic potential and thereby generate a significant hermeneutic bonus. Both in the ways in which the translations appear to remain 'faithful' to the originals (but possibly with different effects from those intended four centuries ago) and in the ways in which they appear to 'depart' from the originals (but possibly implementing a deliberate and artistically motivated strategy aiming for comparable effects), the translations create a slightly dislocated and defamiliarised perception of the originals. In other words, they strip the Shakespearean texts of their familiarity and their self-evidence. They make us think again about their received meanings, which we have always taken for granted, and add new resonances to our understanding of what Shakespeare's words would have meant to audiences four centuries ago, and what they might mean in English today.[23]

A first example of this is the difficulty that Japanese translators of *Hamlet* experience when they have to render the protagonist's most famous line, 'To be, or not be' (3.1.56). The Japanese language has no infinitive form like English; moreover, the closest possible word for 'to be' is 'aru' but this verb has a more restricted semantic range than the English. Japanese translations of Hamlet's line therefore show various solutions. Back-translated, these include 'to exist in this world, or not to exist in this world' (Tsubouchi), 'life or death' (Fukuda), 'to maintain the status quo or to change the status quo' (Kinoshita), 'to stay alive or to disappear from this world' (Matsuoka), and so on.[24] These translational hesitations and variations are not only of interest to the English student of Japanese, or to the experts in contrastive linguistics. They also invite us to reverse our gaze and reconsider the original phrase, whose apparent blandness and sheer familiarity as an overused quote may have blunted our sensitivity to the possible meanings and contextual implications of the words 'to be' in Hamlet's line. Taken one by one, the Japanese translations may encapsulate only one aspect of the original's semantic polyvalence. But taken together, the respective partialities of the different versions can enhance our understanding of what Hamlet may have been trying to say.

My second example is the last six lines of Sonnet 66 as translated by Ernest Lafond, who gave us very first French translation of the *Sonnets* in book form in 1856:[25]

> Et le vrai dont on doute, et l'art que l'on bâillonne,
> Et le fou qui tout haut comme un docteur raisonne,
> Enfin le bien captif du capitaine mal.
>
> Oui! de ce lieu maudit, demeure mal famée,
> Je fuirais, en m'offrant moi-même au coup fatal,
> Si je n'y devais pas laisser ma bien-aimée.   (9–14)

Literal back translation:

> And the true that is called into doubt, and the art that is gagged,
> And the fool who like a doctor reasons aloud,
> Finally, the good held captive by captain evil.
>
> Yes! of this doomed place, ill-fated residence,
> I would flee, offering myself up to the fatal blow,
> If I didn't have to leave behind my beloved [feminine].

The corresponding six lines in Shakespeare's original:

> And art made tongue-tied by authority,
> And folly (doctor-like) controlling skill,
> And simple truth miscalled simplicity,
> And captive good attending captain ill:
>> Tired with all these, from these would I be gone,
>> Save that to die, I leave my love alone.   (9–14)

Clearly, Shakespeare's poem has been 'reformatted' to match the template of the French sonnet form. Like most English sonnets, Sonnet 66 has the rhyme scheme ABAB CDCD EFEF GG, whose logic places the poem's volta or 'turn' between the three quatrains (the description of the world's injustices and frustrations) and the couplet (the suicidal thoughts dispelled by the redemptive power of love). To enhance the acceptability of his experimental translation project, Lafond rewrote the poem as an orthodox French sonnet by using the rhyme structure ABAB ABAB CCD EDE. However, in French sonnets the volta comes in a more evenly balanced position, occurring between the two quatrains (having the AB rhymes) and the two tercets (having the CDE rhymes). Stuck between an English source text with a [4+4+4] + [2] structure, on the one hand, and the [4+4] + [3+3] structure prompted by target-culture poetic conventions, on the other, Lafond decided to refunctionalise the final tercet, placing it after the volta ('Enfin … Oui!') and giving it the counterpoint effect fulfilled by the couplet in the Shakespearean original: [4+4+3] + [3]. It requires a fair amount of padding to produce a tercet (lines 12–14) out of what was only a couplet in the original (lines 13–14); this goes hand in hand with some compression in the preceding tercet (lines 8–11), which was a quatrain in the original (lines 9–12).

French poetry favours the twelve-syllable alexandrine with a caesura in the middle. Lafond's translation accommodates Shakespeare's decasyllabic lines to this convention. A side effect of this move is that it gives the translator 20 per cent more syllables overall than Shakespeare had at his disposal. This increase in length, combined with the mid-line pauses of the French alexandrines and a certain paraphrastic tendency in the translation, slows down the headlong thrust of Shakespeare's original which is iconic of how the accumulation of injustices drives the speaker in the poem right to the brink of despair.

A third striking difference between the original and Lafond's version is that the gender-neutral 'my love' is feminised into '*ma* bien-*aimée*' (emphasis mine); something similar happens in several more of Lafond's Shakespearean sonnets. As it is widely assumed that most of the sonnets are addressed to a man, which entails the possibility of homoerotic interpretations, the significance of such shifts goes far beyond mere grammar or even poetic convention. They make us look back at the original and think again about its deeply ambivalent gender politics.

As these few notes have suggested, a 'stereoscopic' reading of an original and its translation can enhance our understanding of the Shakespearean text (its features as an instantiation of a certain genre, its style and structure, even its submerged meanings). This is true even if the translation happens to be a not very 'faithful' rendering of the original, and perhaps nowhere more so than where it introduces striking translation shifts. Such shifts create some critical distance as well as unexpected new vantage points from where to view Shakespeare's originals, both being conducive to defamiliarised readings that can refresh our appraisal of them.

Despite the easy logic of binary opposites (English/non-English, original/ translation, direct/indirect, etc.) suggesting otherwise, the translations may usefully remind us that there is no neutral translation-free zone from where the Shakespearean originals can be approached today – by anyone. Despite illusions of directness typically nurtured by 'authentic' simulacra such as the Globe Theatre, OP performances, facsimile reprints, and the like, even native speakers of English access the works of Shakespeare in a manner which is necessarily mediated and which involves at least some degree of interlinguistic and intercultural negotiation. In that sense, our involvement with Shakespearean translations surely offers a healthy antidote to the illusion that untranslated or 'direct' access to Shakespeare is possible for anyone at all.

NOTES

1 Dirk Delabastita and Lieven D'hulst (eds.), *European Shakespeares: Translating Shakespeare in the Romantic Age* (Amsterdam: John Benjamins, 1990), p. 19. The phrase was picked up by Inga-Stina Ewbank in her insightful article 'Shakespeare Translation as Cultural Exchange', *Shakespeare Survey* 48 (1995): 1–12.

2 Quoted from Jonathan Bate, *The Genius of Shakespeare* (London: Picador, 1997), p. 30.

3 Albert Lacroix, *Histoire de l'influence de Shakspeare sur le théatre français jusqu'à nos jours* (Bruxelles: Th. Lesigne, 1856).

4 For *BITRA* (Bibliography of Interpreting and Translation), see http:// aplicacionesua.cpd.ua.es/tra_int/usu/buscar.asp?idioma=en. For *Translation Studies Bibliography*, Yves Gambier and Luc Van Doorslaer (eds.), see https:// benjamins.com/#catalog/undefined/e.tsb/main. The data given were obtained on 28 December 2017.

5 Ton Hoenselaars (ed.), *Shakespeare and the Language of Translation* (London: Arden Shakespeare, Thomson, 2004; revised edition 2012).

6 Dennis Kennedy (ed.), *Foreign Shakespeare: Contemporary Performance* (Cambridge: Cambridge University Press, 1993).

7 Among them, we should mention Inga-Stina Ewbank's influential article 'Shakespeare Translation as Cultural Exchange'.

8 A striking exponent of this process is the ample discussion of foreign and translated Shakespeares in the two-volume *Cambridge Guide to the Worlds of Shakespeare*, ed. Bruce Smith (Cambridge: Cambridge University Press, 2016).

9 Susan Bennett and Christie Carson (eds.), *Shakespeare beyond English: A Global Experiment* (Cambridge: Cambridge University Press, 2013).

10 See Ton Hoenselaars, 'Shakespeare and the Cultures of Translation', *Shakespeare Survey* 66 (2014): 206–219, as well as Alexa Huang, 'Boomerang

Shakespeare: Foreign Shakespeare in Britain', *The Cambridge Guide to the Worlds of Shakespeare, Volume two: The World's Shakespeare, 1660-Present*, ed. Bruce Smith (Cambridge: Cambridge University Press, 2016), pp. 1094–1101.

11 Good starting points would be Sandra Bermann and Catherine Porter (eds.), *A Companion to Translation Studies* (Chichester: Wiley Blackwell, 2014), Kirsten Malmkjær and Kevin Windle (eds.), *The Oxford Handbook of Translation Studies* (Oxford: Oxford University Press, 2011), or Yves Gambier and Luc Van Doorslaer (eds.), *Handbook of Translation Studies*, 4 vols. (Amsterdam: John Benjamins, 2010–13; also online).

12 See Roman Jakobson, 'On Linguistic Aspects of Translation', *On Translation*, ed. Reuben A. Brower (Cambridge, MA: Harvard University Press, 1959), pp. 232–239. For the quote, see p. 233. Helpful as it is, Jakobson's model has been criticised, among other things, for being too confident in drawing clear lines between the categories intralingual, interlingual, and intersemiotic. How elastic is the notion of a language's 'sameness'? Or, if *Hamlet* is translated into one of the world's many Sign Languages, would that count as interlingual or as intersemiotic translation?

13 See, for instance, Marianne Montgomery, *Europe's Languages on England's Stages, 1590–1620* (Farnham: Ashgate, 2012), Michael Saenger (ed.), *Interlinguicity, Internationality, and Shakespeare* (Montreal: McGill-Queen's University Press, 2014), and Dirk Delabastita and Ton Hoenselaars (eds.), *Multilingualism in the Drama of Shakespeare and His Contemporaries* (Amsterdam: John Benjamins, 2015).

14 Xiaolu Guo, *A Concise Chinese-English Dictionary for Lovers* (London: Chatto & Windus, 2007); see pp. 26–27 for the example.

15 See Dirk Delabastita, '"He Shall Signify from Time to Time": *Romeo and Juliet* in Modern English', *Perspectives. Studies in Translatology* 25.2 (2016): 189–213.

16 Information obtained on 28 December 2017. See www.unesco.org/xtrans/. This *Index* was developed under the aegis of UNESCO.

17 Jan Willem Mathijssen, *The Breach and the Observance: Theatre Retranslation as a Strategy of Artistic Differentiation, with Special Reference to Retranslations of Shakespeare's* Hamlet *(1777–2001)* (PhD thesis, University of Utrecht), online at: dspace.library.uu.nl/bitstream/handle/1874/22151/full.pdf.

18 Manfred Pfister and Jürgen Gutsch (eds.), *William Shakespeare's Sonnets for the First Time Globally Reprinted: A Quatercentenary Anthology, 1609–2009* (Dozwil TG Schweiz: Edition SIGNAThUR, 2009).

19 Among other things, interesting comparisons could be made here with the reverse (and probably non-symmetrical) way in which English subtitles have had to be produced for non-Anglophone Shakespearean films that managed to achieve international status, such as, for instance, Grigori Kozintsev's highly acclaimed *Hamlet* film from 1964, whose script was based on Boris Pasternak's Russian translation of the play. One expects that in a case like this the Russian-to-English translators would not really 'translate' the Russian dialogues, but 'immediately' look for the corresponding lines in the original Shakespearean scripts.

20 For an excellent first discussion, see Nicolas Sanchez, 'Translating Shakespeare for the Screen', *The Cambridge Guide to the Worlds of Shakespeare. Volume Two: The World's Shakespeare, 1660-Present*, ed. Bruce Smith (Cambridge:

Cambridge University Press, 2016), pp. 1369–1375. Nicolas Sanchez is the author of the first PhD thesis devoted to the topic: *L'étoffe dont sont faits les sous-titres. Traduire William Shakespeare à l'écran* [Such Stuff as Subtitles are Made On: Translating William Shakespeare for the Screen] (unpublished thesis, Université de Nice-Sophia-Antipolis, 2009). It should be noted that the field of AVT also covers forms of mediation such as surtitling in the theatre and audio-description for the visually impaired.

21 This is not to diminish the value or interest of bilingual editions, in which the translations stand 'side by side with' the originals rather than 'standing for' them. With such editions – at least for readers who have the linguistic skills – the translation can function in an auxiliary rather than an autonomous mode, helping to facilitate the semantic access to the original text on the facing page. A similar remark applies to subtitles in Shakespearean productions for the screen.

22 Laura Bohannan, 'Shakespeare in the Bush', *Natural History* 75.7 (August–September 1966): 28–33.

23 For an excellent discussion of how this intuition can be further operationalised with the help of the digital humanities, see Tom Cheesman, 'Reading Originals by the Light of Translations', *Shakespeare Survey* 68 (2015): 73–86. For a more 'old-school' demonstration of the idea in full action, see the anthology *Shakespeare Sechsundsechzig* (3., erneut erweiterte Auflage), edited by Ulrich Erckenbrecht (Kassel: Muriverlag, 2009), which presents and introduces a staggering 168 different German translations of Sonnet 66, 'Tired with all these'.

24 This example is borrowed from Yoshiko Kawachi, 'Gender, Class, and Race in Japanese Translation', *Shakespeare and the Twentieth Century: The Selected Proceedings of the International Shakespeare Association World Congress, Los Angeles 1996*, ed. Jonathan Bate, Jill L. Levenson, and Dieter Mehl (Newark: University of Delaware Press, 1998), pp. 390–402.

25 Ernest Lafond, *Poëmes et sonnets de William Shakespere, traduits en vers, avec le texte anglais au bas des pages, précédés d'une notice et suivis de notes* (Paris: Lahure, 1856). The volume contains translations of forty-seven of the sonnets. The quotation is from p. 20.

14

DOUGLAS M. LANIER

Popular Culture and Shakespeare's Language

In his discussion of speech act theory, Jacques Derrida argues that all language is subject to the principle of iterability, the capacity for language to be repeated in all sorts of new contexts.[1] Each reiteration, Derrida observes, transforms what it is possible for a particular word, phrase, or sentence to mean, as it is extended it to new situations and takes on subtext, metareferentiality, multivalences, or irony. This capacity for reiteration is central to language's status as a living, ever-metamorphosing tool of communication, open to the flow of history. We understand any bit of language by projecting onto it some sense of its context. A reader, without direct access to a passage's originating context, must construe it according to practical systems for understanding signs, systems that depend upon established protocols of contextualisation. Yet – and this is Derrida's crucial insight – because all communication with language involves the capacity to be recontextualised, no one normative context can ever be specified for a particular bit of language, one that would govern its meaning for all receivers. Any word or phrase can be re-sited in a new context, potentially in illimitable numbers of contexts, and so take on all manner of meanings. In everyday life we depend upon principles of salience, shared assumptions about what particular context is most relevant, to guide our understanding of language. But even in 'normal' situations, there is nothing to prevent other ways of contextualising a word or phrase from coming into play. A master's straightforward command to his servant to knock at a door, for example, could be received as a call to violence or insubordination, if it is understood from within a different context.

I'm referring here to the opening sequence of *The Taming of the Shrew*, Act 1, scene 2, lines 5 to 19, where Grumio misconstrues Petruccio's order 'knock'. This moment illustrates two interlocking points. First, it illustrates Shakespeare's career-long fascination with the semantic productivity of language and the slipperiness of interpretive contexts. Grumio's 'misunderstanding' of Petruccio teases out a meaning of 'knock' his master apparently never intended, and that meaning reveals a truth about Petruccio's essential character – his penchant for a fight. Moreover, this example shows how Petruccio, the seeming master of contextual reframing in his encounters with Katherine, cannot himself fully control the iterable nature of language. And, we should not forget, this passage follows upon a reminder (*Shr.* 1.1.247–252) that this exchange is part of a play watched by Christopher Sly and Bartholomew, a cross-dressed performative 'citation' of a woman. Here in layered fashion Shakespeare illustrates the principle of iterability in action. Second, Shakespeare's own words are subject to the same principle of recontextualisation that governs all language. Perhaps it goes without saying, but in the final analysis no one context could ever provide a single, final perspective for construing Shakespeare's language. This is not simply because Shakespeare's language seems to us so rich as to invite various interpretations or because Shakespeare, by embracing iterability as a productive linguistic trait, gives us his blessing to apply it to his words. It is rather because *all* language, Shakespearean or not, is subject to iterability.

This principle bears repeating because the interpretive authority of modern professional Shakespeareans has rested upon two modes of contextualisation that have become firm articles of faith. The first involves placing Shakespeare's language in historical context. Properly understanding Shakespeare's language, so teachers exhort their classes, involves recognising how much the early modern semantic field (which we can glean from the *Oxford English Dictionary* and other sources) differs from the semantic field of contemporary English. When it comes to parsing Shakespeare's words, we should always historicise. To miss, for example, that 'jade' is early modern slang for an old, ill-tempered horse (e.g. 'You always end with a jade's trick' (*Ado* 1.1.107)) or not to recognise the pejorative connotation of 'nice' ('O Kate, nice customs curtsy to great kings' (*H5* 5.2.243)) is to identify oneself as an incompetent interpreter of Shakespeare. We can debate which of the historical meanings of 'jade' or 'nice' are in play, but those debates must respect the limits of the early modern semantic field. One *locus classicus* for establishing this principle is Juliet's line, 'Romeo, Romeo, Wherefore art thou Romeo?' (*Rom.* 2.2.33). The classic error, teachers warn their students, is to read 'wherefore' as 'where' rather than as a Renaissance word for 'why'; Juliet is asking *why* her beloved is named Romeo rather than where he is. To read otherwise is to engage in egregious anachronism and distortion of Shakespeare's plain meaning. To just such misreadings pop culture is prone, as we see in a Bamforth postcard from the 1960s, in which a young, pregnant woman alone on a balcony asks about the whereabouts of her child's absent father: 'Romeo, Romeo, wherefore art thou, Romeo?'

Recognising the historical nature of Shakespeare's language is simply axiomatic, a basic skill a Shakespearean professional must internalise.

The other protocol of contextualisation requires placing Shakespeare's words within their immediate dramatic context. Shakespeare's language must be understood in terms of the character who uttered it, the back-and-forth dialogue in which it is deployed, the goals the character wants to pursue by speaking these particular words, and the indications of subtext, inflection, or irony that might colour the apparent literal meaning. These are *Hamlet*'s or *Shylock*'s or *Falstaff*'s words, specific to their nature, motives, and histories with other characters. Once again, we can certainly debate, say, the meaning of Hamlet's words, but any debate must centre around how critics construe Hamlet's particular psychology, purpose, history, and the like, that is, different understandings of the language's dramatic context. Take, for example, the seemingly simple line, 'though she be but little, she is fierce' (*MND* 3.2.325). In popular culture, this line has become a girl-power maxim on buttons, t-shirts, posters, and smartphone covers – it has even become a popular tattoo. It conveys feminist independence and toughness in the face of men's tendency to underestimate women. In dramatic context, however, the line doesn't carry this sense. It is spoken by Helena, after her one-time friend Hermia has tried to attack her for stealing Lysander. Helena is speaking to Demetrius and Lysander as they try to protect her, though Hermia is in earshot. In this scene the word 'little' has its own history. It picks up on earlier references to Hermia's small stature, irritating a sore spot, something underlined by Hermia's reply: 'Little again? Nothing but low and little?' (*MND* 3.2.326). And 'fierce' too has a history. In dramatic context, it refers not to Hermia's feminist strength but to her easy rage and shrewish tongue, something which, Helena tells us, Hermia exhibited when they were schoolmates. Indeed, it is possible to read this line as a *betrayal* of the feminine solidarity Helena and Hermia once shared as children and students. We might argue about whether Helena wittingly or unwittingly touches upon Hermia's insecurities, whether or not she knows Hermia can hear her, whether this moment constitutes a change in Helena's character, whether Hermia's 'keen and shrewd' nature from her schooldays is real or a fiction, but all such controversies turn upon the conviction that the meaning of Shakespeare's language is located within some plausible construction of the immediate, dramatic circumstances. To read otherwise is take these words badly out of their native, 'proper' context.

These two principles – situating Shakespeare's words in historical and dramatic context – have undergirded the professionalisation of interpretation of Shakespeare's language throughout much of the twentieth century and into the twenty-first. Only a handful of mavericks – G. Wilson Knight comes immediately to mind – have taken a different tack, and even those have rebelled only intermittently. To most Shakespeare professionals these principles seem simply like common sense. For pop culture, however, neither of these principles have much force. On the whole, popular culture is resolutely presentist in its approach to Shakespeare's language, treating it as an antiquated version of contemporary speech and reading it within a contemporary semantic field. The Bamforth postcard treats 'wherefore' as an archaic rendering of 'where'; it reinforces that sense by adding a comma between 'thou' and 'Romeo'. 'Art' and 'thou' read not just as old-fashioned 'are' and 'you', but as comically elevated choices, akin to the language of the Bible or the liturgy where these forms still survive. The sexist joke is that this Juliet remains devoutly attached to her Romeo even after he has abandoned her following a holiday fling. 'Though she be but little, she is fierce' illustrates a second principle: popular culture typically does not see dramatic context as decisive in determining Shakespeare's meaning. Those with this line as a tattoo are not concerned that Helena speaks this line, that it appears in a scene where two long-standing women friends come to blows, that 'fierce' in dramatic context is hardly a compliment. Instead the line is treated as a general truth which can then be made to speak to contemporary gender politics. The fact that this truth is in the third and not first person may actually intensify the sentiment, for it gives the statement a certain declarative objectivity potentially attachable to any 'she'. This is not to claim that popular culture always ignores dramatic context. The humour of the Bamforth postcard depends upon our recognising the balcony scene from *Romeo and Juliet*, particularly its highly romanticised vision of love. But even here the principle of generalisation applies. The name 'Romeo' locates the scene in Shakespeare's play, but here 'Romeo' refers less to a specific character but to a broad type – the lothario who woos, weds, beds, and then rids himself of women. The joke turns upon the gap between the play's character and the pop Romeo-type.

When confronted with pop culture's approach to Shakespeare, the Shakespearean professional's favourite rhetorical move is to reassert 'proper' historical or dramatic context in order to delegitimise the pop alternative. Surveying uses of Shakespeare in the confirmation hearings for Clarence Thomas, Marjorie Garber notes how Senator Alan Simpson cites the famous passage from *Othello* on reputation (*Oth.* 3.3.160–164) without his acknowledging that these are Iago's words, spoken to manipulate Othello.[2] Such examples, Garber argues, illustrate the troubling 'power of this kind of disembodied, free-floating quotation', a mode of reading

Shakespeare that 'authorizes a rhetoric of hero-worship and character assassination' (Garber 157, 165). The same strategy appears in John Drakakis's discussion of pop quotation of Shakespeare.[3] There he chastises the editor of the *Sunday Telegraph*, Sir Peregrine Worsthorne, for using a passage from *Antony and Cleopatra* (4.15.14–15) to lament the political demise of Margaret Thatcher. If replaced in its dramatic context, Drakakis observes, that passage would absurdly cast Thatcher as the dying Mark Antony and Worsthorne as Cleopatra. In the cases he considers, Drakakis stresses how Shakespearean quotation serves the ideological work of political myth-making; by treating Shakespeare as a storehouse of 'exemplary fictions' and 'essentialist meanings' (Drakakis 159), contingent contemporary historical events, cloaked in Shakespearean citations, take on a quality of literary exemplarity and grandeur. What makes Drakakis's dazzling analysis all the more remarkable is that he acknowledges the principle of iterability, even citing from Derrida's 'Signature Event Context' (Drakakis 157–158). As Drakakis presents matters, Worsthorne is engaged in Shakespearean iterability, but Drakakis, in pursuing a historicised, dramatically contextualised reading, is not.

My point in citing these essays is not to take issue with their ideological positions. Rather, I want to draw attention to the interpretive protocols that make these analyses possible. Professional Shakespeareans know well these protocols and the work of legitimation and delegitimation they allow, though they rarely acknowledge them as historically contingent and particular to specific professional subcultures. In practice, we tend to treat historical and dramatic context as if they were somehow attached to Shakespeare's texts as they travel through history and among myriad readers. Indeed, it has been difficult for professional Shakespeareans to recognise these as interpretive protocols at all, particularly since their own hermeneutic authority is bound up with them. One consequence is that pop culture's treatment of Shakespeare's language has too often been delegitimised *a priori*, regarded as 'post-hermeneutic', which is to say, 'non-hermeneutic'. In what follows, I want to lay out some of the protocols that govern pop culture's approach to Shakespeare's language in order to suggest that it is relatively systematic, with its own internally coherent set of axioms and operations. A pop hermeneutic – that is, popular culture's guiding presuppositions about and methods for interpreting Shakespeare's language – proceeds from different assumptions, moves, and aims than does professional reading of Shakespeare. This does not mean that the readings it produces are necessarily socially useful or politically progressive, but it also does not mean that its results are necessarily regressive, stupid, or absurd. Central to the pop hermeneutic are proverbialisation, application, and ironisation.

Proverbialisation

Popular readings of Shakespeare's language tend to treat the Shakespeare text as if it were a collection of *sententiae* or nuggets of wisdom not tied to any particular historical or narrative context. This orientation is driven by several factors, chief among them the powerfully presentist orientation of pop hermeneutics. One way to make Shakespeare's antiquated language relevant to a contemporary semantic field is to treat it as if it were ahistorical, as if its meaning had not changed over time. A second factor is the common expectation, enhanced by the ways literature is often taught, that Shakespeare's language is saturated with ethical significance, that his words teach some essential truth or serve some enduring imperative. Commentators have tended to see proverbialisation as entirely ideological, part of a suspect process of essentialising Shakespearean language by stripping it of its originary contexts and so of its connection to historical processes. Certainly, this is partly the case, but this process is a linguistic operation as much as a political one, driven by an imperative to make historical language legible within a contemporary semantic field.

Because most pop modes of reading Shakespeare's language do not see narrative context as determining its meaning, the Shakespearean text can be freely divided into discrete, quotable segments. Most Shakespearean professionals regard this as a violation of the organic integrity of Shakespeare's text, what Garber characterises as an 'Orphic dismemberment' (165). The analogy is to popular treatment of Scripture, the division of the text into verses that can then be deployed as one sees fit. But this practice has a long pedigree with literary texts as well. Drawing upon classical rhetorical practice, early modern *florilegia* and commonplace books isolated quotable passages from literary texts for later contemplation and citation, in some cases grouping passages under labels that establish some shared ethical or conceptual quality, creating a new integral body from the source. Such is the case, for example, with Robert Allott's *England's Parnassus* (1600), which, so the full title promises, plucks out 'the choysest Flowers of our moderne poets' and reassembles them in alphabetically arranged thematic units, in the process recasting them as a corpus of timeless wisdom and aesthetic excellence, readily available for citation. The film *Shakespeare in Love* (1998) maps this proverbialisation back onto Shakespeare's own compositional processes. As Shakespeare walks the streets of London, we watch him pick up pithy phrases from various passers-by, filing them away for later use in his plays. With a bit of self-conscious irony this representation of Shakespeare's working methods authorises pop proverbialisation, since Shakespeare himself indulges in it.

That said, pop proverbialisation isn't always as complete in its narrative or historical decontextualisation of Shakespeare's language as it might seem. William Dodd's *The Beauties of Shakespear* (1752),[4] the much-reprinted anthology widely credited with setting in motion the vogue for extracting Shakespeare, splits the difference between maintaining the narrative integrity of individual plays and excerpting them according to some thematic regime. Dodd proceeds play by play, scene by scene, singling out quotable passages as he goes and tagging them thematically, supplementing the entire collection with an index that allows the reader to locate passages by topic but also by character and narrative context. Some modern Shakespearean collections betray the same tension between acknowledging and discarding dramatic context. Michael Macrone's *Brush Up Your Shakespeare!* (1990)[5] catalogues famous phrases alphabetically, but each is followed by a paragraph of commentary setting it in narrative context. *The Prince's Choice* (1995)[6] offers much more substantial extracts (sometimes complete scenes) and explains narrative context in little prefaces. In *Bardisms: Shakespeare for all Occasions* (2009),[7] Barry Edelstein surrounds extracts with historical and narrative commentary, and to give his collection a sense of unity, he borrows a scheme from Jacques's 'seven ages' speech, suggesting that Shakespeare's words address the life's major rites of passage, from birth announcements to eulogies.

Other collections seem relatively free of concerns about narrative or historical contextualisation. Louis Marder's *Speak the Speech: The Shakespeare Quotation Book* (1994)[8] identifies quotations by speaker as well as play, scene, and line, implying a barebones narrative context; unusual for such collections, he acknowledges the historicity of Shakespeare's language by including a glossary for archaic words. Quotations are gathered under topic headings (alphabetically arranged), and the sheer number of topics (over 500) suggests the comprehensiveness of Shakespeare's engagement with human experience. Though many topics concern historical issues ('horses and horseback riding', 'hunting', 'royalty') or general ideas ('anger', 'dreams', 'poverty'), some are playfully presentist ('baseball', 'environmentalism', 'plastic surgery') and require parsing Shakespeare's words from a contemporary perspective (under baseball is listed 'fair is foul and foul is fair' and 'a hit, a very palpable hit').[9] Gathering short snippets under random topic headings arranged in no discernible order, John W. Seder's *Shakespeare's Book of Insults, Insights & Infinite Jests* (1984)[10] is of this group of examples the least concerned with historical or narrative context. In his preface, he identifies his target readership as those who 'were turned off by improbable plots, by archaic language full of *thees* and *thous*, and by characters and situations that seemed remote from your experience'

(Seder iii). Accordingly, he fully embraces the pop protocol of contemporaneity, insisting that 'Shakespeare's world is *our world*, the world of today' (Seder iv). Yet even here there is some tension. The book's preface, by combative pundit William F. Buckley, professes delight in Shakespearean invective, the excellence of which Buckley traces to Elizabethan conditions. In that 'moment of flux, anxiety, and opportunity' when social status was unsettled, he argues, 'men competed with words and with swords' and 'relished the sheer sport of contumely' (Seder i).

In practice, pop citations of Shakespeare's language often fasten on an anchor word which identifies the citation's generalised topic which is appropriate to a contemporary context. Victorian and Edwardian postcards often treat Shakespearean citations this way. Holiday cards, for example, involve Shakespearean passages that use words related to specific topics:

- **remembrance** ('I'll note you in my book of memory' (*1H6* 2.4.101); 'Grace and remembrance be to you both and welcome' (*WT* 4.4.76); 'There's rosemary: that's for remembrance; and there's pansies, that's for thoughts' (a lightly edited version of *Hamlet* 4.5.174–175; 'I cannot but remember' (*Mac.* 4.3.224));
- **friendship** ('I count myself in nothing else so happy as in a soul remembering my good friends' (*R2* 2.3.46–47); 'I would be friends with you and have your love' (*MV* 1.3.131));
- **kind thoughts** ('Thou art not further than my thoughts can move, and I am still with them and they with me' (Sonnet 47.11–12); 'how far that candle throws his beams! So shines a good deed in a naughty world' (*MV* 5.1.90–91));
- **good wishes** ('what is best, that best I wish thee' (Sonnet 37.13); 'your heart's desires be with you' (*AYLI* 1.2.190); 'in all mayst thou prove prosperous' (an edited version of *Per.* 1.1.60); 'God bless you with health and happy days' (an edited version of *R3* 3.1.18)).

Read within their original dramatic contexts, many of these Shakespeare citations are spectacularly inappropriate. In the case of the passages above regarding memory, in their respective narratives they involve Richard, Duke of Gloucester vowing vengeance on his enemy, Perdita welcoming the father-king who will soon oppose her marriage, Ophelia in her madness, and Shylock perhaps tricking Antonio into the 'merry' bond. But if the reader regards Shakespeare's language as proverbial wisdom or sentiment not specific to one dramatic situation or historical period, it can then be applied to a contemporary circumstance without irony. The particular occasion indicated on the cards – birthday, courtship, holiday – establishes the salient context that guides interpretation of Shakespeare's words; anchor words suture the passage into that salience; and sentimental or pastoral images establish the subtext-free tone within which these quotations are intended to be read.

Consider 'The Relevant Shakespeare', a series of books produced by the Hallmark Greeting Card company in 1971 aimed at the youth market. Each volume addresses a specific contemporary topic from a counter-cultural angle – sex, pollution, drinking, youth, football, the American dream. Each follows the same formula, photos of the topic at hand juxtaposed with Shakespeare citations. The photos (and book titles) establish the salience that orients interpretation of each Shakespeare passage. Against a picture of a smog-choked cityscape in the 'Pollution' volume is set this passage from *Hamlet*: 'This excellent canopy, the air ... why it appears no other thing to me than a foul and pestilent congregation of vapours' (a lightly modernised version of *Ham*. 2.2.283–286). In the 'Youth' volume a famous shot of two lovers kissing on a hillside at the Woodstock festival is juxtaposed against this quotation:

> And bleat the one at the other; what we chang'd
> Was innocence for innocence; we knew not
> The doctrine of ill-doing, nor dream'd
> We were as twinn'd lambs that did frisk i' the sun
> That any did. (*WT* 1.2.68–71)

This kind of volume follows the hermeneutic pattern adopted by novelty books like *Shakespeare on Golf*, *Shakespeare on Baseball*, *Shakespeare on Lawyers and the Law*, *Shakespeare on Management*,[11] and the like: Shakespeare citations are reread within a particular semantic frame, the link between Shakespeare's language and contemporary context secured by an anchor word or phrase. Syd Pritchard's *Shakespeare: The Golfer's Companion* presents 'what is this quintessence of dust?' (*Ham*. 2.2.290) as if it were Shakespeare's commentary on sand traps and 'This is a sorry sight' (*Mac*. 2.2.23) as the initial response of a golf pro to a pupil's swing.

Again, not all of these kinds of volumes entirely reject narrative or historical contextualisation. A recent series by Katherine and Elizabeth O'Mahoney, *Shakespeare on Doctors & Lawyers*, *Shakespeare on Food & Drink*, *Shakespeare on Foreigners*, and *Shakespeare on Love & Sex* (all 2002), is poised between a pop and a historical hermeneutic, its collection of textual excerpts interspersed with text boxes that offer historical factoids about Shakespeare and Renaissance practices. In Jay Shafritz's *Shakespeare on Management*, Lady Macbeth's exhortation, 'We fail? But screw your courage to the sticking place, and we'll not fail' (*Mac*. 1.7.59–61) teaches how 'the key to success ... lies in overcoming indecisiveness' (Shafritz 43), this even though Shafritz acknowledges the original narrative context of Lady Macbeth's remarks – the planning of a murder. In Shafritz's case, attention to narrative context actually enhances the excerpt's proverbial power: Lady Macbeth successfully motivated her husband. These sorts of citations are forerunners of the Shakespeare internet meme, in which a Shakespearean citation (or something that evokes one) is rendered contemporary (and ironic) through juxtaposition with an image and/or a snarky rejoinder that trades upon one's pop cultural literacy.

Many of the Shakespearean sentiments expressed on the postcards discussed above are utterly commonplace, as is the case with the deployment of Shakespeare in speeches, toasts, and presentations. Why bother with citing Shakespeare at all? That these commonplaces originate with Shakespeare is crucial, for his reputation as a writer of *sententiae* works to intensify the sentiment or idea involved, as well as guaranteeing its lasting truth or special sincerity. Identifying the quotation as Shakespeare's assures that the citation will be read as the author's words and not some character's where irony or subtext might be in play. *Hamlet*, Act 1, scene 3, lines 59 to 80 is chock-a-block with maxims that regularly appear in popular culture as poster-ready nuggets of wisdom – 'neither a borrower nor a lender be', 'to thine own self be true'. If we regard these as Polonius's words, we well might read them as examples of his windbaggery or, in light of his machinations with Reynaldo in Act 2, scene 1, lines 1 to 70, as revelations of his hypocrisy and paternal tyranny. Placing Shakespeare's language under his authorial signature, reading them as *his* words, is crucial to proverbialisation. The identifying name 'Shakespeare' works to establish a specific hermeneutic protocol and gives Shakespearean language a very particular cultural authority. And that authority is subject to reciprocity. It is Shakespeare's inherited cultural status that authorises his words to be read as perpetually contemporary, and the reader's success in reading them that way ends up demonstrating and thus (re)confirming the cultural authority bound up with Shakespeare's uncanny contemporaneity.

A handful of passages have become familiar enough to be recognised as Shakespeare's without his name attached, phrases like 'to be or not to be', 'Friends, Romans, countrymen', 'double, double, toil and trouble', or 'what fools these mortals be'. Interestingly enough, most in this group carry with them some sense of their original dramatic contexts in the popular imagination. As we saw with the Bamforth postcard cited earlier, within popular culture the phrase 'wherefore art thou Romeo' conjures up the balcony scene and is typically regarded as Juliet's, not Shakespeare's, words. Even the rhetorical structure of certain Shakespearean phrases is recognisable enough to make them the subject of pop variations. In the film *Ace Ventura: When*

Nature Calls (1995), Jim Carrey as Ace Ventura calls his army of animals to battle with the line, 'Friends! Rodents! Quadrupeds! Lend me your rears!' without ever identifying its Shakespearean source; the 'to __ or not to __' structure is a favourite mock-Shakespearean antithesis in pop culture. One reason these passages remain identified with their source narratives and not Shakespeare generally is that they are taken from oft-performed or oft-taught plays where readers encounter these phrases in dramatic context. It is clear from nineteenth-century examples in, say, advertising or theatrical burlesques that audiences of that era, regularly encountering Shakespeare in the theatre, could recognise a much wider range of phrases and identify them with their respective speakers and narrative situations more readily than can most modern audiences.

Application

Once Shakespeare's words have been proverbialised, they are then available to be applied to particular contemporary situations, though paradoxically they continue to carry something of their proverbial authority. We can see this instrumentalisation of Shakespearean language at work in two realms where the goal is persuasion: politics and advertising. In political discourse, there is borrowed authority to be had from casting Shakespeare as one's ideological fellow. Addressing the House of Commons amidst the Falklands War in 1982, Margaret Thatcher quoted from *King John* to cast military intervention as a matter of British patriotism – 'Nought shall make us rue if England to herself do rest but true' (5.7); upon Argentina's capitulation in the war, Lord Chancellor Quintin Hogg triumphantly cited the post-Agincourt '*Non nobis*' passage from *Henry V* (4.8.115).[12] In the heat of political debate citing Shakespeare can offer immediate rhetorical advantage over one's opponent; by recourse to Shakespeare's proverbialism, one can appear to transcend the partisan fray and adopt a position of ethical high-mindedness. Several critics have charted how Shakespeare has been used in political discourse, and these analyses often leave the impression that Shakespeare's language has been especially prone to appropriation by the political right because conservatives have portrayed themselves as voices of traditionalism and so are naturally allied to Shakespeare. But there is also a robust tradition of recruiting Shakespeare for leftist causes, though on the left Shakespeare is often evoked sarcastically rather than earnestly. Barbara Garson's 1967 anti-Vietnam war play *Macbird!* consists entirely of reworked lines from all over the Shakespeare canon. Several subsequent lampoons – David Edgar's *Dick Deterred: A Watergate Musical* (1974, on the Watergate crisis), Michael Hettinger's *Macbush* (2003), David Carl's

Trump Lear (2017) – also make comic reuse of key Shakespeare lines. During a 2016 crisis concerning lead in the water system of Flint, Michigan, a crisis precipitated by Republican budget-cutting, an anonymous wag protested the situation by chalking lines from various Shakespeare plays on local sidewalks – 'Be put in a cauldron of lead and usurer's grease, amongst a whole million of cutpurses, and there boil like a gammon of bacon that will never be enough' (*TNK* 4.3.29–31); 'Thy ambition, thou scarlet sin, robb'd this bewailing land' (*H8* 3.2.254–255). In practice, then, proverbialised Shakespeare has no inherent political valence; his words can serve all manner of causes, from reactionary to radical.

The appearance of proverbialised Shakespeare in advertising illustrates the language's penchant for commercial application and its extraordinary semantic pliability. The meaning of Shakespearean passages quoted in advertisements are governed by the principle of salience, established by the product and brand, the ad copy, and the accompanying illustration. The earliest print ads involving Shakespeare's language tend to use citations as if they were testimonials, with Shakespeare positioned as the ultimate celebrity endorser. An 1889 ad for Aspinall's enamel, for example, pictures a woman painting a chair as a man approvingly looks on. The title reads 'Enamelling with Aspinall is "pastime passing excellent" – Shakespeare' (*Shr.* Induction 1.63), while a second set of quotations, identified by their respective plays so that they can be treated as characters' dialogue, establishes the product's benefits for the consumer's relationships: 'She: "I intend but only to surprise him" [*3H6* 4.2.25, misidentified in the ad as *Tim.* 5.2]. He: "Wert thou thus surprised sweet girl?" [*Tit.* 4.1.51].'[13] An 1890s booklet hawking King's Puremalt, a tonic, features illustrations of key Shakespeare scenes; each citation leads in to a marketing pitch. Hamlet, for instance, offers the line 'to be or not to be, that is the question, whether 'tis nobler to suffer the slings and arrows of outrageous fortune' (*Ham.* 3.1.55–57), but the ad goes on to add 'or to take a bottle of KING'S PUREMALT and so cure them all'. Whether the Shakespeare passage is treated relatively straightforwardly or preposterously, the same basic structure of the ad – the suturing of Shakespeare's proverbial words into some contemporary semantic field created by the accompanying copy and images – underlies the basic marketing technique.

Later ads (from the 1920s onward) introduce a more complicated relation between Shakespeare's language, copy, and image. Under the pressure of modernism and an increasing divorce of Shakespeare from popular culture, some ads begin to counterpoise Shakespeare's language and what it connotes *against* the product, as a way of positioning brands as innovative, mass-market, and contemporary rather than traditional, elitist, or old-fashioned. Such is the case, for example, with a 1946 ad for Pacquin's hand cream which sets a quotation from *Romeo and Juliet* over a glamour picture of a woman's face and hands: 'she locks her lily hands one in one' (*Venus and Adonis* 228). At the left, however, is a second picture of a woman's hands peeling potatoes, with the caption, 'but fingers like a lily, Willie, don't come from peeling spuds'. Pacquin's, it is suggested, can help to close the gap between Shakespearean hyperbole and the realities of modern house-work. Though in these juxtapositional ads Shakespeare's language is still read within a contemporary semantic field, the focus is typically on the mismatch between Shakespeare and modern life, and Shakespeare's language is treated with scepticism or mockery. This manifests a growing trend throughout much of twentieth-century popular culture to legitimise its own cultural authority by pushing against qualities associated with Shakespeare's language.

Ironisation

Though pop culture tries to read Shakespeare's language through a presentist lens, there are features of that language – its formal register, eccentric vocabulary, details of historical grammar and syntax – that simply cannot easily be accommodated. Every Shakespearean 'dost', 'thou', or 'prithee' declares its own stubborn historicity. In some cases, those early modern linguistic or stylistic features can contribute to a passage's Shakespearean authoritative feel. Such features are sometimes part of ersatz Shakespeare, proverbial snippets purporting to be Shakespearean.[14] Archaisms are also integral to the peculiar delight of Shakespeare insults, to which have been devoted books, websites, calendars, magnet sets, and iPhone apps. The appeal of Shakespearean invective – whether quoted from plays or randomly generated by computer – springs from the comical extravagance of the language, its deviation from contemporary practice, as well as the willful 'misuse' of Shakespeare's normally anodyne proverbial authority. These antiquated features can also frame a quoter of Shakespeare citation as an eccentric or intellectual villain, an outlaw from the democratic norm, as is the case of the villainous Klingon General Chang's taunting quotations in *Star Trek VI: The Undiscovered Country* (1991). But by far the most widespread strategy for addressing the mismatch between Shakespeare's archaic language and the prevailing pop hermeneutic is irony. This interpretive strategy involves reading Shakespeare's words as if they were contemporary, while at the same time acknowledging (and even heightening) anachronism for comical effect. We should distinguish parody from irony. Irony bears a close relationship to the camp sensibility, restoring cultural value to a product otherwise regarded as outmoded by embracing it with a knowing wink. This approach has the considerable advantage of maintaining the predominantly proverbial quality of Shakespeare's words and their cultural authority, while at the same time wryly recognising that those words do not entirely fit a contemporary context. Since it can be a means for reconciling the pull of two different interpretive protocols at once – professional historicism and pop presentism – it has a special appeal for those educated enough to appreciate the small thrill of transgression in willfully violating 'proper' codes of interpretation.

We've already seen examples of this approach to Shakespeare's language in the Bamforth 'Romeo and Juliet' postcard, the comical books on Shakespeare, golf, and baseball, and the King's Puremalt pamphlet. Indeed, this approach has a long history in popular culture, one that co-exists with a popular tradition of treating Shakespearean proverbialisation earnestly. It can be found, for example, in the ironic readings of Shakespeare passages in eighteenth- and nineteenth-century political caricature.[15] Produced at the very same time as the Victorian greeting postcards discussed above are comic postcards that revel in anachronistic readings of Shakespeare. One such card from the 1890s portrays a boy stealing a drink of wine while his father snoozes, with the caption 'I am thy father's spirit' (*Ham.* 1.5.9). The 'Shakespeare on Poker' series from 1908, one of several card-themed series, pictures poker hands with wry Shakespearean captions; on one we see a spade flush ruined by an ace of diamonds, with the caption 'out, damned spot! out, I say!' (*Mac.* 5.1.30). Almost from the beginning this was an attractive strategy for advertisers, for by citing Shakespeare under the veil of irony, they could lay claim to the language's authority while remaining arm's length from those stylistic features pop culture found problematic. In 1890, Pears' Soap, an innovator in the early days of advertising, ran an outrageous ad in which Lady Macbeth, complaining 'what, will these hands ne'er be clean?' (*Mac.* 5.1.37), is comforted by the gentlewoman with the line, 'Ay, madam. Here, for a shilling, is a *sovereign remedy*, fragrant of "all the perfumes of Arabia"' (riffing on *Mac.* 5.1.42–43).[16] A later Pears ad parodies the anti-Stratfordian technique of reading the Shakespearean text for ciphers. It reads, 'Shakespeare saves his Bacon, for even he recommended Pears' Soap: thus he says – "For soap-_Pears_"' (originally 'For so appears' (*H5* 3.0.16)).[17] A Coca-Cola campaign from 1928, 'what Shakespeare says about Coca-Cola', used citations from ten plays. In each case, the quotations were presented as if issuing from Shakespearean characters (each pictured adoringly holding a Coke) and not Shakespeare himself, complicating the proverbial effect. In the *Hamlet* ad, it is Ophelia who speaks the endorsement, 'the glass of fashion and the mould of form, the observed of all observers' (*Ham.* 3.1.143–144), with 'glass' and 'fashion' as anchor words. The accompanying copy encourages a wry take on Shakespeare's language: 'Maybe Mr. Shakespeare didn't always know just what he was writing about. We can't ask him now. We can only take what he wrote for what it is, and in penning the above he must have had Coca-Cola in mind.'[18] The arch tone allows a readership familiar with the perils of anachronism – the college students to which this ad was targeted[19] – to engage in contemporising with a knowing wink.

By the late twentieth and early twenty-first centuries, the prevailing advertising style was to keep text of any sort to a minimum, and so citation of Shakespeare's language has largely dwindled to variations on only the most familiar passages – 'to be or not to be', 'shall I compare thee to a summer's day', and the like. Contemporary pop culture seems ever more intolerant of linguistic archaisms, so invocations of famous Shakespearean passages in ads often involve comically paraphrasing them into colloquial English. The entire copy of a 2009 ad for Alestra/AT&T reads this way: 'romeo believes juliet is dead. juliet dies because romeo believes she is dead. communication is very important'. Shakespeare's exquisite, complex language is evoked in its absence, set against the deadpan colloquial retelling of *Romeo and Juliet*. Here the cultural authority of Shakespeare's language is residual – it is the *plot* of *Romeo and Juliet* that has a proverbial quality. A TV spot for Nextel from 2008 also makes comic hay of the language of *Romeo and Juliet*.[20] Students in a school production perform on cell phones, reducing the text to eighteen words: 'Romeo – Juliet – I love you – ditto – die – marry him! – never! – no! – you! – ugh – better now – no! – ugh – kids.' This ad registers the loss attendant upon pop modernising of Shakespeare's language while at the same time it embraces the slangy brevity of texting as the new linguistic norm, playing Shakespearean miscommunication against hip modern communication technology. Once again, the poetic texture of Shakespearean language is something to be pushed against, so as to connect youth culture – irreverent, contemporary, cool – with this phone service. The same adaptational strategy underlies a recent spate of novelty books which 'translate' Shakespeare's text into tweets or emojis.[21]

That said, it is important to stress that earlier pop approaches to Shakespeare's language persist, albeit in diminished numbers. A 2005 TV advertisement for Levi's 501 jeans,[22] for instance, suggests the continuing viability of Shakespearean proverbialism for a youth audience. The ad showcases Bottom, a young man in Levi's, walking the mean night-time streets of Los Angeles. The dialogue is taken from Bottom's transformation scene in *A Midsummer Night's Dream* (3.1.96–118):

BOTTOM

I see their knavery: this is to make an ass of me.

GANG MEMBER

Bottom!

BOTTOM

To fright me, if they could.

GANG MEMBER

(TUGGING ON BOTTOM'S JEANS) Thou art changed! what do I see on thee?

BOTTOM

(VOICEOVER) But I will not stir from this place. (TO GANG MEMBER) What
do you see? You see an asshead of your own, do you? (WALKING AWAY)
I will walk up and down here, and I will sing ...

TITANIA

What angel wakes me from my flowery bed?

BOTTOM

... that they shall hear I'm not afraid.

TITANIA

Pray thee, gentle mortal, sing again:
Mine ear is much enamoured of thy note;
So is mine eye enthralled to thy shape.
I love thee.

Drawing heavily upon Baz Luhrmann's 1996 *Romeo + Juliet*, this ad
juxtaposes forbidden adolescent love with a gritty urban setting plagued by
gang violence. Despite the contemporary location, the ad, like Luhrmann's
film, does not modernise Shakespeare's language, instead using its poetry
and archaisms to romanticise the love scenario at the ad's core. Ignored
entirely is the comedy of the language's original narrative context; the love
exchange between Bottom and Titania is instead treated literally and rever-
ently, without a trace of irony. Where in *Romeo + Juliet* there's an obvious
mismatch between Shakespeare's language and contemporary semantic
fields, Luhrmann often recalibrates the problem word's meaning in a quick
shot that highlights his solution to the problem of anachronism, adding a
bit of meta-adaptational wit. Benvolio's and Capulet's references to their
'swords' (1.1.59, 68) are handled as allusions to a brand of handgun. Indeed,
throughout the film this kind of obvious anachronism is associated with
commercial appropriation of Shakespeare's language we see on signs and
logos. The semantic violence in corporate (mis)use of Shakespeare's words
is thereby linked to the physical violence of the feuding families, a point
made early in the film when we first see the sign at the gas station 'add fuel
to your fire' (*3H6* 5.4.70) followed immediately by the first appearance of

Tybalt, lighting a cigarette and joining the gunfight. The romantic passages, by contrast, are free of this sort of meta-adaptational commentary, allowing them to be read more easily in terms of the 'timeless', transcendent, earnest depiction of love pop culture associates with Shakespeare's romantic verse. The *Midsummer* passage in the Levi's ad approaches the depiction of young love in much the same way. Reading anchor words – 'changed', 'asshead', 'enthralled to thy shape' – with their modern meanings sutures Shakespeare's dialogue into a contemporary context, and the utterly unironic tone preserves Shakespeare's status as the classic poet of love.

Conclusion

This discussion suggests that it is not quite right to claim that popular culture's approach to Shakespeare's language is 'post-hermeneutic'. It would be more accurate to say that pop culture follows quite different conventions for contextualising Shakespeare's language than do Shakespearean professionals. Pop culture routinely violates the most fundamental academic assumptions about the nature of Shakespeare's language, as well as the foundations for the academy's claim to be the custodian of Shakespeare's 'proper' meaning. For that reason, it poses a potent challenge to the authority of Shakespearean professionals. Even those who abide by Terence Hawkes's dictum 'Shakespeare doesn't mean: *we* mean *by* Shakespeare'[23] have been reluctant to embrace the full implications of that position. We might be willing to abide modern-dress performance of Shakespeare, transposition of the plays into contemporary settings or application of twenty-first century theory to Shakespeare's texts, but willingness to abide the construing of Shakespeare's language within a contemporary semantic field is a bridge too far, for many the absolute limit of presentism. One virtue of conceptualising pop approaches to Shakespeare's language as an alternative hermeneutic is that it draws attention to the interpretive predispositions and practices scholars and actors routinely bring to bear upon Shakespeare's words. Another is that it raises the question of what sort of knowledge – if any at all – popular presentist readings of Shakespeare's language might be capable of. Might the Bamforth postcard draw our attention to Shakespeare's choice of the word 'wherefore' instead of his much more common 'why', suggesting that perhaps in this case 'where' haunts the line? Does Helena's comment from *A Midsummer Night's Dream* indeed have a subtextual feminist content, despite its apparent meaning in dramatic context? Do popular readings of Shakespeare's words, unhistorical and denarrativised though they may typically be, nevertheless provide evidence for what Deleuze might call the 'virtuality' of Shakespearean language, a semantic generativity that extends beyond the language's originating historical conditions and immediate dramatic context? This is emphatically not to argue that we should utterly reject historical and narrative contextualising of Shakespeare's words, nor is it to argue that we should unquestioningly embrace the presentist hermeneutic offered by modern popular culture or abandon ideological critique. It is to suggest that seeing pop readings of Shakespeare as products of an alternative hermeneutic may allow us to understand better how those outside the Shakespeare industry process Shakespeare's language. And it provides a firmer grasp of the processes that have driven Shakespeare's exceptionally robust afterlife.

NOTES

1 See *Limited Inc*, trans. Jeffrey Mehlman and Samuel Weber (Evanston: Northwestern University Press, 1988).

2 Marjorie Garber, 'Character Assassination: Shakespeare, Anita Hill, and *JFK*', *Symptoms of Culture* (New York: Routledge, 1998), pp. 154–155.

3 John Drakakis, 'Shakespeare in Quotations', *Studying British Culture: An Introduction*, ed. Susan Bassnett (London: Routledge, 1997), pp. 152–172.

4 William Dodd, *The Beauties of Shakespear Regularly Selected from each Play with a General Index Digesting them under Proper Heads* 1752 (London: Frank Cass, 1971). Dodd's model for this collection may have been William Howell's *The Word of God: The Best Guide to all Persons, At All Times, and in All Places* (London: J. Leake for Mary Howell, 1698). Though in his preface Howell claims that this work was intended as a devotional aid, it was probably designed for pastors preparing sermons.

5 Michael Macrone, *Brush Up Your Shakespeare!* (New York: Cader Books, 1990).

6 [Charles] The Prince of Wales, *The Prince's Choice: A Personal Selection from Shakespeare* (London: Hodder & Stoughton, 1995).

7 Barry Edelstein, *Bardisms: Shakespeare for all Occasions* (New York: Harper Collins, 2009).

8 Louis Marder (ed.), *Speak the Speech: The Shakespeare Quotation Book* (New York: HarperCollins, 1994).

9 *The Arden Book of Quotations*, ed. Jane Armstrong (London: Bloomsbury Arden, 2010) follows Marder in format and scope, though this volume, tied to the scholarly Arden editions of the plays, identifies both speaker and interlocutor in an effort to establish a firmer narrative context, and like Marder's collection it includes a glossary of difficult and antiquated terms. In a gesture toward academic respectability, it also does not include the kinds of contemporary categories that Marder does.

10 John W. Seder, *Shakespeare's Book of Insults, Insights & Infinite Jests* (Springfield: Octavo Press, 1984).

11 John Tullius and Joe Ortiz, *Shakespeare on Golf* (New York: Hyperion, 1997); David Goodnough, *Shakespeare on Golf* (London: Robson Books, 2001); Syd Pritchard, *Shakespeare: The Golfer's Companion* (Bloomington: Trafford

Publishing, 2006); David Goodnough, *Shakespeare on Baseball: Such Time-Beguiling Sport* (Fort Lee: Barricade Books, 2000); Edward J. Bander and Jerry Warshaw, *The Breath of an Unfee'd Lawyer: Shakespeare on Lawyers and the Law* (North Haven: Catbird Press, 1996); Katherine and Elizabeth O'Mahoney, *Shakespeare On Doctors & Lawyers (And Other Professions)* (London: Prion Books, 2002); Margaret Graham Tebo, *Shakespeare for Lawyers: A Practical Guide to Quoting the Bard* (Chicago: American Bar Association, 2011); Jay M. Shafritz, *Shakespeare on Management: Wise Business Counsel from the Bard* (New York: HarperBusiness, 1999).

12 Vernon Bogdanor, 'The Falklands War, 1982', Lecture for Gresham College, London, 8 March 2016, transcript at www.gresham.ac.uk/lectures-and-events/the-falklands-war-1982; 'Lord Hailsham quotes Henry V in latin outside no. 10', *ITN*, 14 June 1982, available at www.gettyimages.com/detail/video/lord-hailsham-quotes-henry-v-in-latin-outside-no-10-news-footage/1B07413_0009.

13 *Illustrated London News*, 4 May 1889, p. 579.

14 See Esther French, 'Fakespeare', *Shakespeare & Beyond* blog, 21 February 2017, available at https://shakespeareandbeyond.folger.edu/2017/02/21/shakepeare-quotes-commonly-misattributed/.

15 Jonathan Bate, 'Shakespearean Allusion in English Caricature in the Age of Gillray', *Journal of the Warburg and Courtauld Institutes* 49 (1986): 196–210; 'Nast and Shakespeare', *Harpweek*, 2005, website available at http://staging.thomasnast.com/Activities/NastandShakespeare/HubPages/CommentaryPage.asp?Commentary=01RuscheEssay-02NastLove.

16 *The Graphic*, 1 February 1890, p. 147.

17 *The Graphic*, 6 March 1902, p. 221.

18 *Life Magazine*, 15 March 1928, p. 1.

19 See www.coca-colacompany.com/stories/2010/04/what-shakespeare-said-about-coke.

20 Available at www.youtube.com/watch?v=IqQ9CV9sJCI.

21 See, for example, Mark Hillary, *My Tweets are Nothing Like the Sun* (lulu.com, 2015), or the OMG Shakespeare series from Random House (2015).

22 Available at www.youtube.com/watch?v=_T8OvVa2Ma8.

23 Terence Hawkes, *Meaning by Shakespeare* (London: Routledge, 1992), p. 3.

Appendix

COMPILED BY PETER MACK,
ADAPTED BY LYNNE MAGNUSSON

Glossary of Rhetorical Figures

'What is the figure? What is the figure?' asks an excited Holofernes, the schoolteacher in Shakespeare's *Love's Labour's Lost* (5.1.53). Shakespeare both knew and exploited a wide range of figures of speech, even if he chose to associate this eagerness to name and identify them with one of his more pedantic characters. We offer a list of sixty-two figures, organised thematically to assist with naming and identification, as one of many possible routes modelled in this volume towards the analysis and appreciation of Shakespeare's verbal artistry.

There is considerable variation among rhetorical treatises in the treatment of figures. Often they are divided into two or more categories, such as schemes (figures of sound, which create ornamental figures by patterns of repetition or organisational patterning) and tropes (figures of thought, which 'change' or 'translate' words from their normal sense). Not all figures, however, fit neatly into any of the standard divisions, and we have chosen a simple thematic organisation here. Names and definitions of the figures vary in different treatises, and some authors treat as stylistic figures elements such as vivid description or comparison, which others treat elsewhere, for example, as part of rhetorical invention. Illustrations from Shakespeare have been given for many figures in this list where brief examples can serve, but they are usually omitted for the more extended figures, especially those that are content and audience-oriented.

This glossary is developed from the 'List of Figures and Tropes' in P. Mack, *Rhetoric's Questions, Reading and Interpretation* (London: Palgrave, 2017), pp. 79–84. Figures of word construction and Shakespearean illustrations have been added. For further information see R. A. Lanham, *A Handlist of Rhetorical Terms* (Berkeley: University of California Press, 1991); *Rhetorica ad Herennium*, trans. H. Caplan (Cambridge. MA: Harvard University Press, 1954), Book IV; Quintilian, *Institutio oratoria*, trans. D. A. Russell, 5 vols. (Cambridge, MA: Harvard University Press, 2001), Books 8 and 9; S. Adamson, G. Alexander, and K. Ettenhuber (eds.), *Renaissance*

Figures of Speech (Cambridge: Cambridge University Press, 2007); and Gideon Burton's website 'Silva rhetoricae' at http://rhetoric.byu.edu. Many examples from Shakespeare are offered in Miriam Joseph, *Shakespeare's Use of the Arts of Language* (New York: Columbia University Press, 1947); B. Vickers, *In Defence of Rhetoric* (Oxford: Oxford University Press, 1988), pp. 491–500; and S. D. Keller, *The Development of Shakespeare's Rhetoric* (Tübingen: Francke Verlag, 2009).

Repetition of Words and Sounds

Anaphora: The first word of one sentence or phrase is also the first word of the next, e.g. 'So long as men can breathe or eyes can see, / So long lives this, and this gives life to thee' (*Son.* 18.13–14).

Epistrophe: The last word of one sentence or phrase is the same as the last word of the next, e.g. 'Is this nothing? / Why then the world and all that's in't is nothing, / The covering sky is nothing, Bohemia nothing, / My wife is nothing, nor nothing have these nothings, / If this be nothing' (*WT* 1.2.289–293).

Epanalepsis: The first word of a sentence or phrase is the same as the last word, e.g. 'To know the thing I am forbid to know' (*LLL* 1.1.60).

Anadiplosis: The last word of one sentence or phrase is used as the first word of the next: 'To die, to sleep – / To sleep, perchance to dream' (*Ham.* 3.1.64–65).

Epizeuxis: A word is repeated immediately several times in succession, e.g. 'Never, never, never, never, never' (*Lear* 5.3.282).

Ploce: Repetition of a word after intervening words, e.g. 'Call you me fair? That "fair" again unsay. / Demetrius loves your fair: O happy fair!' (*MND* 1.1.181–182).

Polyptoton: Repetition of the same root word but in a different form, e.g. 'O handle not the theme, to talk of hands' (*Tit.* 3.2.29).

Gradatio, climax: A step-by-step figure in which the end of one phrase becomes the starting point of the next, e.g. 'your brother and my sister no sooner met but they looked; no sooner looked, but they loved; no sooner loved, but they sighed; no sooner sighed but ... they sought the remedy; and in these degrees have they made a pair of stairs to marriage' (*AYLI* 5.2.26–31).

Chiasmus, antimetabole: Repetition of two successive words in inverse order, e.g. 'Fair is foul, and foul is fair' (*Mac.* 1.1.12).

APPENDIX

Alliteration, paroemion: Use of words with the same initial consonant sound, e.g. 'The preyful Princess pierced and pricked a pretty pleasing pricket' (*LLL* 4.2.51).

Homoioteleuton: Use of words with similar endings (close to internal rhyme), e.g. 'Nor fetch in firing / At requiring' (*Temp.* 2.2.157–158).

Word Construction

Prothesis: Addition of a syllable at the beginning of a word, e.g. 'bedimmed' (*Temp.* 5.1.41); 'a thing *enskied* and sainted' (*MM* 1.4.34).

Proparalepsis: Addition of a syllable at the end of a word, e.g. 'the *vasty* deep' (*1H4* 3.1.52); 'climatures' (*Ham.* 1.1.126); 'freightage' (*Tro.* Prologue 13).

Epenthesis: Addition of a syllable or letter in the middle of a word, e.g. 'a *cursitory* eye' (*H5* 5.2.77) for 'cursory'; 'alarum' for 'alarm'.

Aphaeresis: Omission of a syllable from the beginning of a word, e.g. ''twixt'; '*gins* to woo' for 'begins' (*VA* 6).

Syncope: Omission of a syllable from the middle of a word, e.g. 'ne'er' for 'never', 'these rebel *pow'rs*' (*Son.* 146.2); 'a *prosp'rous* day' (*Ant.* 4.6.5).

Synaloephe: Omission or elision of one or two vowels coming together at the junction of words, e.g. 'be't' for 'be it' (*Tro.* 1.3.70).

Apocope: Omission of the last syllable, e.g. 'morn'; 'an *attent* ear' (*Ham.* 1.2.193).

Organisation of Sentences, and Contrariety

Isocolon: Successive clauses of equal length, e.g. Shakespeare's iambic pentameter lines.

Parison: Successive clauses with the same structure (grammatical parallelism), e.g. 'With mirth in funeral and with dirge in marriage' (*Ham.* 1.2.12).

Asyndeton: Omission of connecting conjunctions which would normally be required.

Polysyndeton: Use of many conjunctions, more than would normally be required.

Zeugma: One verb is applied to several subjects and predicates, e.g. 'Give them thy fingers, me thy lips to kiss' (Sonnet 128.14).

Hyperbaton: Disruption of expected sentence order to create emphasis, e.g. 'Himself the primrose path of dalliance treads' (*Ham.* 1.3.50).

Hysteron Proteron ('later earlier'): Disruption of sentence order so that something which should logically be placed later comes earlier than it should, e.g. 'That time of year thou mayst in me behold / When yellow leaves, or none, or few, do hang' (Sonnet 73.1–2).

Antithesis: A style founded on contraries, e.g. 'In respect that it is solitary, I like it well; but in respect that it is private, it is a very vile life' (*AYLI* 3.3.3–5). There are many different types.

Synoiceiosis: The equal intensity of opposites, e.g. 'So much to my good comfort as it is / Now piercing to my soul' (*WT* 5.3.33–34).

Substitution and Change of Meaning

Metaphor: One word is replaced by another chosen because of some sort of parallelism. Ideally, presenting the two as parallel says something new about what would have been expressed by the original word, e.g. 'that sleep of death' (*Ham.* 3.1.66); 'the girdle of these walls' (*H5* Prologue.19).

Allegory: A mode of writing in which one physical element or character consistently stands for a specific abstract quality. This is sometimes called a continuing metaphor. Allegory is also a way of reading abstract meaning from a narrative by interpreting individual characters or elements as abstract qualities.

Irony: Implying a meaning opposite to what the words used apparently mean, e.g. 'But Brutus says he was ambitious, / And Brutus is an honourable man' (*JC* 3.2.88–89).

Metonymy: One word is replaced by another word contiguous to it, typically cause by effect, proper name by epithet (or vice versa). For example, 'the pen is mightier than the sword' (meaning that language or writing brings about more effects than physical force), 'wine speaks the truth' (meaning that wine causes people to become loose-tongued and to exercise less censorship of their thoughts), e.g. 'is it not strange that *sheep's guts* [i.e. music] should hale souls out of men's bodies?' (*Ado* 2.3.50–51).

Hendiadys: A single complex idea expressed as two words joined by a conjunction, e.g. 'My speculative and officed instruments' (*Oth.* 1.3.266) and 'sound and fury' (*Mac.* 5.5.26).

Synecdoche: Part is named where whole is meant or vice versa, e.g. 'Your knees to them, not arms, must help' (*Cor.* 1.1.60).

Onomatopoeia: Inventing a word which sounds like the thing it signifies, e.g. 'Buzz, buzz!' (*Ham.* 2.2.360).

Paronomasia: Play on words, usually replacing one word with another which is very similar but not identical in sound; extended to include playing on the different meanings of a single word, e.g. 'I'll gild the faces of the grooms withal, / For it must seem their guilt' (*Mac.* 2.2.59–69).

Syllepsis: Pun with two meanings in one word, e.g. 'Therefore I lie with her, and she with me' (Son. 138.13).

Antanaclasis: Play on words, where a word is repeated with a shift in meaning, e.g. 'Will will fulfil the treasure of thy love, / Ay, fill it full with wills, and my will one' (Son. 136.5–6).

Antonomasia, pronominatio: Replacing a noun or proper name with a descriptive phrase, e.g. 'Coeur-de-lion' (*John* 1.1.54).

Synonymia, interpretatio: Replacing a word just used with another word or phrase with the same meaning, hence a form of semantic repetition and useful for emphasis and amplification, e.g. 'which here thou viewest, beholdest, surveyest, or seest' (*LLL* 1.1.231).

Content

Enargeia, evidentia: Vivid description, using words to bring something before the eyes of an audience often with strong emotional effect, e.g. Enobarbus's description of Cleopatra's barge on the river Cydnus (*Ant.* 2.2.201–228).

Ecphrasis: Description of a (sometimes fictional) work of art, e.g. 'Look here upon this picture, and on this, / The counterfeit presentment of two brothers' and what follows (*Ham.* 3.4.53–65).

Prosopopeia: Assigning a speech to an animal, object, or abstraction.

Periphrasis: Expressing a simple idea in a more extended and elaborate way, e.g. 'besieged with sable-coloured melancholy, I did commend the black oppressing humour to the most wholesome physic of thy health-giving air' (*LLL* 1.1.221–223)

Exsuscitatio, anastasis: Setting out an argument in several full stages, some of which are embellished, in order to arouse emotion, secure agreement, and present oneself to an audience as authoritative.

Definition: Summing up an idea fully and succinctly to demonstrate secure knowledge and serve as a basis for further arguments.

Expolitio: Dwelling on a point to emphasise and embellish it.

Simile, similitude: A more or less extended comparison with something outside the subject, introduced by 'like', e.g. 'pity, like a naked newborn babe / Striding the blast' (*Mac.* 1.7.21–22).

Comparison: A likeness or difference between two things is used to embellish, prove, or clarify.

Address and Approach to Audience

Apostrophe: Interrupting a text to address directly a god, muse, abstract figure or character; usually introduced by 'O', followed by the name of the addressee.

Aposiopesis: Hesitating or breaking off one's speech as if overcome by emotion, e.g. 'It came even from the heart of – O, she's dead' (*Lear* 5.3.198).

Subiectio: The speaker asks the opponents or herself what can be said against her position.

Hypophora, question and answer: The speaker asks questions and answers them.

Permissio: The speaker indicates that he submits and allows the audience to decide, often in order to arouse pity.

Dubitatio: The speaker seems to ask the audience which of two words had better be used.

Correctio: The speaker retracts what has been said and replaces it with something more suitable, with the effect of emphasising both ways of putting the idea.

Parrhesia, licentia: Frankness of speech, e.g. 'What wouldst thou do, old man? ... To plainness hounour's bound, / When majesty falls to folly' (*Lear* 1.1.140–143).

Occultatio, occupatio: The speaker says that she will not mention something but in fact briefly tells the audience all about it, e.g. 'I'll not remember you of my own lord, / Who is lost too' (*WT* 3.2.227–228).

Prolepsis: The speaker mentions or alludes to something which will be said later, or anticipates the opponent's arguments.

Transition: The speaker recalls what has been said and indicates what will be said next, with the effect of emphasis and making logical connections.

Dialogue: Inventing a speech for a person or a conversation, as a way to make narrative more credible and more moving.

Hyperbole: Self-consciously overstating or exaggerating something, e.g. 'methinks it were an easy leap / To pluck bright honour from the pale-faced moon' (*1H4* 1.3.199–200).

Diminutio: Understating or explaining away one's achievements so as to avoid the impression of arrogance or a sense of entitlement, e.g. 'Sir, praise me not. / My work hath yet not warmed me' (*Cor.* 1.6.16–17).

FURTHER READING

Chapter 1

Barton, Anne, 'Leontes and the Spider: Language and Speaker in Shakespeare's Last Plays', *Essays, Mainly Shakespearian*. Cambridge: Cambridge University Press, 1994, pp. 161–181.

Blake, N. F., *The Language of Shakespeare*. New York: Macmillan, 1983.
  A Grammar of Shakespeare's Language. New York: Palgrave, 2002.

Crystal, David, *Think on My Words: Exploring Shakespeare's Language*. Cambridge: Cambridge University Press, 2008.

Ginzburg, Carlo, 'Style: Inclusion and Exclusion', *Wooden Eyes: Nine Reflections on Distance*. New York: Columbia University Press, 2001, pp. 109–138.

Hope, Jonathan, *The Authorship of Shakespeare's Plays: A Socio-Linguistic Study*. Cambridge: Cambridge University Press, 1994.

Houston, John Porter, *Shakespearian Sentences: A Study in Style and Syntax*. Baton Rouge: Louisiana State University Press, 1988.

Kermode, Frank, *Shakespeare's Language*. New York: Farrar, Straus & Giroux, 2000.

Magnusson, Lynne, *Shakespeare and Social Dialogue: Dramatic Language and Elizabeth Letters*. Cambridge: Cambridge University Press, 1999.

McDonald, Russ, *Shakespeare and the Arts of Language*. Oxford: Oxford University Press, 2001.
  Shakespeare's Late Style. Cambridge: Cambridge University Press, 2006.

Shore, Daniel, 'Shakespeare's Constructicon', *Shakespeare Quarterly* 66.2 (2015): 113–136.

Van Es, Bart, *Shakespeare in Company*. Oxford: Oxford University Press, 2013.

Vickers, Brian, *Shakespeare, Co-Author*. Oxford: Oxford University Press, 2002.

Wright, George T., *Shakespeare's Metrical Art*. Berkeley: University of California Press, 1988.

Chapter 2

Adamson, Sylvia, 'Literary Language', *The Cambridge History of the English Language*, ed. Roger Lass. Cambridge: Cambridge University Press, 1999, vol. 3, pp. 539–653.

Blank, Paula, *Broken English: Dialects and the Politics of Language in Renaissance Writings*. London: Routledge, 1996.

Craig, Hugh, 'Shakespeare's Vocabulary: Myth and Reality', *Shakespeare Quarterly* 62.1 (2011): 53–74.

Crystal, David, *Think On My Words: Exploring Shakespeare's Language*. Cambridge: Cambridge University Press, 2008.

Enterline, Lynn, *Shakespeare's Schoolroom*. Philadelphia: University of Pennsylvania Press, 2011.

Leith, Dick, *A Social History of English*. 2nd edn. London: Routledge, 1997.

McDonald, Russ, *Shakespeare and the Arts of Language*. Oxford: Oxford University Press, 2001.

Chapter 3

Austin, J. L., *How to Do Things with Words*. Oxford: Oxford University Press, 1975.

Calderwood, James L., *Metadrama in Shakespeare's Henriad: 'Richard II' to 'Henry V'*. Berkeley: University of California Press, 1979.

Cavell, Stanley, *Philosophy the Day after Tomorrow*. Cambridge, MA: Belknap Press of Harvard University Press, 2006.

Fish, Stanley E., 'How to Do Things with Austin and Searle: Speech Act Theory and Literary Criticism', *MLN* 91.5 (1976): 983–1025.

Kerrigan, John, *Shakespeare's Binding Language*. New York: Oxford University Press, 2016.

Porter, Joseph A., *The Drama of Speech Acts: Shakespeare's Lancastrian Tetralogy*. Berkeley: University of California Press, 1979.

'Eloquence and Liminality: Glossing Mercutio's Speech Acts', *Romeo and Juliet*, ed. R. S. White. Basingstoke: Palgrave, 2001, pp. 166–193.

Reddy, William M., *The Navigation of Feeling: A Framework for the History of Emotions*. Cambridge: Cambridge University Press, 2001.

Schalkwyk, David, *Speech and Performance in Shakespeare's Sonnets and Plays*. Cambridge: Cambridge University Press, 2002.

'Shakespeare's Speech', *Journal of Medieval and Early Modern Studies* 40.2 (2010): 373–400.

Searle, John, 'A Classification of Speech Acts', *Language and Society* 5 (1979): 1–23. *Speech Acts: An Essay in the Philosophy of Language*. Cambridge: Cambridge University Press, 1969.

Wofford, Susanne L. '"To you I give myself, for I am yours": Erotic Performance and Theatrical Performatives in *As You Like It*', *Shakespeare Reread: The Texts in New Contexts*, ed. Russ McDonald. Ithaca: Cornell University Press, 1994, pp. 147–169.

Chapter 4

Attridge, Derek, *The Rhythms of English Poetry*. London: Longman, 1982.

Well-Weighed Syllables: Elizabethan Verse in Classical Metres. London: Cambridge University Press, 1974.

Crystal, David, *The Oxford Dictionary of Original Shakespearean Pronunciation*. Oxford: Oxford University Press, 2016.

Flint, Lorna, *Shakespeare's Third Keyboard: The Significance of Rime in Shakespeare's Plays*. London: Associated University Presses, 2000.

Griffiths, Eric, 'On Lines and Grooves from Shakespeare to Tennyson', *Tennyson among the Poets: Bicentenary Essays*, ed. Robert Douglas-Fairhurst and Seamus Perry. Oxford: Oxford University Press, 2009, pp. 132–159.

McDonald, Russ, *Shakespeare and the Arts of Language*. Oxford: Oxford University Press, 2001.

Rokison, Abigail, *Shakespearean Verse Speaking: Text and Theatre Practice*. Cambridge: Cambridge University Press, 2010.

Smith, G. Gregory (ed.), *Elizabethan Critical Essays*. 2 vols. Oxford: Clarendon Press, 1904.

Tarlinskaja, Marina, *Shakespeare's Verse: Iambic Pentameter and the Poet's Idiosyncrasies*. New York: Peter Lang, 1987.

    Shakespeare and the Versification of English Drama, 1561–1642. Farnham: Ashgate, 2014.

Vickers, Brian, *The Artistry of Shakespeare's Prose*. London: Methuen, 1968.

Wright, George T., *Shakespeare's Metrical Art*. Berkeley: University of California Press, 1988.

Chapter 5

Bakhtin, M. M., 'Discourse in the Novel', *The Dialogic Imagination: Four Essays*, ed. Michael Holquist, trans. Caryl Emerson and Michael Holquist. Austin: University of Texas Press, 1981, pp. 259–422.

Bourdieu, Pierre, 'The Economics of Linguistic Exchanges', *Social Science Information* 16 (1977): 645–668.

Brown, Penelope, and Stephen C. Levinson, *Politeness: Some Universals in Language Usage*. Cambridge: Cambridge University Press, 1987.

Coulthard, Malcolm, *An Introduction to Discourse Analysis*. 2nd edn. London: Routledge, 1985.

Elam, Keir, *Shakespeare's Universe of Discourse: Language-Games in the Comedies*. Cambridge: Cambridge University Press, 1984.

Herman, Vimala, *Dramatic Discourse: Dialogue as Interaction in Plays*. London and New York: Routledge, 1995.

Kennedy, Andrew K., *Dramatic Dialogue: The Duologue of Personal Encounter*. Cambridge: Cambridge University Press, 1983.

Magnusson, Lynne, 'Dialogue', *Reading Shakespeare's Dramatic Language*, ed. Sylvia Adamson, Lynette Hunter, Lynne Magnusson, Ann Thompson, and Katie Wales. London: Arden Shakespeare, 2001, pp. 130–143.

    Shakespeare and Social Dialogue: Dramatic Language and Elizabethan Letters. Cambridge: Cambridge University Press, 1999.

Matoesian, Gregory M., 'The Turn-Taking Model for Natural Conversation', *Reproducing Rape: Domination through Talk in the Courtroom*. Chicago: University of Chicago Press, 1993, pp. 72–97.

Chapter 6

Empson, William, *Seven Types of Ambiguity*. London: Chatto & Windus, 1930.

McDonald, Russ, *Shakespeare and the Arts of Language*. Oxford: Oxford University Press, 2001.

Shakespeare's Late Style. Cambridge: Cambridge University Press, 2006.

Morse, Ruth, *Truth and Convention in the Middle Ages: Rhetoric, Representation, and Reality*. Cambridge: Cambridge University Press, 1991.

Chapter 7

Aristotle, *The Art of Rhetoric*, trans. R. Waterfield and H. Yunis. Oxford: Oxford University Press, 2018.

Baldwin, T. W., *William Shakspere's Small Latine and Lesse Greeke*. 2 vols. Urbana: University of Illinois Press, 1944.

Barker, William, *The Adages of Erasmus*. Toronto: University of Toronto Press, 2001.

Burton, Gideon O. (ed.), *Silva Rhetoricae*. Brigham Young University, 2016. http://rhetoric.byu.edu.

Cicero, *Rhetorica ad Herennium*, trans. Harry Caplan. Cambridge, MA: Harvard University Press, 1954.

Crane, Mary Thomas, *Framing Authority*. Princeton: Princeton University Press, 1993.

Erasmus, *De conscribendis epistolis*, ed. J. C. Margolin, in Erasmus, *Opera omnia*, I-2. Amsterdam: North Holland, 1971, pp. 205–579, trans. Charles Fantazzi, *Collected Works of Erasmus*, 25. Toronto: University of Toronto Press, 1985.

De copia, ed. Betty Knott, *Opera omnia*, I-6. Amsterdam: North Holland, 1988. Trans. Betty Knott, *Collected Works of Erasmus*, 24. Toronto: University of Toronto Press, 1978.

Hutson, Lorna, *Circumstantial Shakespeare*. Oxford: Oxford University Press, 2015.

Kennedy, George A., *Progymnasmata: Greek Textbooks of Prose Composition and Rhetoric*. Atlanta: Society of Biblical Literature, 2003.

Lanham, Richard A., *A Handlist of Rhetorical Terms*. Berkeley: University of California Press, 1991.

MacDonald, Russ, *Shakespeare and the Arts of Language*. Oxford: Oxford University Press, 2001.

Mack, Peter, *Elizabethan Rhetoric*. Cambridge: Cambridge University Press, 2002.

A History of Renaissance Rhetoric 1380–1620. Oxford: Oxford University Press, 2011.

'Learning and Transforming Conventional Wisdom: Reading and Rhetoric in the Elizabethan Grammar School', *Renaissance Studies* 32 (2018): 427–445.

Reading and Rhetoric in Montaigne and Shakespeare. London: Bloomsbury, 2010.

Rhetoric's Questions, Reading and Interpretation. London: Palgrave, 2017.

Magnusson, Lynne, *Shakespeare and Social Dialogue*. Cambridge: Cambridge University Press, 1999.

Moss, Ann, *Printed Commonplace-Books and the Structuring of Renaissance Thought*. Oxford: Oxford University Press, 1996.

Quintilian, *Institutio oratoria*, trans. Donald A. Russell. 5 vols. Cambridge, MA: Harvard University Press, 2001.

Skinner, Quentin, *Forensic Shakespeare*. Oxford: Oxford University Press, 2014.

Vickers, Brian, 'Shakespeare's Use of Rhetoric', *A New Companion to Shakespeare Studies*, ed. Kenneth Muir and S. Schoenbaum. Cambridge: Cambridge University Press, 1971, pp. 83–98.

Chapter 8

Bakhtin, M. M., *The Dialogic Imagination: Four Essays*, ed. Michael Holquist, trans. Caryl Emerson and Michael Holquist. Austin: University of Texas Press, 1981.

Barber, Charles, Joan C. Beal, and Philip A. Shaw, *The English Language: A Historical Introduction*. 2nd edn. Cambridge: Cambridge University Press, 2012.

Beier, Lee, 'Anti-Language or Jargon? Canting in the English Underworld in the Sixteenth and Seventeenth Centuries', *Languages and Jargons: Contributions to a Social History of Language*, ed. Peter Burke and Roy Porter. Cambridge: Polity Press, 1995, pp. 64–101.

Bell, Allan, *The Guidebook to Sociolinguistics*. Oxford: Wiley Blackwell, 2014.

Blake, N. F., *Non-Standard Language in English Literature*. London: Deutsch, 1981.
  Shakespeare's Language: An Introduction. Basingstoke: Macmillan, 1983.
  Shakespeare's Non-Standard English: A Dictionary of his Informal Language. New York: Continuum, 2004.

Blank, Paula, *Broken English: Dialects and the Politics of Language in Renaissance Writing*. London: Routledge, 1996.

Bourdieu, Pierre, *Language and Symbolic Power*. Cambridge: Polity, 1991.

Chambers, J. K., and Natalie Schilling (eds.), *The Handbook of Language Variation and Change*. 2nd edn. Oxford: Wiley-Blackwell, 2013.

Delabastita, Dirk, and Ton Hoenselaars (eds.), *Multilingualism in the Drama of Shakespeare and his Contemporaries*. Amsterdam: John Benjamins, 2015.

Edelman, Charles, *Shakespeare's Military Language: A Dictionary*. London and New Brunswick: Athlone, 2000.

Görlach, Manfred, 'Regional and Social Variation', *The Cambridge History of the English Language, Vol. 3: 1476–1776*, ed. Roger Lass. Cambridge: Cambridge University Press, 1999, pp. 459–538.

Hope, Jonathan, *Shakespeare and Language: Reason, Eloquence and Artifice in the Renaissance*. London: Arden, 2010.

King, Arthur H., *The Language of Satirized Characters in Poetaster: A Socio-Stylistic Analysis, 1597–1602*. Lund: Gleerup, 1941.

Morris, Pam (ed.), *The Bakhtin Reader: Selected Writings of Bakhtin, Medvedev and Voloshinov*. London: Edward Arnold, 1994.

Musgrove, S., 'Thieves' Cant in *King Lear*', *English Studies* 62 (1981): 5–13.

Salmon, Vivian, and Edwina Burness (eds.), *A Reader in the Language of Shakespearean Drama: Collected Essays*. Amsterdam: John Benjamins, 1987.

Siemon, James, *Word Against Word: Shakespearean Utterance*. Amherst: University Massachusetts Press, 2002.

Sokol, B. J., and Mary Sokol, *Shakespeare's Legal Language: A Dictionary*. London and New Brunswick: Athlone, 2000.

Chapter 9

Basu, Anupam, Jonathan Hope, and Michael Witmore, 'The Professional and Linguistic Communities of Early Modern Dramatists', *Community-Making in Early Stuart Theatres: Stage and Audience*, ed. Roger D. Sell, Helen Wilcox, and Anthony W. Johnson. London: Routledge, 2014, pp. 63–94. [Pre-print downloadable from http://winedarksea.org/?page_id=1990]

Burkert, Mattie, 'Plotting the "Female Wits" Controversy: Gender, Genre, and Printed Plays, 1670–1699', *Early Modern Studies after the Digital Turn*, ed. Laura Estill, Diane Jackaki, and Michael Ullyot. Tempe: Arizona Center for Medieval and Renaissance Studies, 2016, pp. 35–59.

Hope, Jonathan, 'Who Invented "Gloomy"? Lies People Want to Believe about Shakespeare', *Memoria di Shakespeare* 3 (2016): 21–45. [Open access at: http://ojs.uniroma1.it/index.php/MemShakespeare/article/view/14167/13898]

Hope, Jonathan, and Michael Witmore, 'The Hundredth Psalm to the Tune of "Green Sleeves": Digital Approaches to the Language of Genre', *Shakespeare Quarterly* 61.3 (2010): 357–390. [Pre-print downloadable from http://winedarksea.org/?page_id=1990]

Hope, Jonathan, and Michael Witmore, 'The Language of *Macbeth*', *Macbeth: The State of Play*, ed. Ann Thompson. London: Bloomsbury, 2014, pp. 183–208. [Pre-print downloadable from http://winedarksea.org/?page_id=1990]

Tootalian, Jacob, 'Without Measure: The Language of Shakespeare's Prose', *Journal for Early Modern Cultural Studies* 13.4 (2013): 47–60.

Witmore, Michael, Jonathan Hope, and Michael Gleicher, 'Digital Approaches to the Language of Shakespearean Tragedy', *The Oxford Handbook of Shakespearean Tragedy*, ed. Michael Neill and David Schalkwyk. Oxford: Oxford University Press, 2016, pp. 316–335. [Pre-print downloadable from http://winedarksea.org/?page_id=1990]

Chapter 10

Craig, Hugh, 'Stylistic Analysis and Authorship Studies', *A Companion to Digital Humanities*, ed. Susan Schreibman, Ray Siemens, and John Unsworth. Oxford: Blackwell, 2004, pp. 273–288.

Craig, Hugh, and Brett Greatley-Hirsch, *Style, Computers, and Early Modern Drama*. Cambridge: Cambridge University Press, 2017.

Craig, Hugh, and Arthur F. Kinney (eds.), *Shakespeare, Computers, and the Mystery of Authorship*. Cambridge: Cambridge University Press, 2009.

Elliott, Ward E. Y., and Robert J. Valenza, 'Shakespeare's Vocabulary: Did It Dwarf All Others?', *Stylistics and Shakespeare's Language: Transdisciplinary Approaches*, ed. Mireille Ravassat and Jonathan Culpeper. London: Continuum, 2011, pp. 34–57.

Hope, Jonathan, and Michael Witmore, 'The Hundredth Psalm to the Tune of "Green Sleeves": Digital Approaches to Shakespeare's Language of Genre', *Shakespeare Quarterly* 61.3 (2010): 357–390.

Taylor, Gary, 'Artiginality: Authorship after Postmodernism', *The New Oxford Shakespeare: Authorship Companion*, ed. Gary Taylor and Gabriel Egan. Oxford: Oxford University Press, 2016, pp. 3–26.

Witmore, Michael, Jonathan Hope, and Mike Gleicher, 'Digital Approaches to the Language of Shakespearean Tragedy', *The Oxford Handbook of Shakespearean Tragedy*, ed. Michael Neill and David Schalkwyk. Oxford: Oxford University Press, 2016, pp. 316–335.

Chapter 11

Bergen, Benjamin K., *Louder Than Words: The New Science of How the Mind Makes Meaning*. New York: Basic Books, 2006.

Booth, Stephen, *An Essay on Shakespeare's Sonnets*. New Haven: Yale University Press, 1969.

Precious Nonsense: The Gettysburg Address, Ben Jonson's Epitaphs on his Children, and Twelfth Night. Berkeley: University of California Press, 1998.

Cook, Amy, *Shakespearean Neuroplay: Reinvigorating the Study of Dramatic Texts and Performance Through Cognitive Science*. New York: Palgrave Macmillan, 2010.

Crane, Mary Thomas, *Shakespeare's Brain: Reading with Cognitive Theory*. Princeton: Princeton University Press, 2001.

Freeman, Donald, '"Catch[ing] the Nearest Way": *Macbeth* and Cognitive Metaphor', *Journal of Pragmatics* 24 (1995): 689–708.

Lakoff, George, and Mark Johnson, *Metaphors We Live By*. Chicago and London: University of Chicago Press, 1980.

Lyne, Raphael, *Shakespeare, Rhetoric and Cognition*. Cambridge: Cambridge University Press, 2011.

Smith, Bruce, *The Acoustic World of Early Modern England: Attending to the O-Factor*. Chicago: University of Chicago Press, 1996.

Phenomenal Shakespeare. Chichester: Wiley-Blackwell, 2010.

Chapter 12

Barton, John, *Playing Shakespeare*. London: Methuen, 1984.

Black, James, '*Henry IV*: A World of Figures Here', *Shakespeare: The Theatrical Dimension*, ed. Philip C. McGuire and David A. Samuelson. New York: AMS Press, 1979, pp. 165–183.

Escolme, Bridget, *Talking to the Audience: Shakespeare, Performance, Self*. Abingdon: Routledge, 2005.

Eyre, Richard, and Nicholas Wright, *Changing Stages*. London: Bloomsbury, 2000.

Foakes, R. A., and R. T. Rickert, *Henslowe's Diary*. Cambridge: Cambridge University Press, 1968.

Kermode, Frank, *Shakespeare's Language*. London: Penguin, 2000.

Mack, Peter (ed.), *Renaissance Rhetoric*. London: Macmillan, 1994.

Rhetoric's Questions, Reading and Interpretation. London: Palgrave Macmillan, 2017.

Magnusson, Lynne, *Shakespeare and Social Dialogue*. Cambridge: Cambridge University Press, 1999.

McDonald, Russ, *Shakespeare and the Arts of Language*. Oxford: Oxford University Press, 2001.

Rutter, Carol Chillington, 'Shakespeare and School', *Shakespeare Beyond Doubt: Evidence, Argument, Controversy*, ed. Paul Edmondson and Stanley Wells. Cambridge: Cambridge University Press, 2013, pp. 133–144.

Sher, Antony, *Beside Myself*. London: Arrow Books, 2002.

Stern, Tiffany, *Documents of Performance in Early Modern England*. Cambridge: Cambridge University Press, 2009.

Walter, Harriet, *Brutus and Other Heroines: Playing Shakespeare's Roles for Women*. London: Nick Hern Books, 2016.

Other People's Shoes. London: Nick Hern Books, 1999.

Weimann, Robert, *Author's Pen and Actor's Voice: Playing and Writing in Shakespeare's Theatre*. Cambridge: Cambridge University Press, 2000.

Chapter 13

Delabastita, Dirk, and Lieven D'hulst (eds.), *European Shakespeares: Translating Shakespeare in the Romantic Age*. Amsterdam: John Benjamins, 1993.

Ewbank, Inga-Stina, 'Shakespeare Translation as Cultural Exchange', *Shakespeare Survey* 48 (1995): 1–12.

Hoenselaars, Ton, 'Shakespeare and the Cultures of Translation', *Shakespeare Survey* 66 (2013): 206–219.

(ed.), *Shakespeare and the Language of Translation*. London: Arden Shakespeare, Thomson, 2004; revised edition 2012.

Jakobson, Roman, 'On Linguistic Aspects of Translation', *On Translation*, ed. Reuben A. Brower. Cambridge, MA: Harvard University Press, 1959, pp. 232–239.

Kennedy, Dennis (ed.), *Foreign Shakespeare: Contemporary Performance*. Cambridge: Cambridge University Press, 1993.

Chapter 14

Burt, Richard, 'To e- or not to e-? Disposing of Schlockspeare in the Age of Digital Media', *Shakespeare after Mass Media*, ed. Richard Burt. New York: Palgrave Macmillan, 2002, pp. 1–34.

Drakakis, John, 'Shakespeare in Quotations', *Studying British Culture: An Introduction*, ed. Susan Bassnett. London: Routledge, 1997, pp. 152–172.

Garber, Marjorie, 'Character Assassination: Shakespeare, Anita Hill, and *JFK*' and 'Shakespeare as Fetish', *Symptoms of Culture*. New York: Routledge, 1998, pp. 153–178.

Lanier, Douglas, 'Marketing', *The Oxford Handbook to Shakespeare*, ed. Arthur Kinney. London: Oxford University Press, 2012, pp. 499–515.

Maxwell, Julie, and Kate Rumbold (eds.), *Shakespeare and Quotation*. Cambridge: Cambridge University Press, 2018.

Abbott, E. A., *A Shakespearian Grammar*. 2nd edn. London: Macmillan, 1870.

Adamson, Sylvia, 'Literary Language', *The Cambridge History of the English Language*, ed. Roger Lass. Cambridge: Cambridge University Press, 1999, vol. 3, pp. 539–653.

'Questions of Identity in Renaissance Drama: New Historicism Meets Old Philology', *Shakespeare Quarterly* 61.1 (2010): 56–77.

'Understanding Shakespeare's Grammar: A Study in Small Words', *Reading Shakespeare's Dramatic Language*, ed. S. Adamson, L. Hunter, L. Magnusson, A. Thompson, and K. Wales. London: Arden Shakespeare, 2001, pp. 210–236.

Adamson, S., L. Hunter, L. Magnusson, A. Thompson, and K. Wales (eds.), *Reading Shakespeare's Dramatic Language: A Guide*. London: Arden Shakespeare, 2001.

Alexander, Catherine M. S. (ed.), *Shakespeare and Language*. Cambridge: Cambridge University Press, 2004.

Altman, Joel B., *The Improbability of Othello: Rhetorical Anthropology and Shakespearean Selfhood*. Chicago: University of Chicago Press, 2010.

The Tudor Play of Mind: Rhetorical Inquiry and the Development of Elizabethan Drama. Berkeley: University of California Press, 1978.

Aristotle, *On Rhetoric: A Theory of Civic Discourse*, trans. G. A. Kennedy, 2nd edn. New York: Oxford University Press, 2006.

Attridge, Derek, *The Rhythms of English Poetry*. London: Longman, 1982.

Well-Weighed Syllables: Elizabethan Verse in Classical Metres. London: Cambridge University Press, 1974.

Austin, J. L., *How to Do Things with Words*. Oxford: Oxford University Press, 1975.

Bakhtin, M. M., *The Dialogic Imagination: Four Essays*, ed. Michael Holquist, trans. Caryl Emerson and Michael Holquist. Austin: University of Texas Press, 1981.

'The Problem of Speech Genres', *Speech Genres and Other Late Essays*, ed. Caryl Emerson and Michael Holquist. Austin: University of Texas Press, 1986, pp. 60–102.

Baldwin, T. W., *William Shakspere's Small Latine and Lesse Greeke*. 2 vols. Urbana: University of Illinois Press, 1944.

Barber, Charles, Joan C. Beal, and Philip A. Shaw, *The English Language: A Historical Introduction*. 2nd edn. Cambridge: Cambridge University Press, 2012.

Barker, William (ed.), *The Adages of Erasmus*. Toronto: University of Toronto Press, 2001.

Barton, Anne, 'Leontes and the Spider: Language and Speaker in Shakespeare's Last Plays', *Essays, Mainly Shakespearean*. Cambridge: Cambridge University Press, 1994, pp. 161–181.

Barton, John, *Playing Shakespeare*. London: Methuen, 1984.

Basu, Anupam, Jonathan Hope, and Michael Witmore, 'The Professional and Linguistic Communities of Early Modern Dramatists', *Community-Making in Early Stuart Theatres: Stage and Audience*, ed. Roger D. Sell, Helen Wilcox, and Anthony W. Johnson. London: Routledge, 2014, pp. 63–94.

Beier, Lee, 'Anti-Language or Jargon? Canting in the English Underworld in the Sixteenth and Seventeenth Centuries', *Languages and Jargons: Contributions to a Social History of Language*, ed. Peter Burke and Roy Porter. Cambridge: Polity Press, 1995, pp. 64–101.

Bell, Allan, *The Guidebook to Sociolinguistics*. Oxford: Wiley Blackwell, 2014.

Bergen, Benjamin K., *Louder Than Words: The New Science of How the Mind Makes Meaning*. New York: Basic Books, 2006.

Black, James, '*Henry IV*: A World of Figures Here', *Shakespeare: The Theatrical Dimension*, ed. Philip C. McGuire and David A. Samuelson. New York: AMS Press, 1979, pp. 165–183.

Blake, N. F., *A Grammar of Shakespeare's Language*. New York: Palgrave, 2002.
  Non-Standard Language in English Literature. London: Deutsch, 1981.
  Shakespeare's Language: An Introduction. Basingstoke: Macmillan, 1983.
  Shakespeare's Non-Standard English: A Dictionary of his Informal Language. New York: Continuum, 2004.

Blank, Paula, *Broken English: Dialects and the Politics of Language in Renaissance Writings*. London: Routledge, 1996.

Booth, Stephen, *An Essay on Shakespeare's Sonnets*. New Haven: Yale University Press, 1969.
  Precious Nonsense: The Gettysburg Address, Ben Jonson's Epitaphs on his Children, and Twelfth Night. Berkeley: University of California Press, 1998.

Bourdieu, Pierre, 'The Economics of Linguistic Exchanges', *Social Science Information* 16 (1977): 645–668.
  Language and Symbolic Power. Cambridge: Polity, 1991.

Brown, Penelope, and Stephen C. Levinson, *Politeness: Some Universals in Language Usage*. Cambridge: Cambridge University Press, 1987.

Brown, Roger, and Albert Gilman, 'Politeness Theory and Shakespeare's Four Major Tragedies', *Language in Society* 18 (1989): 159–212.

Burkert, Mattie, 'Plotting the "Female Wits" Controversy: Gender, Genre, and Printed Plays, 1670–1699', *Early Modern Studies after the Digital Turn*, ed. Laura Estill, Diane Jackaki, and Michael Ullyot. Tempe: Arizona Center for Medieval and Renaissance Studies, 2016, pp. 35–59.

Burt, Richard, 'To e- or not to e-? Disposing of Schlockspeare in the Age of Digital Media', *Shakespeare after Mass Media*, ed. Richard Burt. New York: Palgrave Macmillan, 2002, pp. 1–34.

Calderwood, James L., *Metadrama in Shakespeare's Henriad: 'Richard II' to 'Henry V'*. Berkeley: University of California Press, 1979.

Cavell, Stanley, *Philosophy the Day after Tomorrow*. Cambridge, MA: Belknap Press of Harvard University Press, 2006.

Chambers, J. K., and Natalie Schilling (eds.), *The Handbook of Language Variation and Change*. 2nd edn. Oxford: Wiley-Blackwell, 2013.

Cook, Amy, *Shakespearean Neuroplay: Reinvigorating the Study of Dramatic Texts and Performance Through Cognitive Science*. New York: Palgrave Macmillan, 2010.

Cormack, Bradin, 'Tender Distance: Latinity and Desire in Shakespeare's Sonnets', *A Companion to Shakespeare's Sonnets*, ed. Michael Schoenfeldt. Oxford: Wiley-Blackwell, 2010, pp. 242–260.

Coulthard, Malcolm, *An Introduction to Discourse Analysis*. 2nd edn. London: Routledge, 1985.

Craig, Hugh, 'Shakespeare's Vocabulary: Myth and Reality', *Shakespeare Quarterly* 62.1 (2011): 53–74.

'Stylistic Analysis and Authorship Studies', *A Companion to Digital Humanities*, ed. Susan Schreibman, Ray Siemens, and John Unsworth. Oxford: Blackwell, 2004, pp. 273–288.

Craig, Hugh, and Brett Greatley-Hirsch, *Style, Computers, and Early Modern Drama*. Cambridge: Cambridge University Press, 2017.

Craig, Hugh, and Arthur F. Kinney (eds.), *Shakespeare, Computers, and the Mystery of Authorship*. Cambridge: Cambridge University Press, 2009.

Crane, Mary Thomas, *Framing Authority: Sayings, Self, and Society in Sixteenth-Century England*. Princeton: Princeton University Press, 1993.

Shakespeare's Brain: Reading with Cognitive Theory. Princeton: Princeton University Press, 2001.

Crystal, David, *The Oxford Dictionary of Original Shakespearean Pronunciation*. Oxford: Oxford University Press, 2016.

Think on My Words: Exploring Shakespeare's Language. Cambridge: Cambridge University Press, 2008.

Culpeper, Jonathan, *Language and Characterisation in Plays and Texts: People in Plays and Other Texts*, Textual Explorations. Harlow: Longman, 2001.

Cummings, Brian, *The Literary Culture of the Reformation: Grammar and Grace*. Oxford: Oxford University Press, 2002.

Delabastita, Dirk, and Lieven D'hulst (eds.), *European Shakespeares: Translating Shakespeare in the Romantic Age*. Amsterdam: John Benjamins, 1993.

Delabastita, Dirk, and Ton Hoenselaars (eds.), *Multilingualism in the Drama of Shakespeare and his Contemporaries*. Amsterdam: John Benjamins, 2015.

Dent, R. W., *Shakespeare's Proverbial Language: An Index*. Berkeley and London: University of California Press, 1981.

Donawerth, Jane, *Shakespeare and the Sixteenth-Century Study of Language*. Urbana: University of Illinois Press, 1984.

Drakakis, John, 'Shakespeare in Quotations', *Studying British Culture: An Introduction*, ed. Susan Bassnett. London: Routledge, 1997, pp. 152–172.

Edelman, Charles, *Shakespeare's Military Language: A Dictionary*. London and New Brunswick: Athlone, 2000.

Edwards, Philip, Inga-Stina Ewbank, and G. K. Hunter (eds.), *Shakespeare's Styles: Essays in Honour of Kenneth Muir*. Cambridge: Cambridge University Press, 1980.

Elam, Keir, *Shakespeare's Universe of Discourse: Language-Games in the Comedies*. Cambridge: Cambridge University Press, 1984.

Elliott, Ward E. Y., and Robert J. Valenza, 'Shakespeare's Vocabulary: Did It Dwarf All Others?', *Stylistics and Shakespeare's Language: Transdisciplinary Approaches*, ed. Mireille Ravassat and Jonathan Culpeper. London: Continuum, 2011, pp. 34–57.

Empson, William, *Seven Types of Ambiguity*. London: Chatto & Windus, 1930.

Enterline, Lynn, *Shakespeare's Schoolroom*. Philadelphia: University of Pennsylvania Press, 2011.

Erasmus, *Collected Works of Erasmus*, trans. C. Fantazzi, 25. Toronto: University of Toronto Press, 1985.

  De conscribendis epistolis, ed. J. C. Margolin, in Erasmus, *Opera omnia*, I-2. Amsterdam: North Holland, 1971, pp. 205–579.

  De copia, ed. B. Knott, *Opera omnia*, I-6. Amsterdam: North Holland, 1988; trans. B. Knott, *Collected Works of Erasmus*, 24. Toronto: University of Toronto Press, 1978.

Escolme, Bridget, *Talking to the Audience: Shakespeare, Performance, Self*. Abingdon: Routledge, 2005.

Ewbank, Inga-Stina, 'Shakespeare Translation as Cultural Exchange', *Shakespeare Survey* 48 (1995): 1–12.

Eyre, Richard, and Nicholas Wright, *Changing Stages*. London: Bloomsbury, 2000.

Fish, Stanley E., 'How to Do Things with Austin and Searle: Speech Act Theory and Literary Criticism', *MLN* 91.5 (1976): 983–1025.

Flint, Lorna, *Shakespeare's Third Keyboard: The Significance of Rime in Shakespeare's Plays*. London: Associated University Presses, 2000.

Foakes, R. A., and R. T. Rickert (eds.), *Henslowe's Diary*. Cambridge: Cambridge University Press, 1968.

Freedman, Penelope, *Power and Passion in Shakespeare's Pronouns: Interrogating 'You' and 'Thou'*. Aldershot: Ashgate, 2007.

Freeman, Donald, '"Catch[ing] the Nearest Way": *Macbeth* and Cognitive Metaphor', *Journal of Pragmatics* 24 (1995): 689–708.

Garber, Marjorie, 'Character Assassination: Shakespeare, Anita Hill, and *JFK*' and 'Shakespeare as Fetish', *Symptoms of Culture*. New York: Routledge, 1998, pp. 153–178.

Görlach, Manfred, 'Regional and Social Variation', *The Cambridge History of the English Language, Vol. 3: 1476–1776*, ed. Roger Lass. Cambridge: Cambridge University Press, 1999, pp. 459–538.

Graham, Kenneth J. E., *The Performance of Conviction: Plainness and Rhetoric in the Early English Renaissance*. Ithaca: Cornell University Press, 1994.

Griffiths, Eric, 'On Lines and Grooves from Shakespeare to Tennyson', *Tennyson among the Poets: Bicentenary Essays*, ed. Robert Douglas-Fairhurst and Seamus Perry. Oxford: Oxford University Press, 2009, pp. 132–159.

Herman, Vimala, *Dramatic Discourse: Dialogue as Interaction in Plays*. London and New York: Routledge, 1995.

Hoenselaars, Ton. 'Shakespeare and the Cultures of Translation', *Shakespeare Survey* 66 (2013): 206–219.

  (ed.), *Shakespeare and the Language of Translation*. London: Arden Shakespeare, 2004.

Hope, Jonathan, *The Authorship of Shakespeare's Plays: A Socio-linguistic Study*. Cambridge: Cambridge University Press, 1994.

Shakespeare's Grammar. London: Arden Shakespeare, 2003.

Shakespeare and Language: Reason, Eloquence and Artifice in the Renaissance. London: Arden, 2010.

'Shakespeare's "Natiue English"', *A Companion to Shakespeare*, ed. David Scott Kastan. Oxford: Blackwell, 1999, pp. 239–255.

'Who Invented "Gloomy"? Lies People Want to Believe about Shakespeare', *Memoria di Shakespeare* 3 (2016): 21–45.

Hope, Jonathan, and Michael Witmore, 'The Hundredth Psalm to the Tune of "Green Sleeves": Digital Approaches to Shakespeare's Language of Genre', *Shakespeare Quarterly* 61.3 (2010): 357–390.

'The Language of *Macbeth*', *Macbeth: The State of Play*, ed. Ann Thompson. London: Bloomsbury, 2014, pp. 183–208.

Houston, John Porter, *Shakespearean Sentences: A Study in Style and Syntax*. Baton Rouge: Louisiana State University Press, 1988.

Hussey, S. S., *The Literary Language of Shakespeare*. London: Longman, 1982.

Hutson, Lorna, *Circumstantial Shakespeare*. Oxford: Oxford University Press, 2015.

The Invention of Suspicion: Law and Mimesis in Shakespeare and Renaissance Drama. Oxford: Oxford University Press, 2007.

Jakobson, Roman, 'On Linguistic Aspects of Translation', *On Translation*, ed. Reuben A. Brower. Cambridge, MA: Harvard University Press, 1959, pp. 232–239.

Kennedy, Andrew K., *Dramatic Dialogue: The Duologue of Personal Encounter*. Cambridge: Cambridge University Press, 1983.

Kennedy, Dennis (ed.), *Foreign Shakespeare: Contemporary Performance*. Cambridge: Cambridge University Press, 1993.

Kennedy, G. A., *Progymnasmata: Greek Textbooks of Prose Composition and Rhetoric*. Atlanta: Society of Biblical Literature, 2003.

Kermode, Frank, *Shakespeare's Language*. Harmondsworth: Penguin, 2000.

Kerrigan, John, *Shakespeare's Binding Language*. New York: Oxford University Press, 2016.

King, Arthur H., *The Language of Satirized Characters in Poetaster: A Socio-Stylistic Analysis, 1597–1602*. Lund: Gleerup, 1941.

Kolentsis, Alysia, '"Grammar Rules" in the Sonnets: Sidney and Shakespeare', *The Oxford Handbook of Shakespeare's Poetry*, ed. Jonathan Post. Oxford: Oxford University Press, 2013, pp. 168–184.

'Shakespeare's Lexical Style', *Shakespeare In Our Time: A Shakespeare Association of America Companion*, ed. Dympna Callaghan and Suzanne Gossett. London: Arden Bloomsbury, 2016, pp. 306–311.

'Shakespeare's Linguistic Creativity: A Reappraisal', *Literature Compass* 11.4 (2014): 258–266.

Lakoff, George, and Mark Johnson, *Metaphors We Live By*. Chicago and London: University of Chicago Press, 1980.

Lamb, Jonathan P., *Shakespeare in the Marketplace of Words*. Cambridge: Cambridge University Press, 2017.

Lanham, Richard A., *A Handlist of Rhetorical Terms*. 2nd edn. Berkeley: University of California Press, 1991.

Lanier, Douglas, 'Marketing', *The Oxford Handbook to Shakespeare*, ed. Arthur Kinney. London: Oxford University Press, 2012, pp. 499–515.

Lass, Roger (ed.), *The Cambridge History of the English Language, Volume III, 1476–1776*. Cambridge: Cambridge University Press, 1999.

Leith, Dick. *A Social History of English*. 2nd edn. London: Routledge, 1997.

Levinson, Stephen C., *Pragmatics*. Cambridge: Cambridge University Press, 1983.

Lyne, Raphael, *Shakespeare, Rhetoric and Cognition*. Cambridge: Cambridge University Press, 2011.

Mack, Peter, *Elizabethan Rhetoric: Theory and Practice*. Cambridge: Cambridge University Press, 2002.

    A History of Renaissance Rhetoric 1380–1620. Oxford: Oxford University Press, 2011.

    'Learning and Transforming Conventional Wisdom: Reading and Rhetoric in the Elizabethan Grammar School', *Renaissance Studies* 32.3 (2018): 427–445.

    Reading and Rhetoric in Montaigne and Shakespeare. London: Bloomsbury, 2010.

    (ed.), *Renaissance Rhetoric*. London: Macmillan, 1994.

    Rhetoric's Questions, Reading and Interpretation. London: Palgrave, 2017.

Magnusson, Lynne, 'Dialogue', *Reading Shakespeare's Dramatic Language*, ed. S. Adamson, L. Hunter, L. Magnusson, A. Thompson, and K. Wales. London: Arden Shakespeare, 2001, pp. 130–143.

    'Grammatical Theatricality in *Richard III*: Schoolroom Queens and Godly Optatives', *Shakespeare Quarterly* 64.1 (2013): 32–43.

    'Language', *The Oxford Handbook of Shakespeare*, ed. Arthur Kinney. Oxford: Oxford University Press, 2012, pp. 239–257.

    'A Play of Modals: Grammar and Potential Action in Early Shakespeare', *Shakespeare Survey* 62 (2009): 69–80.

    'Shakespeare and the Language of Possibility', A Folger Shakespeare Library podcast: Shakespeare's Birthday Lecture 2015, 16 April 2015 folgerpedia.folger.edu.

    Shakespeare and Social Dialogue: Dramatic Language and Elizabeth Letters. Cambridge: Cambridge University Press, 1999.

Matoesian, Gregory M., 'The Turn-Taking Model for Natural Conversation', *Reproducing Rape: Domination through Talk in the Courtroom*. Chicago: University of Chicago Press, 1993, pp. 72–97.

Maxwell, Julie, and Kate Rumbold (eds.), *Shakespeare and Quotation*. Cambridge: Cambridge University Press, 2018.

McDonald, Russ, *Shakespeare and the Arts of Language*. Oxford: Oxford University Press, 2001.

    Shakespeare Reread: The Texts in New Contexts. Ithaca: Cornell University Press, 1994.

    Shakespeare's Late Style. Cambridge: Cambridge University Press, 2006.

Morgan, Oliver, *Turn-Taking in Shakespeare*. Oxford: Oxford University Press, 2019.

Morris, Pam (ed.), *The Bakhtin Reader: Selected Writings of Bakhtin, Medvedev and Voloshinov*. London: Edward Arnold, 1994.

Morse, Ruth, *Truth and Convention in the Middle Ages: Rhetoric, Representation, and Reality*. Cambridge: Cambridge University Press, 1991.

Moss, Ann, *Printed Commonplace-Books and the Structuring of Renaissance Thought*. Oxford: Oxford University Press, 1996.

Musgrove, S., 'Thieves' Cant in *King Lear*', *English Studies* 62 (1981): 5–13.

Nicholson, Catherine, *Uncommon Tongues: Eloquence and Eccentricity in the English Renaissance*. Philadelphia: University of Pennsylvania Press, 2013.

Palfrey, Simon, *Late Shakespeare: A New World of Words*. Oxford: Oxford University Press, 1997.

Palfrey, Simon, and Tiffany Stern, *Shakespeare in Parts*. Oxford: Oxford University Press, 2010.

Parker, Patricia, *Literary Fat Ladies: Rhetoric, Gender, Property*. London and New York: Methuen, 1987.

    Shakespeare from the Margins: Language, Culture, Context. Chicago: University of Chicago Press, 1996.

Porter, Joseph A., *The Drama of Speech Acts: Shakespeare's Lancastrian Tetralogy*. Berkeley: University of California Press, 1979.

    'Eloquence and Liminality: Glossing Mercutio's Speech Acts', *Romeo and Juliet*, ed. R. S. White. Basingstoke: Palgrave, 2001, pp. 166–193.

Quintilian, *Institutio oratoria*, trans. D. A. Russell. 5 vols. Cambridge, MA: Harvard University Press, 2001.

Ravassat, Mireille, and Jonathan Culpeper (eds.), *Stylistics and Shakespeare's Language: Transdisciplinary Approaches*. London: Continuum, 2011.

Reddy, William M., *The Navigation of Feeling: A Framework for the History of Emotions*. Cambridge: Cambridge University Press, 2001.

Rhetorica ad Herennium, trans. H. Caplan. Cambridge, MA: Harvard University Press, 1954.

Rokison, Abigail, *Shakespearean Verse Speaking: Text and Theatre Practice*. Cambridge: Cambridge University Press, 2010.

Rutter, Carol Chillington, 'Shakespeare and School', *Shakespeare Beyond Doubt: Evidence, Argument, Controversy*, ed. Paul Edmondson and Stanley Wells. Cambridge: Cambridge University Press, 2013, pp. 133–144.

Salmon, Vivian, and Edwina Burness (eds.), *A Reader in the Language of Shakespeare, Love and Language*. Cambridge: Cambridge University Press, 2018. *Shakespearean Drama: Collected Essays*. Amsterdam: John Benjamins, 1987.

Schalkwyk, David, 'Cursing to Learn: Theatricality and the Creation of Character in *The Tempest*', *Shakespeare Survey* 66 (2013): 67–81.

    Literature and the Touch of the Real. Newark: University of Delaware Press, 2004.

    Shakespeare, Love and Language: Cambridge: Cambridge University Press, 2018.

    Speech and Performance in Shakespeare's Sonnets and Plays. Cambridge: Cambridge University Press, 2002.

    'Shakespeare's Speech', *Journal of Medieval and Early Modern Studies* 40.2 (2010): 373–400.

Searle, John, 'A Classification of Speech Acts', *Language and Society* 5 (1979): 1–23.

    Speech Acts: An Essay in the Philosophy of Language. Cambridge: Cambridge University Press, 1969.

Sher, Antony, *Beside Myself*. London: Arrow Books, 2002.

Shore, Daniel, *Cyberformalism: Histories of Linguistic Forms in the Digital Archive*. Baltimore: Johns Hopkins University Press, 2018.

    'Shakespeare's Constructicon', *Shakespeare Quarterly* 66.2 (2015): 113–136.

Siemon, James, *Word Against Word: Shakespearean Utterance*. Amherst: University of Massachusetts Press, 2002.

'Silva rhetoricae: The Forest of Rhetoric', ed. G. Burton at http://rhetoric.byu.edu.

Skinner, Quentin, *Forensic Shakespeare*. Oxford: Oxford University Press, 2014.

Smith, Bruce, *The Acoustic World of Early Modern England: Attending to the O-Factor*. Chicago: University of Chicago Press, 1996.

Phenomenal Shakespeare. Chichester, West Sussex: Wiley-Blackwell, 2010.

Smith, G. Gregory (ed.), *Elizabethan Critical Essays*. 2 vols. Oxford: Clarendon Press, 1904.

Sokol, B. J., and Mary Sokol, *Shakespeare's Legal Language: A Dictionary*. London and New Brunswick: Athlone, 2000.

Stern, Tiffany, *Documents of Performance in Early Modern England*. Cambridge: Cambridge University Press, 2009.

Tarlinskaja, Marina, *Shakespeare and the Versification of English Drama, 1561–1642*. Farnham: Ashgate, 2014.

Shakespeare's Verse: Iambic Pentameter and the Poet's Idiosyncrasies. New York: Peter Lang, 1987.

Taylor, Gary, 'Artiginality: Authorship after Postmodernism', *The New Oxford Shakespeare: Authorship Companion*, ed. Gary Taylor and Gabriel Egan. Oxford: Oxford University Press, 2016, pp. 3–26.

Tootalian, Jacob, 'Without Measure: The Language of Shakespeare's Prose', *Journal for Early Modern Cultural Studies* 13.4 (2013): 47–60.

Van Es, Bart, *Shakespeare in Company*. Oxford: Oxford University Press, 2013.

Vickers, Brian, *The Artistry of Shakespeare's Prose*. London: Methuen, 1968.

Shakespeare, Co-Author: A Historical Study of Five Collaborative Plays. Oxford: Oxford University Press, 2002.

'Shakespeare's Use of Rhetoric', *A New Companion to Shakespeare Studies*, ed. K. Muir and S. Schoenbaum. Cambridge: Cambridge University Press, 1971, pp. 83–98.

Walter, Harriet, *Brutus and Other Heroines: Playing Shakespeare's Roles for Women*. London: Nick Hern Books, 2016.

Other People's Shoes. London: Nick Hern Books, 1999.

Weimann, Robert, *Author's Pen and Actor's Voice: Playing and Writing in Shakespeare's Theatre*. Cambridge: Cambridge University Press, 2000.

Witmore, Michael, Jonathan Hope, and Mike Gleicher, 'Digital Approaches to the Language of Shakespearean Tragedy', *The Oxford Handbook of Shakespearean Tragedy*, ed. Michael Neill and David Schalkwyk. Oxford: Oxford University Press, 2016, pp. 316–335.

Wofford, Susanne L., '"To you I give myself, for I am yours": Erotic Performance and Theatrical Performatives in *As You Like It*', *Shakespeare Reread*, ed. Russ McDonald. Ithaca: Cornell University Press, 1994, pp. 147–169.

Wright, George T., *Shakespeare's Metrical Art*. Berkeley: University of California Press, 1988.

Yachnin, Paul (ed.), *Shakespeare's World of Words*. London: The Arden Shakespeare, Bloomsbury, 2015.

INDEX

accents, 134
Ace Ventura: When Nature Calls, 254
acknowledgement, 90
actors
    cued parts, 80
    language cueing performance, 207–25
Adamson, Sylvia, 29, 189, 190
adaptations, 227
Agricola, Rudolph, 122
    De inventione dialectica, 120
All's Well That Ends Well, 183
Allott, Robert
    England's Parnassus, 249
AntConc, 154, 155, 161
Antony and Cleopatra, 20, 23, 75–76, 77,
    78, 94, 162, 182–83, 211–12, 225,
    248, 265
Aphthonius
    Progymnasmata, 115, 117, 121, 122, 123,
    124, 126
application, 248, 254–56
archaism, 237, 250, 256
Aristotle, 93, 123
    Rhetoric, 120
As You Like It, 3, 13, 99, 136–37, 138, 139,
    174, 190, 192–93, 195, 196, 225,
    251, 264, 266
Austin, J. L., 37, 41, 49, 50, 51, *see also*
    speech acts
authorship, 15
    and style, 168–86

Bakhtin, Mikhail, 76, 135, 136, 138, 230
Barton, Anne, 16
Basu, Anupam, 160
Beale, Simon Russell, 210
Beaumont, Francis, 143
Belleforest, François de
    Histoires tragiques, 230

Benjamin, Walter, 234
Bennett, Susan, 228
Benson, John, 226
Bilderdijk, Willem, 233
Blank, Paula, 24
blank verse, 58, 69
Blount, Edward, 140
Bohannan, Laura, 236, 237
Booth, Stephen, 189, 195, 196, 197,
    198, 201
Boroditsky, Lera, 194
Bourdieu, Pierre, 82–83, 84, 85
Branagh, Kenneth, 234
Brome, Richard
    The Jovial Crew, 143
    The Northern Lass, 136
Brown, Penelope, 87
Buckley, William F., 251
Buddingh', Cees, 233
Burgo, Bettina, 75
Burton, Gideon
    'Silva rhetoricae' website, 264

Caesar, Julius, 116
canting language, 136, 142–43
Carson, Christie, 228
Cavell, Stanley, 37, 40, 49, 51
Chandler, Raymond, 96
Chapman, George
    Byron's Conspiracy, 176, 177
    Revenge of Bussy, 176
    The Gentleman Usher, 175
Cheke, John, 28
Cicero
    Ad familiares, 116
    De officiis, 116
    De oratore, 120
Claus, Hugo, 233
Cleese, John, 137

Cambridge Companions to...

AUTHORS